Arthur Erickson

An Architect's Life

Arthur Erickson

An Architect's Life

David Stouck

Douglas & McIntyre

Douglas and McIntyre (2013) Ltd.
P.O. Box 219
Madeira Park, BC Canada VON 2HO
www.douglas-mcintyre.com

Cataloguing data available from Library and Archives Canada
ISBN 978-1-77100- 011-6 (cloth)
ISBN 978-1-77100-012-3 (ebook)

Editing by Barbara Pulling
Jacket and text design by Jessica Sullivan
Jacket photograph by Fred Schiffer
Printed and bound in Canada by Friesens
Distributed in the U.S. by Publishers Group West

We gratefully acknowledge the financial support of the Canada Council
for the Arts, the British Columbia Arts Council, the Province of British
Columbia through the Book Publishing Tax Credit, and the Government
of Canada through the Canada Book Fund for our publishing activities.

Contents

Author's Note

THIS BIOGRAPHY OF Arthur Erickson is grounded in a series of conversations with the architect initiated in the spring of 2005 and continuing until his death in 2009. As I researched his life, interviewing family, friends and clients, and reading through archival collections, I would take him material I had located—letters, interviews, photographs—and they would invariably stir his memories. I read to Arthur passages from the early chapters of the biography and he let me know if I had caught the spirit of that part of his life. From those conversations, always with their slight transporting sense of another world, I have footnoted only matters that may be regarded as controversial. Unfortunately it has not been possible in a single volume to account for all of Arthur Erickson's friendships and business associations, for they were global and legion. —DS

Prologue:
Amiens, 1918

ON AUGUST 8, 1918, at 4:20 AM, the Allies in Normandy executed a surprise attack and made an extraordinary nine-mile advance east on the front line. The goal was simple: to free the Paris-to-Amiens rail line from German interference. On the morning of August 9, after a six-hour delay, the 4th Canadian Division moved into place to consolidate the spectacular gains of the previous day. But while Allied generals were arguing strategy, the Germans brought in their reserves, and the Canadians came under heavy fire. Oscar Erickson, with the 78th Battalion (the Winnipeg Grenadiers), fought his way forward until a shell exploded between his knees, tearing away both of his legs. He would have been carried to a field ambulance tent, his wounds haphazardly bound up. It was a disheartening day for the Allies, with heavy casualties and almost no gains made. It appeared that this massive, carefully planned offensive would make little difference to the outcome of the war, now in its fifth horrendous year.

Oscar Erickson's personal story of Amiens, however, was told differently by his family. In their version, Oscar, who had dropped rank from captain to lieutenant to see action, had been left to die on the battlefield. But a nurse and an officer were making rounds of the mist-covered fields that evening, and, recognizing Oscar as her dance partner from the night before, the nurse pleaded his case. He was taken to the field hospital where doctors went to work, removing the mangled portion of a leg that was still attached. When his condition was deemed stable he was shipped to London for convalescence. The nurse, Elizabeth Pearce, became a lifelong family friend.

This romantic story does not fit exactly with military history. Nurses were kept well back from the front line. Nor is it likely that Oscar Erickson had danced with Elizabeth Pearce as recently as the night of August 8. In a few places along the front line, the Salvation Army set up canteens for the soldiers and informal games of football sprang up, but there were no parties in the tense hours prior to an offensive of this magnitude.[1] And although the fields of Normandy were frequently shrouded in mists that month—most memorably creating crucial cover on the morning of August 8—the war diary for the 78th Battalion records that "weather was clear" for August 9.[2] Nonetheless, the Ericksons' story, distilled from many Sunday dinner retellings, had its own kind of truth. A brave father who lost both legs in a heroically decisive battle, who recovered his ability to walk, to earn his living and sire two sons, had the aura of legend, a family's founding narrative thumbing its nose at chance and fate.

For Oscar Erickson's young sons, the story was especially delightful in its sequel. From his hospital bed in London, the shattered soldier wrote to his fiancée in Winnipeg releasing her from their engagement. But when Myrtle Chatterson received his letter, she wrote back a letter that has become famous in the family annals: "Nonsense. If your head had been blown off, yes; but just two legs— we can deal with that." (In conversation she was remembered to have said to friends: "I'd rather marry a man with two wooden legs than a wooden head.") So Oscar worked at rehabilitation, determined not to be in a wheelchair, and when he arrived back in Canada he made his way down the gangplank of the returning ship on wooden legs and canes—once more "a whole man." This powerful image would be indelibly fixed in Arthur Erickson, the famous son. Throughout Arthur's life, to disembark from a ship or a plane was to be on the threshold of triumph; to be discouraged or bereft was to be "legless."

Part I

A Portrait
of the
Architect
as a
Young Man

1

Child

WHEN ARTHUR CHARLES ERICKSON was born, on June 14, 1924, his parents had been married for nearly five years. Family and friends had assumed Oscar's injuries precluded children. Accordingly, when Myrtle gave birth to a son, there was a heightened feeling of celebration throughout their community. This aura surrounding a special child would persist throughout Arthur's childhood—indeed throughout his life.

Except for his maternal grandfather's family, Arthur Erickson's forebears were recent immigrants to North America. His paternal grandmother, born Bengte Anderson in the region of Gothenburg in 1865, was, according to family stories, raised on a farm where the work was hard and the crops meagre. She ran off with a lover to Stockholm, where they married and then took ship for America, eventually making their home in Ludington, Michigan. In one story, Bengte's husband, Karl Wilhelm Erickson, died shortly after the birth of Oscar, their third child, in 1890. In a story more widely credited, Karl Wilhelm was a womanizer whom Bengte left. She moved to Toronto to live with a friend and there raised her young children. In both accounts, Bengte Erickson made her living by sewing, eventually buying a house and supplementing her income by renting out rooms. Arthur Erickson thought of the Swedish side of his family as practical, hard-working people with admirable qualities but of a frugal and dour nature. His grandmother, whom he would remember as "strait-laced," sitting very upright, strove to be correct in all things. She anglicized her name to Bertha when she arrived in North America and refused to speak Swedish to her grandchildren. She sent her three children to the Sunday school of an Anglican church where Oscar sang in the choir.

Oscar's older brother, Henry, born in 1887, received little formal education, but he apprenticed as a printer's devil and worked his way up in the publishing business, becoming chief proofreader for University of Toronto Press in the 1940s. Like his mother, Henry was an individual of integrity who took pains to preserve his reputation. When the close friendship he had cultivated with his son-in-law, a medical student at the University of Toronto, seemed to cool, Henry's family became anxious. It transpired that at the press, Henry had proofread the university's medical school exams, and he was determined not to give any hint of their contents to his son-in-law.[1]

Oscar's sister, Anna, born in 1888, was "a very upright, serious woman of great character,"[2] who was still working when she died at the age of ninety-nine. As a young woman she made her living as a bookbinder in Toronto. She married Karl Auer, a tailor, and with their two sons they eventually moved to Vancouver. After her husband died, Anna, at the age of seventy, opened a gift shop on West Boulevard in Kerrisdale. There Arthur observed his aunt Annie, an astute businesswoman, at close range: "She had the Swedish eye for china and handsome stemware, and her shop was one of the more elegant businesses in Vancouver at that time." She did not count on passing trade; rather, people sought out her business, knowing she had high-quality merchandise and could advise customers from her significant fund of knowledge. At about age eighty she injured a knee, and doctors were reluctant to perform surgery because of the amount of exercise required to recover its use. When they told Anna, who lived above the shop, that it would be hard to retrain the leg to walk, she replied, "It will when I get through with it." And with the help of her daughter-in-law, Eve, she kept her shop open and continued to use the stairs.

Oscar Erickson, like his older brother, left school early. At only fourteen, he began working for E.H. Walsh & Company, a dry goods firm in Toronto that imported such products as Irish linens and cotton wear from the United States. Oscar developed a close relationship with Walsh who, in a fatherly way, advised the boy on personal matters and gave him special opportunities within the company. When Oscar was in his early twenties, Walsh opened a branch of the business in Winnipeg and made Oscar the western sales manager. On his own in this growing, vibrant city, Oscar expanded the business and quickly made friends, while continuing to send much of his pay home to help support his mother and sister. One of his new friends was Myrtle Chatterson, a lively and unconventional girl to whom he became engaged in 1917.

Oscar was a fine athlete and a champion tennis player, especially strong in track events. With Canada engaged in the war effort, he did basic military training while continuing to work for E.H. Walsh. But in 1917, with the war grinding ever deeper and his older brother, as the chief breadwinner in the family, remaining at home, Oscar's sense of duty led him to enlist with Canada's 78th Battalion, and he soon shipped overseas. After he was wounded in the Battle of Amiens, then sent to a London hospital for recovery, he lay deeply depressed, refusing to eat, with a sheet pulled over his head.

Years later his family would describe a Mrs. Rogers, an English socialite who toured hospitals to cheer the wounded. At Oscar's bedside she scolded him for withdrawing from the world and pointed out that there were many in worse shape than he was. Although this privileged woman may have seemed high handed, she nonetheless rekindled Oscar's sense of duty and, moving about in his wheelchair, he began to help others, fetching things for those who could not leave their beds, reading letters and newspapers to men whose sight was gone or impaired. When he received the letter from his fiancée dismissing a broken engagement as nonsense, his equable nature was restored. (He also received the Military Cross from King George V and was later promoted to the rank of major.) The hospital had wooden legs made for him to use with crutches; although it was necessary to reduce his original height of six feet by two inches to get a sure balance between the new legs and the rest of his body, Oscar was soon able to walk again.

If Arthur Erickson's paternal family was sober and practical, his mother's family can only be described as opposite in every way—high-spirited, imaginative individuals with little concern for order in their lives. In monetary terms, Arthur's maternal grandparents were failures. Charlie Chatterson, of United Empire Loyalist stock, was a large, overweight man with an argumentative streak, a political radical who saw government policies and capitalist finance as the source of human woes. The son of an Ontario teacher, he was a black sheep in the family because he could never settle to one occupation. When he arrived in Manitoba in the late 1800s, Charlie took up farming in the area of Brandon, but he gave up on wheat when a freak tornado demolished all his farm buildings. He moved his family to Winnipeg where he worked as a detective, valuable to the police force because of his remarkable visual memory. It was said that "Ten-Minute Charlie" could look through a file of criminal photographs and, remembering a face, go out into the streets and make a quick arrest.[3] Later, he and his wife moved to Vancouver, where for a time they operated a sweets shop known as Mary Jane's. With its ice cream cones and candy rabbits, the store was a delight for children, but because the Chattersons insisted on using pure cream and the best eggs and chocolate, they never made any money.

Arthur remembered his Chatterson grandparents with great affection, especially his Irish grandmother, Sarah, whom the family called Sadie. As a boy, Arthur thought of her as a gypsy—a fun-loving free spirit who would try her luck at anything. She was remembered by Blackie (Lee) Sparzani, one of Arthur's close friends, as "a marvellous woman, loved by us all... with all manner of Irish sayings never heard anywhere else, such as 'this knife is so dull you could ride it to Dublin.'"[4] Sadie had a great store of superstitions and the perception of a clairvoyant. She read voluminously, and for Sunday visits she would create a narrative merging her readings of that week to entertain her grandsons. Arthur loved the way she sang and danced spontaneously, and could play the piano by ear. She was, as Blackie Lee observed, "a bright presence in Arthur's early years."

Sadie's daughter, Myrtle, inherited every bit of this fun-loving, adventurous spirit—and more. "She was a unique and wonderful woman," wrote Blackie Lee. "She was spontaneous, generous, and interested in everything. She would go out of her way to help someone, even if she didn't have the time or means to do so. She was extremely beautiful throughout her life, but seemed unaware of it and had her mind on other things."⁵ That something "beautiful" about Myrtle wasn't her appearance, exactly. As another family friend recalled, "She really didn't care how she looked—her hair might be askew, her slip showing—rather, it was her love of life and her irrepressible interest in ideas and good conversation that made her seem vibrantly beautiful."⁶ Myrtle had inherited her mother's clairvoyant perception and often told how she had had a vivid dream one night that her engagement ring had broken in two. Next day she received word that Oscar had been injured overseas.

Oscar and Myrtle were married in Winnipeg on June 25, 1919, and later that year moved to Vancouver, where Oscar had persuaded E.H. Walsh to let him open another office for the company. It was assumed that amputees from the war would support themselves on a government pension, but Oscar scorned the idea of living as an invalid. After a brief stay in a small apartment in Vancouver's West End, the couple purchased a lot on the northeast corner of 33rd and Osler, a block from Oak Street in the Shaughnessy neighbourhood, and there they built a two-storey house designed to accommodate Oscar's difficulties. Despite the contractor's objections, the ground floor was placed level with the street, and the master bedroom was built on the main level with a connecting bath and dressing room. For his work as a dry goods salesman, Oscar drove one of the first partially hand-operated automobiles made in Canada (to change gears he pressed down with his hand on one of his false legs), and when he parked at home he was able to walk directly into the kitchen and thence to the bedroom to change out of his business clothes for the evening. One critic has astutely observed that from birth the future architect would have been "privy to an underscored appreciation of function, mobility, access and form."[7]

Oscar and Myrtle Erickson were wonderfully happy together and perfect foils for each other. From the beginning of their marriage they shared a strong interest in the arts. As a hobby, Oscar painted realistic landscapes and flowers in watercolours and oils, and he made his own greeting cards to be sent out at Christmas. Myrtle took great pleasure at the easel herself, producing "interesting but strange pictures," in her son's view. But her special contribution was her public advocacy for improved venues for the arts in Vancouver. She helped establish the Vancouver Art Gallery, and she remained on the Women's Auxiliary of the gallery for the rest of her life.[8] She was especially keen to promote local art, at one point heading a campaign that went under the banner, "Own a Canadian Painting." Later in life, with some of her female friends, she formed a group of painters who worked at what they called the Yellow Door on Richards Street. As many of his childhood friends have observed, Arthur Erickson could not have been born into a family more hospitable to the nurturing of an artist.

In 1924, Vancouver, only thirty-eight years old, was still a small city of just better than 117,000. Except for the two railways, it was cut off from the rest of Canada by formidable mountain terrain. The Trans-Canada Highway through the Rockies was not completed until 1962. There was no bridge yet to the city's North Shore, just a ferry across to what were mostly cottages and a few small businesses along the edge of the forest. Vancouver was becoming an important centre for ocean shipping, but it was still a sleepy little place compared to Montreal, Toronto, or Winnipeg, then the third-largest city in Canada.

Every new arrival to Vancouver goes through a period of adjustment to the heavy rains, but for someone born on the West Coast, the memories of childhood contain as much sunshine as elsewhere. Among Arthur's earliest memories was a girl living two doors down the street who, being two years older, established herself as an older sister. Indeed, in most of the snapshots of Arthur as a blond-haired little boy, Kay Holland seems to be organizing his life: holding his hand as he learns to walk, arranging stuffed animals and dolls for him to play with, setting up formal tea parties on the lawn. Before Arthur was born, Myrtle had wanted her baby to be a girl, so it was natural enough in this loving environment that Kay became like a daughter to her. (Kay continued to help Myrtle with her work until she herself married; the Erickson house, under Myrtle's chaotic management, provided a delightful challenge for a competent and creative girl.) While she was still small, Kay brought her girlfriends to the Erickson house as well. So, until his brother, Donald, was born four years later, Arthur was surrounded by little girls at play.

The neighbourhood in which the Ericksons lived was still being developed, and Nanny Chatterson would take the boys on walks through Shaughnessy's misty forested lots to pick berries and gather mushrooms, in the course of which she would also collect unusual items—pebbles, wild plants, insects—for further examination at home. Her delight in the natural world and her fearlessness lent an aura of excitement to everything she undertook. When they returned home, the air would be full of rich, sometimes strange aromas, and they would sit down to dinner with relatives and friends with almost religious enthusiasm. Those afternoons were so graven on Arthur's memory that they were more vivid to him in old age than most of the scenes from his illustrious career.

Sunday dinner at Osler Street was a ritual during which Oscar and his father-in-law argued politics from opposing ends, the latter a socialist, Oscar a royalist. Although Arthur would always find heated political discussion tedious, he recognized that from his socialist grandfather he had inherited the instinct to challenge the status quo. He was not particularly fond of his grandfather, who viewed his grandson as altogether too curious and serious and nicknamed him "The Professor." Also present for numerous Sunday dinners was Elizabeth Pearce, the nurse credited with saving Oscar's life at Amiens. As Arthur put it years later, she and his father regularly refought the war.

There were picnics and family outings during summer, and Nanny Chatterson usually came along. These would sometimes take the form of painting excursions, with lunches, watercolours, and easels packed into the car. The Capilano River was a favourite spot, which meant the trip began with a ferry ride across Burrard Inlet to Vancouver's North Shore; another option was a journey in the car thirty miles east of the city to the area now known as Golden Ears Provincial Park. Sometimes the whole family would set out to paint, each in their way, a conventionally interesting scene—a mountain, a body of water—but just as often the boys and their grandmother would wander off to explore the surrounding terrain.

Oscar had been a skilled oarsman in his youth, and he liked to put a boat in the water and take his sons fishing. "We were brought up to regard my father as absolutely normal," Arthur observed as an adult. He was never viewed in the family as an invalid; his wife might say, "Get up and fetch the card table, Oscar," and Oscar, in turn, would never plead his disability, no matter how inconvenient or complicated the task assigned. Although just getting in and out of the boat on artificial legs was a challenge, he made light of it. When Arthur was older he recognized the heroic aura that surrounded this practical man. "When I was very small I used to think [my father] could do anything, and I used to boast to my friends that he could play tennis, for he had been a champion tennis player and a champion walker, one of Canada's top athletes. He was also interested in painting, and he always had a paintbox in the house, and whenever he was painting he would give me a brush and I used to paint with him . . . And so when I was very small I became interested in design."[9]

Oscar's influence was felt in public as well. He gave talks to groups of young men who were badly injured in both the First and Second World Wars, and he served for many years on the Borstal boys' home committee for delinquent youth. People admired his courage, maturity, and wisdom, and for a time they pressed him to run for mayor. At the time of his death in 1965 he was chairman of the B.C. Parole Board and a member of the Vancouver Housing Authority. He had received an Order of the British Empire (OBE) citation in 1946.

But the strongest influence on Arthur's life was the lively, eccentric presence of his mother, a spontaneous, sometimes zany individual with a generous interest in the lives of her friends and a keen interest in ideas. Her involvement in painting embraced new modernist forms of expression, her own work often taking the form of collages. She read widely and kept stacks of magazines—*The New Yorker, Vogue*—under the bed for future reference. At the same time, she had a busy social life, which included both the city's wealthy (Babe Taylor, wife of Home Oil president Austin Taylor, was a good friend from Winnipeg) and servants such as the Ericksons' sometime housekeeper, the irrepressible Emma Fox. Myrtle made no distinctions based on class; she simply required that people in some way be interesting.

Her friends certainly found Myrtle interesting and an endless source of anecdotes, for she invariably broke the codes of conventional behaviour. Invited for dinner, she was often an hour or two late. Perhaps, if it was a group, she would offer to bring a chicken, but she was likely to arrive late with the bird not yet cooked. Myrtle herself was an "inspired" cook and liked to give dinner parties on the spur of the moment. These usually involved the whole family in elaborate culinary preparations and house decorations. "When my mother cooked," Arthur would later muse, "there were pots everywhere and sauces on the ceiling."[10] All her kitchen utensils were burned through; unusable ones accumulated on the floor. An invitation for dinner at six often meant not sitting down until nine or ten, though the meal would be memorable for its unusual ingredients. Dinner guests were sometimes anxious when Myrtle brought out the salad, because they had seen her favourite cat curled up in the bowl when they arrived. Oscar was a well-organized man surrounded by chaos; he never knew when—or whether—he would get his dinner. Friends delighted in the excitement Myrtle generated in her home. Oscar's mother and his sister, Anna, on the other hand, were sternly disapproving.

Myrtle generated an equal amount of excitement outside the home. A car, for example, was not a safe instrument in her hands. One day, backing into the street, she pressed the accelerator instead of the brake and sent her neighbour, also backing out, straight back into and through his garage. Continuing on to the golf course, not realizing the damage the "bump" had caused, she encountered the groundskeeper on a tractor. Seeing the speed of the oncoming car, he veered to the verge and, in so doing, rolled his tractor down the slope. Myrtle boasted how quickly she could drive around the city by taking back alleys and never having to stop for lights.

She usually talked herself out of scrapes, but one day, on Vancouver Island with her children and their Auer cousins, she found herself on the wrong road and tried to turn around by backing down a steep lane, but the car went straight into a lake. That day she had to talk to a tow-truck driver. Oscar's presence in the car was no guarantee there wouldn't be an adventure of some kind. When they went shopping in Seattle, for example, to avoid paying duty Myrtle insisted on stuffing some of her purchases—a blouse, stockings, underwear—inside Oscar's hollow legs before they crossed the border. She wore two hats on the return. This worked well for a time, but one day they were caught and, despite the humiliation, Oscar was not sorry.

Oscar's patience was boundless. He would sit in the car waiting for as much as an hour while Myrtle chose what to wear (sometimes the garment needed mending first) or hunted through her vast bag full of nylons for two that matched—though she did not always find a match, and in the end did not worry about it. Because she did not have a lot of money to spend, she kept all of her old clothes, and sometimes, when she needed a new outfit in a hurry, "you would hear her rummaging in the closet, ripping things apart, putting them together again, and going out."[11] In the 1930s she got into the habit of painting her shoes to match an outfit. Sometimes Oscar sat in the car while Myrtle waited for her shoes to dry in the oven.

Myrtle Erickson's casual disregard for the physical world and its timetable was reinforced by her involvement with the Christian Science church. When she first heard her fiancé had been wounded, she wept through the night but thereafter she was never known to cry again. Instead, she looked around for religious counsel and decided that Christian Science, with its positive thinking and its relegation of the material world to illusory status, had much to offer someone in her situation. Mary Baker Eddy preached that everything was spirit and that illness and physical handicaps were simply "errors" in perception. In *Science and Health,* Mrs. Eddy wrote: "Tumors, ulcers, tubercles, inflammation, pain, deformed joints, all are dream shadows, dark images of mortal thought which will flee before the light."[12] One day at church, when Arthur was six or seven, a lady "who always wore silly hats" told him that his father's legs would return if he only believed they would. The boy ran home from Sunday school and shouted, "Daddy, you can walk!" When nothing happened, Arthur lost his literal belief, but he didn't stop attending church until he was in his teens. Eventually he would give the church credit for instilling within him a positive outlook on life. "My mother tried all the denominations after my father was wounded, and found [Christian Science] the most optimistic . . . and [I believe] a religion so optimistic is a lot better than an attitude of sin and guilt. However, I have suffered ever since from trying to adjust to the presence of evil in the world. Deep inside, I am convinced that everything is basically good."[13]

Oscar, who had been raised as an Anglican in Toronto, continued to attend Anglican services as an adult. To him, Christian Science seemed "far-fetched," though there was certainly a vogue for it among those with an interest in the arts.[14] Arthur's brother, Donald, was similarly skeptical. When he was eight, Donald told his mother he would test Christian Science teachings by lying down on the streetcar tracks to see whether or not the passing tram would cut off his legs. Myrtle was frightened and thereafter no longer insisted both boys attend Sunday school.

Donald was four years younger than Arthur, but from the outset there was a solid bond between the two brothers. Although they were not conscious of it as children, their parents were an eccentric couple, and this drew the boys together in unspoken ways. In their teens, when they grew strong enough, they would carry their father, with his heavy, barrel-shaped torso, up long flights of stairs. Neither of them enjoyed sports, and in that respect they were something of a disappointment to a father who, even without legs, played a skilful game of Ping-Pong. But there were ways in which they differed and, like most brothers, from time to time they quarrelled. Most memorable was their long-standing difference regarding the treatment of living creatures. Arthur had a passionate love for wild things, especially birds and fish. He kept tropical fish and he hated his brother's BB gun. One day, when Don was in a tree taking aim at birds and squirrels with a slingshot, Arthur ordered him to get down by the count of ten. When his brother ignored him, Arthur took Don's gun and smashed it. To get revenge, Don turned off the heat to Arthur's fish tank and added cold water for good measure. The fish all died.

But there was a significant artistic consequence to this fraternal spat. Because it was the Depression and funds were scarce, the family could not easily afford to restock the tank. Myrtle encouraged Arthur instead to paint pictures of fish on the walls of his bedroom. Oscar thought the idea was foolish, but Myrtle slipped some of her husband's paints to Arthur and said, "Paint while he's away... and then take him up to look at them."[15] He began by copying two fish from photographs in *National Geographic* and then, with growing confidence, covered all four walls of his room with underwater scenes featuring sunken wrecks, seahorses, sharks, and shrimp. The gloomy north bedroom seemed transformed by the aquamarine walls. Oscar was so impressed that he bought Arthur his own set of paints.

Don then wanted his walls painted, too. Because Don loved Tarzan comics, Arthur converted his brother's bedroom into a jungle, with birds, a black panther, and a family of monkeys. Boys in the neighbourhood were eager to visit Don's room, where they used the creatures on the wall for target practice with their BB guns until plaster started falling away. These murals were so popular in the neighbourhood that one of Myrtle's friends asked Arthur to paint a basement wall with a stylized English hunting scene, lots of trees, and a striking image of a stag. The effect was so pleasing that he was encouraged to carry the project all around the room. This was his first professional assignment; it took him several months to complete, and he was paid $50. The mural would remain a vivid memory in the Shaughnessy community because this basement was where Arthur's young contemporaries often gathered for parties and dances.

Asked whether he had a happy childhood, Arthur would answer in both the negative and the affirmative. Shy as a boy, he was always being sent by his parents to play games with children he didn't like very much. Myrtle Erickson would remember a day when Arthur was supposed to take part in a race but turned to her and said, "Oh, Mother, I don't want to run." On the playground at school, when everyone was chasing the ball, like James Joyce's Stephen Dedalus Arthur kept to the fringe of the line, making little runs now and then. When the family rented a cottage in North Vancouver for the summer, his father expected him to play with a boy the same age next door, but the boy was a bully who would lie in wait for Arthur and chase him with a fish hook—or with a raised axe.[16] One day, as Arthur was running away, he fell, grazing his hand and tearing his trousers. Other children, who had stood up to the bully, gathered around and laughed; Arthur felt sick with shame. Humiliated, he dreamed about a time in the future—when he was eighteen, maybe twenty—when he would not be persecuted by "riff-raff" and would make very different sorties into the world.

In the meantime, there was the great pleasure of his parents' friends: his mother's friends from the art gallery and the social clubs she belonged to and his father's business acquaintances, who sometimes included colleagues from Asia. On summer holidays, the family drove back to Winnipeg to visit. The car held six: the family of four, Nanny Chatterson, and a friend for the boys; each of them got to choose on alternating trips. When it was Arthur's turn, he chose school friend Paul Wright. Like Arthur, Paul was shy, preferring nature and the life of the imagination to sports.

School was a matter of survival for Arthur, keeping clear of boys ready to pick a fight and girls in their smothering cliques. With one girl, however, he had a special tie. Ruth Killam was the daughter of Lawrence Killam, a local lumberman, and when the children were small Ruth's mother, Edith, had given them painting lessons. She was a friend of Arthur Lismer, a member of the Group of Seven widely known for teaching children to paint on Saturday mornings at the Art Gallery of Ontario. Following his example, Edith Killam would cover her furniture on Saturday mornings and let the children experiment with paints and paper.

Paul Wright helped put together a school publication titled *Intermediate Highlights*, to which Arthur contributed poems and prose pieces. At age eleven he wrote a poem titled "Night" that describes Vancouver in wholly visual language as coming alive while humankind sleeps, while "A Ridiculous Story" describes a dream of being confronted by a lion in South America and, having no weapon, reaching into the cat's mouth and pulling the beast inside out. Exotic adventures would always have enormous appeal for Arthur.

Of even more imaginative resonance was Arthur's friendship with Yasuko Ishii, whose father worked for the Japanese Embassy in Vancouver. Before coming to Canada she had travelled to different locations with her family. For *Intermediate Highlights* she wrote an account of a trip they had made across Siberia, in which she imagined being followed by Russian spies. For her travel column, Arthur composed an account of the Mediterranean Sea as he imagined it, with cobalt blue waters, tropical fish, and coral reefs of all colours. But he noted ominously that the sea's name meant "in the middle of the earth" and that in 1935 the world's eyes were watching this centre where fleets from the great powers were gathering, awaiting the possibility of another world war. Years later Arthur would wonder what became of Yasuko, who had returned to Japan and written him letters, but from whom, once the war began, he heard nothing more. These faraway places and fleeting friendships would be the stuff of Arthur's imagination as he explored the world and made a place for himself in it.

2

Prodigy

THE ARTS SCENE IN Vancouver developed slowly, chiefly through a series of short-lived Arts and Crafts societies. When Hill and Nan Cheney moved to Vancouver from eastern Canada in 1937, he a radiologist and she a painter and medical illustrator, Nan was disappointed to find Vancouver still a small Victorian city where doilies and knick-knacks overflowed the parlours. The novelist Ethel Wilson wrote that there was very little art or decoration on people's walls in the early years, just heavily framed pictures of dead relatives.[1] The showing of an artist's work depended on the good graces of local businesses. B.C. painter Bert Binning remembered that in the 1920s there might be a row of watercolours on display in an upstairs room of the Hudson's Bay store annex or, occasionally, an exhibition in one of the framing shops on Robson Street.[2] He may have been thinking specifically of John Vanderpant's photo studio, which exhibited on a couple of occasions pieces by Fred Varley, Jock Macdonald, and Emily Carr. The construction of an art gallery on West Georgia Street in 1931 was a significant step forward, though Garnett Sedgewick, a professor at UBC, lamented that "so much debris from nineteenth-century England had washed up" on the gallery's walls.[3] Cheney quickly joined forces with individuals like Myrtle Erickson who were actively promoting the work of local artists. Nan Cheney had already befriended reclusive Emily Carr, and although it was sometimes a difficult relationship, her correspondence with this eccentric woman, one of the country's great painters, has left a clear and intimate account of British Columbia's art scene from 1937 to 1945.

Cheney and her husband were part of what they called the "Capilano Colony," a small group of artists who during the 1930s and '40s spent summers living close together along the Capilano River in North Vancouver. In addition to the Cheneys, this group included, from time to time, the painter Jock Macdonald; cellist Ralph Cox; Jessie Faunt, an art teacher at Point Grey junior high school; and an English-born journalist and art critic, Sydney Smith, who eventually moved in with Miss Faunt. The group not only shared a love of painting and design but also enjoyed activities such as playing badminton in Jessie Faunt's lighted court and listening to music until midnight ("such a relief from the radio, the newspapers, & the horrors & slaughter of this awful war").[4] They were joined in 1942 by Dr. Ethelyn Trapp, five minutes away on Keith Road, who developed an estate she named Klee Wyck in honour of Emily Carr and which she eventually bequeathed to West Vancouver as an arts centre.

When Arthur entered Point Grey junior high school in 1937, he was certain that he wanted to become a biologist. His consuming hobbies—gathering plants, collecting birds' nests, keeping tropical fish—turned on a fascination with life forms. As he wrote in retrospect, "When [I was] a boy the world was a source of endless wonder to be investigated, collected, dissected, befriended."[5] Sometimes, he would come back from a hike with his grandmother and brother with a salamander for his reptile collection or a wounded bird that he nursed under the bed, where it would likely die and be discovered weeks later in a state of advanced decay. His parents indulged his curiosity. They made no objections to the evil-smelling jars of water full of protozoa and disintegrating organic matter set out on the dining room window ledge for microscopic investigation, though on one occasion his mother drew back when she opened the bread drawer and found a soggy mass of white worms growing there to feed the fish. For a time, Arthur would tell people who asked that he wanted to be an ichthyologist; the word had the right ring.

But the dreams of a young scientist were abandoned when he came under the spell of an unusual art teacher in love with modern painting. This was Jessie Faunt, who travelled across the water by ferry every day from the Capilano Colony to teach her classes. Faunt exhibited some of her own work in local shows, but it was as a teacher that she had a lasting influence. Although she was a short, heavy woman, she seemed to levitate when discussing her favourite painters in class, or when one of her students did well. Nan Cheney wrote in 1938 to Eric Brown, curator of the National Gallery in Ottawa, asking if he had heard of Jessie Faunt, a Vancouver version of Anne Savage: "She has made remarkable progress with her pupils & there are a few very promising ones—Peter Sager age 19 & Arthur Erickson, age 14 to mention two."[6] Cheney made a similar reference to Arthur's promise in a letter to Emily Carr.

As a teenager, Arthur made visits to Capilano Road, sometimes to take painting lessons from Jock Macdonald, but more often to drop in on his teacher and listen to the conversations she had with her friends. Jessie Faunt helped Arthur to see that art was not simply representation but design, composition, and expression.[7] She was the first to expose him to the world of the post-impressionist painters, the Fauvists like Matisse and early abstract painters such as Franz Marc, who emphasized strong colour and painterly qualities. "It was," as he phrased it in the first book he wrote about his career as an architect, "as if a light went on and suddenly all human forms, all landscape, belonged to one design."[8] A feeling of euphoria overwhelmed him at the idea, and he was filled by "a sudden vision of the grand design that pervades nature, the sense of everything following a certain rhythm."[9] In a Blakean vision of totality, he felt that he had the power to see and capture the truth of anything, its deep structure. For the best part of a year he painted day and night, sometimes until two or three in the morning, to give shape to this grand design. Everything he drew, he recalled, whether it was a person, a horse, or a barn, assumed a similar form. Most often he worked in pastels, "since they were quicker and I had so little time to get it all down."[10] Sometimes in the night he felt he was God, for his incandescent visions embraced the universe. In the morning he might wake up still in his clothes.

During that fevered year, Arthur found it difficult to fit into everyday life. He had no interest in the shadowy, banal world of his peers. He didn't want to play baseball or football; the few friends he had were girls. He preferred the solitude of a walk in the woods. But he sought out the company of adults—both because their conversation was interesting and because they encouraged what they regarded as his prodigious gifts. Their praise legitimized Arthur's belief that he was different, special.

One of these adults was a friend of his mother, Eileen Desbrisay, whose passion was to hike to the peaks of local mountains.[11] Eileen was said to have lost a fiancé in the First World War and had therefore never married. She had completed a science degree at UBC, but regarded herself as a strictly amateur botanist. She and Arthur were fast companions for a couple of summers of hiking along the North Shore. She was the first to introduce him to Garibaldi Park, which would be a source of inspiration for him as an artist and an architect.

Arthur had also become interested in landscaping the family property. Neither of his parents were gardeners (it was impossible for Oscar and required more time than Myrtle cared to commit), so they were happy enough to let him create small plots for colourful annuals and a rose bed in the centre of the lawn. At the same time, Oscar was concerned about Arthur's shyness around other boys. He enrolled him in Boy Scouts and, believing that war was almost inevitable for young men of every generation, enrolled both of his sons at an early age with the Seaforth Cadets. Arthur hated these activities, and he would insist as an adult that "any regimentation is anathema to me."[12]

Arthur felt sheltered by his father's protectiveness and shared his love of painting, but he noted that his father was always a little stiffer with him than with Don. His brother fulfilled conventional expectations more easily—he loved to play with soldiers and set out battle formations on the floor. He was also more personable; during the war, Don would imitate Hitler's speeches to everyone's amazement and delight.

In the fall of 1939, Arthur entered Prince of Wales high school, where he became friendly with Bill Baldwin, a comical-looking, good-natured boy who was an outstanding student and, like Arthur, had little interest in team sports. Being new to the city (the Baldwins had moved that summer from Vernon to Vancouver), Bill quickly attached himself to Arthur. They shared a passionate interest in the natural world and would go for long walks to explore different wooded areas and watercourses around the city. In the summer of 1940, after an unrealistic dream of bicycling together to San Francisco, they undertook a two-week hiking trip to Vancouver Island's Forbidden Plateau—the first of Arthur's travel ventures. Both boys had unusually protective parents, who gave permission only on the promise of frequent phone calls home and stays with family friends en route. Bill kept a daybook account of the trip that provides not only an itinerary but also a vivid glimpse of his friend.[13]

On the morning of July 11, with bicycles, bedrolls, camp stove, pup tent, and youth hostel passes, the boys boarded a boat to Nanaimo, where they set out first in search of petroglyphs. They spotted some faint lines on the rocks that possibly depicted "a dragon or a fish," but all that was clearly visible was "John loves Betty and stuff," which they found "disgusting." That evening, after fishing and a swim, they camped at the mouth of a creek on Departure Bay. Next morning, Arthur was determined that they visit a nearby biological station; a professor of zoology from UBC on duty there had extended an invitation to stop by. The professor offered the boys a place to sleep on his boat that night, and the following morning they explored the marine life of the arches and caves along the shore—sea cucumbers, starfish, and sea anemones.

Later that morning, they bicycled north to Qualicum, arriving around noon at the summer house of the Lee family, close neighbours and good friends of the Ericksons. Frank Lee, from the American South, was with Canadian Pacific Railway; his wife, Ruth, dominated the household, which included their only child, Frances Black Lee, known as Blackie. She was already one of Arthur's closest friends. Arthur and Bill stayed for three days and, joined by more of Blackie's friends from the city, helped Mrs. Lee with her "long lists of chores," one afternoon chopping a cord of wood for the fireplace. Every day they phoned home. But the best times were in the evenings, with picnics on the beach and games around a bonfire. "We had hamburgers and ice-cream and real coffee," wrote Bill; "we made donuts, fooled around and sang all night—did I have fun!" And some nights there was dancing at the house, which was what Arthur loved best.

Their goal was to climb to Forbidden Plateau on the mountain chain running down the centre of the island. They left the Lees and bicycled north towards Courtenay but stopped to say hello to the Desbrisays, who pampered them with a big lunch and a bag of donuts for the road. That day ended at Fanny Bay, where the only supper available was at an off-limits pool hall where an old woman served them salad and cookies in a corner. The boys kept bicycling after dark but finally gave up and spent an uneasy night under a railroad bridge.

In Courtenay the next morning, after a breakfast of "3 measly pancakes for 25 cents," they were joined by Blackie's friend John Dayton, who was also heading up to the plateau. They acquired fire permits, had their gear weighed, and then hitchhiked with a logging truck to the base of the climb; the tourist folder had promised tea rooms and comfortable lodgings, but all they found was "a shack, two horses, and a stable."

Next morning, the three boys began a gruelling climb up the trail to Croteau Lake lodge. With provisions tied down on the pack horse, they foraged for berries and drank creek water all day. By nightfall they were at the camp, where they met other hikers, including a group from India, and filled up on "mangy tomato soup, canned beef, and liver." Best of all to Bill was the hot tea, after all the "washy coffee" they had been making for themselves. But it was another fitful night's sleep; the cold and dampness kept them awake.

The boys spent the next two days exploring the hills and lakes on the plateau and made what for reluctant Bill was an exhausting climb to the top of Mt. Albert Edward. To reach the peak, they trekked through patches of "pink snow" coloured by microscopic algae—an effect that was almost hallucinatory.[14] Bill found the view disappointing, but he joined in the race to the top and the ritual "yelling our heads off" and throwing stones over the cliff edge.

The return trip proved to be the biggest challenge of all. With pack horses used only for the ascent, the boys had to carry their packs and camping gear themselves and became hopelessly lost taking a shortcut. It was nearly 7 PM before they reached town and got a room for the night at the Courtenay Hotel. It was three to a bed for $1.50 but nonetheless heaven for Bill; they had hot baths and a corned beef supper, and went to the movies.

Next morning, they reclaimed their bicycles and set out. They stopped first at the Desbrisays, and there, to their surprise, they found Arthur's mother and several other panicked adults. Since nobody had heard from the boys in a week, the police had begun searching for them and their names were in the papers and on CBC radio. The boys were embarrassed by all the fuss, but everyone agreed to let the matter drop. That afternoon they went to a park for a swim and then back to the Desbrisays for supper and dancing before returning to the Lees to sleep. Myrtle took the camping gear home in her car and let Bill and Arthur spend one last night together at the youth hostel at Duncan.

When he expanded his diary jottings into a longer narrative of the trip, Bill presented himself as a bumbling clown, dropping precious powdered milk into the dirt, and wearing socks with so many holes there was little to wash. He depicted Arthur, by contrast, as persistently cool and self-assured, apart from their group and somewhat mysterious, having an experience all his own. Baldwin's intuition was accurate: this trip was a formative experience that fed Arthur's imagination in years to come. Describing for a magazine reporter in 1970 the essence of what he had tried to achieve with his university on a mountaintop, he said: "Have you ever been mountaineering? I remember my first time, climbing out of the treeline, first the meadows, and glimpsing the vistas to come, then climbing to the summit and having that explosion of view . . . Simon Fraser is like that... Education is like that. As you learn more, you are able to see more vistas of human knowledge and experience."[15]

ARTHUR'S MOTHER WAS unstinting in her eagerness to promote her special child. Seeing her son at the easel, she was determined that her artistic friends become aware of his talent. Arthur's relationship with one of Canada's leading painters, Lawren Harris, came about through his mother's friendship with Nan Cheney.

Cheney wrote enthusiastically to Emily Carr about the Harrises moving to Vancouver in the spring of 1941, and later that year, at Myrtle's urging, she arranged for Lawren and his wife, Bess, to visit the Erickson house. Arthur recalled the occasion in eloquent language: "I anticipated the visit with great excitement and remember vividly when they walked up the path to my parents' house how imposing he was—erect, trim, vital, with that corona of white hair framing soft but lively brown eyes and the beautiful Bess at his side. Her beauty emanated not only from startling blue eyes but from the grace that pervaded her manner, her gestures, her voice and what it said. Devoted, radiant, each shone in the other's presence."[16] Arthur showed them his sketches, chiefly pastels he had made of prairie landscapes while on the most recent family vacation to Winnipeg. But while Harris looked at them carefully, he seemed largely indifferent; his only positive comment was "swell." Arthur felt let down after their visit: "I was looking for somebody to say, well, you are a genius, just devote your whole life to it, but they didn't."[17]

A few months later, however, to his surprise, Arthur received a phone call from Harris, who asked to borrow two abstract mountain pieces to be included with an exhibition of his own non-objective paintings that he was mounting for the Vancouver Art Gallery. These were pastels Arthur had done from pencil sketches made when hiking in Garibaldi Park with Eileen Desbrisay and the local botanical club. There was a vogue for working in Garibaldi in the late 1930s. Nan Cheney and Jock Macdonald frequently sketched in the park, and Cheney wrote to Eric Brown on December 1, 1938, that "the material up there is unbelievable."[18] A pastel Arthur had titled "Black Tusk" was of particular interest to Harris. Arthur's sketches received honourable mention in the show, and they drew special attention because they had been done when Erickson was only sixteen, making him probably the youngest artist to exhibit in a major gallery in Canada. The show went on to the University of British Columbia and then to Toronto.

The attention Arthur received brought him into contact with other artists, and he was invited to take lessons with Jack Shadbolt and B.C. Binning at the Vancouver School of Art, then housed "in a bulky wooden monster of a building on Richards Street."[19] He would remember those classes as among the most rewarding experiences of his early life. The lessons in drawing with Bert Binning were especially valuable, because they taught Arthur "how much a simple line could imply the mass and detail of the body, and how the scrutiny of the focussed eye could reveal its mastery over the moving hand."[20] Binning's valuable instruction in how less detail is more would also leave an indelible imprint on Erickson's drawing style as an architect. Vancouver's small community of artists was eager to foster talented young people, and Arthur was regarded as a prodigy—though not by his high school art teacher, who, unlike Jessie Faunt, consistently gave him Bs.

As it turned out, the exhibition with Lawren Harris would be the pinnacle of Arthur's achievements as a painter. He later observed, "My painting ideas were original, but I wasn't very good technically."[21] However, a thoughtful review of the show by Capilano Colony resident Sydney Smith drew attention in an uncanny way to features of Harris's abstract art that would later be attributed to Arthur's work as an architect. Harris's emphasis on basic forms gave his compositions "architectural solidity," Smith wrote, and this scope was immense. Smith was especially impressed by the effects of light in Harris's paintings—translucence and opacity—and the way the problem of "pure vision" was articulated. He was also intrigued by how Harris achieved something like timelessness in his paintings through the element of "perfect proportion," a harmony of relations that simultaneously elicits an emotional response and satisfies an intellectual need. He recognized the qualities of modesty and unpretentiousness in Harris's work as well, a restraint in art that Smith identified as rare and welcome.[22] These were all judgements that critics would later apply to Arthur's work.

Lawren Harris (1885–1970), whose grandfather was one of the founders of the Massey-Harris farm machinery company, was expensively educated in Toronto and in Berlin, where he studied painting for four years. In Canada he went on remote northern sketching trips with J.E.H. MacDonald, was befriended by Tom Thomson, and emerged in the early 1920s as the leader in the creation of the Group of Seven, a fraternity of artists who were inspired to paint Canada's wilderness, giving the country its own artistic tradition. Harris's work stood out sharply for its austere and elemental rendering of northern landscapes. In the 1920s he fell under the spell of theosophy, and in the 1930s his monolithic natural forms became increasingly non-objective. Through abstract painting, Harris sought to portray the realm of spiritual realities—to make the sublime visible.

Lawren and Bess Harris, in middle age, came to Vancouver after living for several years in the United States. With their avant-garde intellectual pursuits and elegant lifestyle, they filled a void in the city's modest cultural life. They regularly opened their home to friends on Saturday evenings. These ethereal "soirées" followed a set routine: after a preliminary period of talk while people arrived, Harris would get up and turn out the lights and "then you sat for three hours in the dark listening to an extraordinary collection of records," on what Arthur assumed was "probably the finest hi-fi in the city, with very interesting people. I was sixteen, and terribly flattered to be included. A whole different world opened up to me."[23] The Harrises' friends included such prominent patrons of the arts as the Koerners, the Grauers, and the Buckerfields; musicians like Harry, Frances, and Murray Adaskin and Jean Coulthard; writers Ethel Wilson and Earle Birney; painters Jack Shadbolt and B.C. Binning; and critic Ira Dilworth, to name a few. With the wartime accumulation of refugees from Europe, there might be guests from outside the city, musicians like Sir John Barbirolli, a guest conductor of the Vancouver Symphony; the composer Arthur Benjamin; visiting dancers; and poets.

Nan Cheney describes those evenings more than once in letters to Victoria painter Humphrey Toms: "We spent most of the evening in the dark listening to the gramophone—music box, they call it, & the last word in recording. They have *all* the symphonies and thousands of records... We had drinks & sandwiches & conversation afterwards."[24] In another letter to Toms, she mentions a more intimate evening: "You should have been with us for dinner at the Harrises as you do appreciate things nicely done. Everything was perfect—the dinner, which was beautifully served by a silent maid—the silver—china—glass—in perfect taste. We sat by the fire & talked & enjoyed it all tremendously."[25] On one occasion Emily Carr was there. Cheney had planned to introduce her to Arthur, but he was absent that evening—something he came to regret because Carr died before another occasion presented itself. The Harrises lived at that time on an elevated section of Nanton Street with a striking view towards Howe Sound. Arthur would write that "those rooms composed of cool silvers and Lawren's abstracts of the blue voids of mountain summits provided a fitting atmosphere for initiation into art and the Eastern philosophies of India and Tibet."[26]

In this exalted ambience, the conversation frequently turned to Buddhist and Hindu texts, to Boehme and Swedenborg, and to those remarkable women, Madame Blavatsky and Annie Besant, guiding lights in the practice of theosophy ("divine wisdom"). Their published meditations and those of W.Q. Judge, an Irish-American who believed he was a reincarnated Tibetan mahatma, proposed the synthesis of all religions into one transcendent whole whereby the unity of humankind under God could be perceived. Not all of the guests on a Saturday evening followed that path, but most were disposed to believe nonetheless that science, art, and religion were moving towards a common goal of peace and happiness. As a painter, Lawren Harris believed that art was meaningful only when it was the expression of a philosophical system, bringing the viewer to see into this realm of eternal life: "Without the philosophy... in the work of a great artist, you have nothing."[27] To render nature's essential elements, he moved steadily towards abstraction in his paintings, "reaching for a universal language that work[ed] on a plane higher than representation" that moved the viewer from the intimate to the ethereal.[28] For a boy of sixteen this was heady, exhilarating talk. More important for Arthur, Harris's non-material approach to the world made possible a smooth and logical transition from a Christian Science upbringing to the more subtle, spiritual religions of the East.

THERE WAS A great gap between this sophisticated world of adults and Arthur's world at Prince of Wales high school, though the praise bestowed on him had given him a degree of self-assurance. His classmates remember him as a self-confident young man, not aloof exactly, but distant, "as if he came from a country where nobody else lived."[29] Paul Wright's cousin Richard, known to his friends as Dick, was Don Erickson's best friend and spent a lot of time at the Erickson home. He recalled that one evening, during a party there, Arthur sat in the middle of the living room reading a book, never for a moment distracted by his brother's friends.[30] There was also self-mocking humour in Arthur's poise. His brother told the story of the time Arthur was supposed to go to a party wearing a white shirt and black tie. Since his white shirt lay rumpled in the laundry basket, Arthur stripped down, painted his chest white with watercolours, added buttons and a little bow tie, and when dry slipped his jacket on.[31]

In the school's *Three Feathers Year Book* for 1940–41, Arthur is described as greatly interested in girls: "He doesn't know much about skiing / But he's never at a loss when she-ing," the editor rhymes.[32] And he remembered himself at that stage as falling in love with a series of beautiful young women. He was fascinated with the way girls dressed, their sense of style and grooming, and with their conversation, which was more likely to be about music or the movies than about another tiresome football match. There were several girls with whom he had intense friendships—Kay Wintemute, Joan Sievenpiper—but the friendship that would engage him the longest, indeed for a lifetime, was with Blackie Lee.

The Lees, who lived two blocks from the Ericksons, were part of a group of close friends who had come to Vancouver from Winnipeg.

Many young men were relocated by their companies to positions in Vancouver after the First World War, Mr. Lee with the CPR being typical. Being from Winnipeg was a special bond for these young families. Myrtle Erickson was friendly with Ruth Lee, but she took special delight in the Lees' daughter, who was sweet-natured and fun-loving, and simultaneously sophisticated and discerning. Arthur appreciated all of those qualities in his friend, and she was drawn irresistibly to his courteous and gentle ways. It was on the dance floor that their relationship blossomed. As Arthur's brother observed, "They were inseparable once a band struck up, and when they danced together others cleared the floor to watch."[33] They started going together to Saturday night gatherings of the Young People's Association at St. John's Shaughnessy Anglican Church, where teenagers enjoyed badminton and refreshments, but what drew Arthur and Blackie was dancing to records. Myrtle Erickson remembered her son moving around the house to dance steps from the time he was a small boy; whenever he heard music Arthur would start to dance. Blackie Lee recalled how they danced together at house parties in the late 1930s and, when they were a little older, at the Palomar, a downtown Granville Street nightclub. They would even set a record going and dance on the front porch in broad daylight. "He was far and away the best dancer I ever met."[34]

Dancing would be a lifelong passion for Arthur, and for a brief season as a teenager he thought seriously of becoming a ballet dancer. One of his most vivid memories as a child was accompanying his father on business trips to Victoria and staying with him at the Empress Hotel. There, a little orchestra played for the ladies drinking afternoon tea. Arthur would dance to the music and they would clap and say how cute he was. He loved the attention and praise.

When in 1941 Blackie Lee went to Toronto's Havergal School for a year, Arthur found other girls to take dancing. Invariably they were remarkable for their beauty and charm as well as their lively grace on the dance floor. And they were girls from Shaughnessy, the daughters of bankers and company executives, who lived in comfortable circumstances. But Arthur was not physically excited by these girls in the way he knew other boys, often crudely, were. In fact, he was quick to criticize the female body for the slightest imperfections. In what might be taken as a misogynist piece of writing, he warns his 1942 yearbook readers in an essay titled "Make-Up" that women, "camouflaged for battle," sometimes appear like a "madman's dream," and he advises the girls in his class: "Do not go around with that red glow on your faces as if suffering from permanent embarrassment. Forget those hideous shades of pink and carmine that fortify your lips as barriers that shout very plainly, 'Scram, you bum,' and leave a gritty and unbecoming smirk on the rims of drinking glasses, cigarette butts and all with which they come in contact. Give us just one peek at what you're trying to cover up—then we will say, maybe, 'Put it back on!'"

Instead of daydreaming about girls, Arthur was more likely to be contemplating his destiny. He did not know yet in what way he was special, or why. Was he to be one of the great men of the world? Had he been given the name of a legendary king by accident or design? Would he be called to fulfill a transcendent destiny (Lawren Harris seemed to be showing him a path), or would he have to create that great destiny for himself? When a few years later he read Joyce's *A Portrait of the Artist as a Young Man*, he found a passage that spoke to him.

> The noise of children at play annoyed him and their silly voices made him feel...that he was different from others. He did not want to play. He wanted to meet in the real world the unsubstantial image which his soul so constantly beheld. He did not know where to seek it or how: but a premonition which led him on told him that this image would, without any overt act of his, encounter him.[35]

This shimmering promise had a potency that belied the injured pride Arthur experienced when he was chased by a bully or scorned for his disinterest in sports. He had one craving—for the power of self-expression in some imaginative form—but to achieve that he knew he would have to acquire a technique.

To that goal he was willing to surrender everything, including the discipline needed to do well at school. Arthur graduated from high school with four B grades and two Cs, no As. He was capable of first-class work occasionally, but being late for class, independent, not always co-operative, he often missed the mark, his report cards a perfect blueprint for the man and the career that lay ahead.

Family life, with interesting visitors at the house, remained the warm, exciting centre of Arthur's world. It was frequently made more colourful by Emma Fox. She was a heavy-set Swedish woman, a widow with a raucous voice who spoke her opinions freely. Those who remembered her said she cooked like an angel, but her language was unprintable. Emma Fox did housecleaning and cooking for various families in Shaughnessy, preferring those who gave good parties. Men drifted into the kitchen to hear her latest outrageous story. She scandalized the Erickson boys with statements like: "That one can put his slippers under my bed." She doted on Oscar, but her own marriage had been one long argument. One day when discussing with Myrtle the possibility of an afterlife, she exclaimed, "Well, I suppose I don't care that much myself, but I just don't want to meet up with Harry [her late husband] again." What especially pleased Arthur were her European-style open-faced sandwiches.

Eagerly learning about the world's different cultures, Arthur proposed to his parents that they find other ways of celebrating holidays. One year, instead of a Christmas tree, he devised a large "kissing bower" like the Druids had fashioned for winter solstice out of oak branches and mistletoe. Another year the theme was Chinese. These alternative celebrations became public events: Christmas Eve was open house at the Ericksons'. Myrtle always planned to renovate or redecorate the house for Christmas, but she never started early enough, and scented candles were needed to cover the smell of fresh paint. One year, when the new living room curtains she had ordered did not arrive, Arthur hung rolls of tissue paper decorated with Chinese-like characters in metallic gold paint over the old ones. The effect, in his opinion at least, was quite striking.

But nothing was quite as memorable as the observation one year of Santa Lucia, the Scandinavian celebration of light. Myrtle, always eager for a bargain, found a large quantity of candles at a good price. She placed them around the living room, and for the centre of the dining-room table Arthur created a spiral of candles in pyramid form. The tapers were lit as the company assembled, creating a warm glow throughout the house. But the guests had barely sat down to their smorgasbord dinner before the first fires broke out. Oscar, on artificial legs, lurched up from the table and managed to contain most of the upsets in the living room, but he was powerless to prevent the pyramid of candles from collapsing onto the dining table. Among the guests that evening were Bert and Jessie Binning. Many years later, Jessie Binning, a centenarian, frail as an eggshell teacup, her concentration fleeting, would still remember that evening. She said in summary of mother and son: "Arthur—Arthur was always buoyant, but Myrtle—well, she was flamboyant."[36]

3

Soldier

WHEN ARTHUR, AGE EIGHTEEN, finished high school in June 1942, the Erickson house was heavy with indecision. Myrtle supported his wish to follow a course in arts at university. But Oscar had concerns about how his son would make his living. Further, with the war in its third year, he wanted Arthur to enrol in the army's engineering course, so that he would get technical training and earn a military rank better than private. Oscar's experience with the general infantry having proven disastrous, he wanted to shield his son from similar exposure.

These matters were not fully resolved when Arthur left home that summer to work at a logging camp at Quatsino Sound on northern Vancouver Island. His employer was Lawrence Killam. Arthur's apprehension about the venture was reduced because Paul Wright was going with him; their friendship had been cemented when Paul saved Arthur from drowning on a family outing.

Arthur and Paul would spend two summers together in the forest. Their assignment the first year was to clear brush and cut down small trees to speed up the growth of the larger ones, especially the Douglas firs. The logging camp was, naturally, rough: meals were served with soup, main course, and dessert all on the same tray, and the boys had to move fast to get enough to eat. The sit-down toilet was set over a stream, and there was always a lineup. The men in camp Arthur would later recognize included renegades on the run, adventurers out for a quick profit, and visionaries. Most of them used language that Arthur and Paul never heard at home. But Arthur had brought books to read, and when he wrote letters home he described the woods and mountain landscapes with such attention to shape and colour that his friends felt they had been shown a painting. The lasting impact of those summers on Arthur was the nature of the forest itself, a wilderness full of mystery and some terror.[1]

For his first year at the University of British Columbia, Arthur enrolled in a wide range of courses, but for second year he and Bill Baldwin entered the Canadian Officers Training Corps (COTC) and took basic engineering as his father urged. He recalled glumly that "they taught you how to take a car apart and put it back together again."[2] Gordon Shrum was his physics professor, and Arthur had doubts about Shrum's depth of knowledge and his pedagogy. When he encountered him later in life, what he remembered first was that Shrum's demonstrations to illustrate principles of physics never worked. His view may have been skewed by the fact that Shrum was also the colonel in command of the COTC, a position that involved six hours of drill and parade every week. Arthur would say of his training on the field that he could never learn so much as "to click [his] heels properly." The horrors of the war struck home in the summer of 1943 when Aunt Annie's popular and fun-loving son, Oscar, was killed in Libya. His death cast a pall over the family.

Nonetheless, the scope for learning at university was broader, and Arthur entered with an enthusiasm best reflected in his ambition to read all the great works of Western literature—if possible, in their language of composition. The horizons for an exciting social life were similarly expanded. Blackie Lee was at UBC, and whenever there was an opportunity they went dancing together, going up to the Green Room over the Old Auditorium. There they would put on records—Latin American dance tunes—and dance with the overtly flirtatious movements that were then fashionable. There might be a choir practising below or a lecture on classical music, but from overhead came the tantalizing rhythms of the rumba and samba.

Blackie took roles in campus stage productions (her deadpan portrayal of a deaf-mute servant was the hit of the theatre season in

1943), so Arthur joined the Players Club and volunteered to work on the sets as head of the "properties committee." He hurried about town borrowing props from businesses and friends. For a "dreadful" pre-war English comedy by Gerald Savory titled *George and Margaret*, he arranged with a local jewellery store, in return for program advertising, the loan of a set of sterling silver. But before the show's run was over, the silver had been stolen and despite all efforts was never retrieved.

Arthur's passion for hiking in the mountains grew stronger, doubtless abetted by strong associations with Lawren Harris's philosophy of persistent upward striving. Mountains for Harris, as for most mystics, lifted the seeker from the confused ruck of humanity to a closer experience of the eternal. He was reported to have once entered a trance-like state on reaching a mountain peak, experienced glossolalia, and broken into an ecstatic, unintelligible chanting.[3] Harris's visual language of mountains and ice and sky was one that Arthur understood well.

His preference would have been to hike on his own, but to reassure his anxious parents he found companions. One successful climbing expedition in Garibaldi Park was undertaken by a group that included Kay Holland, accompanied by her fiancé, Dewar Cooke; Mary Buckerfield; and Blackie Lee. They were equipped with climbing ropes and crampons, and with dried food in case of an emergency, and they hired a guide to take them to particularly striking perspectives. Mary Buckerfield photographed Arthur in a meditative pose in what would become an enduring image of the architect against a mountain background. Future critics, including his brother, Don, would come to see mountains as a major element in Arthur's work, citing especially the ascent to the Vancouver law courts rooftop that proceeds with steps winding like switchbacks, its pathway planted in bushes and grasses, and then the glass ceiling, like a glacier reflecting the sky.

The influence of Lawren Harris on Arthur cannot be overstated. Many years later he would record the strong feelings he experienced in the company of the Harrises: "At that young and searching age I was entranced by [their] lofty concepts for they counterbalanced the awful concurrent violence in Europe that I would have to face in another year. The discussions put the tyrannical tendencies of mankind into a more benign cast of human fate, making them less ominous and disillusioning for one beginning a life's adventure."[4]

Arthur was in awe of Lawren and Bess's spiritual assurance and easy grace, yet he knew from the talk of adults that these were not easily won. Lawren had much in his life he needed to transcend: his father's death when he was nine, an emotional Baptist upbringing, an unhappy first marriage with three children he was responsible for, enlistment in the army, a nervous breakdown at thirty-one, his brother's death in the war, his love for Bess Housser, the wife of his best friend. When, after a divorce not recognized in Canada, he and Bess married, they entered into a celibate relationship, one that they felt brought them peace and a closer contact with the world of eternal spirit. Arthur would write in retrospect that to him, at sixteen, "their 'marriage' appeared to be a blessed relationship of two superior beings who emanated a serenity few could attain."[5] It was an extension of theosophist teaching that humankind has the spiritual power to transcend its "animality," or what Christian Scientists like Bess would call "animal magnetism." In an essay Harris wrote philosophically of his situation: "We must extricate ourselves from the delusions and confusions of earth before we can awaken to spiritual reality. We must transform the desires of the personal man before we can become a beneficent power for good in the realm of consciousness and become aware of the god within."[6] Arthur was deeply absorbed by their way of life and would later reflect: "Their spiritual view of things ... gave me a confidence that this was a way one could view the world. This was a way one could work, and that it had a purpose because they dedicated everything—the way they lived, their house, their work, their association with others—to try through art to bring people closer to that spiritual reality."[7]

To his peers, Arthur already seemed to have achieved the serenity he admired so much. But he had his demons. Like Lawren Harris, who had been raised in a close relationship with his mother, Arthur was struggling to free himself from overanxious parents and to determine for himself what direction his life would take. And he was growing increasingly worried about his sexuality, specifically his lack of physical desire for women. He was aware that his close friendship with Blackie was disappointing to her and that it left him, in turn, feeling lonely. But he could not imagine a physical relationship with his male friends. He was drawn instead to the way of the monk. The only real life for him, he determined, was the life of the mind and the eye, undefiled by emotions or the physical necessities of the material world. This cerebral detachment impressed his classmates at UBC and invested him with a certain mystery.

His reading of another artist's life would serve as a beacon throughout his early life. Perhaps it came in a class at the university, perhaps in a reference made by Harris, but asked when he first encountered the poetry of Rainer Maria Rilke, Arthur could only say that it seemed he had always known Rilke, that he was born knowing what the poet said. At the heart of his love for Rilke was a concept akin to Harris's thought—that God is created by the world's artists, and that the existence of God can only be predicated for the remote future as a final product of the exertion of all artists throughout the ages. In his *Book of Hours*, Rilke writes: "We are building you with tremulous hands . . . God, you are vast."[8]

Yet Rilke's belief was that the artist is a singular individual who has glimpsed the Infinite and is on a return journey in life; alone, he meets everyone advancing in the opposite direction. Influenced by Friedrich Nietzsche's thought and example, Rilke's life and writings spoke strongly to Arthur's sense of being an individual apart from others. Rilke had married a sculptor and fathered a child, but the relationship was brief. He believed in love without possession and lived apart from his family. In *The Notebooks of Malte Laurids Brigge*, he dramatized the idea most powerfully in his recasting of the prodigal son parable from the Bible as the legend of the man who did not want to be loved and described the son's family defection not in the familiar terms of guilt and repentance but as the experience of a man not wanting to impose love on others.[9] Rilke's inverted parable struck home with Arthur. At the same time, he was urgently aware of another of Rilke's famous observations: "Artistic experience lies so incredibly near to sexual experience, to its pain and delight, that both phenomena are really only different forms of one and the same yearning and joy."[10] In step with modernists like T.S. Eliot, Arthur envisaged the possibility of expressing his inner feelings in the guise of impersonal forms. There grew in his mind the idea of art as an expression of the ideal and the artist as a monumental personality set apart, redeemed through art and immune to human weakness and criticism.

In the early months of 1944, there was something like "a miraculous delivery" for Arthur, as he later phrased it. That winter a recruitment officer from the British Intelligence Corps arrived on campus to select young men who could be trained as Japanese interpreters. Those who already spoke an Asian language were given priority; a second tier of recruits was drawn from those who knew two languages. Whether Arthur, unilingual, was chosen on the recommendation of university faculty, or whether his father's continued connection with the British and Canadian armies was instrumental, is no longer possible to determine, but his ability to learn the Japanese language quickly was never in question. Classes of twenty began in early spring and continued for thirteen months. The program extended beyond language to include various aspects of Japanese culture. There were courses on the geography of Japan, its cultural practices in a broad sense, military law, and history.

The school was run by Major Arthur Mackenzie, who had been a professor in Japan. His teenage sons, partly raised in Japan, helped tutor small groups, as did a Caucasian who had worked for years alongside Japanese men in Vancouver. But for Arthur, much more interesting as teachers were two Japanese individuals married to Caucasians. Mr. Ballard, who explained various cultural practices, was a Japanese man married to an English woman; he used his wife's surname. Mrs. Griffiths was a Japanese woman who had married a Welshman working at the British embassy in Tokyo. She was the principal language teacher at the school, remembered as a charming, well-educated woman who deferred to her overbearing

husband in all things, consulting with him before assigning examination grades, walking a few steps behind him.[11] She took the students through the ritual of the Japanese tea ceremony as a way of
introducing them to the sophisticated subtleties of her culture. With
her sensitivity and modest poise, Mrs. Griffiths completely altered
Arthur's perception of the "enemy nation" and made him aware of
the plight of Japanese-Canadian students, reflected in such humili-
ating campus newspaper headlines as "Jap Jitters" and "ıss Aids in
Jap Evacuation."[12] When polled in 1944, nearly 40 percent of UBC
students said they were against Japanese-Canadian students returning to the university after the war: they should be expelled from
the country, some replied, and one person said they should be shot.
Among those answering more positively, a number argued that
returning students of Japanese ancestry should be isolated from all
aspects of Japanese culture to ensure they would be wholly Canadian.[13] But Mrs. Griffiths had won Arthur's heart: he visited her at
her home in Vancouver as long as she lived, and for years he kept
her photograph on a bookshelf in his office. When interviewers later
asked Mrs. Griffiths about her famous pupil, she would say simply,
"He is a genius and a good man."[14]

One classmate was astounded by how quickly Arthur was able to
learn both spoken and written Japanese: he told an interviewer that
Arthur "had an amazing visual memory."[15] This man was George
Swinton, a refugee from Vienna whose family lived in a gracious
home on the edge of the university campus. He was seven years older
than Arthur, but they soon fell in together because Swinton had a
passion for art; he would one day become an art professor at the University of Manitoba and be responsible for creating the internationally famous Inuit collection at the Winnipeg Art Gallery. The men
practised Japanese together and began spending time at each other's
homes, discussing art, literature, and philosophy. George introduced
Arthur to the Jean-Christophe novels of Romain Rolland—with titles
like *Dawn, Morning, Adolescent, Revolt*—which traced the course of
an artist's life. Like the poems of Rilke and Joyce's *Portrait of the
Artist as a Young Man*, these were books that set out for Arthur the

archetypal story of the imagination, and in the story of a musician's development from earliest childhood he recognized some of his own intense experiences. In Jean-Christophe's delirious ambitions, Arthur was reminded especially of the ecstasy he had felt in his early teens: his painter's vision of the underlying structures to everything in the world and his sense that to create art was to be God on earth. But another passage stood in relief—Jean-Christophe's reflections on being in love but not knowing with whom. "Nothing is more wearing than love without a definite object; it eats away and saps the strength like a fever... A known passion leads to excess; it is not a wasting away. Anything rather than emptiness."[16]

Myrtle and Oscar were eager to have George Swinton visit. George was athletic—he had played football at McGill and worked locally as a part-time ski instructor—so he engaged Oscar in easy conversation about sports. He was spirited and strikingly handsome, and his seemingly extroverted, fun-loving nature buoyed Arthur in this critical period. Myrtle had already become friendly with George's mother through a mutual friend.

George had recently married, but he still lived with his widowed mother, two brothers, and "Uncle Hans." The latter, whose connection to the family remained mysterious to Arthur, kept a greenhouse with exotic plants, his prize flora being a black orchid. George's mother, Elizabeth Schwitzer, had belonged to the landowning Hungarian aristocracy and was accustomed to a life of managing servants, testing recipes in her kitchen, and doing needlework. She had organized the family's departure from Austria in 1937 because of her sons' outspoken criticism of the Nazi presence in Vienna and the possibility of undocumented Jewish ancestry in the family. Her husband had been an antique collector, and the family of necessity had left much behind, but the many paintings on their walls and furniture in classic styles made a strong impression on Arthur, who was sometimes invited to dinner. Blackie Lee recalled Mrs. Schwitzer (the sons had anglicized the name to Swinton) as having created "a home with old world culture and charm." The house itself—mansion would be the more accurate term—had been designed in 1912 in grand Tudor style by the pioneer B.C. architect Samuel Maclure. The ten-acre waterfront property, where the young friends strolled in a spacious formal garden, had a panoramic view across the Strait of Georgia and north to Howe Sound. The original owner, a prominent Vancouver lawyer, had given it the name Kanakla, a Salish word meaning "house on the cliff." Mrs. Schwitzer renamed the house Langara, after the eighteenth-century Spanish explorer who had passed through the waters just offshore. Eventually, after two more owners, it would be designated a heritage building, purchased by the University of British Columbia and known thereafter as Cecil Green Park House.

In the summer of 1944 a young woman entered Arthur's life who would also become a lifetime friend. He and Diana Chesterton met at a party on Pasley Island (just off Bowen Island) where the Bell-Irvings, one of Vancouver's premier business families, had a cottage. His attraction to Diana was instantaneous; not only was she strikingly beautiful and spirited, but when the music began to play Arthur could see she was the best dancer on the floor. The feeling was mutual: "Arthur didn't just shuffle around the floor like most young men; he entered into the rhythm of the music spontaneously, and joyfully led his partner like a dance instructor. He was a performer."[17] Blackie Lee was in Montreal that summer, and Arthur started keeping company with Diana, taking her with him to the Harris's listening parties on Saturday evenings; she, in turn, invited him to parties at the Taylors', whose daughter, Patricia, was one of her best friends. The two were eager for house parties where there would be dancing, and Diana was soon enchanted by her new suitor.

The Chestertons lived in a fine home on Laurier Avenue in Shaughnessy; it was called Bickerton after an ancestral property in England. Diana's father, approaching seventy, was at the close of a distinguished career as superintendent for the Bank of Montreal in western Canada. Her grandfather had been an architect in Ottawa. British author G.K. Chesterton was her father's first cousin, and Diana remembered how on a visit G.K., a stout man overflowing one of the dining-room chairs, had brought her a set of Russian dolls.

Arthur was welcomed into Diana's home, which he would remember with pleasure as being quite grand. The atmosphere was hushed on special occasions when a plate was set for Diana's brother, who had died of meningitis at age six.

To Diana's eyes, the Ericksons had an extraordinary household; the doors were never locked, and if a friend dropped by and found no one at home, he or she might stretch out on the sofa for a nap until someone returned. The house was always brimming with different opinions; there might be argumentative visitors such as Earle and Esther Birney. An invitation for dinner did not observe any particular timetable, and the kitchen was invariably a scene of chaos. More than once Diana enjoyed herself in the kitchen, chopping ingredients as Myrtle tried out a new recipe for her guests.

Like his mother, Arthur had little concern for the clock, and to Diana's occasional mortification he would take her to events long after they had started. They arrived two hours late for dinner the first time she met the Swintons. The educated conversation of Arthur's older friends was often beyond the reach of a self-conscious girl just finishing high school. At the same time, she recognized that Arthur's casualness sometimes bordered on naïveté. There was a common phrase at the time: "See you at the bijou," meaning simply, "See you somewhere for a good time." Diana was with Arthur the evening he first heard the phrase, and he led her on a madcap search of the downtown hotels—the Devonshire, the Georgia, and so on—looking for friends in the "Bijoux room."

But Arthur was far from lighthearted. The anxiety he experienced as service in the army grew closer was reflected in one of the intense experiences he often returned to in memory. While studying Japanese, he rode the rails to the Okanagan on a bitterly cold day with a language school classmate who was studying for the priesthood. They stayed with the young acolyte's friends near Kelowna. Out walking under a new moon one evening, they came across an animal's skeleton, and Arthur froze with fright. He experienced the kind of premonition his mother and grandmother were given to—in this case a foreshadowing of his death. His friend walked him back to the room where they were sleeping for the night and calmed him down with religious readings.

When thirteen months of Japanese classes came to an end in March 1945, Arthur, appointed to the rank of lieutenant, was among ten men given a commission for special service as interpreters overseas. Mrs. Swinton held a lunch for Arthur and George, to which Mrs. Griffiths was invited, but in the Erickson home there was no farewell party. Myrtle was distraught at Arthur's imminent departure; seeing her slender, blue-eyed son, now five feet, nine inches, 150 pounds, with his soldier's uniform and kit bag like his father before him, caused her almost unbearable anxiety. But one often-recalled event did take place that spring just before Arthur's departure. At a dance in the Panorama Room on the roof of the Vancouver Hotel, which both the Erickson and Chesterton families attended, Arthur, like many young men, was wearing his uniform. A young Dal Richards led the orchestra in some of the new Latin dance tunes, and near the close of the evening, Diana became aware that the other dancers had melted away to the sides of the room and she and Arthur were giving a duo performance. When the music came to an end, there was a round of applause—a soldier's send-off.

There was one more event that spring that Arthur would never forget—an evening at the Buckerfields' with a celebrated young musician. Sophisticated entertaining in Vancouver at that time was confined to private homes, and Amy Buckerfield had invited some friends to meet Leonard Bernstein, a fast-rising star from New York who was then just twenty-four years old. It was April 1945, and Bernstein was staying with the Buckerfields during a week of rehearsals before conducting a concert with the Vancouver Symphony Orchestra. Lenny, as he liked to be called, was enjoying the success of his first musical, *On the Town,* and at the private gathering he played some pieces from that work, along with selections from Mozart's *Magic Flute.* Mary Buckerfield would later write: "It is doubtful whether [Vancouver] ever experienced in the person of one man so much talent and white-hot enthusiasm. He was so full of music and ideas they were exuding from every pore—ideas ranging from great literature to history and back to music from the Blues to Bach."[18] Arthur was dazzled by Bernstein's gifts, his ideas, and his electrifying physical energy.

ARTHUR LEFT FOR the war in the Far East in April 1945; he wasn't yet twenty-one. "We didn't know where we were going or who we were going with," he told a journalist many years later, referring to the secret nature of many such missions. "No one could have been more incompetent," he added. "It would have been an absolute disaster if we had encountered active combat."[19] Setting out for war was, in his own words, "frightening." But the anxiety of departure was partly offset by the well-travelled, self-confident presence of George Swinton and by the first glimpses of the world abroad. The troop planes had no windows. However, when you lifted the lid off the garbage can toilet and depressed the pedal to flush, the plane opened directly onto the earth below. Arthur remembered especially his first glimpse of North Africa with its blue coastline and palm trees. The destination was Bombay, but the plane made a series of loading and refuelling stops: Montreal, Halifax, the Canary Islands. A three-day stop in Cairo was Arthur's first experience in what would become a lifetime of exploring exotic lands.

When, after a stop in Karachi, the group of ten Canadians finally arrived in Bombay on May 8, there was no one there to receive them. With their commission, fifty pounds of Japanese dictionaries, and little basic training, the young men were supposed to form part of a commando unit with British Intelligence that would broadcast periodically behind enemy lines to demoralize Japanese troops. In Bombay the May heat was intense, the crowds and confusion overwhelming. "Nobody knows anything about us," Swinton lamented in a letter to Saul Cherniak, a member of the language class who remained in Canada.[20] It was several days before they were attached to British Intelligence Force 136 and received orders to proceed inland by train to Poona. As Swinton explained to Cherniak, the confusion stemmed from the fact that Force 136 had nothing to do with the British army; it had been organized by Winston Churchill before 1939 to establish British prestige and was privately financed. During the war, Force 136 gave monetary assistance to underground organizations in France and other occupied areas of Europe and also in the Far East, where greater financial interests were at stake for Britain. The members of Force 136, Swinton wrote, "are not paid by the War Office, but by a Bank in Scotland! It is run by civilians and spends money lavishly, pays extremely well, and only few questions asked. This was what we found in Poona."

The inland heat was even more intense as the Indian subcontinent waited for the monsoons, and when it finally started to rain Arthur said, "All we did was make bamboo furniture and try to keep our Japanese dictionaries from going mouldy."[21] Arthur and George spent time sketching (they were able to buy a few basic art supplies at Indian shops) and critiqued each other's work. They also continued to study Japanese and Chinese ideograms. Arthur spent his twenty-first birthday in the back of a transport truck on a manoeuvre outside a hill station near Poona, the purpose of which was never revealed. George, because of his age and longer period of training, had been made a senior officer for the group, but he suffered more than others in the heat, and a story that followed him back to Canada was of the day he persuaded the Indians at their compound to draw him a bath of gin.

Eventually they were enrolled in a rigorous month-long survival course in the jungle. Part of this training involved surviving on the food they could catch and cook. "The person who taught us was not unlike a Mowgli," Arthur recalled, making reference to the skilled hunter raised by wolves in Rudyard Kipling's *Jungle Book* stories. But when it was Arthur's turn to cook—a deer had been killed—he decided to curry the meat and misjudged the heat of the peppers. The stew was so hot it couldn't be eaten, and he was roundly cursed by his hungry fellow soldiers. Another training exercise involved being dropped off singly in the jungle and finding one's way back to camp by compass. When it came George's turn, his return was long overdue; it had grown dark and the others were worried. Finally he reappeared, but he was ashen and "sort of fell to the floor" before telling his story. Taught that any viper over six feet was likely to be harmless, he had simply stamped his foot at a lengthy snake on the path back to camp, expecting it to slide away. Instead, the snake uncoiled, rose up, and spread its hood, hypnotizing its assailant. George fainted and the cobra left him unharmed, but the next day, unnerved by what had happened, he informed the British Army that "except for learning odd tricks in splitting bamboo, time here was completely wasted." When he threatened to resign, the group was sent to a post near Calcutta.

As a journalist would one day phrase it, this new posting was "more Waugh-like than warlike,"[22] for the group was put in charge of a luxurious mansion on the bank of the Hooghly River where a few Japanese prisoners of war were being held. The villa had been built by a minor raja for his mistresses, and the bedroom walls were covered with stirring erotic art. "It was an enchanting experience," Arthur would recall, "living in a strange house with Japanese captives, walking out occasionally to the Indian villages in the area and befriending the [local people]."[23] Across the river was a temple, and at certain times of day a clashing of cymbals and music called people to prayer. Being an officer in India under the Raj was a very privileged position. That experience was permanently preserved for Arthur in Jean Renoir's 1951 film *The River*, based on a semi-autobiographical narrative by Rumer Godden and shot on location in Calcutta.

The little company was supposed to get as much information as possible from the six Japanese men, who had agreed to co-operate. But captors and captives shared the same quarters, slept in bunk beds in the same room, and what began as a military assignment turned into a leisurely cultural exchange, with discussions of religion and philosophy. This atmosphere was encouraged by the presence of two high-ranking British officers in their company who had important personal connections with the East. One of these was Major Jack Brinkley, the son of an English historian and educator who had spent his adult life in Japan and had married a Japanese woman. Major Brinkley accordingly spoke the language fluently.

He was also a Buddhist, and as such was a close companion to the British officer second in command, Trevor Leggett, an Oxford don and renowned Zen scholar who had translated sections of the Indian *Upanishads* into English. Leggett had also earned a black belt in judo. He persuaded the Canadians to do yoga and practise meditation, with the result that some, though not Arthur, attempted to stand on their heads every morning. Leggett slept in a top bunk next to Arthur's, and Arthur would see him each morning deep in meditation "sitting on his bunk in Samurai scant between-the-legs-up-and-over-tied-at-the-waist-band briefs." Arthur was carrying with him Madame Helena Blavatsky's *The Secret Doctrine*, and Leggett became "an arresting mentor to a twenty-one-year-old seeker."[24]

In addition to reading Eastern philosophy, Arthur and George Swinton bought British novels at local stores—Aldous Huxley, Virginia Woolf, E.M. Forster—and together their minds ranged abroad, "discussing books and ideas and anything in heaven or earth which caught our fancy." Arthur read T.E. Lawrence's *Seven Pillars of Wisdom* for the first time and felt a deep connection to this mysterious figure who had made his experience of war in a foreign setting into a work of art. And for quiet times he had with him a collection of Rilke, his spiritual vade mecum.

Much of the talk between Arthur and George focussed on the plight of India. George's experiences with the British Army were making him increasingly anti-imperial and socialist, and the two followed with great interest Gandhi's passive resistance movement. By July 3 George was mocking, for Cherniak's benefit, his "'brothers' in the mess... here in British India, with [their] long moustaches drooping off tight-lipped mouths holding badly fitted plates, made in England." But as he continued, the comic stereotypes fall off and political realities erupt: "Polo heroes, 'the sun never sets,' Winnie & Beaverbrook, the Bloody Reds... Oh to be in India... the inculcation of snobbish plutocracy and avaricious imperialism, ignorance and super-capitalism. Yes indeed the sun never sets but neither does the misery." He compared the situation in India to "the Negro question [in America] but enlarged thirty times and intensified a hundred." George foresaw clearly enough that debate would be tremendous if Indians were given home rule, but that wouldn't be their fault, he reasoned, because they had been conditioned, the majority successfully so, not to think or be responsible for themselves. As he put it: "If you are being hit on the head every day whenever you want to breathe some fresh air, you finally come to think that fresh air isn't good for you."

In their company of translators from Vancouver, George found in a fellow named Davies a specific example of everything in human nature that he deplored. The young man was from the prairies, and after he and George had quarrelled over what the latter termed selfish behaviour versus altruism, Davies asserted that every man in the army was out for himself. Davies, wrote George in the letter to Cherniak, "never did any work whatsoever, except for opening his mouth to either take in food, or emit hymns in the glory of Moose Jaw or [describe] successful financial schemes he intended to follow up." To Arthur, Davies was just a lanky cowboy, a rather handsome one, but to George he epitomized the spirit of capitalism.

Although Arthur's first response to any situation would privilege geography and art above politics, from his earliest travels he recognized how much politics could shape and distort culture. To his way of thinking, politics was an obsession with raw forms of power, but he listened with interest to his mentor in this field, for George knew equally well the ways of the imagination. Arthur's deepest attraction to the kind of socialism his friend propounded was rooted in a rejection of the status quo and contempt for bourgeois narrowness and complacency. Although Arthur would later identify himself with liberal politics in Canada, his interest would only be roused when he could foresee meaningful changes on the horizon—a commission to promote the arts in Canada, new immigration laws, legislation to ensure equal status and payment for women, or bills that would legalize homosexuality and ensure the safety and privacy of citizens in their own homes.

Calcutta was followed by a posting in Delhi, with weekends free to visit local monuments and to travel outside the city. Arthur would later date his curiosity about the world as stemming from those excursions, in which he saw for the first time such remarkable buildings as the Red Fort in Delhi and the Taj Mahal at Agra. But the site that would have the most impact on the future architect was the dead city of Fatehpur Sikri, some thirty miles outside of Agra. Briefly, from 1571 to 1585, it had been the capital of the Mughal Empire under Akbar but, lacking a reliable source of water, it was abandoned in favour of Agra. Its red sandstone palaces, tombs, and great mosque, in a blend of Islamic, Hindu, and Jain styles, were among the great architectural feats of the Mughal period. But what held Arthur spellbound were the rich effects created by the large open spaces contained by the city's architecture. This would be a frame of reference in the future. On one extended weekend leave, he and George travelled far enough to reach the Himalayas. Again the company of interpreters was enjoying the privileges of a mansion rather than army barracks, and their chief workplace was the Red Fort, where they helped with the translation of documents. Arthur didn't read Japanese well enough to take responsibility for a final translation, but he did some of the groundwork. This idyllic time came suddenly to an end, however, when the Canadians were sent to join in the invasion of Malaya in August 1945.

Back at home, the peace achieved in Europe in May was only a qualified source of celebration for the Ericksons, because war raged on in the East. When the mailman came Myrtle would rush for the letters, hoping to hear from her son, though he reassured his parents repeatedly that his work with Intelligence involved little physical risk.

But before his parents would learn of the dangerous mission Arthur was about to undertake—being dropped behind enemy lines to broadcast propaganda to the Japanese—peace was announced, and Arthur and his fellow soldiers became part of the liberating Western army now engaged in restoring order in war-ravaged Southeast Asia. In Kuala Lumpur, Arthur was assigned the post of program director for the local radio station, though he had never been inside a radio station and had no idea how to run a program there. His first move was to put up an advertisement for volunteer talent from among the troops, and to his delight he snared a BBC announcer, an Old Vic player, and a news writer. He also scrounged up some local talent. He would later reflect with amusement on how he and George fulfilled their assignment: "We broadcast in nine languages, though none of them Japanese. Nobody was listening, but we put on marvellous plays, terrific music, great poetry readings."[25] On Thursdays it was arranged for the company to go boar and tiger hunting. Although Arthur refused firearms, he enjoyed the hikes into the jungle where he could experience the local terrain and observe different species of vegetation. Once again he was living in what he would call "a marvellous house on a hilltop" where the only hardship was the rations.

In October, when George's term of service came to an end, he headed to London, eager to visit relations who remained in Europe. Giving Saul Cherniak a summary account of his experiences overseas, George wrote that "Erickson was no surprise. I expected him to be fine and he was fine. Without him I would have had a very bad and painful time."[26] In the same vein, years later, Arthur would say: "George and I stuck together, because we enjoyed one another so much—in terms of intellectual stimulation and that sort of thing, and our feeling for art."[27] "The war had been a great elation" for him, and something of a "Cook's tour," but that would likely not have been the case without George's companionship.

By Christmas, George was back in Canada, but Arthur was not allowed to return home as fast. A letter to Kay Holland (addressed to dear "Kayo") gives us a glimpse of how he saw his situation. It was written December 22, "too late for an Xmas letter—but, as you know my habits of tardiness [are] born from an utter contempt for time, I hope you will forgive me." After apologizing for not having written to her while in the army, trusting that his parents and Diana Chesterton have passed on his news, he tells her how hard it is to get into the Christmas spirit in the tropics, where "December is like May or June or any other month—the same palms, same blossoms, the same sun and drenching short-lived rains" and where "talk of Christmas... seems very artificial, Xmas carols ring false and discordant."

He wishes he were on a ship in the middle of the ocean where the Christmas ceremony would be simply a toast at dinner or preferably "at some native thanksgiving festival with drums and native dancers." He wishes he could have gone to London with the rest of the Canadians—"I'd love to celebrate with them . . . I get bloody mad thinking of the fun I missed—but the gods haven't willed it!" He concludes his message on a tender note: "Don't think that I haven't thought often about you . . . because, after all, you have been so much a part of the family. And don't think, old girl, that I have the callousness to forget a friend of such long-standing."

Arthur returned to Canada the following spring via Europe. He made his way back slowly, seeing more of the East in Darjeeling, Calcutta, and finally Colombo, Ceylon, where he secured passage on a military transport that carried six men and four hundred servicewomen. In future, the popular media, viewing Arthur Erickson as a ladies' man, would make much of this choice of transportation. And well they might have, for it appears from letters and memoirs that he had his first sexual experience on board that ship. Trevor Leggett had given Arthur the name of a guru in London, whom he had phoned on arrival but had not followed up with because, as he explained, he was "distracted at that time by an attractive young girl who had become an amorata during the long trip back from Colombo to the U.K."[28] In London he did fulfill his father's request to visit Mrs. Rogers, the hospital visitor who, in family stories, was credited along with field nurse Elizabeth Pearce for saving Oscar's life. He found the Rogerses at Number One, the Boltons, an exclusive address in the Kensington area, but felt uneasy amid their stiff courtesies and was happy to leave after the obligatory cup of tea had been served. He was back in Vancouver in March.

4

Student

WHEN ARTHUR RETURNED HOME in the spring of 1946, he had some urgent decisions to make. He still wanted to be a painter, and he was welcomed back into the community of local artists he had come to know at the Vancouver School of Art—Bert Binning, Jack Shadbolt—as well as by Lawren Harris. George Swinton, who already held a degree in economics and political science from McGill, had decided to follow painting at the Arts Students League of New York and was set to leave Vancouver with his wife, Alice, in the fall. But Arthur's father advised there was no future in what he regarded as a hobby, and Arthur turned to the idea of foreign diplomacy. He was teaching his mother how to make special curries to surprise her friends, and he had resumed Japanese lessons with Mrs. Griffiths. With the idea of taking the external affairs exams, he enrolled that summer in two courses at UBC that were requisite for a diplomatic career—economics and political history. He became absorbed in the study of history, though he soon found he could not agree with the basic assumption from which it was taught—chiefly, that history was a series of events turning on wars and coronations, that it was the result of human decisions. He was already convinced that history was about the development of cultures in specific geographical and climatic conditions and that individuals, from that larger view, were merely agents of an evolutionary process.[1] He allowed, at the same time, that politics perhaps seemed absurd to him because he lacked a sporting instinct.[2] The study of economics he found painfully uninteresting and therefore difficult—like mathematics. (Jessie Binning would one day look back and smile: "To this day, Arthur can't tally the bill to pay for his own dinner.")

Diana Chesterton had eagerly awaited Arthur's return, and their courtship was resumed with mutual pleasure. Diana had been training as a wireless operator, preparing to serve in the merchant navy instead of attending university like many of the girls from her social class. Her parents were sometimes alarmed by her maverick ways. She did some modelling, and with her wide, sparkling smile and strong sense of style, she presented clothes with considerable effect. One of her greatest pleasures was her love for animals and outdoor life and she persuaded Arthur to go horseback riding with her. To her surprise he proposed marriage that summer (as he would to another young woman a few years later) but, still in her teens, Diana wasn't ready yet. He gave her a painting he had done, an abstract in blue pastels.

As summer went forward he grew increasingly uneasy about a career in the diplomatic service. He knew that he had fairly good manners, that he could greet and engage people in discussion, but he also knew that he could not take orders and act in a way that he did not believe in. So he started thinking about careers associated with the history of human culture—anthropology and archaeology—and he turned to his friends for their advice. One of these was Bert Binning, a paternal figure fifteen years his senior. A tall, big-boned man, calm and slow-moving, Binning, with his deep, avuncular voice, could more easily have been taken for a football coach than a man engaged in the arts.[3] After a year spent in Europe, he had designed and overseen the construction in 1940–41 of a unique home that embodied many of the features of the Bauhaus style of architecture.[4] Nestled on a hillside in West Vancouver, it surprised visitors with its flat roof, its open, multi-use living area, and its glass wall that let the living room merge with the patio garden and the view of the bay beyond. It was the kind of innovation for contemporary living that fascinated Arthur, especially the single interior

living space, sectioned only implicitly by the arrangement of furniture—the effect was arresting. It was to become an iconic house, a
prototype for West Coast modernist architecture in British Columbia. Binning was also becoming a painter of note with a penchant
for marine subjects, to which he brought drafting skills and an interest in geometry. Bert and Jessie Binning had no children, and they
made their house instead a meeting place for students and others
with a commitment to the arts in Vancouver.

Seeing Arthur's interest in his house, Bert invited him to an evening gathering to meet California architect Richard Neutra. The
Viennese-born architect gave a presentation on modernist aesthetics
to an eager audience gathered informally at the Binning home, but
when Arthur spoke to him in an aside, he was discouraged when
Neutra said he would have to become an engineer before he could
expect to be an architect. "I asked him if he could recommend a
university that taught architecture as an art. 'The best thing for you,
young man,' he said, 'would be to go to MIT and study engineering!'"[5] When Bert Binning agreed with Neutra, Arthur decided he
was not interested.

One of the pleasures of being back in Vancouver was reconnect-
ing with the Harrises. At one of their Saturday evenings, Arthur met
and befriended Gordon and Marion Smith. Gordon's commitment
to painting, as a teacher and an artist himself, gave Arthur further
impetus to pursue this love. He described finally turning to his
revered mentor for advice: "Was it to be painting or the diplomatic
corps? I went to Lawren who gave me the best advice I had ever
received when he said, 'Arthur, it would be a mistake to advise about
your life. It has to be entirely up to you.' I chose architecture."[6]

It came about in this way. One of Myrtle's many friends happened to leave at the Erickson house a copy of *Fortune* magazine,
which contained the first colour photographs of Taliesin West, Frank
Lloyd Wright's house in Arizona. When Arthur saw those pictures
the effect was magical: "Immediately, everything came into focus;
if it was possible to create such a work of art in architecture, I was
going to become an architect." It was late in the summer when he

started wiring all the eastern universities with architecture programs—Harvard, Yale, MIT, University of Toronto, McGill. Because the schools were crowded with veterans returned from the war, he heard back only from McGill. But he packed his bags without hesitation and left for Montreal in September. Arthur told this story many times in talks and in print, and the details changed very little—the events were crucial and decisive. Only once did he embellish the ending of his narrative: "The Dionysian aspect of my nature had suddenly asserted itself, and from that moment I never turned back. Since then each step of my adventure into architecture has always been more fascinating than the last."[7]

Arthur's story of being admitted to McGill at the last possible moment suggests the hand of destiny at work, but in fact the groundwork was efficiently, if belatedly, laid by those who served as his referees. Arthur had achieved very little during his three years of study at UBC, but he had made valuable personal connections with leaders in the academic and arts communities. Strong letters of recommendation were written by Lawren Harris and by senior academics who attended the Harrises' Saturday evenings. One was from Norman Mackenzie, the president of the university, another from Geoffrey Andrew, the assistant dean of arts and science, both of whom had been persuaded by Harris, and by Arthur's sophisticated participation in Saturday night discussions, to press their friends in the McGill administration to accept him. On staff at McGill were Arthur Lismer, a member of Harris's Group of Seven painters, and Gordon Webber, a friend of Harris who taught basic design. Harris asked both of them to use their influence in favour of Arthur's admission, and this old boys' network proved effective.[8]

IN SEPTEMBER 1946, Arthur transferred, with advanced standing, into second year at the School of Architecture at McGill. He took the train east in the company of Douglas Shadbolt, Jack's younger brother, who would eventually become a leading figure in the teaching of architecture in Canada. They had first met by chance on a ferry travelling to Vancouver Island, and before the three-hour voyage was over they had become friends. Doug had apprenticed with Sharp & Thompson, Berwick, Pratt, one of the leading and more innovative firms in Vancouver, and was already an accomplished draftsman and designer, whereas Arthur, in his own words, "had never held a T-square or anything else."[9]

Arthur and Doug were part of the influx of young veterans returning to school with government financial assistance. The architecture program, which during the war had enrolled only five or six students each year, admitted twenty students in the fall of 1946. These students brought with them new ideas and expectations. A student revolt had occurred in the class of 1938–39 — a protest directed against the "arts and crafts" curriculum in favour of modernist theory and the International Style of architecture as defined by Philip Johnson and Henry-Russell Hitchcock — but after the war almost emptied the school the student cause grew cold. Now, with Doug Shadbolt as their leader, Arthur was part of a group that decided to run the architecture school their own way. Invoking those days in a celebratory tribute to Shadbolt years later, Arthur humorously adopted the student language of the sixties — rebellions, walkouts, independence — to describe the events of his first year at McGill.[10]

The School of Architecture was housed at that time in the engineering building, and classes were held all over the campus — drawing and history of art with Arthur Lismer in the arts building, structural engineering in the engineering building, sanitation in the medical building, etc. But with Enrico de Pierro and Gordon Webber, instructors sympathetic to student demands, Shadbolt organized students in the architecture program to meet at a pub on Sherbrooke Street. "You know," recalled Arthur, "if we didn't like courses we'd go in a troop to John Bland [the director] and tell him ... 'We would really like to change this because we don't think it's working.' We really took our courses into our own hands."[11] Later he would say of Doug Shadbolt and himself that "being Westerners, I think we had a certain brashness, but also a freshness and originality ... With a Western background, you don't look to any older culture for standards, so unique solutions are the rule. We really appreciated how free we were, coming from the West."[12]

In 1947, the students were assigned their own building, a four-storey Victorian mansion on University Street. On the ground floor were the principal lecture room and the administrative offices; on the upper floors were drafting studios and staff offices. Although students still attended some classes in other buildings, they enjoyed their new home. Moreover, in the basement there was a common room for social events. The building with its neo-medieval turrets and secret nooks and crannies was a curious setting for the teaching of modern architecture, but students were gratified that "a hard doctrine had found a soft refuge."[13]

Three teachers who appreciated the "freshness" of their western students were especially important to Arthur. Having fallen under the spell of the Bauhaus movement, they too were carrying the banner for change. The teacher who had the greatest impact on Arthur was Gordon Webber, then a part-time instructor in his thirties who taught a second-year course titled Basic Elements of Design.[14] An energetic and incurably optimistic man, Webber was barely five feet tall. He had been born with a severe spinal defect, spina bifida, which resulted in a twisted back and a crippled leg terminating in a club foot. When he was twenty that leg was removed below the knee and Webber was fitted with an artificial one, which gave him greater freedom of movement. His head was unusually large in relation to the rest of his body. A car accident when he was twenty-three brought further disfigurement—in addition to broken ribs and a punctured lung, his face was scarred and several teeth broken. Friends feared the worst, but when they went to the hospital, Webber shouted from the bed, "Come in, come in. What do you think," he laughed—"I have broken my wooden leg."[15]

Webber studied first at the Ontario College of Art, where he came under the mentorship of Arthur Lismer and assisted him with his famous Saturday morning classes for children at the Art Gallery of Ontario. Lawren Harris also saw much artistic promise in this unusual youth. After teaching art for a few years in private schools around Toronto, Webber proceeded on a scholarship in the late 1930s to study art under László Moholy-Nagy and György Kepes, two Hungarian artists associated with the Bauhaus who were teaching at the Chicago School of Design (it later merged with the Illinois Institute of Technology). He came under the special foster-ing of Moholy-Nagy's wife, Sibyl, who encouraged Webber to think of himself as exceptionally gifted and arranged for a tailor to design him special clothing—one-piece sleeveless suits worn with ruffled shirts, Nehru jackets.

Webber followed Lismer to McGill in 1943, where he worked as a sessional instructor. There he cut a unique figure, refusing to wear a gown or a jacket and tie like most professors. He could be seen moving about the campus with debonair aplomb, photographing such unlikely subjects as the texture of a sidewalk, with its bumps and cracks, or a decaying snowbank in winter. He inspired students with his passionate love for all the arts, including music, poetry, bal-let, and theatre, and pursued a busy social life as well as his paint-ing. Blackie Lee, living and working in Montreal for a time during the mid-forties, came to know Webber through a Vancouver Island friend and was invited to one of the parties he gave. "It was a remark-able party," she recalled, "especially because Webber himself liked to dance!" Blackie was game. But for Webber to dance involved elaborate preparations—removing his false leg and locating his wooden crutch—no simple matter after several drinks. "He danced with a crutch rather than a leg," Blackie recalled. "It was really a solo performance."[16]

What delighted and profoundly influenced Arthur was Web-ber's "talk," uniquely phrased and original observations on the arts drawn from instinct rather than anything analytical. Webber gave his students exercises intended to purge their minds of preconceived notions and "to explore the essence of materials, light, line, plane, and volume through drawings and constructs in creative play."[17] One of the exercises that Webber assigned was to fold paper in as many ways as possible; another was to explore the depth of space on paper by means of floating dots and straight lines. Webber had students photographing the effects of light on paper and other solid forms and doing their own work in the darkroom. Some students left his classes upset and worried over the vague assignments—"Create a drawing that represents what architecture means to you" was usually the first one.[18] Some, like Doug Shadbolt, were simply uninterested in pure design; they scoffed at Webber's courses, and the term "Webberism" entered student vocabulary with a note of derision. But others sensed that Webber's approach was valuable. He taught students to see buildings not only as volumes, but as planes and space, interacting transparently. "We didn't understand [his teaching]," recalled Gilles Gagnon, "but we knew there was something in it because we were learning about space relations, textures, colour, three-dimensional feelings of space." He had students "confirm [their] designs by photography."[19]

Webber's pedagogy, in Arthur's view, was remarkable: "He was very vague, never explained anything clearly, which forced you to see for yourself. I don't think I would be as receptive to everything as I am had it not been for Gordon Webber."[20] Further, Webber was neither critical nor full of praise. He was able to see something of interest in whatever a student was doing, though he did not necessarily commend it. This was a way of working with students and employees— even clients—that Arthur would adopt in his career as an architect.

Webber's compelling personal presence was a challenge to many. Doug Shadbolt recalled how one day in a celebratory mood Webber wore his coat turned inside out, because the lining of gold and flaming red satin was so much more colourful.[21] For Harold Spence-Sales, one of the school's professors, "Gordon Webber was a mythical creature—his myth lay in his legs... he moved in a certain sort of way. And I don't think I've ever come across anybody who could less express himself correctly. Gordon's language was mystical—utterly and absolutely inscrutable. You simply loved the man. You excused him. You propped him up... he exerted in some sort of way a vast spiritual sympathy."[22] Arthur summed up the man this way: "Webber exemplified in his dress, manner, observations and thoughts—a new prophet, challenging all cherished precepts, and forcing students into their own creative resources."[23]

Arthur studied architectural history and design with Enrico de Pierro, a flamboyant young instructor the students nicknamed

"Dippy." De Pierro was immediately a challenge for Arthur, because he opposed what he viewed as the dated romanticism of Frank Lloyd Wright, calling Wright's work "muddy architecture." Arthur would start a project with a Wrightian plan and de Pierro would come by his desk and say, "Get rid of all that, you know all those things. Clean it up, clean it up, it's very muddy." It did impress upon Arthur the values of clarity and simplicity of planning.[24] De Pierro's motto was "Le Corbusier or nothing," and he would return to McGill every fall with accounts of Le Corbusier's work, including his most famous *"machine à habiter,"* the Villa Savoye.

Le Corbusier's renown in postwar architectural schools was not derived solely from his designs but also from the more than fifty books and pamphlets in which he set forth a radical vision of architecture for the modern age. At the centre was his promise to elevate humankind to unprecedented levels of both bodily well-being—he advocated rooms as sparse and easy to clean as TB wards—and psychological stimulation. His 1926 "Five Points for a New Architecture," a manifesto of sorts, announced three innovations that were becoming commonplace by the middle of the twentieth century— ribbon windows, amplifying the amount of natural light in modern homes; open floor plans, wherein individuals were no longer sequestered in small rooms but were exposed to the stimulating presence of others; and roof gardens, which have gained increasing currency with awareness of environmental issues. Le Corbusier's vocabulary and his five points—thin piloti columns on which to stand buildings and façades freed from load-bearing structure were the other two— were something like a lingua franca in modern architectural schools.

De Pierro introduced Arthur in a serious way to Le Corbusier's functionalism, his underlying advocacy of the scientific approach to aesthetics—the importance, that is, of taking things apart and showing how they worked. As a challenge to romanticism, this way of seeing art fascinated Arthur initially ("I became for a time a paragon of the new rationalism"), but his enthusiasm would wane, and he referred to this philosophy of art with some irony when he wrote: "In a glass model of a human heart, if you showed all the different valves and how they performed, this became of aesthetic value in itself."[25] Le Corbusier's industrial perfectionism, his machine aesthetic, represented for Arthur a view of the world and the arts that he rejected. But later some of Le Corbusier's ideas would become important to him. Le Corbusier's admiration for classical Greek architecture "came as a revelation," because many historians taught that architectural history really began with the spatial compositions of the Renaissance and Baroque periods, largely ignoring the achievements of Greece and Rome.[26] With its appreciation of timelessness, Le Corbusier's neo-primitivist chapel at Ronchamp suggested for Arthur how a twentieth-century architect could evoke timelessness in a modernist idiom. But most important would be Le Corbusier's apartment block in Marseilles, the Unité d'Habitation, with its vision for communal living—residence, commerce, and recreation all in one building.

Arthur, however, found the presentation of world and contemporary architecture more comprehensive in the classes given by John Bland, the director of the school. Bland's view of architecture as both a physical and an aesthetic discipline made him especially well-suited as an administrator. Although his own field was the history of architecture, he insisted that the curriculum include some engineering courses to tackle the problems of modern building. Bland was especially praised by students for his skill in connecting the history of local buildings to knowledge of the larger movements in architectural history. A humanist who encouraged a wide variety of opinions in his faculty and students, he was wedded to the basic tenets of modernism. In Bland's classes the works of the scattered members of the original Bauhaus design school were discussed with excitement, and one cannot dismiss their general imprint on Arthur's future work: Mies van der Rohe's use of glass, Marcel Breuer and Le Corbusier's use of concrete as a primary medium. These European architects were held up for emulation in Bland's classes, and he took students on pilgrimages to their ateliers in Boston and New York.

In New York the students also spent time at the Museum of Modern Art, which in 1932 had been the site of the first exhibition of modernist architecture in North America. There was still a palpable excitement surrounding this event fifteen years later, because not only had it introduced the new architecture to the public at large— sleek, carefully tooled, geometric buildings highly responsive to technological innovation—its catalogue had identified and named the features of what became known as the International Style. In the catalogue's foreword Alfred Barr, one of the organizers of the show and a director of the MOMA, characterized the modern architect as thinking of his building not in terms of thick columns and heavy masonry but as a skeleton surrounded by a thin membrane. "He thinks in terms of volume—space enclosed by planes and surfaces— as opposed to mass and solidity."[27] Volume, regularity in proportion as constituting beauty, and the avoidance of applied decoration: these were the modern aesthetic principles, and they had parallels in the other arts—the lack of objective reference in abstract paint- ing, the spare aesthetic of imagist poetry, theatre's new bare stage. In Bland's classes students discussed the ideas formulated in catch- phrases like "skin and bones" architecture, "form follows function," "less is more," and "God is in the details"—most of these attributed to Mies.

The enthusiasm of some instructors and their camaraderie with students gave the school its special energy and intellectual verve. John Bland arranged for design exhibitions in the city, most mem- orably perhaps a collection of modernist furniture by the Finnish designer and architect Alvar Aalto at the Art Gallery on Sherbrooke Street (later the Montreal Museum of Fine Arts). De Pierro was instrumental in bringing an exhibition of Le Corbusier's work to the engineering building on campus, which attracted visitors from as far away as New York. Gordon Webber arranged countless social gath- erings at his apartment where students and faculty mixed and ideas were generated.

Among the most memorable experiences for students in McGill's architecture program were Gordon Webber's Sketching Schools, held for two weeks in early autumn, usually somewhere in the Lau- rentians. "We were like a bunch of gypsies going into a small village, sort of taking it over," remembered Gilles Gagnon. "And we'd be perched everywhere doing sketches, people weren't used to that in these small places... We'd have meetings every night and we made crits of our drawings and corrected them sometimes. And we could bring friends and girlfriends. It was like—a picnic."[28] When Arthur went, he befriended Ken Carruthers, who was in the year below his, and they ventured about in the Sainte-Adèle area, getting to know a Québécois family and dating two of the daughters. He would remember it as "quite a mad escapade" and a very "romantic" one because the leaves had changed colour, and he and Ken took the girls on long walks through the woods to a little tea house run by some Austrians. "It was a marvellous time, great conversations, very Oxbridge in its sense."[29] Ken became Arthur's closest companion during the rest of his time at McGill; it was a friendship that stretched into the future. Another of Webber's projects in the Laurentians challenged students to design and put together, with whatever materials they could scrounge, a boathouse on the beach of a lake. This transition from drawing board to physical application, with all its unplanned-for exigencies, was a powerful way to learn. The result, not surprisingly, was very "Miesian."

The four years during which Arthur studied architecture in Montreal also gave him an expanded view of Canada. He deliberately had not applied to UBC's architecture program, which started in the fall of 1946, because he wanted to see and learn more about the country.[30] Montreal was a particularly rich environment, composed of people of every ethnic background and class. This mix was reflected in the makeup of the student body at the McGill School of Architecture, including its inclusion of Jews who had fled from Middle and Eastern Europe. Arthur loved being in a city where the spoken language was French, and he patronized French restaurants and shops to immerse himself in Quebec culture. Montreal was also a "wide-open town," notoriously hospitable to gambling and prostitution and famous for its jazz clubs and nightlife.[31] And Arthur was fully aware, as were many English Canadians, that it was permissive regarding then-illegal forms of sexuality.

But Arthur was not ready to explore such a world. Rather, off campus, he was more likely to spend time with Jean and David Catton, who were friends from Vancouver. The Cattons had recently moved to Montreal where David was employed at the CBC. Arthur and Jean had been friends from the time they attended Prince of Wales high school, where she was known as Tuffy MacTavish; she had often visited the Erickson house, and she had great admiration for both of his parents. Even then Arthur had been known to friends as someone who could visit a home, rearrange a couple of items, and alter a room to great advantage. Accordingly, Jean and David encouraged him in their domestic affairs: he bleached and dyed their curtains, and one Christmas he stuffed the turkey with unusual ingredients. He always felt cheerful there, and they enjoyed him as a bachelor friend with a mutual interest in the arts. They said to Arthur, more than once, "You will have to design a house for us some day."[32]

The architectural students' common in the basement of the old mansion on University Street was known as the "Focus Room" where, after guest lectures, special visitors such as Americans Lewis Mumford and Philip Johnson were entertained on "low divans" (just mattresses stretched on the floor). If from the outside the building looked like a frat house, appearances were not deceiving. As Guy Desbarats, one of Arthur's friends at that time, would later recall, in the common room "it was quite often an all night affair."[33]

Arthur lived at Presbyterian College, across from the main library, where he had been assigned the prize room in a loft called the Tower. He had filled out the residence application identifying himself as a "non-conformist," by which he meant non-sectarian. But non-conformist in Britain originally meant a Presbyterian, and for this historical allusion he was rewarded with one of the most coveted rooms on campus. Arthur was seldom willing to spend his time drinking through the night. He would all his life be somewhat abstemious, preferring one or two glasses of very good wine with a meal to a bout of heavy drinking. His classmates recognized that Arthur had superior gifts, though they did not express any animosity. One called him the class philosopher, with a refined sense of design.³⁴ Another recalled that "Arthur Erickson was always better than anybody else. He was a teacher's pet, but rightly so."³⁵

Although most students found good summer jobs in industry in Montreal, each year Arthur headed home to Vancouver. To expand his knowledge of the continent, he would take as many different routes as possible, both Canadian and American, and as many forms of travel—one summer he hitchhiked most of the way. Sometimes he would drive and deliver a car for somebody at the other end of the country. His mother could hardly wait for his return and overwhelmed him with her doting love and eccentric ideas as soon as he walked in the door. In the background was his father, whom Arthur increasingly admired. With his positive outlook despite his severe disability, Oscar was a role model for another generation of young amputees returning from war. He was often called on to speak to men injured in service and to help them, sometimes on an individual basis, to survive the kind of depression he had initially experienced and to overcome their resentment and bitterness.

Oscar was relieved when Arthur found work in the summer of 1949 with the Vancouver architect C.B.K. Van Norman, an early exponent of modern architecture. Van Norman, in his early forties, was working on some major commissions at the time he hired Arthur, including West Vancouver's Park Royal, the first covered shopping mall in Canada. He also designed and built many private residences, and Arthur remembered how Van Norman would return from a consultation with wealthy clients, stretch out on the office floor, and sleep off the effect of too many drinks at lunch. Another major commission was the redesigning of the Pacific National Exhibition grounds, which had been closed to the public between 1942 and 1946 and used by the military as an internment camp for the relocation of Japanese Canadians. The grounds were to be transformed, just as the name was changed from Hastings Park to Exhibition Park. Van Norman gave Arthur free rein to design a new landscape, introduce water features, and designate building use. For a student, this was work that carried significant responsibility.

That summer Gordon Webber was also in Vancouver, invited to teach a course at UBC's School of Architecture. Arthur included Gordon in his social life, taking him to the Harrises on Saturday evenings and travelling with him to Vancouver Island to spend a weekend near Qualicum with Blackie Lee and her parents. After a short time with Trans-Canada Air Lines, Blackie was now training to be a travel agent and was frequently out of the city, but when she was in Vancouver she and Arthur went dancing. Diana Chesterton, aware that Arthur was not likely to marry her, though not sure why, had accepted a proposal from Patrick Whittall, whom she had been dating while Arthur was at McGill. They were married in the summer of 1949 in a wedding ceremony that graced the social pages of the *Vancouver Sun.* Not surprisingly, perhaps, Arthur's feelings were mixed. Diana was in every way an ideal choice for a wife, but Arthur knew that he really didn't want a wife; he was focussed on becoming an architect, and marriage seemed antithetical to the ambitions of an artist. Moreover, his physical feelings were for men, something he could no longer deny to himself.

ONE OF ARTHUR'S contemporaries has said that at McGill in the 1940s, "Frank Lloyd Wright really wasn't mentioned. As a matter of fact, in an era that embraced machine aesthetics, Wright was frequently laughed at for his feelings towards organic architecture."[36] Arthur, however, though grounding himself thoroughly in the international styles of modernist architecture at McGill, had not lost his fascination for the pictures he had seen of Wright's buildings. On the bus back to Montreal for his final year, he decided to make a visit to Taliesin East, Wright's commune in Wisconsin. On a Sunday afternoon a taxi dropped him at the bottom of the hill. Unable to find an entrance, he made his way through a stable-like garage that contained at least a dozen trucks and cars, all painted in Cherokee Red, Wright's signature colour. From the garage he emerged into a small courtyard girdling the crown of the hill where a single jet of water played with the branch of an overhanging pine. The sound of the water and the swish of the pine branch created an atmosphere of extraordinary peace and quiet. Here in the rolling countryside of America's brassy Midwest, one experienced for a moment "the peace and timelessness of an Italian monastery."[37] Arthur could see that the house was built around but not on the summit, and from that elevation the perspective revealed Taliesin as "'an absolutely beautiful blending of building and landscape.'"[38] Experienced in a flash, it was an achievement that would inspire and direct Arthur throughout his career. From the interior of the house floated the delicate sounds of Bach being played on a harpsichord, and Arthur felt that "'this was what a medieval monastery must have been like.'"[39] He entered the building through a comfortably low space that "unfolded into a broad golden room... empty but charged with a quiet presence."

Later that afternoon, Arthur met Frank Lloyd Wright. He had been apprehensive about meeting him, because rumour painted Wright as a fearsome autocrat—unconscionably rude and opinionated. But Arthur found him a charming individual, full of humour, a mischievous twinkle in his eye, and not self-centred as commonly reported. Rather, Wright asked Arthur about his own background and training, about his ideas and future plans, and at the end of the meeting extended an invitation for Arthur to join his atelier-commune, waiving the $1,100 tuition until Arthur could afford to pay it. Arthur was overwhelmed by Wright's interest and the flattery bestowed by this great man. His feelings, however, shifted a little before the day was over. That evening everyone assembled in the living room in their Sunday clothes. Wright and his third wife, Olgivanna, entered and sat on special chairs, with everybody else at their feet, for conversation that consisted chiefly of adulation of the Wrights by their apprentices. This was followed by a grand procession to the head table in the dining room, where the Wrights sat on a raised dais. In his subsequent assessments, Arthur expressed his dismay at the false ceremonies that took place. He attributed them to the presence of Wright's wife (born Olga Lazovich in Montenegro), a follower of Greco-Armenian mystic George Gurdjieff, whom

Arthur saw as an ambitious person revelling in her power and prestige. Wright himself Arthur regarded as too witty and too absorbed in his creative life to care much about the rituals that went on.[40]

Despite his reservations, Arthur went back to McGill and announced to John Bland, "I'm quitting, I'm going with Wright for a year." Bland, unfailingly helpful and *sympathique* ("a wonderful man, the picture of tolerance"),[41] listened patiently, but he toppled the plan when he told Arthur that, as a top student, he was in line for a travel scholarship when he graduated; it would pay for a year in Europe, where Arthur could learn first-hand from the great works of architecture. Moreover, four hours of manual labour were required every day from the communards at Taliesin. Looking back, Arthur would see this as the most momentous decision he would ever have to make. Taliesin represented a peaceful retreat: "Part of me has always wanted to abdicate from the world and live a monastic life."[42] But the temptation of travel was greater. So he resumed his classes at McGill, worked for days Rilke-like in his Tower room dressed only in pyjamas and kimono, taking Mepacrine (an anti-malaria tablet believed then to induce wakefulness), and completed his thesis, which was a proposal for the first National Gallery of Canada. Although it was drawn freehand and covered with thumbprints, for its originality it was rated higher than the submissions executed with precise drawing board instruments, and Arthur won the MacLennan Travelling Scholarship, the Pilkington Prize, and the Lieutenant Governor's bronze medal at graduation. The awards were an acknowledgement of his superiority in this important respect—he had a conceptual mind capable of remarkable originality. Looking back at this time and the offer from Wright, he would say: "'Sometimes there is a door you could have gone through that would have changed your life, and you are somehow rescued. The idea of peace and retreat was terribly attractive, but I believe now that you have to be in the thick of things. It might have taken years and years to recover.'"[43]

When Arthur graduated from McGill, Myrtle decided to take the train to Montreal for the ceremonies. She brought Don with her, and she managed to recreate something of the excitement and confusion of the Erickson household in their suite at the Ritz-Carlton Hotel. Dick Wright's older brother, Alexander, was graduating in medicine from McGill at the same time, and so Myrtle invited the Wrights and a few others she knew to a party in her room. It was a noisy affair, spilling out into the hall, with messy food and drink and lots of lively conversation. But it was especially unforgettable for Dick, because on his way up to the suite, he shared the elevator with jazz pianist Duke Ellington. Struck dumb by awe and admiration, all Dick could think to do was invite him to the Erickson party. With his unfailing elegance and charm, Ellington accepted, and Myrtle, who had not heard of him, welcomed him royally as another of her son's friends. Arthur's graduation was a princely affair, and when he set out on the road, he did so with every honour that could be bestowed on a young man's future.

5

Traveller

IN THE SUMMER OF 1950, Arthur set out on a journey that would last more than two years and, in his own words, would "change everything I had been thinking up until that time and would bring everything I had been taught...into question."[1] The McGill scholarship, intended to provide support for one year of travel study in Europe, was valued at $1,500, but by adding a veteran's grant of $800 and leading a frugal, vagrant lifestyle, he was aiming to extend his travels well beyond the limits of the scholarship. He hoped to find work that would add to his funds, and he was confident that if he arrived in England midsummer, he could get employment with the Festival of Britain, scheduled to open in May 1951. This national exposition was designed to boost the spirits of the British people, especially Londoners, as they rebuilt their cities after the war, and it was also being held to coincide with the centenary of the famous Exhibition of 1851. What drew Arthur's interest was talk of the new buildings being in the International Style, and he was eager both to witness and to participate. From there he planned to go on to Italy. But circumstances gave rise to a journey and an education in architecture that he could not have foreseen.

One of Oscar's business associates had arranged for Arthur to work his passage across the Atlantic on a freighter. But just before departure from Montreal, he learned that the ship was destined not for Europe but for the Far East and that its first stop would be Egypt. Since a free voyage had been arranged, he carried through—there was just enough time to procure a visa for Egypt if needed. This unexpected change was the prelude to an unsettling voyage. The first thing that puzzled Arthur was that he was the only passenger on the ship. When he inquired about his duties, he was told he was a supernumerary ("We will call if we need you"). He was not called; moreover, he was viewed with suspicion by an unfriendly American in charge of the ship's cargo. Arthur learned that the man was a trader in arms who was taking dynamite and sulphuric acid to India during a buildup of weapons against Pakistan.[2] With his eventual destiny in mind, he retreated every day to a hammock on the upper bridge to study Italian, and when possible he picked up food to take his meals alone in his cabin. When the freighter finally reached the Suez, he, as he liked to put it, "skipped ship."

Arthur would later reinterpret this inauspicious journey as good fortune in disguise. He would even give it a mythic cast when he described setting foot on land and seeing a goat fall to the ground in front of him to give birth—a propitious omen, he was told by one of the locals.[3] When he started his travels in Egypt, he "had no interest whatsoever in historical architecture."[4] McGill had thrown off the yoke of traditional, beaux-arts training, and he, accordingly, had adopted a disparaging view of the past. He had set out for Europe to see what was new. But once in Egypt, "with its revelations of the extraordinary beauty and vitality of the past," he decided to follow the path of Western civilization from its origins in the Middle East. His journey, an "odyssey" through the Middle East to Greece, Italy, France, Spain, and finally England and Scandinavia, would comprise some of the most formative years of his professional life. His experiences would deepen his conviction that meaningful history was about the imagination, "the great adventure of the human spirit."[5]

His adventure in Cairo began with a lesson. He had contacted a young Vancouver couple, Fredericka and George Sweet, who were working for a time in Cairo, and they arranged a comfortable *pension* for him. The affluent couple arranged expensive meals and entertainments and suggested some popular but not very interesting sights to visit. (Especially disappointing for Arthur was the fashionable Modern Art Museum, with its collection of Arabic paintings imitating worn-out European modes and paintings of pyramids by Europeans executed, he felt, with the lifeless sentimentality of tourist postcards.) In less than two weeks, nearly a quarter of his funds were gone. He recognized the value of these Vancouver friends in making the bewildering transition to Cairo; as he wrote home, it was "a shattering chaos of traffic, animals, people, and vehicles and deafening noise," and finding one's way was no simple matter. But after leaving the Sweets, carrying only a rucksack containing a scant supply of clothing, a good Rolleiflex camera, and a portfolio of his designs, he turned to cheap accommodations, food from street vendors, and third-class bus and train fares, determined to make his time abroad last as long as possible.

Arthur's letters home, which Myrtle would later type up as a travel diary,[6] focus from the outset on his self-education as an architect. From his first forays into the streets of Cairo he realized that it would not always be straightforward. Since he didn't speak or read Arabic, the dates and functions of buildings would be difficult to determine, although in terms of materials, structure, proportion, and decoration, the buildings spoke for themselves.

With a guide named Rene Harari, arranged by his friends, Arthur was taken around the city. He experienced the tourist's fascination with the clamour of the markets and their impact on the senses— sacks of raw cotton soft to the touch, sweet prickly pear peeled by the vendor for immediate consumption, and everywhere the confusing aroma of dung permeated by jasmine and spices. But what caught his eye and was captured in his letters was the impact of lighting: the glare of the sun on house walls, or the pleasant filter of light created by the raised screened balconies, the *mashrabiyas* from which members of the household viewed activities in the streets below: "The effect of the light piercing the dusty streets in shafts, and illuminating at the bottom of the street a counter of brilliant textiles or gleaming copper or brass, was superb."

He requested that Rene take him to two remarkable sites in Cairo. First was the City of the Dead in an old native quarter. Here the streets comprised one- and two-storey houses, but, remarkably, there was an eerie quiet and no inhabitants to be seen. Rene showed him how each house surrounded a tomb and explained that on certain festivals people brought baskets of food to the houses to stay overnight with their dead. But the quiet was deceiving: when Arthur tried to photograph a tomb with its stela in Arabic script, he was suddenly "surrounded by a mob of angry Arabs threatening [him] for disturbing the dead. Seemingly they had emerged from nowhere." Until this point, only India's Taj Mahal, also Islamic, had made him reflect on the housing of human remains for the next world. But a two-day visit to see the tombs and mortuary temples at Luxor would extend that thinking further.

The more significant site Arthur visited in Cairo was arguably the world's oldest institution of higher learning—Al-Azhar University. Dating back to 975 CE, with a mosque at its centre, Al-Azhar began in a unique way by including secular as well as theological studies—grammar, astronomy, Islamic law, and philosophy. In a letter, Arthur described entering the large main court surrounded by an arched colonnade where pilgrims waiting for passes for Mecca were lying on a white marble floor or conversing in huddled groups. The pilgrims, from all parts of the Arab world, were allowed to stay in the court to share their experiences and ideas while in Cairo. In the space beyond were the students, and Arthur's description signals the germination of an ideal that would one day inform his designs.

> The atmosphere was one of great serenity—the endless quiet repetition of columns and arches, the rich crimson carpets that covered the entire floor. Looking back to the court from where we had entered, the dividing wall between the court and interior was merely of wooden mashrabiya screens, so that the sunlight filtered through and gleamed crimson in bright patches on the floor. Students with open books walked noiselessly along the aisles or sat discussing quietly. Here would be the place to study, and study here I am sure would be effortless.

The repetition of architectural motifs, the strategies for managing natural light, and the generous accommodation of students studying in quiet, informal groups—these would all be fundamental in the architecture for the two universities he would build.

Arthur's letters also reveal the powerful impact of geography on his artistic sensibility, anticipating the way climate and setting would be crucial elements in his work. Passing through desert on a bus from Cairo to Alexandria, he is absorbed by the purity and starkness of "the four ancient elements"—the pre-vital landscape of sand and sky ("yellow brilliance throbbing against blue brilliance"), waiting for rain and the warming fire of the sun to make the desert bloom. In Lebanon, having sailed from Alexandria to Beirut, he finds an idyllic mountain landscape of orchards and vineyards, not unlike California, that elicits description rich in poetic phrases and metaphors. From terrace vantage points his eye fastens on "pencil slim cypresses," umbrella pine trees with their "floating dirigibles of needled green" (described elsewhere as a myriad of "balloons strung to the mountainside"), and, below, the "peacock coloured" waters of the sea. Without the foresight of what was to come, he observes how friendly the people of Lebanon are and concludes that "a beautiful environment is conducive to a generous temperament" and a benign way of life.

Arthur had a specific reason to praise the country's generosity, because when he was picking up his mail at the office of Mitchell Cotts Industries, a young Lebanese employee there named Jean invited him to spend the night at his cottage in the mountains. After a refreshing swim in the sea, they made a breathtaking drive through terraced groves of olives and figs and down precipitous cliffs, which brought them to the cottage. There Jean's wife prepared a meal reflecting the country's multicultural cooking traditions: Lebanese aperitifs of pickled eggplant, hummus, and flatbread, olives, cheeses, and nuts; frog legs fried in the French manner; Greek patties of meat, parsley, and garlic; and finally Turkish coffee with watermelon, all presented on a balcony that hung out over the slopes. There were friends and other family members present and a mixture of languages spoken: while French was the common denominator, some conversations took place in Arabic, and Arthur was most comfortable speaking to Jean in English. The evening had a magical quality for Arthur, which is reflected in his poetic account of the advancing night:

> As we talked the shadows deepened in the valley and each mountain bore a corona of lights. The night was dark and brilliant, stars mixing with the lights of villages. As the moon rose, its pale radiation drew a mist out of the valley. A long white tongue of mist sought the crevices of the hills, separated into white streamers billowing moonward, and suddenly, ending the act, obliterated everything, even its generator, the moon.

The morning was much less romantic as Arthur struggled with an Arab-style shower positioned over the toilet, which was a hole in the floor. To his embarrassment, he discovered the walls were merely screens separating the lavatory from the kitchen, where the family was already busy preparing breakfast.

While still in Lebanon, Arthur made his way to a sixteenth-century monastery situated on a "magnificent" promontory that commanded a view of Beirut and the surrounding valleys. The site had been occupied by the Romans and by different groups before that. An old man, whom he found "reading La Fontaine," showed him through the monastery's disintegrating vaulted halls and around the littered remains of a Roman village. Arthur writes: "It was serene, this ageless crag, and one marvelled at the supreme aesthetic and military sense of the ancients to choose such a site." And of the old man: "He maintained a solitary command—the warden of a deserted fortress—supervising the wreckage of thirty centuries and half as many civilizations." For the young man from Vancouver, where so little evidence of human time's passage was visible, this experience helped to lay the foundation for his sense of architecture as monumental, not only serving the needs of the present but evoking buildings from the past and their relation to a specific site.

In Syria, he made his way to another such building—the Krak des Chevaliers, one of the castles of the thirteenth-century crusaders—but the approach was more adventurous. Missing his bus connections to this remote spot, he secured a ride with an Anglo-American oil truck as far as a military post near Talkalakh, from which the castle was visible ten miles in the distance. It was evening, so he decided to walk the rest of the way and spend the night at the castle in his sleeping bag. On the road, in brilliant moonlight, he was overtaken by three horse-mounted gendarmes to whom, in white cap and knee socks, he looked suspicious. But one of the men spoke some French, and Arthur was able to explain that he was just "a foolish Canadian" who wanted to see a castle, whereupon they changed heart, insisted he stay in their village of Omar El Hosn, and gave him a mount. At that point he was grateful to Diana Chesterton for insisting he learn to ride a horse. They lost sight of the castle as the landscape became more mountainous; then, rounding a bend in the road, "it stood across a gulley and above us. Everything enhanced its magnificence. I stopped in wonder." This was the castle T.E. Lawrence deemed "the finest castle in the world" and where, alone, he had stayed for three days at the time of his twenty-first birthday. In the moonlight, Arthur wrote, the height of the castle, the depth of the valleys, and "the great distances of range upon range of hills of quiet incandescence gave a sense of an unearthly extent of space equivalent to that inherent in the resounding depth of the deepest register of the kettle drum." That night, after a meal of lamb, rice, and yogurt, he slept on the floor of a little village house.

Travelling by train through the treeless desert of Syria, Arthur was fascinated by mud villages where the dwellings were shaped like cubes and cones, with no vegetation to relieve the relentless geometry. He was assured that the tall cones with their thick windowless walls were cooling, though it was hard to imagine any relief from the terrific heat. In the city of Aleppo, he was invited to join a group of Americans attending a convention for an Arab village feast and festival out in the desert. There, whole cooked sheep were served on huge trays with rice and pistachio nuts, cucumbers and tomatoes, and the guests used their hands to tear the sheep apart, sometimes ending with a jawbone or an entire hind leg.

By late September, Arthur was in Turkey exclaiming over "one of the most thrilling city sites" he had ever seen, ancient Bergama (Pergamum), "perched on a mountain top." There was little left of the city, much of it removed and "reconstructed in the Berlin Museum," but the plan of the acropolis, with its "hellenistic flamboyance," was still visible, and its siting would be an inspiration for his work to come.

In Istanbul he was struck first by the stark contrast between Hagia Sophia and the delicate grace of the Blue Mosque, its galleried minarets suggesting "the most graceful and indolent movement of any architecture that I have seen." And although the old part of the city, in his view, received its special character of submission and tranquility from the rounded profile of the mosques, his admiration was focussed on Hagia Sophia, which he viewed as "tremendous" and of a different spirit altogether. Sitting in a vacant lot at sundown reading his mail from home, he looked up from time to time and felt the shock of actually being there and of beholding Sophia's great mass, "its huge buttresses and inclined planes piling up in almost a frenzy to the dome." To him, the simplicity of its unornamented exterior and its plain plastered walls made the play of light and shadow on the building's "huge tumbling planes" powerfully dramatic. Only the minarets, added when Sophia was transformed from a church into a mosque, seemed out of place. But his strongest praise is reserved for the building's interior: entering from a long gallery and through a huge doorway, the effect, he writes, is "stunning." With its galleries and naves, the enclosure is immense and the mosaics and marble very rich. He could imagine how much richer it would have been with the original dome of mosaics in translucent gold glass. Architecture for Arthur was an art involving movement through spaces, and his account of Hagia Sophia sketches the experience of a building in theatrical terms.

While in Istanbul, Arthur made contact with members of the Whittall family, into which Diana Chesterton had married. A branch of this English family had established businesses and lived in

Turkey as far back as the late 1700s. In his letter home he describes them as a "remarkable clan." Hugh and Ken Whittall, Patrick's uncles, with whom Arthur dined and spent some time, arranged for him to work his passage as a deckhand on a freighter bound for Athens. The captain let him sleep on a sofa in the salon. After "searching frantically for a place to stay" in Athens, the prices being "fantastic" there, he ended up in his sleeping bag on the floor of the YMCA. Things brightened when the Canadian embassy put him in touch with Kaye Derby of Ottawa, who was living in a handsome apartment with two other girls and was engaged by the embassy to take Canadians on excursions of the area. She invited Arthur to join them for supper, spend the night in their living room, and join a party that evening for a tour of the Acropolis: "So I first visited the Acropolis by moonlight and the Parthenon by floodlight."

His experience would have an indelible impact on his conception of public spaces. In his letter home, he conveys the ritual nature of encountering the greatest architectural achievement of Western antiquity:

> It is impossible to describe the feeling of mounting those old stairs to the many columned Propylaea which stands above you at the top of the stairs, its pale shadowy columns seeming to support the night sky... As you climb the stair the columned wings of the Propylaea extend above you to each side. On the left a tall and solitary pedestal once bore a monumental statue. To the right, like an exquisite jewel the temple of Nike stands—unprotected in the wide night air... The buildings seem to stand in a profound space—separate and isolated from each other.

The Parthenon he viewed as a monumental work of sculpture rather than architecture. It was built, he would argue, not by mathematical engineering—the exact measuring of spaces between columns—but according to the eye of the architect, who "felt" the possibilities of the space and worked out the proportions on site in the way a sculptor works with stone. As a result, the building, supporting thousands of tons of stone, seemed weightless, effortless. Arthur used poetic language to convey the effect of the Parthenon, describing its balance as uncanny, almost mystical, the slight curvature of the columns making the building a living thing. Your eye, he said later, moves with unhindered ease over surfaces where each weight is applied with god-like surety, the power of the great temple going much deeper than sight. Later he would write to John Bland at McGill to say that the architecture of Greece was the yardstick by which all architectural achievements must be measured.[7] On subsequent returns to the Acropolis, he would begin his photographing of Western architecture in earnest.

At McGill, Arthur had been friendly with a Greek student a year behind him in the architectural program. When he won the travel scholarship, she urged him to make contact with her father in Athens, who was also an architect. Arthur was invited for much of October to stay at the Zoumboulides home in an affluent suburb of the city and to accompany his friend's father on a two-week business trip that took him to different parts of the country. "Mr. Z" was chief architect for the National Bank of Greece, and they travelled comfortably—by ship, plane, private car, and sometimes by bus, when it was the best transportation available. Arthur's host paid for everything. Although Mr. Z was an architect and businessman, Arthur could not help but think of him as a professor as well.

Their first destination was Crete, and to Arthur's surprise he found himself on an overnight ferry that had once been the *Princess Adelaide* in service with Canadian Pacific, on which he had often travelled between Vancouver and Victoria. This suggested to him, subsequently, parallels between Greece and the landscape of British Columbia: the harbour and surrounding hills of their Cretan destination "could easily have been Victoria," the Peloponnesus reminded him of B.C.'s mountainous interior with its western towns, and the setting and wide streets of Sparta, he reported to his parents, reminded him of the town of Chilliwack. For Arthur, these were not nostalgic reflections but attempts to think about universalities in geography and culture.

The travellers had two destinations on Crete—the ancient Minoan palace at Knossus on the north shore of the island and Phaestos on the south. In the late nineteenth century, British archaeologist Sir Arthur Evans had begun excavations on Crete in search of physical evidence for the legends of King Minos, and in 1900 he uncovered a palace complex at Knossus where he could identify with certainty a throne room, a theatre (reputedly built for Ariadne by Daedalus), and walls that might have been part of the legendary labyrinth. Evans engineered a restoration of the site that clarified the ground plans, at a cost of millions of dollars, but for Arthur its relative newness greatly diminished "the awesomeness that one feels in witnessing the riddle of ancient ruins." What thrilled him instead were the original frescoes in the throne room and the contemporary character of some elements of the palace: the clerestories—"windows of the most modern fashion giving both excellent light and ventilation to all rooms," the multi-storey construction with terraces and stairwells, the elaborate and expert drainage of the sites. None of this existed anywhere else in the second millennium BCE.

But Phaestos, for Arthur, proved a far more moving experience of ancient Minoan culture. Here the palace was only excavated, giving one a more direct experience of its original comprehensive plan (including ancient renovations and later Hellenic additions) and its magnificent mountain situation. Arthur was especially taken with its eight-tiered theatre ("much more finished and splendid than Knossus") and its sacrificial well and terraces, some of which had fallen into the valley. From the theatre, one could apparently mount directly to the king's quarters. The great court was flanked with colonnades, and on its sides were apartments and storehouses. Its terminus, like part of the theatre, had disappeared over the side of the cliff. But there another powerful effect was achieved, for "as one stood in the opened court, all the distant mountain peaks seemed to rest on its brim."

In the evening, Arthur slipped out of the little two-room hotel to wander the grounds. His written descriptions are steeped in the loneliness of his traveller's life:

I walked again down to the palace. The stars swung on long threads from the sky, down the wide processional stair to the hushed terrace of the theatre, and the crowd seemed to be there in the deep shadows, watching in silence. Figures in full skirts descended the steps noiselessly, coming down from the palace which loomed in the darkness into dimensions that you could not see. Darkness filled the palace and made it whole. The wind touched me lightly and the hollow space about me echoed a sigh that seemed to come from the distant mountains that separated lover from lover, or was it the weeping of the crowd that crouched against the sombre stones of the theatre wall. Weeping over the broken terrace that lay in the lower valley, or over that last tragedy enacted in the theatre when the palace crumbled. Or was it Pisces fingering the wind that caused such utterances?

In a passage written the next day, that loneliness is identified more specifically as sexual, as he describes a flower opening in the office of the hotel: "Its six long stamens reached to the light dangling six heavy masculine anthers thick with pollen, and curving up from the centre rose the pistil even further... ending in a bud-like cap, full ripe for pollination. So this delicate flower, which seemed to have no substance, in the thin rays of its purpose contained such virility and intensity that the whole room seemed to wait breathlessly with it for the entry of the Tarquinian invader." What is the "morality" of the flower, he asks. And his swift reply is that all the academic talk of art and architecture, all proud human convictions fall away as water when compared to the "clarity of purpose and magnificent fulfilment" of the flower's pollination. "Why can't we distil our lives into such clear beauty and then accept it as such," he asks, instead of being "distracted by distraction into destruction"? After the flower has fully opened, he observes, "the faintest scent sweetened the room for an instant."

After a brief return to Athens, Arthur and his "professor" set out again to do business and visit sites in the Peloponnesus: Corinth (to Arthur, another Midwestern North American town), Argos, Tripolis, and Sparta. But what filled his letter was his exploration of the Byzantine ruins of Mistra at the base of Mount Taygetos, overlooking Sparta and the Laconian plain. Wide distances, intimate courtyards—all possible dimensions—unfolded in sudden succession, so that he describes himself by the end of the morning as "weeping inside, an exhausted soul, teary-eyed from the wonder of feeling joy upon joy." From ruined churches there was a vista of soft grey olive orchards in a landscape punctuated by solitary, heaven-yearning cypresses. But words completely fail, he states, because Mistra can only be experienced by being in motion. The situation of this medieval city two thousand feet above the plain was central to his excitement. But as everywhere in Greece's ancient ruins, he read the lesson of civilization's fragile nature and the passage of time

FROM ATHENS, ARTHUR took a boat to Naples, where he met with Blackie Lee, who was touring Europe as part of her training for Foster's Travel Agency. They had little time to see the city, but they did find a hotel with a small orchestra on the rooftop, where they could dance and Blackie could share some of the news from Canada. The next day they took a train to Genoa, and when they said goodbye it was the last time they would see each other before Blackie married Al Sparzani the following year. Arthur's parents were said to regret that the twelve-year friendship had not culminated in a marriage, but there are no further references to Blackie in Arthur's letters home. Presumably they said nothing to him of their disappointment.

Myrtle naturally was anxious for her son's health and welfare on this long journey. Often she attempted to send him some money in a foreign currency; as backup she would sometimes enclose "ten dollars from Nanny"—an American note twice folded and placed in the centre of the letter to avoid detection. She never cautioned her son against taking risks but instead gave his desire to see the world generous emotional support. She believed there were few limits on what her son could accomplish. In return, he adored his mother for her curiosity about the world and the unpredictable shifts of her imagination.

By mid-November, Arthur was writing home from Venice to say that after two weeks in northern Italy he was temporarily "in a critical state of saturation" and needed to stop for a while and "see nothing." His focus had shifted from architecture to art, and for the first time in his travels, he had a negative response:

> I never knew that so much bad painting had been done in the world, and trailing through these vast galleries, which are the boasted possession of every little town [he had visited Pavia, Cremona, Parma, and Mantua before reaching Venice], one becomes quite cynical about Renaissance painting. Animals and human nudes writhe and wriggle over the gallery halls in a seemingly meaningless expenditure of frantic effort… A face, a hand, a body pose are so much part of the designer's pattern book that one ceases to be impressed by the technical skill of the modelling, and even the masters produced poor canvasses. I have seen more sloppy Tintorettos and Tiepolos, downright bad paintings, and I have yet to see a Titian that isn't a messy composition.

But Venice had features that delighted him. For one, it was a city made for people, not for cars. For another, it was a city of endless variety—twisting streets and shops scaled to human dimensions, palaces and piazzas, canals and bridges, and various forms of water transportation. What could be more efficient and pleasing than to be paddled to the door of the symphony hall? He wondered if St. Mark's Square might not be "the most splendid city space in existence" and if the *piazzetta* fronting the Ducal Palace along the wharf wasn't the most romantic. He spent an afternoon approaching the latter from every possible angle, each time feeling "an honest dramatic tension before the climax of bursting upon its whole openness."

While the Lombard and Romanesque architecture of the Veneto impressed him, he was disappointed by the high Renaissance architecture in Venice. Heavy decoration destroyed the surfaces of structures and set buildings into a churning movement. To him,

"St Marks [was] not in any sense a beautiful building." He appreciated its human scale, yet the interior, despite the finest marble floor
he had ever seen, was lacking. There was "none of the elixir of space"
as in Hagia Sophia; there was no central dome to draw one forward,
no centre—all the cupolas were the same height—and space inside
the church was static. The mosaics were gaudy and full of disturbing
movement, and "all the various accoutrements to the church—small
altars, great altars, chandeliers, pulpits, and so forth, were distracting rather than harmonious to the whole." "What might be mistakenly called an oriental ambiguity of space," Arthur observes, "to me
is, I think, ineptitude rather than orientalism." The glass industry
reflected his view of the city in many ways—fine craftsmanship in
glass-blowing producing terrible-looking objects.

On two evenings, he stopped at a small café that was the nightly
haunt of the city's young artists—English-speaking residents as well
as Italians. One night he joined in making a record, reading a passage from one of T.S. Eliot's *Four Quartets*; on another he became
engaged in an argument that pitted the flat space division of Man-
tegna against the "cubism" of Tintoretto. In the debate that filled
the café, Tintoretto was held up as the first of the moderns for his
attitude towards "man" and space. In essence, the discussion was pit-
ting reason against emotion, classicism against romanticism. But the
important idea Arthur took away was that the artist must never lose
himself—the artist's person was the shaping presence in every painting. Returning to his lodgings very late through deserted streets, he
decided Venice was best seen at this time, when the lagoons and
canals were quiet and the scattered lights made deep shadows in the
recesses of the street. Thenceforward, he would try to arrive in a city
late at night or in the predawn, so that his first impressions were tender ones—of a city's innocence and its potential. It was also a way of
seeing its fundamental outlines, its essential structures, before they
were blurred by crowds and daytime usage.

6

Europe

IF VENICE WAS A CITY marked by excess and decadence, Florence would come to represent for Arthur the most perfectly realized city in the world—not only for its art and architecture but also for its history as a city state. He arrived in late November 1950 at the fabled city on the Arno, hallowed by the creative presence of many great architects and painters—Brunelleschi, Giotto, Masaccio, Donatello, Leonardo, and especially Michelangelo—and mantled by literary associations from Dante to the Brownings to E.M. Forster. To Arthur, it seemed that each stone and cobble must have felt the impress of a famous footstep. Jacob Burckhardt guidebook in hand, he made his way down the narrow streets, seeking out in historical order the city's treasures—the Baptistry and Duomo, the Uffizi Gallery, the Bargello, the churches, chapels, houses, piazzas, and countless museums.

He soon realized that he wanted to go through Florence "inch by inch," and so, to stretch his resources, he rented a non-functioning bathroom in a *pension* where the owner put a board and mattress over the bathtub and charged him fifty cents a night. This constituted his lodgings for almost eight months. In a basement tavern on the Via Cavour where on dark, rainy evenings students gathered to eat, play guitars, and socialize, he got a full-course meal for twenty-five cents, and there he met Carl Massa, a young Italian-American sculptor and painter. Massa took Arthur to his nearby studio to show and explain his work to him and to discuss for hours the relative merits of the Renaissance artists to be studied in Florence. Massa was "a passionate worshipper of Michelangelo" but had strong views regarding the shape and significance of Michelangelo's career.[1] He scorned the sculpture of David and the early *Pietàs*, regarding their concern for detail—the veins in the arms, the curls of hair, the folds in the garments—as concessions to Florentine taste at the time. Instead, he showed Arthur, in their visits to museums, how Michelangelo's later work moved beyond contemporary taste by leaving the surfaces rougher, the details obscurely suggested, until in his final works, sometimes referred to as his *prisonnières*, the figures barely emerged from the stone, making manifest the tragic imprisonment of the human spirit in mortal flesh. Great art, Massa insisted, always broke with the taste and conventions of the artist's time to reveal the creator's genius.

To John Bland, Arthur wrote that until coming to Italy he had been able to approach five thousand years in the development of architecture in a clear, logical way: "Greece was the culmination of what had gone before and even of what came after the Roman invasion." But in Italy each city contained examples from all stages, so "you don't really know what you are seeing, whether such and such is a Romanesque development of the Gothic or a Gothic development of the Romanesque." Often the differences were subtle, and architectural guidebooks, he lamented, were vague. In addition, winter light in Tuscany, especially in the small cities and towns in the hills surrounding Florence, made it hard to be discriminating: "You spend an afternoon in one of the cold, damp, badly lit galleries, working through endless rooms of huge canvasses to find three or four, or perhaps only one, painting that really interests you. But... that one, or three or four, is so much worth the trouble that you will endure the... dreariness, all to dig out a treasure in the next gallery."[2]

No discovery quite matched his excitement when he first beheld the paintings of Masaccio in the dimly lit Brancacci Chapel of the

Myrtle Erickson holding Arthur Charles, born June 1924.

facing, top left Arthur, age four, and Kay Holland, his childhood playmate.
PHOTO COURTESY STEPHEN COOKE

facing, top right Arthur and his parents. ERICKSON FAMILY COLLECTION

facing, bottom Myrtle Erickson and her teenage sons, Arthur (*left*) and
Donald. ERICKSON FAMILY COLLECTION

above Arthur looking out over Diamond Head in Garibaldi Provincial
Park, c. 1944. PHOTO: MARY BUCKERFIELD WHITE

facing, top Arthur with friends hiking in Garibaldi Provincial Park, c. 1944. *Left to right, back row*: Mary Buckerfield, Kay Holland, Dewar Cooke; *front row*: Blackie Lee, Arthur. PHOTO COURTESY MARY BUCKERFIELD WHITE

facing, bottom A picture from the home front: *left to right*: Diana Chesterton, "Nanny" Chatterson (Arthur's maternal grandmother), Oscar Erickson, and Donald. PHOTO COURTESY DIANA CHESTERTON WHITTALL

above Arthur and Diana Chesterton, 1945. "When they danced together, others melted away to the side of the room." PHOTO COURTESY DIANA CHESTERTON WHITTALL

right George Swinton, Arthur's wartime companion. PHOTO COURTESY MOIRA SWINTON

below McGill University graduation photo, May 1950: Myrtle and Arthur, with Arthur's irrepressible instructor, Gordon Webber, on the left. ERICKSON FAMILY COLLECTION

above Arthur and Guy Desbarats in Carcassonne, 1951. PHOTO: GORDON WEBBER. GORDON WEBBER COLLECTION, JOHN BLAND CANADIAN ARCHITECTURE COLLECTION, MCGILL UNIVERSITY LIBRARY

left Robert Filberg. COURTESY FILBERG HERITAGE LODGE AND PARK

FEBRUARY 1961 25¢

CANADIAN Homes

The New Magazine of Canadian Living

Special feature: 34 Prize Houses and Floor Plans

5-page cover story: THE MOST FABULOUS HOUSE IN CANADA

The Filberg house, Comox, B.C., featured in *Canadian Homes* in 1961 as "The Most Fabulous House in Canada." COURTESY SIMON SCOTT PHOTOGRAPHY

Carmelite church. Here was the extraordinary work of a painter who had died in his mid-twenties but had developed a three-dimensional painting technique that, like Brunelleschi's architecture, would gradually revolutionize painting and be foundational to the Italian Renaissance. The expulsion of Adam and Eve from paradise and the baptism of a young man were paintings that spoke to human feeling far beyond the technical achievements of the Renaissance. Arthur went back to see the Trinity at Santa Croce and to find whatever else Masaccio had painted, for the "universal feeling in those pieces was tremendous."

So, despite the wet and cold of December, he wrote home, he could not stop counting his pleasures: "Florence, of all cities, is the one which I would rather never leave. It is the one city one cannot see and be done with; here, one must stay, and staying, grow." The houses of the Alighieris, the Buonarrotis, the courtyards of the Medicis, the pulpit of Savonarola, the workshops of Giotto were "only understood with time, and to understand these things is veritably to grow to consciousness." In a passage frequently quoted later by Arthur and others, he writes: "Collected in this small space is most of what has given us the reason and desire to reach this present moment in history. Here, in one city of the world, was gathered the impetus to send us staggering to now."[3]

In this letter home, only partially preserved, he suggests that Florence is most deeply experienced in the Palazzo Vecchio (Piazza della Signoria), with its massive square palace, its tall central tower, and the loggia with its three vaulted bays where nobles would assemble to watch festivities. The spirit of that age, he wrote, lingered in the gigantic glowering sculptures of Hercules, Neptune, and Perseus, and the copy of David, and "when you walk among them suffering the glares, the raised clubs, and crippling swords, you feel that never have you walked in a space of such grand dimensions." He creates in a single sentence a coloured panoramic view of the city from the Piazzale Michelangelo: "When the low winter sun of late afternoon leaves the yellow walls of the houses of the city, it moulds the dome of the Duomo in orange, and the Giotto Campanile in pink and white and, when it first strikes the crisp black and white marked face of San Miniato above the David, then David's flanks are luminescent green against the gunmetal clouds gathering over the hills of Fiesole." In sharper focus, he moves to the Santa Croce church, with its tombs of illustrious Florentines and Giotto's powerful fresco of the death of St. Francis in the Bardi Chapel. But what elicits his highest praise are the cloisters to the right of the church and especially the exquisite Pazzi Chapel, designed by Brunelleschi in 1444 — "my choice of all the buildings in Florence."

Mid-December, Arthur set out for the medieval towns south of Florence — Arezzo, Perugia, and Assisi. He was drawn to Assisi, with its two-tiered thirteenth-century basilica and magnificent frescoes, their "penetrating character studies" attributed to Giotto.[4] Here was a particularly striking example of Italian Gothic, that synthesis of Romanesque and French Gothic that Arthur often found puzzling. But in a letter to John Bland, he extols another medieval hill town:

> I am now in that most aristocratic of all cities, Siena. In its small area there seems to be more evidence, in the old buildings, of style than anywhere I have visited. Although there are no *great* buildings, there are some of the richest and most original in Italy. Here the many palaces, the consistency and charm of the streets, its traditions that to some extent persist, make for its patrician character. Here, even the *restauranti populare*, which in other cities is not much more than a breadline, is a brick-walled vaulted room studded with old coats-of-arms and half filled by a great staircase that works up to the once *piano nobile*.

After returning briefly to Florence, he set out to spend Christmas in Rome. Although in mid-life he would spend considerable time there and see it as suited to his maturity,[5] his youthful impressions were of an imperial city, whether Roman, Christian, or Fascist, and were not very positive. The architecture, he wrote, "seems cut out of unwilling stone by a sure, exuberant, sometimes florid hand. It has not the tapestry of Venice or the grace of Florence; it is not really rich, nor very subtle, never quiet nor very human—from the beginning it has involved great dimensions, encompassed great spaces in an exultant manner."[6] Later, thinking about the Italian Renaissance, he would identify Florence, with Michelangelo's *David* and Botticelli's *Venus*, as embodying youth; Rome and its monumental architecture as signifying maturity; and Venice, with its Tintorettos and Titians and its ornately surfaced palaces, as reflecting the decay of old age. This organic sense of places as living creatures would eventually dominate his way of talking and writing about buildings and cities.

But Arthur did more in Rome than reflect on its alienating spaces; he attended the Christmas Eve service at St. Peter's Basilica, which made him think about its place in one of the oldest of human rituals—the winter festival of light marking the rebirth of the sun. From his reading, he knew this worship of a birth that would bring light to the world was embodied in such ancient events as the northern tribes gathering evergreens, adorning them with tapers, and worshipping their deities until the trees caught fire and turned night into day. The Romans had filled their homes and streets with lamps and torches to celebrate the birth of the sun-god Mithra, and the ancient Syrians, at the first hour of the winter solstice, came out of their temples crying, "The Virgin has brought forth—the light is waxing," carrying a newborn child in procession. Arthur came to St. Peter's prepared for an ancient miracle, and though he waited for hours in the rain for the service to begin, he was not disappointed, as his exhilarated account attests.

The ritual at St. Peter's began with the singing of "Ave Maria" and "O Holy Night" in the piazza. When the doors of the great church were opened, Arthur was lifted off his feet by the fierce pressure of the crowd "surging forward, carried backwards, choking and shouting for breath... until [they] were inside," running headlong down the length of the nave towards Bernini's bronze canopy that rose over the altar. Arthur pulled himself up on the pedestal of one of the central columns supporting the dome and helped a young woman up beside him; from that vantage point he looked over the great human tide of some sixty thousand pilgrims. Singing echoed

from the vaults and remote corners of the church, the consumma-
tion of the vastness and richness of what he was seeing: "Vaults of
shimmering sheaths of gold sprung from polished piers of rose, lav-
ender and grey marble. Gilt host of heaven flurried in gilt skies over
chapel altars. Giant white prophets peered from niches between
tapestries of gold and scarlet and pointed up—or down." And finally,
preceded by Swiss guards and knights with stiff Elizabethan ruff col-
lars, His Holiness entered the church carried on a gold and scarlet
throne and flanked by guards in scarlet tunics and black helmets. A
trumpet voluntary accompanied his movements. Under the Bernini
canopy, in the purity of his white-and-gold vestments, the Pope's
blessing of the books, the chalice, the bread and wine of the sacrament were in slow, graceful measure with the chorus of the Sistine
choir hidden in a screened balcony. Arthur turned to comment to
the young woman he had pulled up to the pedestal beside him, but
her face was drawn and drained of colour, "conscious of nothing but
her own rapture that transgressed the mere spectacle before her."
Then he recognized the full power of what he was witnessing: "It
was a pageant such as I had never experienced before, an enactment
of something as ancient, as inevitable as the dilemma of life and
death, of some positioning of the human spirit, some superb reaching of the human imagination."

But after the service was finished and the vast crowd had dispersed, the euphoria of this powerful rite ebbed away, and Arthur
was once again the lonely, uneasy observer of imperial, political
Rome.

I waited until the square was deserted to see in its purity the
baroque century—the immense flow of space cupping to the steps
of the basilica, the tumult of columns climbing the façade, the
strong surge of the dome ending in a crown. Then I wandered
through deserted streets when a city reveals its ghosts and climbed
the wide steps to the capitol, where . . . stood the antique statue of
Marcus Aurelius [and] the remains of the pagan city stretched to
the distant shadow of the coliseum. Stairs, sacred roads, marble

platforms, and columns, white as bones in the night, stood in the grass... But the triumphal arches—the still flagrantly jubilant triumphal arches—proclaimed the persistent spirit of the place.

He was glad to be back in Florence by the beginning of January 1951: "I return as if to home, revelling... in the train of pleasures encountered by an aimless walk through the streets of the city."

As Arthur learned more about the art and architecture of Florence, one name kept recurring—Bernard Berenson. The famous connoisseur and long-time leading authority on Italian Renaissance painting, born in the Pale of Settlement in a Lithuanian village in 1865, had been raised in Boston and educated at Harvard, but in his early twenties he had come back to Europe. Before he was thirty, Berenson had made Florence his home, eventually purchasing a villa in the hills at Settignano. Arthur decided to write and ask if he could visit Villa I Tatti, where for more than fifty years so many had spent long hours in the company of Berenson and his wife in conversations about the Renaissance. Arthur felt intense excitement when he received a reply and an invitation for tea from Berenson's secretary and intimate companion, Nicky Mariano. The American writer Elizabeth Hardwick, who called on Berenson in 1950, compared him to an innkeeper whose fear was that he might miss someone, "almost as if [his] countless visitors and travelers had a secret the exile pitifully wished to discover."[7] Guests at Villa I Tatti were first invited to stroll the grounds of the seventy-seven-acre estate, then browse the villa, where they would see works of famous painters such as Giotto, Bernardo Daddi, and Simone Martini, as well as lesser-known Sassettas and Lorenzo Lottos. Arthur was especially moved by the penetrating character studies in Giotto's *Entombment of Christ*, a painting dated c. 1300 and regarded as the jewel of Berenson's collection. He was also amazed by Berenson's multi-roomed library complex of nearly fifty thousand books. "What a vast consumption the man must have," he exclaimed in the account he sent home.

Visitors were eventually shown into the living room and joined by secretaries and librarians for conversation over tea and white Sienese biscuits. The latter were tissue-thin wafers, the same, a secretary explained, as those of the holy sacrament but, she carefully added, "unblessed." Berenson himself, tired from a walk, said he would meet with one of the group in his study upstairs. Because Arthur had said he was in Florence for a short time, Miss Mariano took him to the study, where he found the great man resting on a chaise longue with a cup of tea on his lap. To Arthur, Berenson appeared extremely old, "much more [frail] than I expected," breathing and talking with difficulty. But he pinned Arthur with quick blue eyes, led him into conversation about the countries he had visited, chaffed him for the many things he had neglected to see in Italy, and suggested what he should not overlook in Spain. He also declared the United Nations headquarters building in New York, designed in part by Le Corbusier, an abomination—"simply not Art." And then, as the session concluded, he startled his visitor by saying, "I should like to burn all books on Art, including my own."

Arthur's thoughts lingered on this parting pronouncement. Berenson had devoted himself to connoisseurship, to art criticism, and to creating the most aesthetically beautiful life possible. His worship of art, so tangible in his home and his collections, and especially in the books he had written, embodied for Arthur something like the perfect existence. Yet Berenson had denounced the significance of his life's work. Was it physical age, ill health, loneliness? (He was a widower but surrounded by companions.) Was it bitterness evoked by his enemies in the art business—"the pig trade," as Berenson's wife had called it? Or was it simply a way of saying that great works of art stand on their own—that they need no explication, and only one's love for the paintings was of lasting value?[8] Arthur preferred to think it was the latter.

But the unsettling words made him think also about Michelangelo, whose extraordinary career was shadowed by his mercurial temperament and angry self-doubts. Carl Massa praised Michelangelo's late sculptures—the figures not fully released from the marble—as being greatly superior to the polished statues of David or Bacchus. But Arthur remained aware that the *prisonnières* could be read as part of Michelangelo's crippling inability to finish his work, as unfulfilled commissions such as the sculptures for the tomb of Pope Julius ıı piled up in his workshops. As an old man, Michelangelo had turned in a rage against some of his work, most notably smashing the Florentine Pietà with a hammer. The dark side to artistic genius had registered with Arthur, especially from reading about Rilke's treatment of his wife and child, but with his youthful optimism he was not given to dwelling on it for long. Instead he pondered Berenson's assertion that the new United Nations building was "not Art," and he pressed himself for a definition that would explain art's "timelessness," its *longue durée*, rather than its associations with social and economic opportunities or with bitterness and betrayal. He thought back to Lawren Harris's belief that a work of art is a weaving together of parts into a unity that achieves order and "inevitable structure," a structure that once achieved cannot be altered and will produce "ecstasy" in both the creator and the audience.[9]

Arthur had been told that he could not succeed in architecture without an engineering background, and so he took refuge in the fact that Michelangelo had no professional training in architecture, that his stupendous originality and competence and his grasp of architecture's mathematical content were "seemingly instinctive." Nothing demonstrated this better than the San Lorenzo library in Florence, where a dark vertical vestibule in grey sandstone and white plaster creates a dramatic prelude for entering into the brightness of the long horizontal reading room. But the vestibule is not just darkness; its walls, divided into three sections, are richly decorated by double columns, scroll-shaped corbels, and gabled niches formed by pilasters that taper as they rise to heighten the drama of ascent up the staircase. While these decorative features have no structural function, their dramatic impact is powerful, testifying in Arthur's eyes to the fact that greatness in architecture went beyond high modernism's strict rule that form follow function.

Michelangelo likely held Arthur's fascination for another reason as well. The great Renaissance artist, who had never married, was long said to have been attracted to men. His mother had died when he was a boy, so he grew up in the company of his father and four brothers, and all his life he was surrounded by men. Although there is no extant record of his homosexuality, Michelangelo's greatest works of sculpture and painting feature potent male nudes, and his best poetry was addressed to young noblemen like Tommaso de' Cavalieri. He was also devoted to his manservant, Urbino. But both Tommaso and Urbino were married men, and Michelangelo was a puritanical follower of Savonarola, the monk who exhorted Florentines to renounce the pleasures of the flesh. One might surmise that in 1951, Arthur, a self-described monastic, was also the captive of his austere and fastidious inhibitions. With his cautious nature and a nurturing idealism, he was probably not yet ready to confront the demands of his sexuality in a social situation. Except for his description of the flower in the hotel at Phaestos, his aesthetic raptures were remarkably chaste.

IN FEBRUARY 1951, Arthur left Florence for an extended visit to the south of Italy. He embarked for Sicily, where over the centuries so many cultures—Greek, Roman, Byzantine, Arabic, Norman, Spanish, Italian—had left strong memorials of their presence. Travelling on his own, he was able to linger over the buildings that interested him most. He was especially fascinated by the way styles merged; in a ruined cloister near Palermo, for example, he found an unroofed wall of Arabic arches on slender columns topped with Corinthian capitals. Similarly, the fine cathedrals at Monreale and Cefalù revealed how the Norman conquerors of the eleventh century had used Arab craftsmen to create great riches in glass, marble, and mosaics.

Then came what Arthur described as "three of the most perfect days I have ever spent," when he explored the island's Greek ruins, especially those at Taormina. "I climbed through cactus and the pink Greek lily, the odd small tree of pink almond blossoms, moonlit white, until I stood high above the village ... of Taormina; very far below, lights girdled the great sweep of the bay. In the distance, just under the moon, was Etna, majestic, her fires reddening the smoke issuing from her side wound."

In Sicily, Arthur met a young American, Michael, who was resolved to climb Mount Etna and invited Arthur to join him. Arthur had been wary at first: while companionship dispelled loneliness, it also exacted compromises, and it sometimes involved emotional entanglements that Arthur found difficult. They hiked a good part of the way to the crater, but very strong winds forced them back to a ravine. "Here my friend pitched his little yellow tent and I put on all the clothes I had and most of his and spent the night out under a raincoat on his ground sheet." Next morning, they descended the hill for a train to Messina, where they bought more camping equipment in preparation for hiking together on the Aeolian Islands.

But like Odysseus, Arthur and his new friend found travelling the Aeolian Islands by ship more of an adventure than they had bargained for. They started at the island of Lipari, but heading for Stromboli a heavy storm blew up, and they were stranded for a week on Panarea, a tiny island with only three hundred inhabitants. In the island's half-deserted village, they rented a room from an old couple who provided meals, but it was scant fare—eggs on "boiled weeds," lemons, and bread—because the wind was too fierce for the fishermen to go out, even for the old woman to venture into her garden. She cursed the storms and muttered, "*Marzo è pazzo,*" meaning the weather in March is madness. Arthur came to understand that all year round the island was so windswept it produced very little for its inhabitants—some fig trees and lemons grew in sheltered spots, but most people had only a small vegetable garden, a few goats, and chickens. The old couple were raggedly dressed, yet for a time they had known something of a different life, because the old man had spent twenty years working in the United States—on their walls were photographs taken in Brooklyn in the 1920s. On Panarea there was a saying that when the sea raged and a fisherman couldn't make land, he would wave to his family and head for America.

When the seas calmed, the two young men escaped to the nearby island of Salina, where they camped in Michael's tent in a fertile valley lying between twin volcanoes. In a perhaps somewhat fictionalized version of this adventure, given as a talk,[10] Arthur heard the short, dark inhabitants of Salina whispering amongst themselves as they looked up at Michael towering over them—blond-bearded, open, sunny—and he made out the words, "*Gesù Cristo...* *Gesù Cristo.*" From then on in their companionship, Michael was Gesù and Arthur, with two weeks' worth of nondescript stubble on his chin, was his disciple Pietro.

Finally, they boarded a steamer for Stromboli, the island famous for its active volcano and given notoriety by recent erotic interest in a film made there with the same name, directed by Roberto Rossellini and featuring his lover, Ingrid Bergman. The approach to the island was too shallow for a steamer, so passengers crowded onto a high-prowed fishing boat that was swept by the waves onto a black-sand beach. What immediately fascinated Arthur on this jet-black volcanic island was that the villagers had painted their houses pure white—"in a desperate attempt it seems to save themselves from the terrible gloom of this ashen landscape." The houses, he wrote, stood "stark and jewel-like on lava teeth over the azure sea." He admired, too, the sculptural look of their buildings and other paraphernalia—all plastered white. And the churches were white inside.

But the deepest call to Arthur was the rumble of the volcano. He and Michael, now closely bonded by their adventures, climbed the mountain twice, mesmerized by the cascade of fire and the precipitous view to the sea below. In his letter home, he describes the volcano's eruptions in language with sexual overtones: the mountain "sighing and gasping" and then the cone "throw[ing] the molten stuff high into the air." The mountain summit generates an excitement curiously Miltonic in its epic language and its reference to demons:

> The crater erupted every few minutes and we climbed to it by day and by night. From the ridge, frozen rivers of lava swept down to the sea. Ash as soft as snow silenced our footsteps and muffled the sighs and the thunder of escaping gases. Gases swept the ridge, flashing with fire around us at night. Within the old crater two smaller cones gasped and sputtered like monster demons with boiling lava until what clogged their throats spewed out or burst with a thunderclap

high in the air. There were seconds of silence as the meteors fell, then thudded into an invisible bed and for a moment studded the cone with molten stars before cooling into darkness.

He also describes their "unforgettable" night descent by torchlight with the thunder and fire behind them.

After more than a week on Stromboli, Arthur and Michael boarded a ship for Naples. No sooner were they out in open sea than another storm struck, much worse than the ones they had experienced before. Suitcases, bicycles, and crates of chickens hurled back and forth. Crawling on hands and knees, Arthur reached a bench and strapped himself to it with his belt. Things banged and people shouted through the night; Arthur was too seasick to tell if there was a call to "abandon ship." With morning, there was no diminishing of the storm, but the ship found its way into a sheltered bay and the passengers were rescued by some fishermen who braved the heavy seas to row them ashore.

On land, they were still dogged by the storm. Bridges and roads had been washed out, and there was no way to cash traveller's cheques. After walking for hours, they came to a station, and by boarding the next train and locking themselves in the toilet, they managed to reach Paestum. When they emerged from hiding, Arthur saw startled faces on the platform as Michael hovered over them for a moment in his white plastic raincoat and hood. As they fled into the night, he heard again the words, "*Gesù Cristo, Gesù Cristo.*"

What fascinated Arthur from the outset about the three Greek temples that remained from the ancient colony of Poseidonia was that the style of the temple built last was the simplest and the most powerful. Named the Temple of Neptune, it was built in the fifth century BCE just before the Parthenon, in the classic Doric manner. Here was proof to Arthur's mind that progress for the Greeks was a matter of simplifying, not multiplying and ornamenting—and he could not help but draw a parallel with modernism. He concurred with then-current thought that the Temple of Neptune was second only to the Parthenon in Western architectural achievement:

"The impression of simplicity and grandeur, the beauty of clear-cut sculptural forms is something you feel nowhere else but with such a temple." In his letter home, he called that feeling "something indefinable," something magical, but in a talk he would later give that included the visit to Paestum, he defined that magic as "an acclamation of life itself, an exultation [in stone] of being alive." And he added: "Its mystery was in its balance, its uncanny equilibrium in stone, as of action just completed or about to begin." Seeing the temples at Paestum reinforced his view of architecture as a form of sculpture, as the product of the imagination, not mathematics.

It began to snow as Arthur and Michael left the temple enclosure the next morning. They parted in Naples, not to meet again, but Arthur would never forget the details of the two weeks spent in the physically confident and cheerful presence of his American acquaintance.

BACK IN FLORENCE, Arthur received word from Montreal that Gordon Webber and Guy Desbarats, one of his McGill classmates, were coming to France and hoped to join him there. Webber's unconventional antics and Desbarats' youthful enthusiasm to see something of Europe for the first time made for a stretch of rollicking adventures. First, there was the matter of the car they had shipped over. Webber, because of his disabilities, couldn't drive, and after Arthur had taken the wheel a few times, Desbarats decided to take sole charge; as he recalled years later, "I tried to let Arthur drive, but I soon feared for my life and for my car."[11] Then there was Webber's erratic behaviour. Careless with his possessions, he lost his wallet, and it was soon apparent that he could never keep the value of foreign money straight, so Desbarats had to take over his finances. Gordon also managed to lose his passport several times—in the glove compartment, in the depths of his overlong sleeping bag—and when it was gone for good, to the horror of the others, he was jubilant. "A free man at last!" he cried. Gordon's presence was important to Arthur because he read art and architecture from a wholly unconventional point of view. He could still make Arthur see things in a different light, even the buildings in Florence he knew so well.

But there were disadvantages to travelling in company with friends. Arthur's serious study of the history of architecture involved, when possible, a strict procedure, which was to make his first foray of a city's streets at night and then the next day "start with the earliest buildings and progress up to [the point of] losing interest in the contemporary buildings."[12] Such a routine was seldom possible with Webber and Desbarats in tow. Further, camping was proving a trial because France was plagued with rainy weather all through spring. So in June, after the three had visited Carcassonne in southern France, Arthur set off on his own again for a time.

On his way to Albi, a small city in the French Pyrenees known for its cathedral in the southern Gothic style, he happened to read about the cathedral at nearby Conques, a relic stop popular with medieval pilgrims on their way to Santiago de Compostela. Making this side trip brought him to "one of those unusual places where everything . . . is in key and full of great interest." The village, almost unchanged since the twelfth century, spread up unaccommodating hillsides in half-timbered houses of local copper-coloured limestone, "fish scaled with blue tiled roofs," in a coherent pattern "almost untenable in our century." From their midst rose the Romanesque cathedral, one of the finest cathedrals in France. It, too, was constructed from the warm-coloured local limestone—and, as Arthur pointedly observes in his letter home, "It belongs to the village and the village to it." To his delight, the interior of the cathedral terminated "not in the frenetic confusion of Gothic ribbing but in the calm barrel vault and round arch"—the kind of "harmony that is so easy when [it is] an arrangement of graceful arches." The people, he writes, with their leather or wooden Dutch shoes and black habits, were so much a part of their village, in this valley setting of extreme isolation, that "one need not make any of the usual allowances for a time and change." In other words, here one had a perfect example of the architectural coherence of life in the twelfth century—an ideal instance of houses, church, and setting as an organic whole.

He joined his friends again in northern Spain, and from there they travelled through France, Switzerland, and Holland, where in The Hague Gordon finally secured another passport. In August, they crossed over to England. When Arthur arrived in London, he was excited to be again at the centre of the once-powerful nation his father had fought to defend, in which the architecture spoke forcefully, sometimes eloquently, of that era of empire. But the appeal proved short-lived. England, Arthur writes, "is a troubled country peopled by quite unnatural beings," and he goes on to describe a society of repressed individuals who are unfailingly polite, seldom speaking out of turn, but whose reasonableness and intelligence stifle spontaneity to the point "where they are justifiably accused of being a cold, cold people." He says he is "choked with admiration" for the good conduct of the English, yet "calculation dogs every move, and a calculated joy can't be other than joyless."[13]

Part of Arthur's negative feeling about the English was no doubt generated by his experience of again visiting Mrs. Rogers, the overbearing woman credited with saving his father from starving himself to death in a military hospital. Arthur was shocked to find her blind as the result of a violent attack on her person and even more shocked to learn that the assailant was her husband. The only reason she had survived was because he had experienced a heart attack during the struggle.

Until mid-September, Arthur and Gordon stayed at the home of an English couple Gordon had befriended. The woman was in Arthur's view very sweet, a friend of the hairdressing Sassoons, but her husband was despondent and tight-fisted. He frequently referred to rationing and would go so far as to split matches to economize. Gordon used their phone to make leisurely long-distance calls, so the atmosphere was not comfortable. Things became less tense once Gordon paid his phone charges; not knowing the difference between a pound and a shilling, he refunded his hosts extravagantly. But things ended badly when the couple went away on a little holiday, leaving their guests in charge. Gordon decided to repaint the house interiors as a gesture of gratitude. That might have been appreciated, for the walls had gone a dirty cream with age. But Gordon decided each wall should be painted a different colour. Moreover, when he and Arthur painted the closet doors, they did not notice the clothing pinched in the hinges, which soaked up some of the paint. They fled before the couple returned.[14]

As noted, one of Arthur's purposes in going to London was to seek employment with the Festival of Britain. Much of London was still in ruins, and one goal of the exhibition was to promote models for contemporary design in the rebuilding of cities throughout Britain. The architect in charge, Hugh Casson, was only thirty-eight, and Le Corbusier's influence was evident in much of the architecture at the central site on London's South Bank. Arthur could see at once that these buildings, including the Royal Festival Hall, which would be permanent, suggested new possibilities for the waning conventions of high modernism. This way of building came to be known as the Festival Style in Britain and would be incorporated into the housing and office blocks of the so-called New Towns—extensions to historic centres built to accommodate the swelling population. With its extensive use of concrete, the style would also be referred to as the New Brutalism, *"béton brut"* being the French term for concrete.

In a letter to his brother, Don, Arthur explains that he has lost faith in the International Style of the contemporary world because it had opted for machine function instead of beauty: "I can see how we can be duped by the excitement of the curious and the novel— how in architecture, so beautifully expressed by the South Bank, we can become machine neurotic, when as Frank Lloyd Wright so often warned before, the machine is becoming the thing of beauty and not the agent of beauty."[15] Arthur may also have been thinking of John Ruskin, who had written one hundred years before in *The Stones of Venice*, "Exactly so far as architecture works on known rules, and from given models, it is not an art, but a manufacture."[16] At McGill, Ruskin's rejection of mechanization and his nurturing of the Arts and Crafts movement were regarded as antiquated and irrelevant by the exponents of modernism, but Arthur's exposure to Wright's organic architecture had left him receptive to Ruskin's "medieval" idea that buildings should be sympathetic to local environments, should use local materials, and should involve the whole community.

In October, after Gordon and Guy had left for Montreal, Arthur met with Ken Carruthers, his junior classmate at McGill, with whom he had spent some "romantic" evenings during the Sketching School; he had strong feelings for Ken, and a new, more complicated chapter in his travels unfolded. Ken was the 1951 recipient of a McGill travelling scholarship, and they found themselves a room in a down-at-the-heel rooming house near Hyde Park, overlooking Kensington Gardens. The challenge for Arthur was to find employment so that he could remain in Europe for at least another year. His success was limited. He had been carrying his portfolio in his backpack for more than a year and, bent and "mouldy," it did not make a good impression. Moreover, as he lamented in a letter home, he was becoming threadbare, and he asked his mother to have socks, a sweater, a jacket, and an overcoat sent over. He also asked if she would inquire if the *Vancouver Sun* would be interested in buying some of his travel letters as a way of staving off his "approaching financial crisis."

After making the rounds in London, he eventually secured a couple of months' work with Ernst Freud on a competition project for the Royal Institute of British Architects. It was set up in Freud's garage in St. John's Wood, and Arthur's task was to "generate ideas." Ernst Freud, the son of Sigmund Freud, had first established an architectural practice in Berlin in the 1920s, but with the rise of Nazism he had emigrated to England, where he picked up commissions for private homes and blocks of flats in Hampstead. Arthur felt Freud was not a very good architect, but the work was fascinating because of the people he met. Every afternoon he was invited to have tea in the house, where visitors included the architect's famous sister, psychoanalyst Anna Freud, and Ernst's son Lucian, who would make his mark as a celebrated English painter. Arthur might have stayed for the winter, but the salary he was paid—in Canadian funds only about $35 a week—was not enough to live on.

There were, nonetheless, compensations in London, most of them provided by Oscar Erickson's English friends, the Suttons and the Adamses. He had promised his father he would visit with these wartime acquaintances, and in his reduced circumstances he was happy to avail himself of their generosity and kindness. The Suttons twice took him to dinner at Claridge's, to see John Gielgud and Flora Robson in "a magnificent performance" of *The Tempest*, and to a performance of *The Magic Flute* at Covent Garden. But best of all, perhaps, was meeting the Adams family, with three lively sons and daughters-in-law, and receiving an invitation to spend Christmas with them. Their holiday celebrations included a solemn Christmas Eve communion in the "barest" of barn-like country churches. Christmas Day, complete with "stockings scraping the hearth... bulging with breakfast fruit and Penguin books," an elegant meal of chestnut soup, turkey with bread sauce and stuffing, and a flaming pudding, with wines for every course, broke with custom twice. Gifts unwrapped, the family spent the afternoon watching television; in the evening, "Noels were forgotten, and a fantastic, undisciplined hot jazz ensemble carried on hysterically into the night."

Arthur and Ken had planned to spend Ken's scholarship year together, travelling in northern Europe and Scandinavia, but at their rooming house Ken had become interested in a slightly older woman from Australia nicknamed "Happy." To Arthur, she bore an uncanny resemblance in manner and dress to Lady Brett Ashley in Ernest Hemingway's novel *The Sun Also Rises*. "She was a lot of fun," Arthur would recall later. "She had red hair, and a long cigarette holder... a tam, and wore slacks. She was a real character." But she was also an enchantress, and Ken announced they had become lovers. Instead of spending the winter months with Arthur, he was going to Spain with Happy.

Arthur, feeling "cut out," set off on his own in early 1952 to see the English cathedrals and contemporary works like Wells Coates's Isokon, an ultra-modernist apartment building completed in 1934 and regarded by many as far superior to anything done by Le Corbusier. He went as far north as Edinburgh and then over to the continent to Scandinavia, the home of his paternal ancestors, seeing several cities in Germany en route. What northern Europe impressed on Arthur further was the impact of climate on the artistic imagination. Gothic spires reaching upward and lost in mist was an architecture inspired by little light; the Romanesque, in contrast, was a shielding against the sun. He would later appreciate what Mies van der Rohe meant when he said that in Greece a Gothic cathedral would look like an old spiderweb.[17]

By late March, he was writing to his parents of his "joyful return to Spain." The sensuality of life there became the dominant motif in his letters. Even churches and religion assumed an earthy, sensual physicality in his descriptions—cathedrals were like cliffs, "sculpted by the wind" and "carved by the sun's knife." Only in the churches of Spain, he writes, did mystery remain; a sensuous appetite invested religious practice with the passions of love and cruelty. Coming into Valencia, he encountered an unforgettable dawn "as opaque as brilliant pigment smeared on a blue-glazed plate," and then the sun like "a daub of umber hanging motionless above."[18] In another letter he identifies the sun as the "tomenter" of Spanish culture: "Here where the sun so grates one's life, each activity is sun tied—to avoid the sun's heat, the intensity of light. The sun is the reason for the character of the people, the character of their art. This light and this heat arouse the senses, deaden the mind... but having heat like this and above all light, the things created are a veritable glorification of light and heat."[19]

Perhaps his experience of living "at the finger tips of sensuousness" was connected to the conditions of his travel for part of that summer in Spain: he had joined Ken and Happy. They were now travelling with another woman who, Arthur quickly recognized, was in love with Happy. She identified herself as a skilled sailor and the daughter of a wealthy American businessman. These were complicated relationships, exciting and disturbing. In his letters, Arthur seems to project some of his feelings onto the land itself, describing the Andalusian countryside as "threateningly romantic and dangerously stimulating to the senses." With his own feelings for Ken still intense, he describes himself in a letter as being tempted to surrender to the sensual life and be like the people "who enjoy the richness of life that is only possible when one cannot be bothered to achieve anything."[20] Arthur took no photographs of his friends;

just buildings appear in the numerous rolls of undeveloped film he mailed back to Canada. Ken, Happy, and the American woman are shadowy figures in his letters.

Arthur's most profound experience of Spanish architecture was his visit to the Alhambra in Granada, the seat of Muslim rule in medieval Spain. There, "the Court of the Lions" recalled for him the Taj Mahal, demonstrating, he wrote, "the refinement and grace of [Muslim] culture which that of the west has never really equalled. It is oriental, very delicate, feminine, almost bodiless. It seems to swim in its reflecting pools."[21] He would make numerous subsequent references to the pleasure of Middle Eastern architecture: "What Arab architects do is build their dreams. There is something insubstantial about [the Alhambra]; it's like a vision. That's part of its beauty. It's unreal, but it's a very sensual building. Everything about it is about the pleasure of being there. The pleasure of views. The pleasure of wind."[22] There would be strong echoes of this experience in Arthur's first acclaimed building, his house for Robert Filberg.

Another space that would be echoed in his work was the great square, the Plaza Mayor, in Salamanca. His description anticipates one of the large effects he would strive for in the design for Simon Fraser University's quadrangle: "From ambiguous streets one suddenly burst into [Salamanca's] plaza that at night had the splendour of a crystal and mirrored ballroom. It was a great precise, chiselled, arcaded square ... a magnificent sky-topped room as no other plaza in the world."

Two intense episodes captured for Arthur the at-once primal and sophisticated nature of life and art in Spain. One of these was attending a bullfight, "a terrible spectacle," colour ritualized through violence. But more powerful was discovering the record of animal life in the prehistoric cave paintings near Altamira, amazing to Arthur for the way the figures of the animals were given a three-dimensionality by the shape of the rock's surface—"a bison springing in attack on some protrusion." He was stunned by the way every attitude of the bison was drawn over the ceiling surface, with some, like an unfinished head in black line, "as sensitive as the brushstroke of a Chinese poet." The mystery of this art was not only how it moved beyond symbolic representation but in how lines depicting "figures caught in the moment of vital action, could be as vital as African sculpture and yet as elegant and refined as that of oriental." Echoing Picasso's exclamation that after Altamira Western art was all decadence, Arthur wonders in concluding his account whether even at this natal stage, humankind was "producing a culture that experienced the gestation of all cultures to come, from crude vitality to mastery, refinement and final decadence." And he wonders if a single cave could have the cultivating effect of a city.[23]

By late summer, the woman who was pursuing Happy had left the group, but the relationship between Ken and Happy was diminished, and Ken was anxious now to fulfill the terms of his scholarship. Since he wanted to see Greece, Arthur gave him the name of the energetic secretary at the Canadian embassy, Kaye Derby, who had first shown him the Acropolis. Ken did meet with Kaye, spent the rest of his year abroad in Greece, and eventually they married. Arthur continued to travel with Happy, and they became lovers. They were a puzzle to the Spanish people they met, who could not understand the relationship of a young man to an older, seemingly eccentric woman. In their view, she was not attractive, and some drew cartoons of her in pants brandishing a cigarette holder. In September, in the Basque country, they were joined again by Happy's friend, who was determined to take her to America. Relations among the three grew tense, with the friend becoming increasingly hostile to Arthur. His revelation of his deepest sexual feelings might have eased relations, but he chose to remain silent. As a result, Happy's friend bought him a ticket to return to Canada—"to get rid of me."[24]

Before leaving, Arthur went back one more time to Florence. As Mary McCarthy observed in *The Stones of Florence*, except for the Duomo, the bell towers, and the two churches of the preaching order—Santa Maria Novella and Santa Croce—Florence is not a city of spires and towers, and viewed from across the river at Piazzale Michelangelo it appears, except for the Duomo, almost a level city. In the period of Florence's first democracy in the thirteenth century, to reduce the civic turmoil generated by the ambition, pride, and rivalry reflected in ever-higher buildings, orders were given to reduce the height of all buildings by two-thirds, to a height not to exceed ninety-six feet.[25] Perhaps this feeling for horizontal building, continuous with the power and rhythm of Greek trabeation (column and entablature, or post and beam), was to be the strongest practical legacy on Arthur of his experiences in this city.

Arthur made his way north again and boarded a ship at Southampton bound for Montreal, arriving home in September.[26] His travels over the previous two years were the best thing that had ever happened to him, he thought—an estimate that would remain unchanged for the rest of his life.

7

Apprentice

BACK IN VANCOUVER IN the fall of 1952, Arthur, now twenty-eight, felt himself to be a very different man. He told a reporter, "I had lived in Italy very much as an Italian. I don't think I drank water in two years, and when I got back, my hair, which had been blond, was black, and my skin was oily."[1]

But he was more than physically changed. The ideas he had formulated in his travels were wholly out of step with North America's postwar euphoria about the great future ahead. As he had anticipated before his return, Vancouver, with its limited historical references, seemed to him mean and superficial, defined only by "our miserable western materialism."[2] In Europe, he had been thrilled by the originality and audacity of the early builders; their works, based in religious faith, "exuded an inner life" that had become his criterion for great art. As a North American abroad he had been looking for his roots, which he located in medieval Europe—"our culture, thought, sense of form and space [are] very much part of the Western experience from the twelfth century on." He began to think more frequently, like Rilke, that the life of the imagination was lived backwards: "that everything is already known and that we have to go through it once again."[3] That fall, as the days shortened and fog settled over the city, he was haunted by nostalgia for Europe, especially Florence, which he now romantically regarded as his first home.

One of the first things Arthur did on his arrival back in Vancouver was to follow up a letter he had sent to Fred Lasserre at the School of Architecture at UBC, inquiring about a teaching position. His travels would give him an edge, he thought; architectural history was often taught by instructors who had never seen the great buildings their lectures described, and they knew little or nothing about the architecture of the Middle East, which Arthur now regarded as one of the great sources of Western art. However, when they met, Lasserre said bluntly: "Well, no, you really don't have the experience or anything else."

Arthur felt the rejection keenly. But with his reputation as an exceptional student at McGill, he quickly found work with one of Vancouver's top firms, McCarter & Nairne. In addition to a number of conventional high-rise office buildings, this company had designed and built the art deco–styled Marine Building at the corner of Hastings and Burrard, recognized as one of the city's outstanding works of architecture. In this spirit of innovation, Arthur attempted to bring modernist concepts to a new post office competition the firm had entered. He designed a building in glass, so that its enormous mass would seem less heavy and there would be an illusion of depth. He included glass *brise-soleil* for heat control. But his employers thought it was "an absolutely crazy building" and began to view him with suspicion. Moreover, in the pristine company offices in the penthouse suite of the Marine Building, Arthur went around with a loaf of French bread under his arm, sometimes leaving it lying with a piece of cheese and a bottle of wine on his drafting table or sticking out of his desk drawer. His fellow employees saw him as affected; his employers, in starched white shirts and armbands to keep their cuffs off the drafting board, saw him as unsanitary. Arthur was not surprised when after six months they let him go.

Looking around the province with his now-educated eye, Arthur found little architecture of interest. The most famous buildings had been designed by British émigré Francis Rattenbury (1867–1935), whose works included the Parliament Buildings and the Empress Hotel in Victoria. These landmarks were designed by a man who became famous for his self-promoting, arrogant personality and for the fact that he was murdered as a consequence of a sensational love triangle after he returned to England. Rattenbury's buildings offered no directions for a young architect, because they were simply copies of Victorian-era styles—the legislative buildings in heavy Renaissance Revival, the Empress in the French Château style.

More sensitive to the local setting was the work of B.C.-born Samuel Maclure (1860–1929), who exhibited some concern to use native wood and stone and to place his buildings harmoniously within their setting. But the style of Maclure's most famous houses was early Tudor—the shingle-style, half-timbered houses familiar to Arthur from his visits with moneyed friends like the Swintons and the Taylors. In a foreword to Janet Bingham's 1985 monograph on Maclure, Arthur wrote, "I remember from those years what could have been called the Shaughnessy Style—substantial, comfortable homes with grand central halls, honey-coloured wood panelling with details reminiscent of the Arts and Crafts movement which then I thought much too old fashioned."[4] In their buildings, both Maclure and Rattenbury affirmed the Canadian national identity as colonial.

There was, however, in the city an architectural firm of long standing that was receptive to new designs. Under the names of its two senior partners, Sharp & Thompson, the firm had been in business since the early part of the century; their work included the design and construction of the first UBC buildings in 1912, the Victory Square cenotaph in 1924, and, in 1927, St. James' Anglican Church at Gore and Cordova in East Vancouver, which Arthur regarded then as the finest building in the city. By 1953, known as Sharp & Thompson, Berwick, Pratt, they were Vancouver's largest architectural firm, riding the postwar institutional boom, building schools, hospitals, and transportation facilities. The company was also building modernist post-and-beam houses adapted to the steep, wooded slopes of the city's North Shore, reflecting specifically the California influence of architects like Rudolph Schindler and Richard Neutra. The most talented designer of the partners was Ned

Pratt, who previous to joining the company had distinguished himself as an engineering student at the University of Toronto and as a bronze medal winner in pairs rowing at the 1932 Olympics. When Pratt started courting Charles Thompson's daughter, his friend Bob Berwick persuaded him to switch from engineering to architecture. While still a student in 1940, Pratt worked on the drawings for Bert Binning's self-designed house, a project subsequently regarded as initiating modernism in British Columbia. The firm's work was eventually dubbed the West Coast Graduate School of Architecture, a finishing school for some of the city's finest architects.[5]

When Arthur began working for the firm early in 1953, he was put under Ron Thom, earmarked as a leading talent in the company. Thom was only a year older than Arthur, but he had taken a more direct route in establishing himself as an architect. In 1940, he had enrolled in the Vancouver School of Art, where he studied painting and architecture, and, after serving in the Royal Canadian Air Force during the war, he graduated from the school in 1947. As an exceptionally gifted student, Thom was invited to stay on to teach first- and second-year courses in architecture at VSA and, the following year, courses in design at the recently established School of Architecture at UBC. Like Arthur and many others, Thom was greatly influenced by B.C. Binning, who, he said, "taught me to see, and taught me to think. He was one of the most important teachers in my life. The strongest thing he taught us, which has had a profound influence on everything I've done in architecture since, was that every aspect of the design had to respond directly to the world around it, whether it be colour or form, or where the light came in, or the views looking out."[6]

What Binning had been teaching his students were the fundamentals of architecture as theorized and practised by Frank Lloyd Wright. Eager to put those theories into practice, Thom indentured as an architect at Sharp & Thompson, Berwick, Pratt, where he soon established himself as their most innovative designer, marrying the horizontal Wright house to the geography and climate of the West Coast and placing B.C. residential design in a league of its own. As such, he would pave the way for Arthur to design some of the most imaginative architecture that West Coast modernism would produce.

But in 1953, Arthur was, in his own words, an awkward apprentice, trying to follow Ron Thom's version of the Wright style but "ill suited to the dynamics of architecture as a business." Looking back, he would acknowledge he was a dreamer and not of much use to the company; he wasted a lot of their money and eventually was fired.[7] He liked to boast, in fact, that he was the only architect ever fired from STBP, a remarkable accomplishment given its reputation as a "generous, happy go-lucky firm, good to work for and ready to welcome past employees back."[8]

Arthur was still living at home at age twenty-nine, and his father was again becoming anxious about how Arthur would make his living and with whom he would "settle down." On board the ship returning from Europe, Arthur had met a girl from Vancouver, Joanne Sheppard, with whom he struck up a friendship, and they became dancing partners during the voyage. It was not a shipboard romance, exactly, but they enjoyed each other's company and agreed to be in touch once they were back in B.C. Joanne become one of Arthur's "dates" during the 1950s when an invitation required one; parties at some of the larger homes in Shaughnessy included a dance floor, and sometimes friends got together on their own simply to dance to records.

But a more significant and emotionally powerful friendship was established in 1953 when, at the Binnings' home in West Vancouver, Arthur was introduced to a tall, handsome Harvard-trained architect. Geoffrey Massey was a fourth-generation member of the Massey family, distinguished in Canada's manufacturing community for the farm machinery company started in 1870 by Hart Massey and Alanson Harris. In generations to follow, the family name acquired lustre through philanthropy in education and the arts and with the appointment of Vincent Massey as the first Canadian-born governor general. Geoffrey was the son of Vincent Massey's brother, Raymond, an actor well-known for his roles in such films as *The Scarlet Pimpernel* (1934) and *East of Eden* (1955). Raymond Massey had

had three wives; Geoffrey was the sole child by his first, Margery Fremantle. Born in London, England, in October 1924, Geoffrey was just four months younger than Arthur. He had also served in the Canadian Army. They took an interest in each other at once, and their relationship would lead to one of Canada's most renowned architectural partnerships and a lifelong friendship.

Arthur and Geoff had the self-confidence of young men who were focussing on careers in architecture at a time when it was the most dynamic of the arts in western North America. Self-confidence also came from their families, though in very different ways. For Geoff, it was the security and privilege of being a Massey; for Arthur, it was having parents who bestowed extraordinary amounts of love on their children and a mother who believed her oldest son was a "golden child." There was a bond, too, in the shadow side of family. Geoff's parents had divorced when he was a small boy. He had been raised by a stepfather and had endured the loneliness of private prep schools in the U.S.; when young, he had a distant, formal relationship with his biological father. Geoff envied Arthur his intimate experience of "home" and quickly grew fond of Oscar and Myrtle, adopting both the Ericksons and the Binnings as "family." For Arthur, however, family meant living up to high hopes and expectations he was confident he could eventually fulfill professionally but not likely in his personal life. Arthur and Geoff also had in common the friendship of Gordon Webber. Looking for work after graduating from Harvard, Geoff had moved to Montreal where he met Gordon through architect and Harvard friend Jeffrey Lindsay. When Geoff could not find permanent work in Montreal, Gordon suggested there might be possibilities for employment in Vancouver. With Geoff and Arthur both working there, Gordon became a frequent visitor to the city.

It was not long before Arthur and Geoff decided to become housemates. They found a small place on Chilco Street in Vancouver's West End that was owned by an Egyptian businessman. Arthur would remember it affectionately as a "wonderful old prefabricated house from San Francisco that had been shipped north—with Ionic columns, a wonderful porch, and a classical Italianate garden with fountain."[9] When he learned his tenants were trained architects, their landlord offered them free rent in return for the design of a six-storey apartment building to replace the house. He also promised payment when the building went ahead. The building did eventually go up, but the owner left for Egypt, not to return, and their final payment was a big American car he had left behind. In the meantime, Arthur and Geoff had fun painting the little prefab in stark black and white (black doors and floors, white walls) and gave some memorable parties there, with young artist and architect friends such as Jack Shadbolt, Ron Thom, Barry Downs, and Takao Tanabe, taking little care about doing damage since the house was going to come down. The apartment block, named "The Residency," stands in a nicely landscaped area of the street—an early modernist concrete shoebox.[10]

Another early business adventure was to design and manufacture the kind of narrow ties that were fashionable in Europe but had no currency yet in Vancouver. They called it the Aerig Tie Company, and the Erickson house was headquarters. In the morning, Arthur's brother, Don, would take samples to the clothing stores and bring back orders; in the afternoon, Myrtle would buy fabric; in the evenings, family and friends set to work at the dining-room table, designing, cutting, and sewing. Ruth Killam, Arthur's childhood friend, would often be at the table, working well past midnight.

Geoff had also found work with Sharp & Thompson, Berwick, Pratt, but he and Arthur were eager to work on their own. Their first joint architectural project was to build in 1954 a house for two struggling artists in West Vancouver—painters Charles Stegeman and Françoise André—who had a ravine lot on upper Stevens Drive in the British Properties. To get started, Arthur got a loan from his mother's banker. He and Geoff worked at the project weekends and evenings, supervising the construction of a large studio: a pure cubic structure, with a small kitchen, bathroom, and bedroom attached. As businessmen, they teetered on bankruptcy. Building costs went far beyond Arthur's ability to calculate, chiefly because of the difficulties of a ravine lot where, for example, a crane was required to place the beams. The studio house pleased the Stegemans, who had asked for double-height ceilings so they could paint in ideal light, but it was deemed "just a big empty box" by some of Arthur's architect friends.[11] Certainly it was the most Bauhaus-like of any of Arthur's buildings. But its functionality would give it a long life: after an addition, it became a Unitarian church, then a home again, where two leopards roamed. Eventually it would be further expanded by architect Brian Hemingway and, with its deeply wooded lot, used as a set for the sensationally popular *Twilight* movies based on a series of vampire romances.[12]

At the same time, they secured a commission to build a house for another artist couple, Gordon and Marion Smith—she a weaver, he a painter—whom Arthur had first met when listening to music at Lawren and Bess Harris's home. Gordon was English born but had come with his mother and brother to Winnipeg while in his teens. His meeting with Marion Fleming led him to visit Vancouver and, after service in the Second World War, he moved to the coast, where he studied art and then taught, first at the Vancouver School of Art and then as a professor in the faculty of education at UBC from 1956 to 1982.

Gordon developed his talent as a painter in the modernist tradition and was highly praised for his abstract landscapes, so the first requirement for his home was a studio with filtered light. Accordingly, Arthur and Geoff designed and executed a small one-bedroom post-and-beam house for the Smiths (barely fourteen hundred square feet), with kitchen and living room and a second storey at one end that was exclusively a studio. Glazed overhangs were provided at the windows on the second level to admit precious light and protect the windows from rain. In Erickson's words, it was "a blend of Bauhaus formal concepts with West Coast sensibility to wood construction." Gordon did some of the carpentry work himself.

The lot on which the house was erected turned out to be a prototype for numerous sites that Arthur would develop in West Vancouver during the course of his career. It was an acre of sloping land, densely wooded in cedar, with numerous rock outcroppings. Only a few trees were cut to let some light into the studio. Arthur persuaded his clients that the house should be lifted one storey off the ground to create something like a bridge, so that they would be living in the trees and could leave the forest floor with its ferns, moss, and rocks largely intact. This respect for the physical place in which a building was situated would be a fundamental principle in all his work and would lead him to observe more than once that he was as much landscape designer as architect. "To me, architecture means unifying the duality of site and building... It is the dialogue between building and setting that is the essence of architecture."[13]

However, the dialogue between designer and client did not always go smoothly. It was Arthur's first experience of having to modify a project in the face of a client's wishes and, because it was a wholly experimental enterprise, costs were soon out of control. Gordon, slight and high-strung, was normally gentle in behaviour, but he grew edgy and increasingly alarmed as the bills kept coming in. Geoff did not always take criticism lightly, and one day a quarrel ensued over costs; Gordon became angry and raised his voice. In an interview fifteen years later, Arthur admitted that the architects and client "parted *not* too good company at the end of the job."[14] In a summary of that period in his career, Arthur made a veiled reference to the tensions that arose: "It is one thing to win over a client in your own office-lair and another to dictate on site to one who is serving as his own carpenter."[15] But for 1954, the house won the first Massey Medal in the category of a single-house dwelling under $15,000, and the Smiths, by then well pleased, would ask Arthur and Geoff to build them another house, much larger, ten years later.

On the basis of this early success, Arthur and Geoff were eager to start an architectural firm, but neither had the financial resources. They needed more than a loan from Myrtle's bank; they needed money up front, and they both needed to be free from other work to focus on getting a business started. Arthur still had his eye on a teaching position at UBC, which he saw as employment compatible with starting a company, but his applications were not successful.

While Arthur was struggling at age thirty to establish himself as an architect, to many in Vancouver's arts community he seemed to possess already the sophisticated self-confidence of a man of considerable accomplishment. There is a glimpse of him in a recollection by man of letters George Woodcock, who first met Arthur at the home of Jack and Doris Shadbolt in Burnaby. Woodcock observes that since the mid-1950s was an age of "sartorial self-effacement," drab clothes and hair trimmed short, it was the way someone spoke that left the strongest impression, and he remembered Arthur for his "peculiar rounded utterances... a rhythmic way of speaking in phrases that sounded as though they had been deliberately crafted."[16] He was in Woodcock's view an urbane conversationalist, with a striking talent for good description that made his stories vivid. Woodcock especially liked Arthur's tales from the war, when he had lived in the villa on the Hooghly with officers who were Oxford dons and Buddhist scholars. His other impression of Arthur from that first meeting was that he seemed much younger than he actually was—perhaps still in his early twenties. This would not have meant much to Arthur at that time, but as he grew older, his youthful appearance became a matter of considerable personal vanity.

RUTH KILLAM SPENT part of 1953 travelling in Europe, studying art, and when she returned home the next year she came to see Arthur about waterfront property where she could build herself a small house. By now, Arthur and Geoff were renting a house on Bachelor Bay in West Vancouver, where at high tide the water came almost over the wall and into the house. They showed Ruth what was available in their area. She chose a lot at Whytecliff with a spectacular view of Howe Sound, but she selected a particularly challenging site for the house—a narrow peninsula of rocks jutting out into salt water. Arthur's response was to design a house that spoke to the place and its geographical history. The one-storey flat-roofed house stretched out on the rocks, with the bedroom directly facing the sound. To bring light into the north end of the house containing the kitchen, dining, and living-room areas, he designed a skylight in the shape of a pyramid that was a geometrical version of the rock outcrop. And "to honour its marine location," the house was painted lighthouse white with silver wood infill.[17] For its inventiveness, this house would also win a Massey award for architecture, much to the chagrin of competitors Thompson, Berwick & Pratt, for whom Geoff was still working.

But the project would also change the relationship between the two architects. Although Arthur felt sexual attraction in their friendship, this was not the case for Geoff. It would be several years before Geoff realized his friend was gay. The client and architect relationship between Ruth Killam and Geoff, however, had grown into something else, and when the house was completed in 1955, they announced their plans to marry and live there. Arthur withdrew as much as possible from the building site. The only public hint of his troubled feelings came in a few terse lines in an interview years later: "I was acting as a supervisor on the house site until one day Ruth said, 'Look, Arthur, don't you get the point?' and I said, 'Well, what point?' And she said, 'I want Geoff to come and supervise the house!' So I got the point!"[18]

A more dramatic indication of his feelings was his departure for Eugene, Oregon, directly after the September wedding, at which he served as Geoff's best man. Arthur had received a phone call a couple of weeks earlier from Douglas Shadbolt about an assistant professorship in the School of Architecture at the University of Oregon. Five faculty members had quit, and there was a "big revolution" taking place at the school over pedagogical methods. Doug had not yet completed his own degree at McGill—he had repeatedly failed two courses in engineering mathematics—but after a brief meeting with the dean of the school, he had been assigned a job there teaching drawing and design and would be able to study part-time himself. "But this is a very strange school," Doug advised his friend. "They have no set curriculum. No time frame. Everybody passes. You can't criticize. You can only ask questions."[19] After accepting the job, Arthur wrote to Geoff that this was the chance they had been waiting for. He would save his salary—it was generous—and when he returned the two of them could go into business together.

What Arthur found when he arrived at the architecture school in Eugene was a pedagogy along the lines of Louis Sullivan's "kindergarten chats." Students were free to choose their own projects, their own mentors, and they could take as long as they wished to finish a project. Arthur was thrilled to be part of this experiment. It helped him forget the disappointment at home. The fundamental teaching principle was Socratic; the professor would offer no opinion or advice, thus forcing students back on their own resources. As Arthur would later explain, it put the student in a desperate state, grasping at whatever would save him or her, and then, for the good student, would come the revelation. "It was the most mature educational experiment, I think, in the United States at that time. It was really remarkable... I guess there were a number of fairly chaotic years, but I think very fruitful years. Certainly, the experience for me was remarkable."[20]

Doug had separated from his first wife, and he and Arthur shared a house that winter. Doug was already "an invaluable down to earth mentor" for Arthur, who had set out for McGill with "a vast innocence of what architecture was altogether." Now he was inspiring Arthur to show students what exciting things could be done with space and a few planks of wood. They became intrigued with ideas for urban planning and, knowing that the city of Victoria was going to make major changes, they worked out a plan to redesign Victoria harbour. While their submission fell short of the city's overall needs, it was credited as being influential in the work as it went ahead.[21]

On his own, Arthur started work on a design that completely re-envisioned Vancouver's West End peninsula. One of his parents' friends had a significant amount of real estate to sell in that part of the city, and instead of the heterogeneous mix of apartment buildings that exist there today, Arthur proposed two massive spiralling structures terraced from the English Bay shoreline to a height of one hundred storeys, with the centre open to the bay. This was urban planning on Le Corbusier's sweeping scale, something like the latter's 1925 "Plan Voisin" for the demolition and rebuilding of Paris's Right Bank as a great park dotted at intervals with eighteen sixty-storey cruciform apartment towers. Later Arthur would concede that the scale of his design was inhuman and that "it was just as well it was never built."[22]

Together, Arthur and Doug taught courses in design and landscaping, and, in Shadbolt's words, "We were a pretty powerful team."[23] As foreigners, they felt they could experiment with new ideas, and so they decided that the final project for their courses should be a party held at a beach on the Oregon coast. Eventually, the whole architecture school decided to take part—professors, lab assistants, physical plant planners, ceramicists—and they drove to the coast in a caravan. Each group had to erect its own wind shelter on the dunes, where they would live while preparing the three-day feast. Students were called on for their ethnic specialties—one from China cooked a pig, basting it with maple syrup, ginger, and soy; another, from Iran, marinated a lamb for several days in wine, onions, and spices, then dug a pit in the sand to roast it. The ceramicists made ceramic masks and armour. A student from Colombia provided music, inventing instruments and putting wind chimes and noisemakers on long poles for various ceremonies enacted. As Arthur would fondly recall, "We had a great celebration with processions and performances and everything else. It was an extraordinary thing, and it became a tradition [for a time] at the University of Oregon."[24]

The Oregon beach party was both a major social event and a significant pedagogical exercise (Gordon Webber would have been amazed by the aesthetic possibilities of bamboo poles and sheets of plastic[25]), and it created a kind of instant fame around Arthur in the West Coast architectural community.[26] But its most immediate result was the offer of an assistant professorship at UBC for the fall of 1956.

Before returning to Vancouver, Arthur travelled to Scottsdale, Arizona, to visit Taliesin West for the first time. He was accompanied by the student from Colombia, and they camped out in sleeping bags and hitchhiked for part of the trip. The Wrights were not in residence, so, undistracted, Arthur was able to take the full measure of the extraordinary building that first inspired him to follow the path of architecture. On this trip he also travelled to California, and then to Mexico, where he had his first formative encounter with Aztec and Mayan architecture.

Before he returned, Arthur learned that, with money from his wife's family, Geoff had created an architectural firm and was already in partnership with Ted Watkins in an office in Gastown. The hurt he felt was reflected in the uncharacteristic bitterness he expressed in a letter to Alan Jarvis, director of the National Gallery in Ottawa, making it clear that he, not Geoff Massey, had designed the medal-winning houses. The only thing Geoff had suggested for the Smith house, Arthur wrote, was a sewer pipe for the footings; for Ruth Killam's house, Geoff had designed metal supports for under the columns and, under Arthur's supervision, a work bench for Ruth's studio.[27] Arthur considered establishing himself somewhere else, where opportunities for an experimental young architect might not be so meagre. But ties to his family were strong, and British Columbia exerted a pull that only his poetic meditations could articulate: "What is it about Vancouver that keeps many of us inescapably under its spell? Is it because we succumb so heedlessly to the sheer beauty of its setting—to the haunting melancholy of a summer evening's light or to the spring air washed with sea salt and the sap of alder?"[28]

FROM THE START, Arthur viewed his teaching position at UBC as a necessary sinecure, the kind of material support, once provided by the Church or individual patrons, that artists had relied on historically while they developed their ideas and their craft. Architecture was housed in army huts on the campus's West Boulevard. Arthur's office there quickly became a drafting studio and the place from which he conducted business as he undertook, now on his own, additions and renovations to homes in the city. He regarded the classroom as a place where ideas could be exchanged, but he gave little time to preparation. His lectures consisted of observations and anecdotes designed to stimulate discussion, but Canadian students were reticent to respond; they exhibited little of the "joy and experiment" Arthur had encountered in their American counterparts.

In contrast, Arthur was deemed brilliant in studio workshops, where he proceeded to "unteach" his students. Many, not long out of high school, were initially frustrated by his seemingly casual, Socratic method. But the good ones would look back on those studio sessions as their most creative experiences in a classroom. Bruno Freschi, one of Arthur's bright students, later gave one example.

> One of the most poetic problems [Arthur] created was called "Seven Stones." He said to the class one day, "The assignment is to choose seven stones, and present your project in three weeks." It was terribly generative. Some students danced with seven stones, some glued them to a piece of cardboard, and one got seven beautiful stones from the beach and presented them in a velvet box, clanking them together for everyone to hear. It was a little performance. Arthur looked and said, "Why are you wearing a blue sweater?" The kid was dumbfounded and replied, "That had nothing to do with the problem!" And Arthur said, "No. It's a performance, and your clothing is part of it.[29]

Arthur liked to quote Gertrude Stein on her deathbed; when asked by Alice B. Toklas, "What is the answer?" Stein replied, "What is the question?" "All my exercises," said Arthur, "were to force the students to probe their own resources for the meaning of things and not to do anything by habit or convention. None of us knew what the problem was, and the whole exercise was to find out." Another version of the Seven Stones exercise, more like a game, was meant to illustrate the organic nature of architecture. "Each player was given a stone to be located in harmony with the shape of an existing field. Each placement influenced the judgment of where to site the subsequent one. The resulting pattern could not be planned in advance, but was the outcome of an organic series of decisions along the way."[30]

The same tangential, open-ended process could be applied to architectural design. John Roaf recalled that designing a restaurant for Arthur's class meant learning about the larger culture surrounding food, what people ate and what instruments they employed, how they sipped wine, what light they found most conducive to pleasure when eating, how they used space: "Arthur was like a Zen master."[31] While the class was at work, he would look over the shoulder of each student. As Gordon Webber had done at McGill, Arthur would neither praise nor disparage the work in progress but rather ask questions and suggest further possibilities. Even if the work showed little or no promise, he would say "Very interesting," though students eventually realized what this meant. Especially gifted students were invited to participate in some of the projects Arthur was working on himself.

But teaching sharpened Arthur's growing conviction that art had little to do with intellectual pursuits, and he doubted that its study should be part of a university curriculum. His thinking was akin to statements being made in the U.S. by architect Philip Johnson, famous for his modernist Glass House in Connecticut. "Art should be practiced in gutters—or in attics," Johnson proclaimed in a controversial address he gave at Harvard in 1954. "You can't learn architecture any more than you can learn a sense of music or of painting. You shouldn't talk about art, you should do it."[32] Johnson's ideas, in turn, were closely aligned to those of English art critic Geoffrey Scott, who asserted in *The Architecture of Humanism* that the crucial element in art was taste—something beyond measurement or proof, something that could not be taught.[33] By extension, Arthur was increasingly skeptical of reason's primary place in the hierarchy of human experience. "Salvation" through knowledge seemed doubtful: knowledge that mattered was not argued in communicable points but experienced directly in art—in tragedy, paintings, sculpture. "I always advised my students not to think—but to feel and to respond to their instinctual inner voice."[34] He held an increasingly low opinion of the dialectically derived systems of Western epistemology.

One of the most valuable experiences for Arthur's students was to see some of his work. Jim Strasman, a gifted student who would later be one of Arthur's employees, recalled vividly that the Smith house "made me understand for the first time what space was about, and proportion." It was a sensation revived again and again in the presence of Arthur's buildings.[35]

One of the bright spots of Arthur's years at UBC was the presence on campus of Abraham Rogatnick, known to his close friends as Abe. He joined UBC as a professor of architecture in 1958, but Arthur had known Abe since his arrival in Vancouver in the fall of 1955. Born in Boston in 1923, Abe had studied at Harvard under Walter Gropius and, like Arthur, had served in the army during the Second World War. He came to live in Vancouver in happenstance fashion: at Harvard, Abe had shared a room with Geoffrey Massey, and he decided to pay him an impromptu visit. With Alvin Balkind, he drove out to the West Coast and arrived when Geoff and Ruth were on their honeymoon. Arthur, hearing about the two men through a phone call from Bert Binning, agreed to let them stay at the house on Chilco Street while they were in town. Abe and Alvin were so taken by the city and its possibilities that they decided to stay. Within weeks of their arrival, they rented commercial space in West Vancouver and opened the New Design Gallery, the city's first modern art establishment.

Abraham Rogatnick, small in stature, quick-witted, mischievous, quickly became a leading presence in the arts community. His gallery would revolutionize the visual art scene in Vancouver, but with his love of theatre he also became involved in founding the Arts Club Review (later the Arts Club Theatre) and introduced theatre-going audiences to several avant-garde plays. To make his living while Alvin ran the gallery, he eventually used his Harvard credentials to secure a teaching position at UBC. Many of the mostly male students were initially uneasy around Abe, who was not just small, but sexually ambiguous—but soon he became one of the most popular teachers on campus, for he made his classes multimedia events that were not only informative but irresistibly entertaining. Arthur was aware from the outset that Abe and Alvin were a couple. They made no attempt to hide the nature of their relationship, something relatively rare then in Vancouver. Arthur enjoyed their company immensely, and Abe was one of his closest friends for the rest of his life. Abe travelled and knew Europe's art world intimately, especially that of Venice, and in campus politics, attempting to raise the profile of fine arts, he and Arthur were allies.

But Arthur did not have Abe's kind of dramatic energy. A brief excursion into television broadcasting in 1954 had made that clear. He had persuaded a local producer to let him host a show titled *Looking at Art*, which featured conversations with local artists such as jeweller and carver Bill Reid, but Arthur's interview style was passive, and the show drew so little interest it was discontinued after eight weeks. Arthur also knew that good teaching in lecture halls required an extroverted, spontaneous manner that ran counter to his meditative style of speaking. Accordingly, he continued to pursue design commissions. His clients in the mid-1950s were most often moneyed family friends, and some of the projects were modest: a porch to be closed in, a living room extended, a kitchen remodelled. When the Buckerfields engaged Arthur to design a terrace roof and patio for their home on Southwest Marine Drive, he experimented, using two layers of fibreglass between which wood shavings were sandwiched.[36] The effect was both novel and attractive, and for some years the structure held.

A more ambitious project was to design a new garden terrace and a pool house for the Grauers, his first clients in what Arthur would describe as the "Medici mould." Dal Grauer, as the head of British Columbia's hydroelectric corporation, had power almost equal to that of the premier. But in contrast to W.A.C. Bennett, Grauer had been a Rhodes Scholar and, with his family, was actively involved in the arts. They knew of Arthur's unique capacity to articulate aesthetic principles. Indeed, Grauer's mother-in-law, Zipporah Woodward, felt "diamonds and pearls fell from Arthur's mouth."[37] They had high expectations.

The large Grauer home was in the Riviera style fashionable in the 1910s. The pool complex was at the back of the house, in what Arthur would describe as "the most unpleasant part of the garden."[38] As an "impertinent" centrepiece to distract the eye, he designed a cabana to shelter a lounging and social space adjacent to the pool— "a 'petit' Trianon to the main house." The vaulted canopy consisted of eight tulip-shaped fibreglass shells sprouting from steel pillars that were hollow to drain off the rainwater. The design was sound, but the manufacture was a nightmare. The first plaster mould for the shells collapsed, and the next one also proved defective. Eventually, production went ahead successfully, but just when the shells were finished, Blythe Rogers's plastics company went bankrupt, with some of the forms still in the factory. Desperate to finish the project and not let the Grauers know the company was in receivership, Arthur rented a truck and during the night broke into the shop and removed the remaining panels. It was a "hair-raising" adventure, but when the cabana was completed, the Grauers enjoyed the praise their guests lavished on this structure with its Moorish appearance. The roof of tulips on their slender stems gave the building a lightness, as if it were floating, an illusion enhanced further when the shells were lit up from inside at night.

There had never been anything quite this "frivolous" in Vancouver, and it would be seen locally as ushering in the New Romanticism of the late 1950s. Arthur arranged for Selwyn Pullan, a skilled local photographer, to take some pictures. He ambitiously sent photographs and suggestions for an article on his work to the arts editors at the *New York Times* and *Architectural Forum* and was refused by both.[39] But an illustrated article in the *Vancouver Sun* credited Arthur for leading a rebellion against the starkness of modern architecture and creating an effect at the Grauer residence "associated with the splendour of a Persian garden."[40]

Arthur also aimed to develop a presence in the local arts community by doing practical service. In 1957, he joined the Vancouver Centennial Committee, which was preparing to celebrate British Columbia's one-hundredth birthday. He headed a subcommittee celebrating the province's creative and cultural activities, which included Ron Thom, Ted Bethune, Bruno Bobak, and John Dayton (with whom Arthur had climbed to Forbidden Plateau in his teens). Arthur put himself in charge of "decorations"—pennants and street banners, flower baskets and tubs to make a street of roses, a street of carnations. He arranged for merchants to display equipment and products from the past and for radio stations to play vintage music. These were detailed and time-consuming commitments.

At the same time, Arthur became associated with the expatriate Canadian architect Wells Coates, who had built himself a considerable reputation as a modernist in England but returned to Vancouver in 1955 and set up Project 58, a far-reaching program for the advancement of the visual arts in Canada. Coates's reputation for original ideas (he was designing a monorail rapid transit system for Vancouver thirty years ahead of its time) was such that his work was often overlooked, but back in Vancouver he was funded by Dal Grauer. It was to Project 58 that Arthur submitted his "Plan Voisin" for the massive apartment building to occupy most of the West End. The work of the group came to an end in June 1958 with Coates's sudden death. Arthur and others in the arts community, such as Gordon Smith, would be haunted by Coates's memory: "He was a little too flamboyant for Vancouver I guess. England had given him a kind of French flourishing manner, and so one didn't know how to take him. He wasn't able to get much work. He very sadly lived alone in the West End."[41] Coates was said to have died of a heart attack, but there were rumours that he had drowned himself in English Bay.

WHILE ARTHUR WAS teaching and rapidly expanding his client base as an architect, he was also looking for a piece of property where he could make his home. In 1957, he chose a 66 × 120–foot lot with a very small house at the northeast corner of Courtenay and West 14th Avenue in Point Grey. It was close to the university, and the purchase price was only $11,000. What attracted him was the fact that the house, instead of being in the middle of the lot, was on the lane, and the remainder of the lot, facing south, was an expanse of garden—a lawn and a colourful English herbaceous border (roses, delphiniums, phlox), concealing a vegetable and raspberry patch, a rose-covered arbour, and some fruit trees, all surrounded by a white picket fence. The house, partly covered by a grape vine, was in fact just a garage with a lean-to, built in 1917, and was only meant to be lived in while a proper house was being built. The English owners had temporarily converted it into a domestic dwelling, dividing it into a set of minia-ture rooms. But they never went any further with their plans—the Depression intervened, and then advancing age. Their only addition was another single-car garage that was being used for storage when Arthur bought the property.

Arthur, too, planned some day to build himself a full-scale house on the property, but in the meantime he set out to make his little garage house comfortable and interesting. The first thing he did was hire a "sailor-handyman" to take down all the partitions and make it a one-room house.[42] One day during this process, Arthur arrived back in time to prevent the collapse of the roof by propping it up with a wood and terracotta column he had salvaged from the demolition of another house nearby. Hard-pressed for cash, he furnished the new room with marble slabs retrieved from the men's room of the old Vancouver Hotel and with seating made from the straw benches of former trolley cars. On the walls, he affixed Chinese gold dragon's blood paper rendered antique with many layers of pigmented lacquer, and for the little kitchen area he built teak cabinets. He slept on the trolley car benches. The smaller garage became a guest room for visitors like Gordon Webber, though it served as such only in summer because it was not heated.

The garden was changed more dramatically and would eventually become famous. By the second year of Arthur's residence, the property was overrun with uncut grass, and the English garden looked romantically deserted—"the kind of secret garden that children love, saturated with weeds but with the flowers still growing."[43] By the third year, there were no flowers except for a few roses hanging off the trellises. His eighteen-hour work days left no time to care for a garden, so Arthur decided to create a natural garden that would look after itself. He arranged for a bulldozer to clear and contour the lot in a way that would solve another problem—the view of the ugly door and brown-shingled porch of his neighbour to the south. To accomplish this, the whole of the English garden was excavated and mounded up near the end of the property in a berm. Arthur hired one of his students, Werner Forster, to line the resulting hole with roofing felt, to tar and cover it with a layer of sand and gravel, and to fill it with water. The edges of the pool were lined with rocks gleaned from the property. Aside from a bathing pool adjacent to the smaller garage, the rest of the garden was paved with concrete bricks so there would be no lawn to mow. It was not long before a new ecosystem was establishing itself: first lichens and mosses, then water beetles and spiders. Frogs arrived to provide a chorus for the neighbourhood the following spring. By removing the English garden, Arthur had returned the site to its original character of a forest clearing.

To the garden he added both native plants (salal, skunk cabbage, ferns) and exotic grasses. After the planting of a row of poplars, a cedar hedge, bamboo on the berm to further screen the south end, more bamboo on the east side, and masses of rhododendrons and azaleas on the west side, the vegetation was allowed to develop on its own, creating a "green laboratory" in which the architect was able to study how a site changes and evolves with time.[44] But it was, and remains today, more than a wild garden that has been "let go." Writer David Laskin astutely identifies an austere, elemental structure of strong horizontal surfaces, one of water, the other of granite and brick, in rhythmic interplay with the curving lines of the pond and the foliage, as being the source of the garden's powerful effect on the viewer. It is also, in the words of another writer, a masterpiece of "illusion": the fish-filled pond at the centre is like a lake, and the eight-foot mound of earth and bamboo planting at the far end camouflages the property line like a low mountain and jungle. The effect is of a spacious landscape "continuing into the beyond." Everything appears bigger than it really is.[45]

Arthur's living quarters were similarly altered to create an illusion of greater space. In the early 1960s, he bridged the two garages together with a new kitchen, a bathroom, and a central skylight overhead. The second garage was now his study. Under its roof he made a sleeping loft, accessible by a carpeted ladder. A futon and down comforter on the floor, bookshelves, and a small television comprised its furnishings. But this tiny space was made to seem larger by means of a trap-door skylight. Similarly, the rest of the house seemed much larger than its actual 850 square feet—an effect achieved by mirrored entryways and sliding glass doors leading to a small greenhouse and then to the garden. Arthur would often say that architecturally the house was so bad he didn't like to admit living there. But, in fact, it was the perfect expression of his essential philosophy that a building must harmonize with its setting. Surrounded by shrubs and situated far back on the lot, the house is hardly noticed as one enters the property from a gate on the west side. Giuseppe Mazzariol, a Venetian architectural teacher and critic, would one day describe this *"piccolissima casa"* as a dwelling of "elegance and refinement. It is made of nothing. There are no extraordinary things inside, only colours and materials, but it is a place where a man feels hugely rich and cultivated."[46] For Arthur, throughout the rest of his life, this most elemental of shelters would be his refuge. It was a pastoral dwelling, nostalgic for places of origin, set in a garden where one was part of nature and uninterrupted by the world's passing.

Not everyone admired what Arthur had achieved, however. When he began excavating the garden, his neighbours chatted with him over the fence, happy to believe they were no longer going to have a "nonconformist garage dweller" in their midst. Regarding the expanse of water at the centre of his lot, he overhead two neighbouring women conversing as they peered through a gap in the old picket fence. "It's a tragic story," one said. "This poor fellow started to build his house, and when he dug he struck a spring and it all turned into a swamp!"[47] When Arthur replaced the pickets with a seven-foot cedar fence, suspicion arose in the humdrum, middle-class neighbourhood of stucco houses and open lawns, and that grew into hostility when the pond brought marauding wild creatures—herons, wild ducks, and raccoons whose depredations spread throughout the area. There was further friction when Arthur started giving noisy parties for his students and artist friends. His neighbours eventually took their complaints to city council to make Arthur comply with the regulation fence height of four feet. In a protracted conflict, he brought the fence down to six feet, then down another four inches, finally achieving a truce. But as his parties grew more frequent and the music louder, skirmishes erupted, with Arthur's address becoming well-known to police. The latter, however, knew that there might be treats for them at West 14th and Courtenay—canapés and casserole dips, beer if they were interested—and so he managed, Gatsby-like, to maintain his privacy and remain the exotic centre of speculation.

8

The
Filberg House

AS A SELF-CONFIDENT YOUNG MAN of talent and
promise, Arthur was much in demand socially in the late 1950s.
Ambitious and testing for a direction, he was receptive to invitations,
particularly from potential clients and patrons. Some connections
came through his parents. Babe Taylor, for example, was one of his
mother's many friends from Winnipeg, and this connection proved
invaluable throughout Arthur's life. Babe's husband, Austin, who
had made a considerable fortune in gold mining, was head of the
Home Oil Company and raised racehorses in Langley; the Taylors
lived in the house in Shaughnessy once owned by sugar manufacturer B.T. Rogers. From an early age, Arthur was a close friend of
their daughter, Pat, who married the American spokesman for conservative thought, William F. Buckley Jr., and became a doyenne of
fashion and opinion in New York in the 1960s. Other connections
Arthur made on his own—with the Southams, for example, and with
the Grauers, the Buckerfields, and the Bell-Irvings. If there was an
invitation for an evening of dancing he continued to take Joanne
Sheppard but otherwise he was a bachelor, and he played the role
of the extra man smoothly. His manner was always conservatively
debonair, appropriately *dégagé*.

But at the same time, there was Arthur's longing for a close male
companion. Early in the evening at a lavish party given by the Taylors in 1957, Arthur became aware of a good-looking, well-dressed

young man watching him from across the room. When the man came over, he straightened Arthur's tie, then introduced himself as Rob Filberg. The two had seen each other in passing as students at UBC, but this was the first time they had spoken. For Arthur it was as if the party had suddenly stopped; he could not remember afterwards what he and Rob had talked about, but he knew at once that an important friendship was unfolding. It was a portentous meeting.

Robert Filberg Jr., also known as Bud and Buddy, was born into a life of privilege on Vancouver Island. To the people of the Comox Valley, his father, Robert J. Filberg, president of the Comox Logging and Railway Company, was lord and master. Born in Colorado in 1890, the son of an itinerant Swedish tailor, Filberg Sr. was an energetic, "bull-of-the-woods" logger who had pulled himself up by the bootstraps to become a chief engineer at the company and eventually marry Florence McCormick, the daughter of the vice-president. Later, as company president, he managed the province's largest logging operation, remaining in this managerial position when the company became a subsidiary of the Canadian Western Lumber Company and becoming a director when it was sold in 1954 to Crown Zellerbach Canada Ltd. In the classic pattern of such relationships, Rob Filberg Jr. had no matching ambitions. Unlike his demanding father, an anti-union man and a "heller with the women," Rob was gentle in spirit; he was interested in the arts and education and placed high value on the utopian dream of world peace.[1]

At university, Rob Filberg was singled out in *The Ubyssey* as one of the smart dressers on campus in his blazer and grey flannels.[2] He exhibited a boyish charm, especially in his relations with older people. Although he had easy access to affluent society and world travel, Rob energetically cultivated a small circle of friends in Comox, where he took part in the local Little Theatre. He was also a patron of the local art scene, buying canvases from E.J. Hughes, Joe Plaskett, and Jack Shadbolt. But there was another side to this affable young man; he was subject to periods of depression and spent long stretches in seclusion in the family home. Things came to an excruciating head when his mother committed suicide.

After leaving UBC, Rob had married Marie Foley, the daughter of another family prominent in logging, but by the time Arthur met him at the Taylors', the marriage had been annulled. He was now engaged to Melda Buchanan, a part-time instructor in mathematics at UBC, who would one day become known for her passionate environmentalism. Rob Filberg was struggling to find a role for himself; he was also struggling with alcohol.

Before Arthur left the Taylors' party, he had accepted an invitation to visit Vancouver Island and look at a twenty-five-acre property Rob's father had deeded to him at Comox. Part fields and part forested, it was located on a bluff two hundred feet above the Strait of Georgia, a stretch of water sometimes referred to as British Columbia's "inland sea." Arthur would regard it as the most dramatic site he ever built on. Not only were there coastal mountains to the east, but the vista looked west to the magnificent Comox Glacier, and to the south the eye swept for miles down the strait to more mountains and islands. On a very clear day one could see as far as the volcanic cone of Mount Baker. A century earlier, Arthur liked to reflect, the canoes of the First Nations had passed through the waters below.

What Rob proposed building there was a small conference centre and retreat where world thinkers and leaders could gather to discuss global problems, especially issues of peace. In addition to the main building and its facilities, there would be cabins scattered around the property for visiting politicians, scholars, and artists. Rob conveyed to Arthur that this centre would represent a "cleansing" of his family's life, which had been focussed on the ruthless pursuit of wealth and power at the expense of others. Rob Filberg was exactly the individual Arthur had been searching for—his first real patron, as he put it, "a wealthy man who was willing to back a full-scale architectural expression of my artistic nature."[3] Walking the site on his first visit, Arthur recognized that whatever was constructed should be designed like a pavilion for viewing the landscape—so that the fields and forest, the bluff edge and distant glacier could all be seen at once and one's spatial imagination would be prompted to embrace the world at large. The aesthetic problem, as Arthur saw it, was "how to cast lines into this vast space, draw it into the complex of a building and release it without decreasing but rather enhancing its energy; how to find a building that would not interrupt the space but stand aside as a good conductor or eloquent guide to the pleasures of the site."[4]

On that first visit, the two friends discussed reworking the landscape to emphasize its features, and the next time Arthur went up to Comox, he found Rob on a small bulldozer, scraping and moving the soil. Together they planned to act "on behalf of the centuries"—following the way weather and geology would work—forming a rise under a stand of maple trees to create a natural fall of land to both the east and west. They also cut a tunnel south through the forest; its dramatic descent opened to a view of the beach below, so that before the house was designed, four powerful axes were established. When the building began, the house was placed to draw one "through and away from the house towards the many points of view."[5] Enhancing the flow of space in what he thought of as both a Himalayan and a Mediterranean setting, Arthur established a different viewing place at the end of each axis: to the east a balcony or morning terrace; to the north a stone platform under the maples, from which the serrated outline of the Coast Range was visible; to the south a landing above the beach; and to the west an evening terrace overlooking the bay and village and the glacier beyond. He used glass liberally as walls to dissolve the transition from inside to out.

The design was also sensitive to Rob's chronic problem with depression, especially in winter, and so to the importance of light. Rob was living in a cottage on the property nearby, but when Arthur visited, they would tent on the proposed site together "to understand better the play of light."[6] Arthur would write shortly after completing the house: "Light brings life to a building. With its constant change of colour, intensity and position, it is the most important of building materials."[7] Arthur was almost certainly thinking here of Lawren Harris's belief that light was the passageway to a higher world. In a poem titled "Darkness and Light," Harris writes that light is weightless, with the mystical power to quicken and transform.[8]

From the outside, Arthur planned for the house to appear light in structure, as if it belonged to the sky, an effect to be achieved not only by the glass walls but by a roof that flared upward and outward from the posts. The base and lower masonry walls of the Filberg house would represent a solid mass emerging from the sandy field, "as if they had always been there and had only been swept clean to receive a new superstructure."[9] A creative tension was to exist between the house's rootedness and its desire to float free.

Arthur felt from the outset that he was in a race against time, that Rob Filberg's depression was gaining the upper hand. In the fall of 1959, Rob was drinking heavily. "I had a feeling that... if I could get him into his house with the grand scheme working, he would have the motivation he needed," Arthur told an interviewer several years later.[10] But on April 5, 1960, before the house was completed, Arthur received word that Rob had died in his cottage, asphyxiated on his vomit, a death that would be described as an "accidental suicide." On the night of Rob's death, Arthur's phone had rung at 3 AM, but he had not answered. He would always believe that the caller was Rob.

Robert Filberg Sr. had no wish to pursue his son's vision of an international peace centre, but he commissioned Arthur to finish the building. In the spring and summer of 1960, in mourning for their tender relations, Arthur lived in Rob's cottage and continued work on the house. It was not easy to take up a task that required the calm and chaste strength of a craftsman, but he could not let Rob's vision simply slip away. He introduced into the house, as he and Rob had discussed, elements from Andalusian Islamic architecture— delicate filigreed screens to fend off the direct sun, highly polished terrazzo floors, and a reflecting pool. With its glass walls, skylights, and the sheen of its floors and pool, the house recorded the slightest variations of light, including the drama of moonlight and starlight. At the same time, to emphasize its connection to the site, Arthur instructed the builders, Qualicum Enterprises, to use local materials as much as possible—the visible framing and finishing wood in clear yellow cedar, local pink granite to conceal all mortar.

In his will, Rob had made Melda Buchanan his beneficiary. That summer, she began disposing of some of the items in the estate and presented Arthur with a Buddha's head from Rob's collection—a piece fifteen inches high in greenish-brown marble (possibly jadeite). When he purchased it, Rob had been told that it was stolen from a temple by a sailor and had since passed through several hands. It would remain in Arthur's hands for the rest of his life, as a concrete symbol of a friendship and a dream of an ideal world.

In the late summer of 1960, a group including the Binnings, the Smiths, and the Parnells made an excursion to see the Filberg house. Word of this unique building soon circulated in the country's arts community, and the house occasioned the first public celebration of Arthur's talents as an architect. In its December issue that year, *Western Homes and Living* would announce a "special award" for the Filberg house, describing it as a "fabulous" home, a radical "adventure in the 'poetic geometry' of Mediterranean Baroque—rich, lavish, delicately graceful, and highly imaginative." One of the picture captions reads: "As high art, it is a sensitive combination of fragile screens that look too delicate to touch, massive granite walls of almost overpowering strength, and voluptuously curved ceilings. None of these elements seem to touch each other; they appear more like the textures and colours of a painting than the walls of a building."

Arthur reported in a letter to Alan Jarvis, now editor of *Canadian Art* magazine, that the Canada Council was discussing making the Filberg house an artists' residence, an idea that attracted him immensely.[11] In November 1960, accompanying a set of photographs by Herbert McDonald, *Canadian Art* published an article about the house by Arthur, which he titled simply, "The Design of a House." In it, he touched on some of his theories about light and the importance of a building's relationship to its site. He also described some of his strategies for giving the building its pavilion-like quality. He concluded with a heartfelt tribute to his client, saying that if the house had achieved "a measure of grace, an abundance of light, a handsome or noble bearing," it reflected the spirit of the man who first conceived it.[12]

Although Arthur had at first been reluctant, because of his grief, to write about his experience of building the house, he had not hesitated to send photos and a brief description to leading architectural magazines, hoping for publication. In June of 1960, he was turned down by both New York's *Architectural Forum* and London's *Architectural Review*, but making the personal acquaintance in Vancouver that summer of Rita Reif secured him a feature later that year in the *New York Times*. The article appeared with many of Reif's own impressions of the house, most notably a picture caption that drew attention to the living room's "oversized brass chimney that shimmers in the sun on a bright day."[13]

In December, *Canadian Architect* ran photographs of the house, along with the first discussion of it by an instructor of architecture. In a florid appreciation, Abraham Rogatnick finds himself at the outset beggared for language to describe the lyrical beauty of the house: "One gropes for apt comparisons," he gasps. "Taj Mahal? Parthenon? Shangri-La?"[14] When he recovers himself, Rogatnick argues that this beauty is achieved, in fact, by the building materials of the present age, specifically steel and glass as articulated by the modernist idiom. For example, he posits that the visual poetry of the building lies in the transparent glass which, like the eye-deceiving painted perspectives of the Baroque era, draws space through walls and unites the inner confines with the outer landscape in a layering of planes that seemingly flow into infinity. That same glass at night, he suggests, seems to disintegrate the building's structure by producing a maze in which reflected planes intersect with real ones "in a cubist symphony undreamed of in the mirrored halls of other centuries." The clean lines of Erickson's design, he argues, allow for no compromises, no disorder.

But in one of Rogatnick's summary descriptions, his comparisons encourage a view of Arthur's work that has often been problematic— that its appeal is to the leisured, affluent classes only. After describing Rob Filberg as a wealthy bachelor, an art collector, and a lover of quiet luxury with no interest in the common comforts of the middle class, Rogatnick writes of the house:

There is a touch of Versailles here. The sweep of the architectural lines against the landscape, the orientations which seek to capture the most distant views, the dramatization of the nearer landscape with long stairways to precipitous terraces, the fountain and pools, even the curtainless master bedroom suggesting the levée of Louis Quatorze, all culminate in the kind of inevitable formality which fine clothes, epicurean tastes, and a luxurious atmosphere unconsciously impose. This house will be hated by Puritans, as it will be loved by purists.

The charge that Arthur was an elitist architect would dog him throughout his career, and it made more than one potential client shy away.

Arthur's own view of the Filberg house contradicted Rogatnick's claim that it was "purist" in the Bauhaus sense of that term. He sometimes called it his Florentine house and pointed to its Mediterranean way of mixing Western and Islamic styles as fundamental to its illumination. He recognized early that the minimalism of the Bauhaus aesthetic quickly exhausted itself and that its reductiveness left its practitioners in an expressive cul-de-sac. Although he would remain faithful to certain fundamental principles of simplicity—clean lines and the use of industrial materials—the Filberg house was a measure of how far he had moved beyond the International Style in his work.

In a later, more theoretical discussion of the house, Rhodri W. Liscombe would identify its special quality as a tension between the architect's use of industrial materials and his refusal to be bound by their utilitarianism. The Filberg house combines pictorial and fanciful effects with underlying functionalism. But even more significant, he argues, is that the house reflects Arthur's move beyond Bauhaus functionalism to an interest in the effect of region and climate and the spirit of the times—all of which had been minimized by the industrialization of architecture. Arthur embraced visual delight as one of the architect's prime responsibilities, a task beyond that of the engineer. Liscombe would argue that the Filberg house, especially in its consciousness of site, represents a major contribution to the development of modernism in Canada.[15]

In 1961, *Canadian Homes* magazine described the Filberg house as "The Most Fabulous House in Canada" in an article of the same name, and the house received a Pan Pacific Citation from the American Institute of Architects' Hawaiian chapter for outstanding contribution in the field of design. These acclamations put a solid foundation under Arthur's career, one upon which he would steadily build. To become famous at age thirty-six was uncommon in a profession on which the traditional aspirations of most clients and the hard necessities of commerce place enormous constraints.

The Filberg house, in the meantime, would continue to blend beauty with sadness. When it was finished, Melda Buchanan could not afford to maintain it. She sold it to a middle-aged couple, Bill and Alice Smitheringale, who made no changes. The property ticked away with time, unaltered, until in old age Bill, a geologist, was in a car accident, developed pneumonia, and died. Alice sold the house to an Inuit doctor who had been raised in Canada's Far North. Ironically, the new owner found the house, with its three sides of single-pane glass, too cold, and, to his taste, filled with too much light in winter. He removed the cedar latticework at the windows, enclosed the whole house with studs and plywood, cut out small windows, and covered the new framework in pink stucco. The Filberg house now looked like a small third-rate motel. Simon Scott, Arthur's photographer, referred to it as "a stucco coffin"; he was afraid to go inside.[16]

When the house was purchased in 1999 by Douglas Field, the owner of a renowned fishing lure business in Courtenay, its architectural fortunes were reversed. Doug undertook to restore the building to its original state. No detail was spared. He contacted Arthur on occasion to check on the materials he had used and where they might best be sourced forty years later. But before the work was complete, he and his wife were divorced, perpetuating the shadow of misfortune that seemed to persist over the site. Arthur wrote that the house survived alone on its promontory, a knight's pavilion, with a large audience room and a single empty bedroom.[17]

Part II

The
Weight
of
Heaven

9

Japan

IN 1958, WITH A GRANT from the Carnegie Foundation, Bert and Jessie Binning made a long-awaited trip to Japan. They had been planning the trip for several years, motivated in part by fond associations from childhood. Jessie's father had been an importer of goods from the Far East, and when she was in her teens he had taken her on one of his trips to Japan. For Bert, the sights and smells of products from the East, when as a boy he had watched the ships unload, triggered a yearning for faraway places. "Our only physical contact with any foreign land," he told an interviewer, "came to us by way of those great *Empress* liners which docked at the foot of Granville Street."[1] When they returned to Vancouver, the Binnings brought back more than hints of a unique culture on the other side of the Pacific: they brought reports of Japanese art and architecture and a way of life that fired Arthur's interest to see the country for himself.

Like the Binnings, Arthur had memories of being taken to see ships like the *Empress of Japan* disgorging their cargo in the port of Vancouver and of his parents' friends leaving for the Orient amid streamers and brass bands. His early memories of school included his friendship with Yasuko Ishii, the daughter of Japan's ambassador to Vancouver. The time he had spent with Mrs. Griffiths, his wartime language teacher, had also left him with a strong feeling for the country. But these associations acquired significant focus when Bert

Binning observed that the arts in Japan already embodied everything modernism was striving for. Bert's work as a painter had undergone a major transformation—he had moved away from marine illustrations and complicated designs to the simplest of forms, to colours and textures suggesting the late Matisse or the American abstractionist Mark Rothko—and the Binning house had become a museum of Japanese pottery and calligraphy.

Arthur applied for funding from the Canada Council to spend the summer of 1961 travelling and studying in Japan. In an eloquent and supremely confident application, he stated that through Frank Lloyd Wright and later pioneers of the modern movement in the early twenties, "Japanese architecture has become known and given rise to much of the present day vocabulary of domestic architecture: the 'open plan,' post and beam construction, the lightweight wall partition, the sliding panel, the raised house deck... The taste for natural finishes, for simple unadorned surfaces, for lightness of construction... is to a great extent of Japanese origin." Arthur wanted to examine in person, he stated, the Japanese mastery of space, their ways of siting a building, and their response to climate. That the Japanese had used such impermanent materials as wood for even their largest buildings, and that these had lasted in some cases since the seventh century, was of particular importance to the West Coast architect. He concluded by pointing out that architecture was a fine art like painting or sculpture, and until it was recognized as the most fundamental and powerful of the arts, shaping our lives through environment, it would remain "an awkward and undeveloped handmaiden."[2]

Arthur received word in late February that he had been awarded a fellowship and left for Tokyo in early May. Unsure of his language skills and increasingly fastidious about his appearance, he prepared a note in advance in Japanese that read: "Cut my hair with scissors, not clippers. Cut my hair shorter all over the head. Do not make the neck-line too high."[3]

ARTHUR'S INITIAL IMPRESSIONS of Japan were surprisingly negative. In the first of nine letters he wrote to Gordon Webber[4] (Webber was teaching a course at UBC that summer and living in Arthur's house), his response is almost hostile. He describes people on noisy, crowded streets as small and ill proportioned, with large heads and short, thick legs. They move with "that peculiar Japanese gait which consists of falling forward and yet keeping upright by a pigeon-toed shuffle." More surprisingly, he writes that "Japanese buildings look dull and drab" and emanate a "black moodiness." The codes of etiquette were also proving difficult to master, and his first response was to see all the bowing and refusals of gratitude and praise as elaborate forms of hypocrisy.

But when he writes to Webber again the following week, he starts by saying his first impressions are now "almost reversed," beginning with "the great number of good looking people" he sees on the street.

> Well dressed young women whirl through the stores swinging marvelously wrapped packages. All the young men seem to wear spotless and starched white shirts, clipped continental suits and American hair-cuts. Strangely too, soap and polish extends, through the tradition of the bath I suppose, to the bodies, for one is amazed how sweetly, in a sweaty climate, every one smells. Fresh smelling deodorants fill the air.

He realizes that what he is appreciating, on the surface, are North American ideas and values carried even further than occurred in America, "approaching at time caricature, but with such enthusiasm." He wonders, at the same time, about the "dark and morose" houses distant from the bright centre of Tokyo, about "the squat little woman, tucking her kimono into the tops of her boots and donning a police jacket and belt" to direct traffic for the well-mannered school children and bowing deeply to thank the cars for having stopped.

A bridge to the more traditional Japanese world would be created for Arthur by Canadian friends living in Tokyo: Kon Uyeyama, an architecture graduate from UBC who had done some work for Arthur while a student, and Jim Koyanagi, a young architect from Toronto. To Kon and Jim, Arthur admitted that he found Japanese architecture strange: "You know, I just don't get the sense of the buildings, and also the surroundings. I can *see* that their places are beautiful... but I don't quite get the sense of it." They assured him that if he stayed long enough, he would.[5]

Geoffrey and Margaret Andrew from UBC were also spending time in Japan, and they took Arthur out for a dinner he describes for Gordon as "beyond belief"; among many dishes, it featured bear steak, lotus root, fried endive (said to be especially popular in the Imperial Palace), and pickles in place of a sweet dessert. The meal concluded with a large cup of hot sake containing a potentially lethal blowfish tail. Arthur recognized that his initiation in Japan was just beginning.

At the suggestion of Vancouver artist Takao Tanabe, Arthur contacted Bill Crowley, an American painter living in Tokyo. Crowley invited Arthur to join him and two others on a special visit to the home of a Japanese family named Takeda, a family so devoted to the craft origins of Japanese culture that they had relocated a centuries-old farmhouse from northern Japan to their property on the outskirts of Tokyo. This visit proved a magical introduction to the finely tuned, closed world of the upper middle class, where the observance of tradition in landscaping, architecture, and social rituals spoke to Arthur of a rarified sophistication.

At the Takeda house, a lane led down to an unpromising gate of lashed bamboo. It was a hot, steamy day (typical summer weather in Japan, he was finding out), but inside the gate a forest path had been freshly sprayed with water so that the air was cooled and the leaves and stepping stones glistened. The path branched left through a grove of bamboo leading to the old farmhouse hidden by tree branches. Removing their shoes, the visitors entered what had once been the kitchen and granary and was now an entranceway sitting room, a space enjoyed especially by Japanese guests, they were told. The room was open to the underside of the roof, and the heavy beams and bamboo poles were blackened with centuries of smoke. What also caught Arthur's eye were "marvelous bizen storage pots, Chinese bronze drums, and pottery of the Sung period... and exquisite flower arrangements... a small spray of azalea amongst uncurling stems of bracken... unopened buds of white iris." From the sitting room they stepped up to the formal living room, then passed into the dining room where they sat on tatami mats to be served sweet bean cakes and tea. Presiding here was the host's mother, whom Arthur judged to be a woman of great charm and taste. She ordered the translucent shoji screens opened to reveal a garden that stretched through carefully pruned maples and pines into a seemingly endless glade lit by forest-filtered skylight.

After conversation and cakes, they proceeded through the garden to Arthur's first experience of a full tea ceremony. Following a path to a huge stone cistern, they were made to pause at a small basin with a bamboo ladle where they washed first the left hand, then the right, rinsing their mouths and the handle of the ladle, all in a rite of purification. They then entered the simple tea house, removed their shoes, and crawled in ceremonial humility through the small opening. Mr. Takeda had preceded them and made preparations for the ceremony, placing five cushions around the room, which indicated they would relax after tea. (A more formal ceremony would have been without cushions.) The informality of this occasion was also reflected in the *tokonoma*—the small, raised decorative alcove— where a scroll depicting children playing at tea was hung, with a single violet clematis flower below it contrasting vividly with the ochre walls. The utensils of the ceremony were arranged to the left of the *tokonoma*—the stone brazier, the water cauldron on a polished lacquer board, a Bizen ware cold-water container, and the tea caddy. The host's sister served the guests small sweet cakes; then the host entered, bringing two bowl-shaped cups, one black and one white, and the ritual of tea began—first the cleaning of instruments "with a strict and formal grace," then with a spoon placing the tea in the bowl, pouring in water from the cauldron, whisking it with a small bamboo whisk, and placing it for the mother to pass to the first guest. She bowed to the floor on offering the bowl and the guest bowed on receiving it, placing it on the flat of the hand, turning it twice, observing the bowl for a moment, and then drinking the hot, strong brew. Then the cup was carefully studied and returned to the hostess.

After all the guests had been served in this lengthy process, they were invited to relax on the cushions; the instruments of the ceremony were washed and then brought forward for examination and discussion. Arthur learned that the teacups had been produced in the early eighteenth century by Ogata Kenzan, a Kyoto potter and one of the great masters of the tea ceremony. His host explained what each ritual observance signified and how the Japanese ceremony had acquired its characteristic form from the Zen tea masters, who put simplicity and humility at the centre. Concentration on the forms and details of the ritual was a way of separating the self from one's quotidian existence, a way of emptying the self in a process whereby the individual is renewed and can return invigorated to the concerns of ordinary life. But what impressed Arthur at this point was the austere aesthetic of the ritual—the single flower chosen with great care for the *tokonoma*, the simple clay bowls for the tea.

After the ceremony, the company returned to the house, where the male guests were offered beer and Scotch. This was followed by a meal served by the host's wife—the food "all served in quite splendid bowls." After dinner, a series of scrolls by a famous Zen poet were brought out for examination: "each beautifully matted and each presenting a greater problem of translation until the last, done in his final years, which was apparently meaningless." As the Takeda family puzzled over the words of an obscure poem, Arthur was experiencing the thrill of trying to decipher his first intimate experience of Japan.

Professionally, although he may not have realized this at once, there was another experience of architecture in Tokyo that would have a profound influence on his future career. On his way to visit the National Museum in Ueno Park, Arthur "stumbled on" the newly opened Tokyo Metropolitan Festival Hall (the Bunka Kaikan), and in his letter to Webber he calls it "the most spectacular recent building that I have seen anywhere." The architect, Maekawa Kunio, had worked for Le Corbusier in Paris between 1928 and 1930, and the influence of the International Style was evident in the technological achievements of the hall—a long building of reinforced concrete, crowned by a hexagon and a cubic structure over the roof of the main auditorium. But the design was drawn from many sources: the foundations and a moat made a direct reference to the sloping base of earthquake-proof Japanese castles; the gently curved eaves suggested Buddhist temples and Shinto shrines (and possibly Le Corbusier's Ronchamp chapel); there was a pyramid roof over a smaller concert hall; and Arthur viewed as American the recessed "starlight" illumination and use of bright colours inside the building. Its references, in fact, were international.[6] But what struck Arthur on this first visit was how far an architect could run a horizontal line and how "unbelievably beautiful" raw concrete was—the lumber forms had been fitted so tightly that the bronze-toned concrete had the appearance of smoothly polished wood, the work of ancient craftsmen.

By coincidence, Arthur would later meet Maekawa Kunio when he was visiting an architectural historian at Nippon University. He learned then that Maekawa had taken part in designing the International House in Tokyo, where Arthur had secured a room, and that Maekawa had assisted Le Corbusier during the building of the National Museum of Western Art, situated directly across from the Festival Hall in Ueno Park—in Arthur's opinion "a singularly unsuccessful building." Their conversation stayed with subjects like their mutual delight in having met Richard Neutra and Arthur's curiosity about the blending of the Japanese vernacular with Western modernism. Although he could not help feeling that Maekawa strongly patterned himself after Le Corbusier in manner and dress as well as architectural ideas, this did not detract from his view that the Festival Hall displayed an elegance in forms that was "breathtaking."

FROM THE OUTSET, Arthur's travel plan in Japan was to replicate what he had done elsewhere, visiting the oldest places of civilization first and then tracing the development and changes in architecture over the centuries. His starting point would be a week in Nara, one of the ancient capitals, followed by a month in Kyoto, but first he travelled down the Ise Peninsula to visit the ancient Shinto shrine there, "said to be the one truly Japanese building." The fame of this shrine was puzzling to Arthur because the buildings were not monumental in size; moreover, every twenty years they were replaced in exact replica by new ones. In a letter to Gordon Webber, he acknowledged that the shrine's buildings were "beautifully proportioned, severely restrained and superbly crafted," but the craftsmanship practised for more than a thousand years, where not a hairline showed between the satin finished boards, remained a mystery, because one could not enter the inner shrine. The continual renewal of the buildings, he learned, derived from Taoist philosophy and the idea of reincarnation and eternal youth—"the empty site beside the new building being a stirring demonstration of life and death" together, of permanence in transience. The refusal to render the shrine buildings in greater size and more splendid and permanent materials was at the heart, he suspected, not only of Japanese philosophy but of taste as well.

The journey to Nara by bus was slow and tiring, the search for his lodgings at Jikko-in, a Zen Buddhist temple established in 1013 at some distance to the north, was almost impossibly difficult. The Japanese Arthur had acquired from Mrs. Griffiths was of little help when he asked for directions on a dusty country road. Although relieved to finally reach the temple, he was disoriented by his initial aesthetic experience there—a garden whose foreground was so severe it drew the viewer's eye at once to the scene beyond. But later, writing to Webber, he asks, how could one come here and "not find something strange and difficult to understand?" In fact, learning to "read" Japanese gardens and the shaping of landscapes would be one of the challenges and the significant rewards of the journey.

At Jikko-in, Arthur tried to decipher the effects achieved by the garden, the tea house, and the use of *shoji* to manipulate space. He learned that the garden at the Jikko-in temple, divided in the middle ground by a pond or reservoir, had been designed to embody a cosmology. The austere foreground of raked sand, a clipped hedge, two carefully pruned pine trees, and one tiny azalea represented the familiar world of everyday experience; beyond the reservoir, the

November-flowering cherry trees, the maples, the glimpses of Nara and the distant hills represented paradise, a garden where something was in bloom all year round. The contrasting effect was dramatic. For Arthur, the framing of that scene, which began with the temple tea house, was architecturally amazing as well: "Framed by the spacing of the posts—an opening about six feet high and twenty feet wide—[it was] a seemingly immense space for a beam only about fourteen inches deep" to span. Pulling back the *shoji* to reveal the view was like unveiling a painting. The technique, known as the "borrowing garden," framed distant vistas in a way that extended immediate space to infinity.

At Nara, the ninth-century capital, Arthur spent most of his time examining the seven great temples, which were at first a disappointment: "I could not understand them. To me they were rather feeble wooden structures, alone and unprepossessing, the antithesis of what my reading had led me to expect."[7] He wrote to Webber positively about the five-storey Horyu-ji pagoda, known as the oldest wooden structure in the world and the first centre of Buddhism for all Japan— "an unbelievable building" for its intricacy and proportions, the top storey being exactly half the dimensions of the first. He fell momentarily under the spell of the massive Todai-ji temple, said to be the largest wooden structure in the world, housing the country's biggest statue of the Buddha. But once away from the temples and their treasures, his feeling was of architecture without exuberance or joy, only "a somber, medieval resignation" and the "darkness of ancient associations." Wandering the streets of Nara at twilight, Arthur was overwhelmed with a "feeling of depression"—one he attributed in part to the darkness of the Japanese villages with their unpainted wood and heavy thatched roofs (sometimes black tile). "It may be part of the secret of Japan," he speculates, "that in spite of Tokyo's brilliance, the medieval age is still very much alive here with its headquarters in the farmhouse." He was reading Lady Murasaki's *Tale of Genji* and Sei Shonagon's *Pillow Book*, and he found in the fleeting emotional life recorded in clear detail nearly one thousand years before another haunting juxtaposition of transience and permanence.

In Nara, Arthur was not very comfortable—his bones ached from sleeping on the floor, and the vegetarian diet of soup, dried seaweed, and rice left him feeling undernourished—but more painful was the isolation he felt linguistically. He was surrounded by people at all times—in the communal bath, in the dining hall—but there were no English-language provisions for tourists; he saw no one from North America.[8] His loneliness was also now a matter of age—he was thirty-seven. While travelling in Europe ten years earlier, he had been exploring the origins of his culture and his own identity, but in Japan he was an alien, frequently without bearings. During pre-arranged engagements with Vancouver friends in Tokyo he was buoyant and curious, but alone in the spare room of a Zen hostel in rural Japan, he reflected on a melancholy that he detected underlying all the elegant and austere forms of life and art in Japan.

To dispel these feelings after arriving in Kyoto, Arthur arranged to meet with Bishop Kojo Sakamoto. He had met this friend of the Binnings the previous year, when the bishop had brought with him to Vancouver an exhibition of the paintings of Tomioka Tessai, a Japanese painter who died in 1924, and who was of growing interest in the West because his rough brush strokes were closer to those of Cézanne and Van Gogh than to the Japanese court-painting tradition. The eighty-nine-year-old bishop invited Arthur to visit at his temple in Takarazuka near Osaka. He arranged for a car and an interpreter to pick Arthur up and insisted that he stay for two days. During their first lunch together, attended by two priests in white robes, the bishop told Arthur he had been deeply impressed on his visit to Vancouver that "a country so young and with so few people could reach such a standard of culture... and that we seemed to take time to enjoy things."[9] Through the interpreter, Arthur tried to explain that the civilization and quiet the bishop had enjoyed in Vancouver were in fact unique to the secluded Binning house; most people in the city lived busy lives exposed to their neighbours and moved house, on average, every five years.

Arthur flourished as a guest in the tastefully appointed grounds of the temple; his curiosity and spirits quickened as he was shown

through the buildings and some esoteric features of Shingon Buddhism were explained to him. Through the interpreter, he was able
to enjoy a discussion of religion and to appreciate the bishop's commentary on his art collections. He was especially delighted to be
able to discuss with the bishop how Japanese buildings differed in
design from those in the West—the subtle balancing of structural
members, windows seldom the same size or shape on different walls,
the extraordinary subtlety of colour. He was intrigued by the way
the gallery connecting the bishop's rooms to the guest quarters and
the tea room was approached indirectly, at an angle. The grounds
were endlessly delightful: a tea room displayed Tessai's essential
accessories; the *shoji* throughout were covered with the bishop's calligraphy; a basin for washing one's hands was hung from a tree, with
a container of fresh flowers and a towel also suspended among the
branches—all accessible from the window of the bathroom. Arthur's
box of Rogers' chocolates from B.C. seemed a paltry gift at parting;
in contrast, he was given two scrolls done by the bishop and a "huge"
book titled *Japanese Art Treasures*.

IN KYOTO, WHICH would be the heart of Arthur's trip to Japan, a
room had been reserved for him at the Daisen-in temple, part of the
Daitoku-ji complex of Zen Buddhist temples founded in the early
fourteenth century. He was the only guest, and the rhythm of the
day was set by the routine of the monks: the gong at 6 AM and the
husky sound of sutras being chanted, the tinkle of a bell and then
the shuffle of receding footsteps and the smell of sweet incense
seeping out from under the screens. He took breakfast with a view
of one of the most famous gardens in Japan—an arrangement, in a
narrow space, of large rocks and a river of white sand representing
the journey of life. The sharp rocks and ravines creating rapids and
constricting the flow of sand were placed to represent birth and the
vicissitudes and challenges of youth, with the river widening and the
rocks becoming smaller in middle life and then opening to a wide
expanse of white sand representing, as Arthur explained to Webber,
death and "the final purification in the ocean of nothingness." The

life of the spirit was dramatized in a far corner of the garden by two gravel cones at either side of a bodhi tree, the cones representing the obstacles to enlightenment. The tree blossomed while Arthur was staying at the temple—on the day of his birthday. The priest told him this was very auspicious.

Arthur wrote to Webber about an aspect of Japanese aesthetics that the temple revealed to him: "How easily and effectively the spaces [are] changed by the arrangement of the shoji and the opaque fusuma (sliding panels)—from extreme intimacy with the immediate garden to expansiveness as one glimpses parts of the furthest garden—but never, of course, the whole thing at any one time from any one point." Arthur was increasingly aware that the Japanese aesthetic preferred the *idea* of a thing, its memory or promise, to the thing itself. "The Japanese never reveal much at a time—certainly never a complete view—one never sees more than a little and the vision of the whole can only be an accumulation of one's remembered experiences."

While at Daisen-in, Arthur received some letters from home. His mother reported that Gordon Webber was looking after his house very well and filling the garden with all kinds of flowers. Gordon and Arthur's good friend Jane Clegg were going over to the Island, and Myrtle was sending Arthur's letters with them for Melda Buchannan to read. Arthur was shocked to read that Bert Binning had had a heart attack while in Toronto and would have to stay there for two months' recovery.

Arthur had first met Jane Clegg when she travelled to Comox with some of his UBC students to see the Filberg house, and she became a lively presence in his life and his date for parties and dances. She was from an old Vancouver family but was trying to establish herself with a career in the contemporary arts. She rented a small flat above Takao Tanabe's studio in Gastown, and Arthur liked to take friends there because of its striking view over the water to the North Shore mountains. They sometimes travelled together to Vancouver Island to visit Melda— Arthur "always late for the ferries and driving like a maniac in his little Hilman."[10] Arthur frequently took

Jane to meet his clients, and Myrtle and Oscar viewed her as another candidate as a wife.

One letter from his mother made him realize in a fond way how closely attuned they were. Her opening paragraph was about redesigning the North American kitchen; the walls, she said, should all consist of cupboards instead of being clinical blank spaces. And kitchens should be places to live in, not just workshops. He would have appreciated most her account of an art teacher who came once a week to the Yellow Door art studio that Myrtle and some of her friends had organized:

> Miss Walker... is quite an old conservative biddy, but lots of things I can learn from her about mixing paints, colours, etc. although she puts up her hands in horror when she glances inside my paint box. I mentioned that you were in Japan and how you marveled at the taste of the Japanese and I said it was something handed down through the ages... And she said "No, it is discipline. We are not a disciplined nation. Look at the way you use your brushes. Do you go home every evening after painting and wash them carefully in soap and water, revolving them in the palm of your hand? One of your brushes is an especially good one. You have never noticed the quality of that brush, the workmanship that has gone into the making of that brush." And perhaps she is right.[11]

Staying for nearly a month at Daisen-in, Arthur came to know the temple priest and his family. Out of both politeness and gratitude, he agreed to assist the son, an unusually dynamic young man, in his preparation of an English guide to the temple. It became a tedious chore of translation, and Arthur's Japanese-English dictionary was not always adequate. But he found himself very attracted to the boy, who in his person represented something like a hermaphroditic ideal—the male voice and energies in a smooth, female-like body. One of Arthur's friends in Tokyo had given him a translation of Mishima Yukio's *The Temple of the Golden Pavilion,* which also stirred in him a sense of the erotic in Japanese life.

Arthur took his evening meal with the family. They were strict vegetarians except for serving on one occasion "the long cold arm of an octopus," which Arthur managed to down. Near the end of his stay, he began to crave meat and something sweet to end the meal— the craving suddenly so great that he would leave for another lodging a few days before departing Kyoto.

But, for the most part, he was successful in submitting to the disciplines necessary to adapt to Japanese life. Another experience he shared with the family was the hot bath—usually before the evening meal and sometimes with the gardener. His first bath became a favourite anecdote to relate. The water was very hot, but knowing how the Japanese scorned the timidity and modesty of foreigners, Arthur slowly immersed himself. The water was so hot that the sensation was one of cold, the body setting up an insulating layer, but on emerging, the sensation was of being parboiled. The gardener entered to have his bath as Arthur was finishing, felt the water, and immediately turned on the cold tap, asking how Arthur could tolerate water that hot. In a moment of giddy bravura, he replied that the water was just right—"usually I find Japanese baths not quite hot enough."

In letters to Gordon Webber, Arthur continued to describe his puzzlement while visiting famous Japanese sites. Ryoan-ji, the most revered temple garden in Japan, was "disappointing because it is so small." He could see that it was a "lesson in arrangement... depending on number, texture, colour, kind of rock," but its meaning eluded him "because it is so intricately tied up with the complexity of Zen." About a tea house near Daisen-in he had read that the thin, pinkish-green light allowed in by lower walls of dark plaster and grey paper was to suggest *sabi* and *shibui* (the spirit of melancholy, in this case something akin to the feelings evoked by the last light of the evening sky), and the overall effect was to convey *wabi* (a refined simplicity achieved by complex means). The white paper door, with its round-headed frame, represented purity. But his frustration was mounting, as he later wrote: "After I had been in Japan for about a month, I felt that I still couldn't understand... I couldn't see through the eyes of the person who made this, as to *why* they did this, and what their basic feeling about the building was."[12]

Something like a crisis occurred for Arthur at the Saiho-ji temple (more commonly known as the Kokedera or Moss Temple). Here was located one of the most revered tea houses in Japan, built in the mid-fourteenth century by a distinguished Zen priest, Kokushi Muso, and repaired in the seventeenth century by the son of the great tea master Sen Rikyu. But to Arthur, it appeared to be nothing more than a shack, a rustic conceit at best. "I felt I was being very stupid . . . but the building annoyed me because one post came on to a stone, and another post was in the earth, and another post was on a beam."[13] Nothing was level, and the garden site looked neglected— just a few aged pieris shrubs. He decided that he would go back the next day and stay, without food or drink, until he solved the mystery.

The following morning he wandered the moss garden, approaching the tea house from different sides, still unable to feel or understand its architecture. He went to rest on the other side of a little lake in the centre of the garden to ponder the problem further; just when hunger threatened to break his resolve, he heard a rustling sound in the distance, as if a flock of birds or monkeys was moving through the trees. Instead, a dozen or so women emerged from the foliage, dressed in special blue kimonos pulled up between their legs and tucked into their obis. They had come to trim the trees and bushes. Accustomed to gardeners in Canada using saws and pruning shears, he was amazed to see these workers using something like nail scissors, trimming the ends of the pine needles "as if clipping hair" and plucking individual leaves from the maples. "What difference is that going to make!" he thought to himself, but when they had finished he was amazed—for two reasons.

First, there *was* a difference—the trees now seemed to "breathe" in an openness that allowed each plant "to fulfill itself with grace." Relieved of the need to compete, each tree and bush could become "a more perfect expression of its species."[14] Second, the trees looked as if no human hand had ever touched them, yet they were so much more beautiful than before. And then Arthur came to what he believed to be the secret of things Japanese: the people had an understanding of nature—an appreciation of plant and tree forms— that underpinned their approach to life and their aesthetics. It seemed to Arthur that the Western aesthetic put the human figure at the centre; therefore, Westerners looked in art and architecture for the characteristics of the human body—strength, vitality, grace, symmetry, and finality: a foot at the bottom and a head at the top. "But in Japan where natural forms are the basis of aesthetics, there is no finality, no base to a tree, because the roots go on and on until they disappear. And there's no top to a tree, because the branches grow on and on. And there's no symmetry in the human way. So it's an entirely different way of seeing."[15] For Japanese artists, grace of movement had nothing to do with the line of the human body, but with the line of grass or trees; the abiding source of their inspiration was plant morphology.[16] Arthur would put it this way subsequently: "In Japan, man doesn't enter into the composition except as an observer. Instead, it is nature that is built around, which infuses the design."[17]

By the time Arthur left his seat by the lake, it was clear to him that the architect of the tea house "was trying to imply within that static structure the same reaching out and upward that occurs in the tree form"—both a rootedness and a fluid spiralling that began with the posts grounded at different levels. The rough walls of mud and straw, the building's irregular shape, the paper at the windows— these were all part of the organic nature of the structure, something he had admired in Wright's Western version of this style. Arthur also understood now why Japanese buildings often looked frail. Instead of mirroring the physique of an individual, they exhibited a linear grace like the plant whose expanding roots, getting smaller and smaller, disappear deep into the earth and whose branches, reaching upward, grow smaller and smaller in leaf and bud. A series of observations tumbled forth from this insight: "And you find that this is the line that is essential in Japanese architecture and painting, Japanese flower arranging, everything—it's the line of movement that disappears into infinity... They are not concerned about vitality or any of the physical aspects that give our buildings character." The Japanese were concerned instead with the incomplete line, arrested as if it were in mid-air, and with mood, most often stimulated by the seasons and light—"when the last winter snow falls on the first spring blossoms, or when the last of the evening light is in the sky."[18] Arthur wondered if the upward curve of a roof in Japan did not correspond to the lift at the end of the pine branches. In a talk, he would extend these insights further, suggesting that "the architecture of Japan is probably closer to that of medieval Europe than anything in existence today, because in Japan neither the individual nor three-dimensional space in our sense exists."[19]

With this way of seeing nature as central to the Japanese aesthetic, Arthur now understood what Okakura Kakuzo meant in *The Book of Tea* about the tea room as the embodiment of fugitiveness, where the frailty of slender pillars, cedar shingles, or thatch roof, and all the other commonplace materials, represent the process of growth and change. Where the Western ideal of symmetry represented completion, a permanent perfection achieved, the Zen conception of perfection was focussed in the *process* through which perfection was sought. And so, as Okakura wrote, the tea house "does not pretend to be other than a mere cottage."[20] Arthur was right to view the Saiho-ji tea house as a shack, but it was purposely so, an ephemeral, imperfect structure, "leaving something unfinished for the play of the imagination to complete." Nature, guiding human behaviour, "established also the canons of proportion and composition that differentiate the architecture most distinctively from the west."[21]

Arthur's story of his determination not to rise and take nourishment until solving the mystery of the Saiho-ji tea house seems self-consciously reminiscent of the Buddha's vow not to leave the bodhi tree until he achieved enlightenment. At the same time, there is no doubt he was trying earnestly to understand Japanese spiritual practices. In his teens, he had been caught up in the discussions of transcendentalism at the Harrises', and during the war, he had listened intently to Trevor Leggett expound his knowledge of Buddhism. Here in Japan, the spiritual quest to loosen the grip of the

ego and be free of the cravings and delusions that bind humankind
to the physical world were manifest everywhere around him. His
mother's Christian Science beliefs were also an attempt to transcend
the suffering and imprisonment of the physical world, but there was
an important difference: Christian Science was a cheerful religion
grounded in the optimism of the New World, whereas the Zen
Buddhism of Japan based its meditative practice on the knowledge
that human life as part of nature was finite and filled with suffering.
Underlying all Japan's art was the Japanese acceptance of nature as
a force of both life and decay to which human beings and their built
structures must submit and which they can never overpower.

Arthur's new understanding prepared him for his supreme
experience—a visit to the Katsura Imperial Villa, which, he wrote
to Webber, "climaxed all previous experiences, and nothing—no
description, photograph, film—can convey anything of its effect. It
is the most complete work of art in Japan, and, I think, in the whole
repertory of architecture, one of the greatest compositions." The
seventeenth-century villa was not a single building but a complex
comprising palace, tea houses, pavilions, and garden. It was created
and situated by Prince Toshihito, the emperor's younger brother,
in a rural retreat, in deliberate rejection of the grandeur of the
city palace. Its architect, Kobori Enshu, was also a tea master, and
he designed Katsura to express the Zen values of rustic simplicity.
Accordingly, the landscape and buildings were completely fused.
Arthur wrote: "The buildings without the garden would be nothing—
the gardens without the buildings—nothing." He insisted that, more
than any other place in Japan, "it demonstrates the sense of refinement, of severity, of melancholy, of simplicity that Japanese taste can
achieve . . . and cannot be surpassed." He wondered how such refinement could be possible: "Enacting the rituals of manner, of poetry
and tea is to imagine a life of such art and artifice as to be almost
completely abstracted from reality."

Arthur visited the villa three times, and he noted that as one
moved through the buildings, the rooms unfolded with each one a
little offset from the other, so that the line of movement seemed to

have no beginning or destination. He would later place this observation in a larger comparison of Western and Eastern cultures: "Western culture with its evangelistic focus on destination uses rhythm to mark our progress to our objective. In Japan, space is non-directional. The passage, not the destination, is what matters." And rhythm "com[es] slowly into the audible range and fad[es] lightly out of hearing into infinity."[22]

The Katsura Imperial Villa, above all other sites, demonstrated for Arthur the idea of beauty founded in a philosophy of transience and futility, making Japanese architecture concerned foremost with moods beyond verbal communication. The villa was also a supreme example of how fine works of Japanese architecture responded to climate. It was most lovely in Japan's typically muted light—the sunless white skies of summer, the overcast skies of autumn and winter—when no shadows were cast. He would later write: "The [Japanese] inclination for the transient, the incomplete, the taste for bitterness and melancholy *(shibui)* are all fused at Katsura in a composition of extraordinary character and strength. The strength is not physical, for the building hardly touches the ground—but it is the intensity of feeling."[23] That feeling also spoke to Arthur's hard-won understanding that the deepest principle in Japanese architecture was an organic one—that a building should not simply stand on the ground but should be rooted to that place like a plant and grow from it.

ARTHUR SPENT MOST of July exploring the different cultures of Southeast Asia. In a letter to Webber marked "En route to Macau, July 3, 1961," he writes that although it had the variety of smells and luxuriance of colour missing in Japan, Hong Kong was a disappointment architecturally: "Simply a rather messy collection of buildings in a superb setting." But Vancouver friends Leonard and Dallis Boultbee had arranged for him to meet some interesting people among their acquaintances in Hong Kong, including the architect John Howard, who had one of the largest practices in the city. Howard was completing the design for the Mandarin Oriental Hotel, which would rocket to fame as one of the world's top ten hostelries.

He shared a house with his friend Godfrey Moyle on the other side of the mountains from Kowloon. It overlooked a deep valley and, just as Arthur arrived, a storm dramatically illuminated the view with lightning that cut off the power. They took their evening meal in candlelight, and Arthur found it all reminiscent of Somerset Maugham. He was curious to see how these two men lived so comfortably together (were they homosexual? he wondered) and how it did not seem to affect their professional lives. Arthur discovered that Howard had been one of his colleagues with British Intelligence Force 136 during the war, though he had no recollection of meeting him.[24]

The Portuguese colony of Macau received Arthur's praise for its "complete fusion of the colour and vitality of the Latin countries and the rich essence of the East." What especially drew his interest was to be "back in a place where the architecture of the street and the town have importance... where the populace lives on the street—and the street, though filthy sometimes, has the appearance of a place that is lived in and enjoyed." In Japan, he would later observe, "The city street is not a meeting place, the living room in the Mediterranean sense, but only the place between, to scurry through, the place of conflict, the sewer, the negative space of the city."[25] In his description of Macau's exuberant, sometimes frivolous spirit, he extols the delicious baked fish and chicken, the wine and olives—"all the rich foods [I] had been missing for so long."

Arthur spent the next two weeks in Thailand and Cambodia and sent Gordon Webber a haunting description of exploring the grand ruins of Angkor Wat. While there, he fell into a discussion with the French director of the conservation program, who surprised Arthur by dismissing Japanese architecture, mostly wooden, as inconsequential—"merely a highly refined craft." At Angkor Wat, the French conservationist pointed out, only the stone masonry had survived; the wooden structures of the vast complex had rotted away. It was a claim Arthur would give further thought to. In response, he proposed his tree theory about Japanese aesthetics. That apparently intrigued the Frenchman, who agreed that nature was central to Japanese culture.

But the experience in Southeast Asia that would have the most lasting influence on Arthur was the eight days he spent in Bali, Indonesia—an experience "far beyond anticipations."[26] What impressed him from the outset was that this was a traditional culture whose religious myths were still as vital and visible as when they were brought to the island more than fifteen hundred years before. A unique form of Hindu dharma blending Hinduism, Buddhism, and indigenous animism still informed every aspect of life. Bali had scarcely been touched yet by the materialism and skepticism of the twentieth century, and it was closer to Arthur's medieval ideal of a holistic community than any he had ever seen. Especially amazing was the fact that this spiritual life was "celebrated with a high degree of art that penetrated to all levels of people and through every performance in their lives," from the daily offerings made to the demons and the gods to the most sophisticated forms of gamelan music and dance.

Describing Bali for Gordon Webber, Arthur marvels at the rice paddies sculptured in wavy terraces from the steepest hillsides, where the beauty of the topography was a perfect synthesis of form and function. "The rice fields," he writes, "so carefully patterned— so complete in all the arrangements for growing, harvesting, resting, and worshipping—are like the most civilized places on earth." He describes workers from the villages harvesting rice as if their labours were a staged performance—the women "moving in columns across the paddies... tying the rice in neat bundles that are then carried like huge Edwardian hats back to the village... the men with the sheaves carried across poles, beating their three pronged hoes in rhythm." In the evenings, women carried offerings to the temples in processions through the fields or village lanes: "These are carefully arranged compositions of food and flowers, piled on silver or lacquer bowls, often to the height of three feet and carried on their heads—to be blessed in the temple and returned later to the household to be consumed." What thrilled Arthur in this spectacle was his perception of a community founded on the interdependence of every aspect of life—practical, religious, and aesthetic—and where "everything is a celebration."

During his time on Bali, Arthur stayed at a hotel in Ubud, a village that in the 1930s had become a centre for the arts, and for two days he shared a rented car with other tourists, travelling the island's narrow roads through lush jungle gorges into the mountains. Frequently they came upon villagers gathered to bathe at a river pool. Often they first heard laughter and singing from one of the precipitous recesses, and unless they brought out a camera as they approached, the bathers would make no effort to conceal their nudity. Arthur conveys explicitly his sense of a prelapsarian paradise on Bali when he describes himself in the company of two others, "an agitated American and a Swiss," coming upon a naked young husband and wife and an older man and joining them for a nude plunge into the sea.

But his most rewarding time was spent on long walks around Ubud, where he learned to decipher the architecture that was fundamental to the communal and religious life of the villages. The temple, he discovered, its uniquely Balinese outer gate "like a pair of flamboyant wings lifted against the sky" (no lintel), was a compound of black-thatched pavilions on raised platforms for different functions, including a pagoda and bell tower. A family household within external walls comprised separate thatched-roof pavilions on raised platforms and included a barrel-shaped granary or rice barn. He managed to visit one of these family complexes and was amazed at what he found: it consisted of a shrine for the household's gods, a room for musical instruments and masks, a kitchen and a shrine for the kitchen, rooms for the family's daily life, and at the centre a room for newly married couples, a room for birth, and a room for dying. The "house" was not only for living in but for celebrating all the basic events of life. He asked himself, "How can I put that same strength of meaning, that profound symbol of existence, into whatever I build?"[27]

"And the remarkable thing," he writes to Webber, "is the impression of order, of completeness, of care and careful craftsmanship that characterizes all of these complexes. Nowhere, and this is perhaps the precarious virtue of Bali, is the open wound of the 20th century ['the ugly baked enamel glare of advertising'] in evidence." Arthur was seeing Bali when only Denpasar, the main city, and its newly opened airport had electricity, before tourism brought major resorts and commercial development to the island. He had an intimation of what might come when a local man told him that what a Balinese craved most was a suit of Western clothes and a transistor radio, and when he observed the local woodcarving and framed paintings for sale to tourists around Ubud. "Both of [these] are a misdirection of talent," he writes, "in a culture whose architecture has almost no walls." Their craft should still be applied, he asserts, to carving posts and painting ceilings.

While all facets of Balinese life had a ceremonial aspect, in Arthur's view, "the one ritual that is beautiful beyond belief is the dance... and its music the most thrilling thing of all... Truthfully I have seldom heard such beautiful music—from strong almost brutal sounds to the most delicate sounds imaginable, full of the sounds of the forest, almost entirely with percussion instruments—drums, gongs, bells and xylophones." Around Ubud and out in the smaller villages, he writes, "Music and dance seemed to be in the air at night," and he watched two or three performances each evening: the Legong court and temple dances with "young girls of exquisite grace, their fingers vibrating like excited night insects against the slow movement of arms and body"; the Kecak dance with about one hundred men seated in a circle like a Greek chorus making rhythmic sounds from whispers to shouts to full-throated shrieks as the main dancers acted out a story from the *Ramayana* ("theatre in its most moving form"); and the sometimes frightening Barong and monkey dance full of witches and demons, with its contemporary satirical improvisations on the Hindu epic stories. The iridescent music of the gamelan and the physical grace of the dancers was a source of enormous sensual pleasure, but what especially stirred Arthur in retrospect was that this folk culture was innovative in its artistic expression, firmly grounded in its ceremonial origins but always adaptive to life in the present. Moreover, the innovative performers were not artists set apart from society but often menial workers during the day who gathered in the evenings to entertain each other.

The example of Bali would inform Arthur's work in subtle and specific ways. In general, it reinforced his conviction that the bonds of community were at the centre of all civilized enterprises and that those bonds were foremost spiritual and artistic. It sharpened his interest in folk cultures, particularly the indigenous cultures of the Pacific Northwest. Bali also significantly extended his grasp of landscaping as fundamental to architecture—the desirability of terracing steeply graded building sites and building office blocks and homes in terrace formation. He would even design a home in the Pacific Northwest (the Puget Sound house), consisting of a series of separate-function buildings, like a Balinese family compound. Secretly, he took great delight when he was told that an architect in Bali was almost invariably first a priest.

ARTHUR HAD ANOTHER goal that summer—to visit China—but all tours to the country were cancelled. He returned to Japan with the plan of seeing some of the buildings of Tange Kenzo, a young architect who had worked with Maekawa and was rapidly becoming one of Japan's foremost architects. Tange's city hall in Kurashiki was a raised horizontal building of concrete beams with sun-shielded windows—in Arthur's words "a virtuoso display of proportion recalling Michelangelo."[28] After the fire bombings of the Second World War, the Japanese had turned from wood construction to concrete for their public buildings. The Japanese tradition of carpentry pervaded Tange's use of concrete, as it did in Maekawa's Festival Hall. Tange's concrete was rough, but it suggested enormous power. Seeing Tange and Maekawa's use of the castle and storehouse wall, Arthur appreciated more fully how the new forms of architecture in Japan, even in concrete, were still "redolent with traditional meanings vital to the Japanese imagination." In an essay titled "The Weight of Heaven," written on his return, he observes:

> The former significance of the parts of the Japanese building is present in the modern work. The roof as shelter and the resolving line between earth and sky; the wall as fortification, the base as brace

against the trembling earth; the column in the universal sense of
the tree or upright man... In architecture I don't believe there is a
more poignant sense of meaning than the act of setting a structure
in its environment. Architectural form is only eloquent in context.[29]

Context for Arthur now meant region as determined by climate
and terrain. Japanese architecture was sombre in response to the
harsh realities of earthquake, fire, and typhoon, but rich in sensitivity to the qualities of light and seasons—the muffled luminosity of
mist, the shadowless illumination of the deep forest, the melancholy
of fading light, the remote white light of heavy, sunless skies in summer. Maekawa's Festival Hall, he wrote, while strikingly modern in a
Western sense, with its asymmetrical upper structures (the cube and
hexagon), was still responsive to its Japanese context—its bronzed
concrete like gold foil in the glow of the low winter sun, its upswept
eaves like the Japanese temple roof.

Matters of politeness, honour, and shame had frustrated Arthur
during the first part of his trip. But as he acquired a greater understanding of Japanese art and architecture, he found himself attracted
to this culture of evasion and deference, where to boast was to
behave shamefully, and where you never burdened someone else
with your troubles. Japanese modesty and reserve touched in him a
core of similar feelings.

The last days of his trip were spent in Kyoto, "reminiscing and
visiting old haunts... [it was] too hot to do much else," and in Tokyo,
spending time again with Kon and Jim, the Japanese-Canadian
architects. He went to see a six-hour performance of kabuki, which
he describes for the Binnings as "full of invisible feelings that are the
essence and dilemma of Japan." But most important for his future
as an architect, he saw the Bolshoi Ballet perform in Ueno Park at
"the crackling building of Maekawa." Its acoustics, he observed, were
"miraculous."

Arthur returned to Vancouver in September, feeling he had made
the most important trip of his life. Asia had opened his imagination
to another world altogether. Architecture, he had discovered, could

express something very different from the human adventure with physical space, "where man is the centre and measure of all things"; it could instead foreground the moods of nature and forms of spiritual discipline. Seeing architects like Maekawa and Tange adapt Japanese architectural idioms—the lifting roof, the sloping wall—to the bare bones of modernism opened a way for Arthur. He saw himself becoming a cultural anthropologist, curious and respectful of other ways of doing things. This expanded view made him more objective about his own work, more determined to avoid fashions and doctrines and to focus on the realities of a specific context. How could he not fall in love with Japan, where in times past when someone became ill an architect was called in first, rather than a doctor?[30] The trip to Japan had created for Arthur another spiritual home.

10

Public Lecturer

ARTHUR RETURNED FROM JAPAN in September 1961 teeming with ideas, and his desk was stacked high with opportunities to put them to work. Although few people had actually seen it, the Filberg house was acclaimed in photographs and articles, as was the fibreglass cabana for the Grauers.[1] In 1960, he had done something similar in a living-room addition to the E. Leonard Boultbee home; with lacquered steel pillars supporting an exotic glowing roof, this use of fiberglass made a striking photo in *Architectural Digest*. The editorial policy then of not naming the architect only made readers more curious to know who had designed these unique Riviera-like structures.

But the work he had done before visiting Japan now seemed to him romantic and excessive, a false attempt to be Mediterranean in a part of the world where rain and low skies prevailed for a large part of the year. Japan's architects made an aesthetic virtue of sunlessness, fashioning their buildings in materials that were black and white and designing their gardens in a variety of greens. Then, wrote Arthur, when against the austerity of grey walls and green gardens a splash of colour appeared—a woman wearing a bright kimono, a pool of purple iris—it was breathtaking: "You almost choke on it."[2] The design of Japanese buildings was such that simple activities such as looking out of a window, walking from one room to the next, or sitting on a bench were invested with a sacramental gravity. One felt the existential weight of wood, stone, water.

Arthur determined to build more austerely, with less detail, emphasizing the elegance of simple, rugged materials. "After Japan," he would write, "my houses ceased to be composed of a variety of materials and instead became as much as possible expressions of one material—reminiscent, almost, of sculpture."[3] At the same time, he was uncomfortable transposing another cultural tradition to British Columbia. He was painfully aware that indigenous traditions had been almost completely exterminated and that Europeans had no real roots in B.C., no relationship to the land. Only by seeing aboriginal culture, with its pantheistic reverence for nature, as Oriental could he justify bringing Japanese traditions to bear on his work.[4]

Arthur managed to persuade his new clients to let him experiment. A house for Ted Bayles in 1963 in West Vancouver was a striking example. Here, Arthur used rough-cut lumber for the crossbeams and internal support, but the rustic look was carried further: first by the use of peeled tree-trunk posts set upside down, and then with roofs covered in mosses to complement the moss- and lichen-covered rocks on the site—the effect anticipating the "green" movements in architecture.[5] Instead of the usual northwest cedar shingling of sides and roofing, Arthur sought a clearer demarcation between what was natural and what was manmade. He had observed this repeatedly in Japan, where beauty was not simply in nature but in the human intervention to civilize it. The best example in Vancouver, he felt, was the seawall around Stanley Park, where land and sea were divided and defined by the craft of the stonemason.[6]

For the friend of his youth, Bill Baldwin, now an obstetrician with a young family, Arthur designed a frame house on Deer Lake in Burnaby of rough-sawn cedar and glass. Its chief strategy was to exploit the proximity of the house to the lake to suggest that it was floating on water, like a Katsura tea house. As one entered through the dining room, the spaces beyond bloomed with natural light from several sources, including a wraparound clerestory, a skylight overhead, and a view of the water from the living room that reflected the light of the sky. Walls of glass brought the landscape into the interior of the house, and the creation of a shallow pond to one side seemed to bring the lake right up under the house.

Designing and constructing the Baldwin house was not straight-forward, because this proximity to the water was in contravention of Burnaby municipal regulations. Bill had first approached Arthur in 1960; the house was designed in 1962, but there were long delays before the builders could proceed, and it was not completed for occupancy until 1965. But Bill and his family were thrilled with their house; to them it was like holidaying at a cottage all year round.[7] Despite the legal hurdles and subsequent problems with roof leaks and heating costs, the Baldwin house has had a happy history, and it exemplifies the essence of West Coast post-and-beam archi-tecture. A specific Asian borrowing was the use of chains instead of drainpipes to lead away rain water. Arthur liked to think of the over-all effect as similar to the lake pavilions of Mughal India,[8] though the delicate appearance of the house evokes a specifically Japanese reference.

A house for John Laxton in 1964 on a precarious West Vancou-ver slope was, to Arthur's mind, perhaps the most Japanese of his buildings in intention and effect. The house was placed on long cedar poles to fit its cliff-face site, and Arthur liked to compare the exposure of its wood frame and stilt-like bracing posts to that of the famous Kiyomizu Temple in Kyoto (popularly known as the suicide temple). The horizontal structure of the house followed the edge of the cliff, stepping down on several levels and maximizing, with its generous windows and outdoor decks, the exposure to southern light and a spectacular ocean view. Its bracing posts echoed the straight tree trunks of the forest, and the drooping arches in the roof line were designed to suggest the lowering boughs of the trees. The Lax-ton residence was chosen as "House of the Year" by the Architectural Institute of British Columbia.

Arthur also brought influences from Japan to bear on the details of his own property—most strikingly in the addition of a moon-view-ing platform to his garden pond. It consisted of a piece of travertine from the Vancouver Hotel placed on the north side of the pond, where it created a central focus for the property. It became a site for ceremonies and special performances: one of the first was his language teacher, Mrs. Griffiths, preparing a tea ceremony there. It was a place from which a robed Japanese flute player, under a basket-like hat, might send forth the sheer and haunting notes of the *shakuhachi.* On the east side of the pool, Arthur created a moss terrace, reminiscent of Saiho-ji, and placed there a stone water basin of the kind used for ritual cleansing before a tea ceremony. On the berm he established a stand of blue fountain bamboo that arched over the path like Hokusai's great wave. These details reinforced his belief that one could live simply and well in small spaces.

The second house Arthur built for Gordon and Marion Smith, in another forest clearing, might also be seen as Japanese in its effects because it was built with a central courtyard around which were wrapped, in non-directional order, the living spaces. The visitor entered the studio and could proceed from it in either direction, stepping up one level at a time through the living spaces and continuing outside in a series of terraces that inferred an endless spiral. This echoed, to Arthur's way of thinking, the welling in concentric circles of a Japanese house that merges with the spaces of nature—the garden, the forest, the sea.[9] Like the Japanese house, the Smith house was designed to be attractive from all aspects. As Arthur would say, "There should be no back or side or front... all parts should have an equally vital relationship with the site."[10]

The Smith house was also part of Arthur's program to simplify his use of materials—just rough fir beams and sheets of glass unbroken by mullions. The experiment in simplification went a stage further than in the Baldwin house, with both posts and beams being cut from the same size wood. Eliminating the appearance of tension between thin columns and deep beams was meant to create, for the sensitive eye, an effect of "extraordinary repose." Arthur conceived of the Smiths' busy lives and their art set against "an almost sculptural consistency and quietness."[11] Ignoring the different structural purposes of the posts and beams surprised, even horrified, some

of his colleagues, but, as Arthur said, "I never let structural verac-
ity interfere with aesthetic purpose."[12] This kind of statement made
clear his determined move away from architecture as engineering
and towards its endorsement as fine art.

The enormous power of the horizontal, which Arthur had first
observed in the Parthenon and whose modern possibilities he then
became so conscious of in Maekawa's Festival Hall, was here fully
realized in his work for the first time. Its power, despite his references
to tranquility, depended on a tension, not in the building's structure,
but in a dialogue between form and setting as determined by a reaching for light. It existed most powerfully perhaps in the living room,
which spanned a rocky crevasse with floor-to-ceiling glass on either
side and a view of the sea to the south. Here, with the surrounding
forest, was a place of both containment and release, where Arthur's
friends, he liked to say, were temporarily "suspended in light."

John Fulker, a skilled B.C. photographer, had been making a pictorial record of Arthur's buildings, but to publicize his work Arthur
hired the popular Los Angeles–based photographer Ezra Stoller.
Stoller was regarded as one of the best photographers of architecture
in the U.S., and with his pictures it was easier for Arthur to persuade
Rita Reif to feature the Smith residence in an article in the *New
York Times*, where she described it as "a house with motion built in,"
emphasizing the way the house spiralled upward on five levels but at
the same time, by means of its simple materials, gave the feeling of
serenity.[13]

A house Arthur designed for David Graham near Horseshoe Bay
in 1963 descended spectacularly in three storeys a steep cliff to the
sea. Arthur thought of the house as something like a ladder placed
against a cliff face. The drama and the pleasure of the house, which
was built of raw wood and sheets of glass from floor to ceiling, were
in the act of descent, with the water and island vista revealed more
fully with each drop. The many glimpses of water, amplified by a
swimming pool on one side and a reflecting pool on the other, made
Arthur think of the Villa d'Este near Rome and its composition of
fountains. Beams of different sizes created tension and were also

in contrast with the rough board and batten on the sides. The Graham house became a showpiece for Arthur's increasingly bold style, establishing his reputation as "the architect you went to see when you had an impossible site."[14]

But the story of the Graham house might well have served as a cautionary tale to future clients. David Graham was the son of wealthy businessman and philanthropist F. Ronald Graham. In the summer of 1963, David and his wife, Penny, a good-natured, sociable couple, were travelling in Europe and sending Arthur greetings from far-flung places like Turkey and Sweden; they were carrying their house plans with them and had already invited several overseas guests to stay once it was built. In a form Arthur asked prospective clients to fill in, the Grahams had indicated that they generally entertained four times a week and that the house should accommodate twelve for dinner and fifty for cocktails, with rooms for one or two servants as well as their two children and guests. The cost agreed upon was $35,000, with a completion date set for spring 1964. But design revision and construction went slowly, and a cave-in of the bank at 6997 Isleview Road caused a major delay. Still hopeful, the Grahams sold their home in preparation for the move, but when little progress was evident, Erickson's office received a series of urgent messages from his clients saying they would be homeless by the first of July. After living in temporary quarters for three months, the Grahams moved to Isleview Road in October, but there was a great deal of work to be finished, including the carport at a time when fall rains were becoming heavy. It wasn't long before the house was plagued by leaks; tiles curled and loosened, some dropping from the walls. Garry Hanson, the project manager on site, arranged for repairs and tried to reassure the Grahams that the problems would be solved, but they were not.

In 1966, David Graham wrote Hanson a letter detailing nine major problems and omissions, including stains throughout the house, unlevel beams, and red water in the swimming pool from some mysterious source of rust. Hanson's reply addressed the matter of leaks, insisting that faulty caulking of the roof flashing was the problem rather than faulty design. An angry David Graham was left to sue the construction company, but the settlement barely covered his legal fees. In June 1969, Graham was writing to say that two major problems remained: "First, the constant and persistent leakage, which has not only required additional maintenance annually, but also re-design of the house." Secondly, there were different rates of settlement between the house and the swimming pool, especially alarming where the pool attached to the house at the bedroom. In the classic photo of the Graham house taken by Ezra Stoller there was little evidence of this turmoil; nor was there concern in Arthur's office correspondence with the Grahams, in which he characteristically distanced himself from the problems at hand and wrote instead about paintings the Grahams had purchased in England. But the office file on the house told another story: it had cost not $35,000 but more than $79,000 and was at times a source of great anxiety and unhappiness for its owners. Like the Filberg house, the Graham house seemed destined from the outset for an unhappy future.[15]

WHEN ARTHUR WAS in his third year of teaching at UBC, he had become aware of an attractive woman in his classes who was slightly older than the other students but brighter, more sophisticated, and, especially, more eager to learn. Her name was Lois Spence. Her then husband, Robert, was a foundations engineer, and they had three young daughters. Lois's intense curiosity about design and her personal sense of style set her apart. Arthur was drawn to her subtle vibrancy, her imagination, her shrewd sense of how to get things done. With something like soul affinity, they became lifelong friends.

For a 1962 thesis project, Lois proposed something new for Vancouver: a townhouse complex. At that time, Vancouver housing was either single-family dwellings or apartment blocks. Driving along the Point Grey Road waterfront in early 1963, Lois came upon a 198-foot stretch of property with a dazzling view of the North Shore mountains and the city nestled between False Creek and English Bay. She envisioned removing an old house that still stood there in weeds and tall grass and making this the site for the townhouse complex she had drawn up. The property had already been subdivided into six thirty-three-foot lots, and once her husband had verified that the bluff would support a five-unit building complex, she made the land purchase for $80,000, with one of the units to be the Spences'. Arthur was in South America, so he delegated two architects working with him to draw up designs, but their work didn't meet Lois's expectations. When he returned, Arthur took on the assignment.

There was no legislation on the books in Vancouver for dealing with contiguous single-family dwellings. City planners wanted six separate houses with side yards. The idea of five owners for one building was outside their frame of reference—they could understand only one owner to a building or one company leasing to five tenants. Lois presented her plans to city hall three different times as the months dragged on. On one occasion, the proposal was sent back with instructions to remove a mutual driveway in front of the five units. Later there was the issue of the city reserving riparian rights, because there were plans afoot for a break wall and a four-lane highway with arc lights along the beach side of Point Grey Road, though, in the end, the city's plan never went forward. Although Arthur cited housing practices in different parts of the world, including some in North America, it took more than two-and-a-half years of perseverance on Lois's part to break down resistance at city hall. Finally the building went up—an outer framework of used bricks, with each unit inside designed specifically for the individual owners.[16] Lois would be identified as the first woman in Canada to have a six-figure loan from a bank without a male co-signature.

Arthur was excited to see the project realized but dismayed by local resistance to new ideas. He felt the end result was far from an aesthetic success, because each unit was required by the city to have an ungainly garage opening on to the street. The way a committee could diminish an imaginative concept by insisting on compromises would be the source of frustration throughout his career. But the Point Grey Road project inspired a lecture by Arthur on housing that was eventually published as a pamphlet by the Canadian Housing Design Council in Ottawa.[17] In it, he envisioned cities of the future comprised largely of massive townhouse complexes. The modern apartment, he asserted, did not satisfy basic domestic needs. Typically, he reached into the past to build his argument, beginning with some observations from Pompeii, where excavations had revealed a society with housing problems akin to those of the mid-twentieth century. There, as in Vancouver, he said, self-indulgence and personal vanity had created a rambling cityscape where those who had amassed fortunes from wars were building flamboyant, incoherent houses in an attempt to outdo one another while the poor lived in tenement housing.

A house, Arthur argued, is the hardest architectural problem to define. It is inhabited by a complicated social group—the family— and in addition to their physical needs, it must accommodate all the souvenirs and trophies that individuals hang about themselves to perpetuate their identities. Radically different relationships can also be established between the house and the street. In the Mediterranean village, for example, much social life takes place in the street; in Japan, the house and internal garden are kept aloof from the street, which is a lane for traffic and sewage. In North America, he said, housing was rooted in the British legacy of the Georgian house, with its central entrance and stairway to the sleeping quarters dividing the main floor into dining on one side, living on the other. This New England–style village architecture, with its accompanying regulations, cultural values, and moral restraints, was "the spectre of our streets."

In the contemporary village, Arthur argued, people connected with others through their occupations, shared interests, or leisure pursuits, not communal neighbourhood values. They demanded privacy, their unique identities preserved. "The more demanding the pressure of urban life," he asserted, "the more we need a home to be a retreat, hidden behind walls." The vertical apartment building was not the answer, because it meant giving up so much—independence, free expression, privacy, fresh air, and garden living.

Arthur made two radical suggestions. First, "Why not build vertical real estate in many layers—providing the services the city provides now at the ground, at every level?" Such buildings could be as much as fifty storeys high, with an architect for each unit and a guarantee at every level of garden terrace spaces, privacy, and an unobstructed view. Second, a complex of this size would be part of a mixed zoning area, with single-family residences, light industrial, commercial, etc. The whole city could then be shaped with buildings to appear like hills in a landscape. Streets and lanes would be replaced with roadways sculptured with curves and high embankments. He concluded his talk by insisting that individual buildings were largely a thing of the past, and building complexes of the kind he described were both a step forward and a return to the medieval city of the past. Arthur had not yet given up his earlier vision of rebuilding Vancouver along Le Corbusier's lines.

HAVING TRAVELLED SO widely, Arthur more and more saw his home city as a small, "out-of-the-way place" where any experimental offering in the arts left its audience "bewildered or outraged." This was the gist of a speech he gave in 1963 at the windup of UBC's Festival of the Contemporary Arts, an annual event initiated two years earlier by Bert Binning.[18] With the city's main venues for the arts—an international festival, the art gallery, and the Vancouver symphony—languishing because of civic apathy, the university was attempting to create a spark in future art patrons. In its short history, the UBC festival had brought in some remarkable avant-garde talent, including poets Robert Creeley, Robert Duncan, and Lawrence Ferlinghetti, musician John Avison, painter Robert Lavigne, and an exhibition on the architecture of Brasilia. Most memorable, in Arthur's view, was the appearance in 1962 of musician John Cage, who "disturbed the mothridden dignity of the auditorium" with two pianos rigged with contact microphones, along with bolts and clamps on the strings, to accompany a performance by the Merce Cunningham dancers. Cage's performance at the piano was full of silences while those on stage danced on. Cage, who had submitted to long courses of Zen discipline, was one of the first artists to incorporate chance and uncertainty into the creative act. His concerts were notoriously challenging: audience members weren't always sure whether an intermission was taking place or, indeed, if the event had suddenly been cancelled. What fascinated Arthur was that this aesthetic of chance and indeterminacy helped to remove the presence of the ego. How, he wondered, could this transfer to architecture?

Arthur concluded his talk by blaming modern technology, especially television, for making the UBC festival another spectator sport. The dull, timid people of Vancouver had no experience of living culture; it was just something they viewed on screens. Fellow architect and UBC instructor Barry Downs observed that although Arthur may not have put together coherent lectures for his students, he engaged the public by taking contrary views and a line of reasoning that was never predictable. He wanted people to think.[19]

If Arthur was beginning to sound openly arrogant and elitist, it was in part because his career was changing; he was making important contacts in the architectural world outside Vancouver, which gave him growing confidence in his work and his ideas. This was greatly accelerated by his first international award. On January 14, 1963, he had received a citation from the American Institute of Architects for outstanding contributions in the field of design. His friendly meeting the year before with Philip Johnson, one of the leading opinion makers in the field, was probably a crucial factor in Arthur's being named for this honour, which was bestowed by the Pacific chapter of the institute at its meeting in Hawaii. His address, "Architecture: What *Is* the Question?" kept Arthur's fellow architects riveted for the best part of an hour as he connected their discipline with significant issues of contemporary and classical cultural theory, referencing ideas stretching from Tao to Marshall McLuhan, with examples drawn liberally from ancient, Renaissance, and Japanese architecture. This speech would serve as something of a template for speeches to follow in the years to come.

Arthur opened by dramatically asserting that two thousand years of Western reasoning (the logic of cause and effect; linear, historical time; the Euclidean view of space; the moral view of right and wrong) was giving way to new forms of reality in which language as the prime source of knowledge was being challenged. Citing McLuhan's *Gutenberg Galaxy*, he argued that we gain knowledge through a mosaic of impressions, and so other forms of communication, especially visual ones with international currency, were becoming pre-eminent—road signs and magazine illustrations being good examples. Architecture, he argued, is a kind of visual language that references the essential terms of the human condition: the roof represents the absence and the need for shelter, a column is a potent symbol of support, etc. The strongest human motivation, he asserted, is the pursuit of freedom, a struggle that architecture dramatizes more powerfully perhaps than any other art form, because all forms of freedom contain the forms of confinement. To the mystic and the sage, Arthur pointed out, freedom and containment are one, but to the rest of humankind the concepts are in perpetual conflict. Architecture embodies that contest. "As the human is motivated by spirit and bound by flesh," he told his audience, "so architecture is charged by space and contained by structure... At the needlepoint of equilibrium, architecture communicates with eloquence and fluency of style." The Parthenon was supreme because it achieved freedom within the stifling confines of trabeated structure, demonstrating that the stronger the prison, the more heroic the breakthrough.

Modern architecture, he asserted (with exceptions such as Le Corbusier's chapel at Ronchamp), rarely had this power, because the architect had become confused with the inventor. Traditionally, the architect's role was not to invent new forms but to invest existing vernacular forms with new significance—the Greek farmhouse became the temple, the Tuscan townhouse the Florentine palace. Thus the ordinary was ennobled; an inner world was made manifest. This was the real concern of the architect—not comfort and convenience but the inner life. Among modern architects, he suggested, the Japanese were fortunate to have a traditional basis for architectural language. Their new buildings had adopted the bare bones of Western modernist architecture, but the flesh—the style of expression—was traditionally Japanese. He drew two outstanding examples from his travels: Tange's Kurashiki city hall, a virtuoso display of proportion recalling Michelangelo, with a wall that might suggest Le Corbusier's Marseilles apartment units but more profoundly recalled the massive, earthquake-proof walls of Japanese castles and storehouses; and Maekawa's very modern concert hall, which intimated the ancient temple roof with its upswept eaves. The temple roof, gracefully accepting the weight of heaven, was another way of visualizing the artistic equilibrium of confinement and freedom.

In North America, Arthur reminded his audience, the most powerful visual symbols were power poles rather than church steeples, the traffic exchange rather than the pedestrian square. Where to find the indigenous forms that were waiting to be discovered and transformed was the specific question he posed for his audience. Architectural form is eloquent only in context, he said, and in a poetic vein continued: "The act of siting betrays to us the tenor of human aspirations, the shape of God, and the worth of man." His examples reflected the range of those aspirations and their worth— the Greek temple, the Gothic spire, ornate French palaces. In New York City, new buildings clamoured for attention, appropriate perhaps for the stock market of the world, but he saw this jostling as tragic, because it made no reference to the fundamentals of climate or terrain. Beyond the social complex, the shaping influences of nature persist. The clarity of Mediterranean light induced crispness of form and sensuousness of surface; in architecture farther north, weak light fostered tenuous, dark silhouettes—Gothic steeples rather than simple white structures. Japan had developed an architecture sensitive to moods and states of feeling—to beauty found in severity, astringency, isolation, melancholy. One statement in particular was central to Arthur's aesthetic as an architect: "It is with light that we can bring soul and spirit back into architecture."

At the close of his lecture, he returned to his central claim—that contemporary architects in North America needed a vocabulary of forms that drew meaning from the contexts of environment. He gave as an example the difference between houses on the east and west coasts. Philip Johnson had said to him once that buildings without basements were not architecture, but Arthur countered that no building could sit on such a predetermined base on the rugged, volcanic west coast. Stable, unobstructed building sites in the east had promoted geometric and abstract independence, whereas the difficult coastal topography of the west resulted in incomplete forms, with the site itself an indispensable part of the building complex: "This coupled with an often misty climate as against the clear light of the east induces a poetic rather than a formal approach to design." Arthur warned against the blight of developers—probably startling some members of his audience when he advocated enlightened central authority or public ownership of land for the common good. It was vital to listen to architects, he insisted. They were the ones who must be approached to deal with the issues of housing and the redefinition of the city—"more urgent problems than atomic warfare."

This speech was important because it outlined some enduring tenets of Arthur's faith as an architect. And although he would later argue that art was a product of the "unconscious intelligence," his 1963 address also identified him as a poet-philosopher, one for whom architecture was inextricably bound up with ideas.

11

Simon Fraser University

IN LATE MAY OF 1963, anticipating the baby boom demand for higher education, the B.C. government announced an architectural competition for a new university to be built on Burnaby Mountain. The premier of the province, W.A.C. Bennett, had chosen Gordon Shrum, retired UBC physics professor and co-chair of B.C. Hydro, to take charge of the project. "We want you to be chancellor," Bennett told Shrum in a peremptory telephone call. "Select a site, and build it and get it going. I want it open in September 1965."[1] The time frame was almost unprecedented,[2] but Shrum had a reputation for getting things done. The fact that he would not be paid was immaterial.

Gordon Shrum (1896–1985) was a classic instance of the self-made man. The son of unprosperous farmers from Ontario's Niagara Peninsula, he put himself through the University of Toronto, saw action at Vimy Ridge in 1917, and distinguished himself as an academic. He served as dean of graduate studies and director of the extension program at UBC and as a member of the National Research Council at a time when its primary concern was the future of nuclear energy. His fame for ignoring red tape was best illustrated when, after the war, while municipal councillors vacillated, he commandeered the removal of more than three hundred army huts, some from as far away as the west coast of Vancouver Island, and had them barged and trucked to the UBC campus to accommodate the flood of army veterans entering university.[3] A tall man with a dour expression, Shrum was famous for his enormous energy but also for his gruff, inflexible manner. Arthur remembered Shrum as a formidable presence on the COTC parade grounds at UBC: "He had a real Prussian streak in him... always in uniform, very strict. He wouldn't accept any deviations."[4]

Forced into retirement from the University of British Columbia at age sixty-five, Shrum welcomed with almost vindictive relish the opportunity to create a new university.[5] UBC administrators had originally envisioned an off-site undergraduate extension of their own campus, but Premier Bennett's hostile relations with UBC made him receptive to the idea of a separate and completely independent institution. When Shrum, as chancellor, called the first meeting of his board of governors, he made clear his ambitions for his new university—it would have graduate students and it would seek excellence in the same arena as UBC.[6] It would welcome experiment and innovation.[7] Most important of all, it was to have a campus and buildings that would be a showpiece. "Nobody goes to Mexico City," he said, "without seeing the University of Mexico."[8] The national university was famous for its architecture and murals. Its status as a near-separate region within Mexico City, with its own governing council and regulations, was also not without interest to Shrum.

In a comprehensive history of Simon Fraser University titled *Radical Campus*, Hugh Johnston records that Gordon Shrum had his mind set, from the beginning, on a site "that was largely removed from the normal world."[9] Shrum had flown over the city in a twin-engine Grumman Goose amphibian, and Burnaby Mountain seemed to him the perfect situation. Shrum also jotted down ideas about the buildings in a series of brief notes to himself. Among these was the comment that "architecture determines the nature, the inner philosophy of a university," a claim that Arthur would have no quarrel with. More specifically, based on a visit Shrum made to the graduate centre at Harvard was the idea that there should be "covered walks" inviting students to use the library, an idea especially favourable to a rainy mountaintop. He also noted more sweepingly: "We have a general artistic responsibility to the whole public to create buildings that set a high standard of beauty and efficiency."[10] Shrum had only one pedagogical conviction that would influence the architectural design: that teaching was best done with a combination of large lectures and small tutorials.

In setting up an architectural competition with the assistance of British-born architect Warnett Kennedy, Shrum insisted that submissions be simple—just three sheets of drawings (a site plan, an aerial view, and building profiles) and one legal-size page of written explanations. It was a contest for B.C. architects only, and the modest requirements meant that young, independent architects, without the resources of a large office, could participate. The five judges were national and international, including three from the United States. In newspaper interviews, Shrum expressed his hope that the architects would provide a unique vision for the university.

When Arthur heard about the competition, his mind was immediately rampant with ideas. His thesis at McGill had focussed on university architecture, specifically New College at Oxford, and he had incorporated an examination of the architecture of learning going back to Cairo's Al-Azhar and including Bologna, Salamanca, Paris, and Cambridge. These venerable institutions had one thing in common—a philosophy of education in which all knowledge was related and all its seekers were members of one community. He remembered Al-Azhar especially, with its tranquil courtyards and its carpeted mosque where students seemed to gather "almost informally" around men of learning.

The B.C. competition specified the usual separate locations—an arts building, a science facility, library, theatre, and gymnasium—reflecting the North American concept of the university as a site for many specialized areas of knowledge, with faculties isolated from each other. To Arthur's way of seeing things, "that concept existed for bureaucratic convenience rather than educational goals... and echoed Newton's mechanistic view of knowledge rather than Einstein's theory that all was connected."[11] Of his own experiences as a student he said, "McGill was charming, but it was just a factory that turned out architects. UBC was appalling. It was no place for students."[12] Architecturally, UBC was "a jumble of cacophonous, rambling personal statements."[13] The only place on campus students could meet was in a basement cafeteria—"a sordid place." Each building was like a fortress set up against the intrusions of rival disciplines—jealous enclaves with no exchange. Specialization encoded this way in the campus architecture negated, Arthur felt, an open approach towards the total body of knowledge. The most important places on a campus, in his view, were those where students gathered with their confreres and their teachers, not necessarily the classrooms. Surely the academies of Greece, with just a wall in Athens or a colonnade on the mountaintop of Pergamum, had been open and inclusive sites for learning. Only when this condition was recovered on university campuses could comprehensive, interdisciplinary knowledge exist once again.[14]

There was just a two-month period in which to put together a submission. Arthur could barely sleep as he worked feverishly on a master plan for the university. But he knew he could not do it on his own, so he approached Geoff Massey, who was running his own architectural firm at the New Design Gallery on Pender Street and employed a staff that included some of Arthur's brightest students, like Ron Bain, Ken Burroughs, Bruno Freschi, and Bing Thom. When Arthur and Geoff agreed to join forces, they headed into "the most frantic summer any of us had known."

One of the first things Arthur did was to fly to Mexico City to see what had so impressed Shrum there. In an interview years later, he recalled "the proportions—the very low, long proportions... that occurred in many of the buildings... I was very impressed by that." More significantly, he flew on to Oaxaca to see the ancient site of Monte Albán. His idea of an east-west axis, he said, came from there.[15] Arthur's vision of a university was so contrary to the competition's requirements that he came to an impasse. "Part way through I said, 'Geoff, do we want to win this competition or do we want to show what we believe in?'"[16] The question was really rhetorical, but it cleared the air, and from that point they committed themselves to working out a design for a university unlike anything built in North America before.

Arthur and his team designed a campus around four areas to create the widest possible interaction among students. The first of these was the mall—a gathering place and a crossroads where all activities merged in a "town square" consisting of library, theatre, bookstore, and student services, an area amply supplied with notice boards, a speaker's lectern, benches, containers with trees and shrubs. The mall was to be covered, so that it could be used year-round, and the covering would be glass to admit as much light as was available. The mall was to remain open air—a galleria in which pedestrians mingled and large public groups convened.

The second space, on a higher elevation, was the academic quadrangle enclosing a garden—a tranquil space where one could stroll, talk, and think. "Perambulation," Arthur observed, had in classical Greece, in Buddhist temples and Christian cloisters, "always been conducive to deep thought."[17] The philosopher's walk (found in Cambridge and Oxford) could here be taken in the garden or, in rain, under the protection of the raised storeys of the quadrangle. The serenity of this space was enhanced by the rhythmic repetition of its surrounding structures—the monotonous pattern of pillars and windows and "fins" (even the bathroom windows would have clear glazing for consistency); only the views within the garden would change as one walked, opening up across a broad pool, compressing behind a berm or group of trees.

The third space, west of the mall, would allow for raucous student activity—a sports complex, student union and co-op, a café and cinema. The fourth space, adjacent and farthest west, would be residential. Even though SFU was to be launched as a commuter campus, Arthur believed strongly, as did Shrum, that dormitory life was essential to all great universities.

The major spaces, then, were designed for students. The administration building and president's residence would be at the east end of the campus. The mall, running east to west for the length of the campus like a main street, would serve as a spine to which all present and future buildings could be connected; the campus would thereby be flexible and could expand down the slopes without disturbing the proportions and appearance of its centre.

The other important aspect to Arthur's design was the university's relationship to the Burnaby Mountain site. There would be no high-rise buildings, no university towers; rather, the buildings were designed to be horizontal, contoured to the lay of the land in the manner of Wright's best work. From his travels in the Far East, Arthur had learned that a building cut into a mountainside became part of the mountain and shared its imposing presence. With the landscape of Bali in mind, he proposed terracing all elements of the university—its buildings and playing fields, parking lots and improved areas—so that everything, like the Balinese rice terraces, would be part of one composition.[18]

Arthur postponed final decisions about how the buildings would look. Ken Burroughs remembered: "Erickson was constantly thinking of ways of refining things... he held on until the last minute. We finished [the drawings for SFU] about 4 AM. He was at my shoulders while I was drawing perspectives, that was in the last three or four hours. They had to reach the competition office by noon the next day."[19] Arthur's own observation was that "crisis always energizes everyone. But usually I keep people waiting because I haven't made the final decision myself. [We work] until something seems right and it all comes together—and that's very quick at the very end and everybody is in a panic. That's the way it happens."[20]

For the competition, the main ideas had to be tersely summarized in the explanation accompanying the three drawings. After making reference to a cohesive philosophy of education and the exigencies of site, climate, and circulation, the report focussed on the plan of a single complex rather than separate buildings, a mall running at its centre along the ridge of the mountain, and incremental expansion in the form of terracing down the mountain slopes.

The entry deadline was noon on July 30. There were seventy-one submissions, but the judges had their decision ready by July 31. It was a sunny morning when a curious crowd gathered at the Vancouver Art Gallery on Georgia Street to look at all the drawings on display. The announcement of the winners was to be held that afternoon at the pavilion in Burnaby Mountain Park. After viewing the entries, Arthur and Geoff almost didn't go to the ceremony. Almost all of the other entries observed the designation of at least five separate buildings on the top of the mountain; Rhone & Iredale went even further and placed three separate colleges (the Oxbridge model) around the ridge. Some of the entries were highlighted in colour; Erickson and Massey's was very plain. But out of curiosity about their colleagues' work, they drove up to the mountain park along with five hundred other architects, academics, and politicians. To their astonishment, Premier Bennett read out their names as the winners.

The five judges had been unanimous in the decision. Beyond the revisionist philosophy of interdisciplinary education, what impressed them most was the flexibility of the design in terms of coherent future growth. The judges recommended to Chancellor Shrum that every effort be made to have the winning design built without destroying the overall concept. To this Shrum publicly agreed. And to actually have a university ready to open its doors in September 1965, the four runners-up were told that they would each take charge of a particular section of the complex, under the design guidance of the winners.

Arthur and Geoff's exhilaration was shared that evening at a party at Arthur's house arranged by Lois Spence and a young male friend of Arthur's who had seen the design and was certain the two would win. He and Lois arranged to rent glasses and to purchase hors d'oeuvres, wine, and liquor, and when they got the news at 4 PM, they invited as many friends as they could reach and raced off to pick up the supplies. It was a party that Arthur's friends (and outraged neighbours) would remember for years—the pool lit with floating candles, music throbbing through the streets, exotic canapés and drinks replenished from a seemingly inexhaustible source. Arthur and Geoff did not arrive until the party was in full swing, and Ruth rushed to her husband, threw her arms around him, and shouted for joy—this was the real ticket for success in a young family overawed by the achievements of their ancestors.

But the euphoria subsided when it became clear that Shrum was deadly serious about his timetable for a September 1965 opening. The following morning, he met with the five prize winners in his B.C. Hydro office and said he would replace any of them right away if they had reservations about the project. "I want you all to understand that this university has to be built in 18 months—and if anybody can't do it, there are a lot of other architects that want the job."[21] Shrum also set out the terms of payment. The standard fee was 6 percent of construction costs, but they would all receive 5.5 percent instead, and the 0.5 percent deducted would go to Erickson and Massey for coordinating the project. When some of the architects queried this arrangement, Shrum reminded them that he had others on his list who would be willing: "I'll substitute somebody else for you right this morning."[22] Arthur and Geoff asked for four months to reconsider their proposal in a more realistic light, "for we knew how rash and romantic it was." But Shrum would only give them one month, and in that time he wanted a clear plan of how they would divide up the work. "Our joy was dampened by the enormity of what we had to do," Arthur remembered. "We didn't know how or where to start. I've never been through fire like that."[23]

The two young architects trembled at the prospect of dealing with Shrum. Arthur's experience of him on the COTC training grounds had been one of "pure fear." Although Shrum talked a good line about doing something different, he was now motivated to enhance his reputation as a man who got the job done. He told Arthur and Geoff outright that their submission had not been his first choice—"it looked absolutely crazy," not what he wanted for Burnaby Mountain; but he had agreed to be guided by the jury's decision. He instructed Arthur that he was to quit his teaching job for the next two years and told him directly that he didn't have much respect for him; Arthur was too malleable, and his head was in the clouds.[24] Shrum had more confidence in Geoff, who would handle the administration and business side of the operation.

But Shrum would also have seen a letter to Warnett Kennedy from Stewart Williams, one of the American assessors, who wrote from Palm Springs, California, "I cannot tell you how impressed I was with the potential of the #1 scheme submitted by Erickson and Massey. It seemed to fit the gently rolling crest of Burnaby Mountain like a well-cut cloak, tailored to fit the exact shape of the owner." Williams was equally impressed with the "possibilities of future expansion down the mountain slopes," and he concluded his letter on a cautionary note: "I believe that SFU stands a better than even chance to become the most beautiful, best planned university in the world if both administration and architects treat their initial scheme with the respect it deserves every time they make an important decision."[25] Although Shrum's administrative view was now sharply juxtaposed to the creative view of his architects—necessarily so, as he saw it—he was, at the same time, not deaf to such praise.

In the early stages, Shrum could sometimes be supportive. He said to Arthur and Geoff: "If you have any questions, come to me. Don't worry. Don't spend all your time looking for things. I'll tell you what to do." They cowered when they had to make a report to his office—indeed, "we never knew when we went into a meeting whether we'd be thrown out the door"—but they grew to respect Shrum's indomitable will: "We had the idea and he made it happen." Thinking later about the relationship, Arthur said: "I guess the nervous tension he inspired made you perform to your utmost capacity. We did meet deadlines."[26] Shrum respected the architects when they stood up to him, defending the integrity of their design. But he told them bluntly, "Do what is essential now—there will be no opportunity in the future."[27] By this he meant the mall, library, gym, swimming pool, and theatre. There would always be government money later for classrooms and laboratories.

But the deadlines required superhuman effort. In one month, they had to work out a master design for something that had been, in Arthur's words, a complete fabrication—a wild guess on our part."[28] And they had to present details for the other architects to work with. Like many architects, Arthur revised endlessly, leaving a trail of

190 I ARTHUR ERICKSON

hundreds of sketches. He found it extremely difficult to cut this process short, because his approach to designing remained almost mystical. "You cannot speed up your rate of absorption and concentration,"
he would argue, "because most of the creation takes place in the
subconscious." One had to wait until "suddenly things are right."[29]

At the office that was set up for SFU, Ron Bain recalled that
Arthur's sketches were in shorthand, two-dimensional diagrams that
were close to what he wanted to see in the finished building. But
this information had to be turned into three-dimensional models.
"Arthur's method was to get the design team to do all the analyses
of the spaces, volumes." One of the main problems was making the
diagram work on points of the site where the slope was not sufficient
for terracing, and in other parts where it was too steep. The so-called
"ridge" of the mountain was a series of hills and valleys, so it was a
matter of putting this large building across the entire site with as
much as sixty feet of excavation in some locations. A series of models
was created, beginning with one of the site itself, seven feet in length,
scaled at one inch per hundred feet. Models of the individual buildings were larger in order to understand the structural methods and
the finishing materials.[30] The final version was forty feet long.

After winning the competition, Arthur and Geoff added several
young architects to their office; they included Rein Raimet, Genje
Ogawa, Fred Dalla-Lana, Dan Lazosky, and Leo Ehling, who had
worked with Arthur on the Filberg house. Ron Bain recounted the
way they would typically work: "We would have a big evening with
half a dozen people around cutting cardboard and styrofoam and
messing around until we modeled the entire project... I can remember the sort of esprit de corps where people would work intensely
half the night until we had brought the model to a point where we
could refine it to the next stage."[31]

The biggest challenge was to work with the four other architects
and their teams. In order of their placement in the competition, the
five firms were each instructed to choose a building. Erickson and
Massey at first considered the academic quadrangle, viewed as the
jewel in the crown, but felt the pressure to take on the mall and

transportation centre, the heart of the project. After seriously considering the AQ, Rhone & Iredale chose the science centre, because it would expand and provide their company with future work. Zoltan Kiss took the academic quadrangle, Robert Harrison chose the library, and Duncan McNabb and Associates were left with the gymnasium and theatre buildings. Erickson/Massey did preliminary drawings (plans and sections) for each building and sent them by mid-September to the other architects.

Tenders were called, and building was underway by the early spring of 1964. It was, for Arthur, a chaotic experience, though he was diplomatic in working with others. It gave him an insight into what a film director's life must be like. "Geoff and I had never done anything much larger than a single house and now we were immersed in the utter confusion of coordinating four architects and five contractors on five contiguous sites."[32] The five contracting companies, pouring foundations more or less at the same time, had to have their own yards and offices. Ten cranes and a variety of other machines were in almost constant use. Of course, major problems arose. More rock had to be dynamited for the library's foundation than the core sample indicated; the contractor claimed an additional $300,000 and was not willing to go ahead until payment was made. Arbitration equated conglomerate rock with hardpan, as identified in the original contract, so the contractor was awarded only an additional $32,000, but time was lost. And more time was lost when the foundations for the theatre were laid twenty-seven feet too far to the east because the contractors were working with a site plan that had been recalled and replaced by another one.[33] The project required an exceptional amount of co-operation, and several times a week meetings were called to settle differences. Shrum was watchful and concerned there be no holdups caused by disputes.

Despite its challenges (at any one time there were as many as five hundred to eight hundred construction workers on the site), Arthur was supremely confident in the project. "It is a monumental scheme," he said to an interviewer. "It is going to be the one monumental thing that people in Vancouver will see. They have never seen anything like it and probably never will again. It will have great spaces which I feel are important—in scale to the landscape and the site." (His comments are reminiscent of Michelangelo, who wrote about his plans for Pope Julius II's tomb: "I am certain that, if it comes to be made, there will be nothing like it in the whole world."[34]) Arthur regretted the rush, but his expectations could not have been higher.

> It will unfortunately be rough, brutal, but I feel it is better to be rough and brutal in the materials and in the way it is built, rather than to pretend refinements, when there hasn't been time to apply these. It will be as I think architecture should be in this city—down to earth, rank, open, no nonsense, applying itself with as much harmony as possible to its setting and to the climate... but also with something that takes the human out of his ordinary, humdrum fireside existence. Ennobles him, lifts him.[35]

Arthur and Geoff both attended meetings that involved Shrum and other university personnel. Otherwise, Geoff was the administrator; he went to all meetings and coordinated scheduling, surveying, and relations among the architects and contractors. He took the brunt of the criticism. Arthur, who hated meetings, focussed on design, materials, and the architectural language of the buildings. He made choices, such as how the concrete was to be finished in different parts of the building: whether plain, with the impressions of the formwork clearly visible in a way that had impressed him in Maekawa's concert hall, or sandblasted or bush-hammered for different textural effects. The division of labour between Arthur and Geoff sometimes had a comic aspect. When it was discovered that one of the concrete slabs was not thick enough to bear the required weight, Geoff burned up the telephone lines, shouting at various contractors and suppliers to deal with the problem at once. Simultaneously, Arthur was on another line trying to track down a certain type of gold-scaled koi for a reflecting pool.[36]

Only one of the other four architect groups had aesthetic concerns that sometimes challenged Arthur's. Zoltan Kiss, Arthur's

Hungarian-born contemporary, had arrived in Vancouver in 1951 via Denmark and completed his architectural training at UBC in 1952. Arthur probably met Kiss when they were both working at Sharp & Thompson, Berwick, Pratt in 1953, and they knew one another socially. Modest and soft spoken, Kiss nonetheless had firm ideas, and he brought the sharp eye of a European architect to the project on Burnaby Mountain. As project architect for the new Vancouver International Airport and designer of several buildings at UBC—including the original Buchanan Building and the Koerner graduate centre— he also brought considerable local experience. Kiss had been as amazed as Arthur and Geoff were to have his submission included in the top five, and he readily acknowledged the overall superiority of the Erickson/Massey submission. (His design also hugged the mountain landscape but did not so easily accommodate expansion.) But his modernist sensibility was not quite as austere as Arthur's, and they had to negotiate some differences as Kiss fine-tuned his work on the academic quadrangle with its Corbusian stilts. Arthur had specified that the interiors should be "like monastery walls, white or off white, with only a work of art for colour,"[37] but Kiss insisted on wood panelling to give warmth to the rooms and corridors on the second and third floors. Kiss extended his aesthetic claims to the exterior of the AQ by doubling the number of vertical fins shading the windows and proposing they be finished with marble chips and white cement. Arthur argued that doubling them would make the exterior too busy. Moreover, if they were white instead of grey concrete, it would distract from the unified effect of the campus, which was to have the look and character of sculpture. Shrum decided in favour of Kiss, and, given the iconic status the AQ façade took on, featured subsequently in almost every photograph of the university, one cannot help feeling that Shrum was right. Perhaps to smooth the waters, Shrum judged in Arthur's favour when he and Kiss argued about the windows to the washrooms on the AQ; Kiss, conventionally, wanted to use opaque glass, but Arthur, again concerned for the unity of effect, argued for clear glazing, with moveable screens for privacy. That too appears to have been the right aesthetic choice.

In addition to the transportation centre and mall, Arthur and Geoff took on numerous other small contracts such as the water tower, the fire pump house, and outdoor lighting. They were especially concerned with ensuring uniformity throughout the campus, and no detail was too small for their attention. They wanted uniform signage and, after considerable research, chose a sans serif typeface to be used throughout (though it wasn't in the end), and they chose the carpets, drapes, desks, chairs, coat racks, and the paint colour for the lampposts—"Simon Fraser green."[38] They even selected bedspreads for the women's residence. Their commitment to the best materials continually got them into trouble. For example, the drapery material they chose had to be flown in from Europe; it was held overlong in customs, then delayed at the local manufacturer's who had, in the meantime, taken on other assignments.

Despite it all, the "harrowing adventure"[39] of designing and building a university was marked by moments of euphoria for Arthur. "I remember the exhilaration," he told interviewer Ruth Sandwell, "when, after the surveyors had cleared a line through the thick forest, we climbed stumps to look out and there at the end of the long swath we could see the green of Stanley Park and the Lions Gate bridge, magically appearing just as we had predicted."[40] Everyone seemed to share the exhilaration as work on the mall was nearing the end; the Italian tile layers would "race down the Mall with fork lifts swaying, singing Neapolitan opera in the mountain air at the top of their lungs." Arthur had to reassure the chancellor and the president that the tile layers were not taking their job lightly; they were singing because they were enjoying their work—and because they enjoyed their work, they would be finished on time.[41]

And it did open on time, its motto "*Nous sommes prêts*" (We are ready) generating its media nickname, "the instant university."[42] There were 3,550 guests for an opening ceremony. Not all of the buildings were done—the academic quadrangle was not landscaped, the mall roof not finished, and there were "instant" leaks that needed repairs—but on September 9, approximately 2,500 students were enrolled and, with the media attention, the eyes of the country

were on this experiment in university architecture and the new education it was designed to foster.

Arthur was the ideal spokesman for what had been achieved; in
Marshall McLuhan's term he was a "cool" personality—self-confident,
eloquent, intelligently aloof—with a sense of mystery that left his
audience wanting more. In interviews, he grounded his descriptions of the university in references that were historical and poetic,
invoking physical sitings as well as architectural inspirations. He
compared Simon Fraser's mountaintop setting to that of the Greek
acropoli, not just in Athens but in Pergamum, Turkey, describing
a hilltop university as "an urban compression, a fragment of utopia suggesting a pattern for the ideal city."[43] In this city, he added,
"everything depends on the space between—the common ground"
where disciplines and information overlap. The siting of the gymnasium on the westward slope of the mountain with a view of the
city and ocean evoked another reference to Pergamum. He told one
reporter that his first impression of Pergamum "certainly influenced
me, and I have felt since then that the way the Greeks used the
mountain, to occupy the temples of their gods, is how the twentieth
century should use the mountain to build its universities."[44] His way
of siting buildings has been described as "talking to the distances."[45]
He had tried to use everything he had admired in his travelling, he
said. "This was the one chance to put them all into a composition,
but there wasn't any imitation. It was the spatial experience itself
and the composition too."[46] The Bauhaus practice, in which everything had to be new, now seemed very limiting to Arthur. Finding
out from study what made old buildings beautiful and powerful and
translating that essence into the contemporary idiom was the course
he would follow.

His inspiration was also of a local nature. To a reporter, Arthur
recalled his climb with Bill Baldwin to Forbidden Plateau and seeing the vistas unfold. Simon Fraser, he said, was like that: "You
come out of the lower transportation area and you climb up terraces
past classrooms and laboratories and into the roofed-in mall, and
you get glimpses of the vistas you can see from the mountain. Then

you climb higher, to the summit, to the upper quadrangle, and you see the whole world around, with the realization it has wide, limitless horizons. Education is like that. As you learn more, you are able to see more of the vistas of human knowledge and experience."[47]

The ideas and powerful feelings that Arthur injected into the creation of Simon Fraser University stirred excitement in the public and the press. Early headlines set the bar high. "Higher Education Rides a Rocket in B.C.," shouted the *Financial Post* in March 1965, and a reporter for *Time* magazine announced in April "A Flowering up North." When the university opened in September, the headlines were full of praise, such as "Dynamic Design for a Daring New Concept" in the *Victoria Daily Times*. Even the conservative *Business and Financial Chronicle* prefaced its report with "On Burnaby Mountain—A Miracle of our Times." The *Architectural Forum* ran an article headed "In Canada, the Continent's First Single-structure Campus." Vancouver had never before been in the spotlight this way. Montreal architect Ray Affleck wrote in the March 1966 issue of *Canadian Architect*, "Seldom have I ever been so impressed, so excited by the nature of a concept... It expresses architecture as a space-time continuum related to experience and action, rather than a composition based on formal or structural ideas."[48] And in 1966, three British journals, including the *Architectural Review*, gave the new university top marks. *Interbuild*, in an article titled "Canada: Sermon on a Mount," called the university an architectural "masterpiece," and to Arthur's delight astutely identified some of the important reasons why: "The bold nucleus... gives Simon Fraser University a distinctive and total identity— which is revolutionary on a continent where campuses are too often a far-flung and mutually hostile sprawl of pedagogic tribal encampments... Some of the spaces for gathering, like the Mall, are exciting intellectual agoras." The reviewer concluded by predicting the university would be mandatory viewing on any North American architectural pilgrimage.[49] For his part, Arthur was careful to acknowledge that a similar, though perhaps not so dramatic, experiment was being undertaken at Scarborough College in the suburbs of Toronto, where John Andrews was also "striving to decompartmentalize the rigid enclaves of academia and to propose instead a pedestrian freeway along which education becomes a series of planned and unplanned events."[50]

Canadian Architect devoted the whole of its February 1966 issue to Simon Fraser University. Two articles were of special interest to Arthur. Lionel Tiger, a UBC sociologist, lauded the fact that "SFU is a classless building; it flatters no social class." Nor was there ancestor worship, Tiger added, in the naming of buildings for the deeds of dead people. This was a modern university, with its numerical realities reflected in the epic scale of the wide flights of steps approaching and leaving the mall. Only the location of SFU elicited Tiger's scorn: "Since most students are being trained for urban jobs it is fanciful to secrete them atop a mountain because of some tedious illusion about peace, quiet and Wordsworthian pantheism... Simon Fraser University on its mighty peak [has] been sterilized by a retrogressive situation."

In contradistinction, Ron Thom asserted in "Architecture of the Indefinite" that it was in every sense an elevating experience for the student to leave behind the "depressing, mean-minded" streets of Burnaby and climb the mountain. He recognized an essential aspect of Arthur's vision when he described, in a slightly altered version of the same article, the approach by road, emerging from a cleft in the trees at the edges of the playing field, then catching a first glimpse of the buildings "appearing as a delicate crown inseparable from the top of the mountain."[51] But what pleased Arthur most was Thom's recognition that the university's form was the embodiment of an academic idea—the belief that expanding boundaries of knowledge could not be contained.

What no reviewer mentioned was Arthur's enormous debt to contemporary Japanese architecture. This was his first project in concrete, executed with all he had learned through his encounter with the buildings of Maekawa and Tange.

Abraham Rogatnick, who one day took Walter Gropius on a tour of the campus, composed an article about SFU that would eventually be published in Britain's *Architectural Review*.[52] In a flow of superlatives, he suggested that the music of Beethoven should accompany one's ascent to SFU, specifically the Ninth Symphony, because SFU was designed as a place of brotherhood—of equals—and a glimpse of utopia. That suggests today another way to think about SFU's achievement, one Arthur fervently endorsed—namely, that Simon Fraser University is a work of epic imagination, an expression in architecture of communal needs and aspirations, though not in any nationalistic sense. Ancient building sites such as the Greek acropoli or Mexico's Monte Albán envision a people's future, not its past, and in a seven-page document dated September 2, 1965, Arthur identified the unified structure of the campus as embodying a course for the future. Only by the physical overlapping, even merging, of disciplines in constant intellectual and social interchange, he argued, could anything like "the universality of human culture" be recognized. His further goal, he asserted, was to redefine the university in contemporary terms to make it "meaningful to the whole community." The ascent from arrival on campus at the transportation centre to the mall, then further to the AQ, with its tranquil garden and view, replicated the climbing of a mountain and, in Arthur's view, the course of *every* human life.

Arthur's intense feelings about the university he had created were acted out one evening on campus in the company of friends. The issue was landscaping. The original plan called for the removal of all trees on the high slopes and the planting of grasses and wildflowers to give the campus a bucolic setting, but the groundskeepers were cutting the grass, creating lawns instead of meadows.[53] Arthur decided that surely the colourful flowering of wild poppies would keep the grass cutters away. One sunny evening in late April, he invited some colleagues from the office and several faculty and students to gather on the slopes below the theatre around Helen Goodwin, a dance teacher at UBC. They had twenty pounds of poppy seed and several bottles of Faisca. Each person was given a yard of red cotton to adorn themselves and a musical instrument, and in the delicate spring air and splendid colours of the evening, they danced through the fields, scattering the seeds, strips of red cloth flying, cymbals and tambourines ringing. They were overcome with Bacchic exuberance. Then, forming a procession, they twirled and danced around the running track, up the stairs to the mall, and across the mall to the foot of the quadrangle. In Arthur's words: "It was a truly pagan rite, and just as the sun was lowering, Helen mounted the Quad steps like a high priestess and each one of us, without bidding, came forward silently to lay our instrument at her feet as she invoked the setting sun." Some bewildered tourists wandered onto the mall, and Arthur thought they must have believed what they were seeing "were the ghosts of the original tribe that had built this mountain temple."[54]

12

Francisco Kripacz

THE EUPHORIA ARTHUR experienced on the meadows at SFU was a momentary heightening of the exhilaration that he had been experiencing steadily for nearly three years. His personal life had changed dramatically by 1962. The young friend who, with Lois Spence, had arranged the champagne party for the SFU winners had become his partner.

His name was Francisco Kripacz, and they met at a party in Vancouver's West End in December 1961. Arthur, encircled by admirers, became aware of being watched by a dark-skinned, handsome boy of about nineteen, who eventually came over and introduced himself. It would be interesting to know what Francisco said, for there was, and still is, considerable mystery surrounding his identity. Arthur's account was a stripped-down immigrant narrative of a boy born in Slovenia in 1942, whose parents fled Yugoslavia after the war, endured many hardships, and eventually settled in Venezuela. In this story, Francisco had come to Vancouver to visit his younger brother, José, who was being schooled at St. George's, a symbol of the family's eventual success, and it was at that time that he and Arthur met. Privations in childhood, however—not enough food, no fixed home for many years—had left Francisco insecure and anxious for material possessions. It was a story that Arthur told to elicit sympathy for Francisco when his behaviour strained the patience of Arthur's friends.

Quite a different account would be given in the cover story of the January 1985 issue of *Interiors*, the magazine of the National Society of Interior Designers, where Francisco was celebrated as "Designer of the Year."[1] Here he is said to have been born in Caracas in 1944 into a family with money and artistic taste. His father is identified as the founder of an important Venezuelan publishing firm, a man who had studied design and graphic art in Germany and who had not only furnished their home with discernment but had designed much of its furnishings. He had influenced his son's taste for fine things by taking him to the best shoemaker in Caracas to have his shoes custom made. According to the *Interiors* article, as heir apparent to a publishing empire, Francisco received an education "specifically planned to equip him with the cosmopolitan sophistication necessary to assimilate and interpret world events." Accordingly, he was sent to a series of exclusive private schools: at age six to Le Rosey boarding school in Switzerland to learn French and German; at ten to The Lodge School in Barbados to learn English; at thirteen to Florence ("which his father considered the cradle of culture") to the Jesuit Badia di Fiesole, where Italian became his favourite language. By fifteen, Francisco was beginning to chafe under the strict discipline of the Jesuits and, pleading homesickness, he persuaded his parents to let him go to school in the United States. While his parents investigated prestigious preparatory schools such as Exeter and Andover, Francisco on his own initiative selected the more permissive Pine Crest School in Fort Lauderdale, a school established in the 1930s for children of privileged families wintering in Florida. His family, we are told, somewhat reluctantly gave in to his choice. After graduating in 1961, Francisco attended New York University to study journalism. But in a short time, the young man realized the family business was not going to satisfy him. He came to Vancouver when his brother enrolled at St. George's but stayed, the article said, because his parents had decided to build a house in the city designed by Arthur Erickson. The magazine tells us that Francisco fell under the spell of Erickson's "spectacular and subtle architecture" and eventually became his business partner, running an office in Los Angeles. There the story ends.

This glamorous biography comes up against the more sober facts of Francisco's life in Vancouver as remembered by Arthur and his friends. There was no Kripacz house built in Vancouver; nor, according to Arthur, was one ever contemplated. In fact, Francisco's parents were divorced by the time he and Arthur met; his flamboyant mother had a lover whom she followed to Vancouver with her younger son in tow, and Francisco, who joined them, took design courses at the Vancouver School of Art in 1962. Among the languages mentioned in the *Interiors* article, there was no reference to Hungarian, which, according to several of Arthur's friends and acquaintances, including Zoltan Kiss, was the language Francisco's family was known to speak. Lois Spence (later Milsom) remembered that Francisco's birthplace was given on his passport as Budapest, and she recalled his mother speaking in Hungarian to a local tailor. Still, in what was once the Austro-Hungarian Empire, the family could well have been Slovenian, as the name Kripacz suggests, but used Hungarian as a lingua franca.

But the Geneva archives for Second World War refugees provides yet another account of Francisco's origins.[2] A boy with the Germanic name Franz Leopold was born to Leopold and Carla Kripacz on April 8, 1942, in Hungary. The boy's father is identified as originally having had an Italian name, Leopardo Cripacio; his mother is listed as Carla Sandro-Cripacio. Assuming the family also lived in Slovenia, their peripatetic life might suggest Roma origins. More than once, Francisco was mistaken as someone from India or Pakistan. The subsequent Spanish names, Francisco and José, reflect the New World myth-making of the *Interiors* article. In what Lois knew of the family, Francisco's father lived for a time in New York City, where Francisco was briefly enrolled in law school. When he missed classes, spending weekends in Florida, his father cut off his allowance, which was why Francisco was with his mother and brother in Vancouver.

Lois's first meeting with Francisco was in October 1962, when she and her first husband, Robert Spence, were about to leave for New York City and to travel from there to Pakistan. They were attending a production at the Arts Club; Francisco was there with Arthur's friend Jane Clegg as his date, but not far into a conversation with Lois he made it clear that Arthur belonged to him. Despite the bluntness of this claim, Lois took a quick liking to Francisco; with their mutual experience of cosmopolitan eastern cities they were both feeling marooned in a small town, and Francisco's campy humour at the expense of Vancouver kept them laughing all evening. Francisco arranged a farewell party for the Spences, employing some musicians who performed at the theatre that night to entertain them a few evenings later.

Arthur had a deep conviction that temperamental opposites were strongly attracted to each other. His own restrained, Apollonian nature was drawn fatalistically to the Dionysian—in this case to a young man who was flamboyantly outgoing, not unlike his mother. For Arthur, Francisco was a thrilling person to be around, someone who charged everything with a higher level of intensity. He was an energetic companion and an exuberant conversationalist; his talk was nimble, smart, funny—nothing was sacred. Francisco was always full of plans and gossip, speaking quickly, his imagination constantly taking flight. To Arthur, life seemed so much bigger and more exciting in Francisco's presence. On that first meeting, "it seemed we had known each others for years." Or, as one of their friends put it, "It was as if Francisco had rolled out a magic carpet into the future for Arthur and said 'we will travel on this together.'"[3]

But Francisco's vibrant personality did not charm everyone; most of Arthur's friends took a strong dislike to him. Abraham Rogatnick saw Francisco as an ambitious social climber who viewed Arthur's friends with contempt. Some thought him predatory, living without employment off Arthur's earnings. But to most of Arthur's friends in 1963, Francisco was an embarrassment, a flagrant statement that their discreet, gentle friend was a homosexual, someone other than he portrayed himself to be. This was when the Masseys first understood Arthur's nature, and they did not feel comfortable around Francisco, who seemed to be laughing at them. Kay Cooke and some of her family felt the same; Francisco's flamboyance was such a startling contrast to Arthur's reserve. Blackie (Lee) Sparzani enjoyed dancing with Francisco, and she felt a certain relief to learn that Arthur had not rejected her for another woman, but she could not help suspecting Francisco's motives—who was this boy, almost twenty years younger than Arthur? There was something almost sinister in this relationship, it seemed to her—it was not just a matter of sexual preference.

Arthur sensed how his friends felt, and he regretted their lack of enthusiasm for his companion. But the reaction of his family was much more troubling. Myrtle and Oscar were deeply upset about Arthur's relationship with Francisco. It was particularly difficult for Oscar. To Francisco's effusive manner, he could not respond in his usual genial way; in conversation he could find no common ground. Myrtle, usually so open to new ideas and people, seemed to withdraw into a conservative frame of mind, and it took several years for her to feel relaxed in Francisco's presence.

Oscar did not have that much time. On May 4, 1965, he died of a heart attack while he and Myrtle were on vacation in California. Arthur was usually Zen-like in a crisis—he went forward calmly, as if untouched—but when news of his father's sudden death came, his legs gave way and he lay down on the office floor as he spoke on the telephone. He was shattered.[4] The obituary in the *Vancouver Sun* was titled "A man of courage, he helped others," and it read: "A man has to stand on his own two feet even if they are artificial ones." Arthur consoled himself that his father had lived to see him succeed as an architect; his anxieties about his son making a living had finally been put to rest. His cousin's wife, Eve Auer, who rode with Arthur to the cemetery, remembered that the funeral director's chauffeur pointed to the top of Burnaby Mountain and said—"Look, from here you can see where they are building the new university." Arthur thanked him for pointing it out.

There was a haunting repetition of events in November of that year when word came from Montreal that Gordon Webber had died suddenly of a heart attack. He was only fifty-six. Like Arthur's father, Gordon had learned to live a full life with legs that were badly compromised, and he had always been optimistic. Like Myrtle, Gordon had been irrepressibly curious about life and had given Arthur a fresh way of seeing. But Arthur's feelings on Gordon's sudden death were tinged with the guilt of someone who has moved on and achieved much more than his mentor—for Arthur, in the creation of Simon Fraser University and in finding a life's partner.

There were two family members who had a very different view of Francisco; they were Donald Erickson's sons, Christopher and Geoffrey. Raised in a conventional and not especially affluent home (Donald made his living variously as a writer and a teacher; his wife, Eleanor, was a homemaker), Arthur's nephews, in their early teens, were awestruck by the lavish lifestyle of their uncle's friend. Francisco's clothes were custom made by tailors in Los Angeles and New York. He drove a Triumph TR4 roadster. He was immensely generous, giving the boys rides to school and passing on smart items of clothing that made them the envy of their friends. Arthur and Francisco also purchased exotic gifts: for Chris and Geoff they brought daggers from Damascus and swords from Africa; for the boys' little sister, Emily, they would buy a doll in each of the countries they travelled to.[5] They brought native costumes from the countries they visited— vests, sombreros, kimonos—and for Myrtle unique fabrics to be made into dresses by her tailor. It was like Christmas when they returned from a trip. On birthdays and holidays, they staged exotic entertainments. One Halloween, after having recently returned from Shanghai, they invited the boys to the house for a private, park-style display of fireworks that alarmed the neighbours and brought the police.

But one of Chris and Geoff's most vivid memories was taking the train to Montreal by themselves to stay for a holiday in the apartment that Arthur and Francisco had rented for the period of Expo 67. On a trip to South America in the mid-sixties, Francisco had discovered the modernist-style furniture being designed by Jorge Zalszupin. He brought a couple of catalogues back to Vancouver and found such enthusiasm for the Brazilian's work that he decided to import furniture as a business venture. Because Expo 67 was on the horizon for Arthur—he had been commissioned to create two pavilions for the Canadian government, Man in the Community and Man and His Health, and to work on the Venezuelan pavilion with that country's premier architect, Carlos Raul Villanueva—Francisco decided Montreal would be the logical location. In 1966, he opened a showroom there called Francisco Ltd. Contract Furniture, and to the work of Zalszupin he added contacts (catalogues and sample pieces) for contemporary European designers including Dino Gavina from Italy and Haimi Oy from Finland. Francisco was probably their first exclusive representative in North America. In Vancouver, he had worked informally with Arthur, advising on interior design projects, but in Montreal, he became one of the designers Arthur drew on heavily.

Arthur's young and impressionable nephews were witness to many things that summer: the frenetic energy both Arthur and Francisco expended in their work, the intensely glamorous social life they engaged in with the powerful people present in Montreal for the exposition. Among the rich and famous the boys might have glimpsed were the Duke and Duchess Pini di San Miniato, who had homes in both Montreal and New York. The duchess was Canadian-born Gladys Wilson, daughter of a senator and heiress to a considerable family estate. Arturo, the Italian-born duke, was her third husband, and as American president of the National Society of Interior Designers he was a man of great interest to Francisco. Arturo had been an antique dealer with a gallery in Bologna, but he moved to New York in 1953, where he began working as an interior decorator; a royal apartment suite at the Waldorf Towers for the Duke and Duchess of Windsor and the oval reception room of the White House were among his commissions. Arthur was dazzled by the antiques in the Pini di San Miniatos' Montreal home, especially by a Chinese bronze said to date from 1000 BCE that sat on an eighteenth-century inlaid Chinese chest. As for Chris and Geoff, Arthur felt his nephews' visit likely started them on their career paths: Chris to become an architect, Geoff an interior designer.

One of the young architects making a sensational debut at the fair was Moshe Safdie with his seminal work, Habitat. As Arthur remembered it years later, "No project caused quite the stir that Habitat did with its freshness, ingenuity and boldness—a flying city of apartments piled up into sloping planes... suggesting a way of increasing the density of a city without the inhuman impact of skyscrapers."[6]

Montreal was not Arthur's first exposition. While still in the throes of completing Simon Fraser University, he had erected a pavilion for Canada at the 1965 Tokyo International Trade Fair. In stark contrast to the refinement and finish of Japanese craftsmanship, he had assembled a structure of rough-cut lumber like a massive log cabin to suggest the crude, unfinished, but raw power of his young country. The open interior even had a pool for log-rolling exhibitions. Wood was again his construction material for the Montreal fair, and the Man in the Community pavilion that resulted was something like a pagoda-style pyramid with a 140-foot-high cone. Thirty-seven layers of composite glulam and plywood beams were laid in a series of diminishing octagons that each rotated 45 degrees, so that the corner of the one above rested on the sides of the one below. This was engineer Jeffrey Lindsay's solution to Arthur's goal, which, in keeping with the fair's international theme of *Terre des Hommes* (Man and His World) was "to create a space which was infinite—both vertically and horizontally."[7] The illusion was further enhanced by a long reflecting pool in the centre. Early in the season, *Interiors* judged Arthur's theme pavilion for the fair "best by far," and the lavish magazine was very visibly displayed in the Montreal apartment.

From the beginning, Arthur viewed Francisco's taste as unerring, blending elegance with simplicity so that one felt the powerful energy of underlying restraint. "I have complete trust in his sensibility, understanding and sympathy for my buildings," Arthur would repeatedly assert, adding that he sought Francisco's advice even at the conceptual phases.[8] In the second of Arthur's books, he would clearly state the importance of their professional partnership:

> Over the years, Francisco's work has fleshed out my architectural bones without in any way denying the thrust of the design. Long ago I concluded that the architect's mind is more suited to envisioning space and structure than the subtler materials and colours that adorn interiors. Preoccupied with the purity of our spaces, we tend to overlook them. And when an architect does attempt an interior, the result is always recognizable for its lack of that final,

complementary step of definition—the tying together on the intimate level dominated by furnishings and their details. At the same
time, the architect with no control at all over his interiors finds his
work more often compromised than enhanced by the work of the
interior designer, for whom a set of rooms may be but a stage for
presenting a quite unrelated visual order. It takes a sure affiliation
of purpose and spirit between architect and interior designer to
achieve that rare building that is a conceptual unity throughout. As
an associated partner, Francisco has given my practice this added
strength.[9]

Francisco had critiqued the design for Simon Fraser University as it unfolded. He had also tried to bring balance to Arthur's
life, coaxing him out from the lean-to garage where he sometimes
spent twenty-hour stretches wrestling with the spaces that would
constitute his epic achievement. Yet their professional partnership
remained unofficial for many years. Francisco's name was not on the
payroll until he was set up to manage an office in Los Angeles in
the 1980s. In the business files that comprise the University of Calgary's Erickson collection, ranging from the 1950s to 1972 (some 111
boxes), Francisco's name seems to appear only twice—as sharing a
room with Arthur on an invoice for a 1964 Christmas vacation at
Ochos Rios in Jamaica, and as addressee in a formal business note
Arthur dictated when the firm was redesigning the prime minister's
office in 1971.[10]

Arthur was similarly circumspect about making his relationship
with Francisco known to the public, especially in Vancouver. In the
late 1960s a gay bar functioned in the basement of a building on the
corner of Robson and Seymour Streets. When Arthur encountered a
university faculty member there, he said he was present owing to the
curiosity of a friend from out of town.[11] Francisco felt no reluctance
to hide his sexual identity, but as Arthur put it in later years, "To be
openly gay at that time would not have been good for business."

13

Huckster

THE POSTWAR BUILDING BOOM in North America had created an unprecedented demand for young architects graduating from universities. In that heady time, more than ever before, architecture was viewed as supreme, the mother of the arts that made civilization possible. Many architects viewed their work as also providing solutions to social problems. Professors and students accordingly nurtured a high sense of their value, and many of those who had come into the profession via schools of architecture felt it was unbecoming to seek work; the world should come to them. Ayn Rand built her story of Howard Roark in *The Fountainhead* around this idea of the architect as a superior man guided solely by his own vision. In practice, clashes inevitably resulted between those who saw themselves as creative artists and those who considered themselves engaged, even more importantly, in the *realpolitik* of public administration and bureaucracy. As Arthur's practice and reputation expanded, these radically diverging interests more and more became a source of conflict. He was especially frustrated, on the local and provincial level, to be critiqued by those he regarded as dull and uninformed. His response was to become a showman, a favourite with the media, which gave him the leverage needed to deal with philistines. His secretarial staff sent out publicity notices for the office on a regular basis.

Although Simon Fraser University was nationally and internationally a great triumph for Erickson and Massey, locally their achievement was frequently disparaged. From the outset, professors and students were ambivalent about this campus of *béton brut* (raw concrete). Historian Hugh Johnston quotes a department colleague, Charles Hamilton, as saying that "on a sunny day the university was breathtaking, but on a foggy winter day the unpainted concrete in addition to the isolation could make it feel like a prison."[1] Some local art critics took a similar view. David Watmough, unaware of the contemporary Japanese aesthetic, wrote in the *Vancouver Sun* that Erickson had created architecture for a Mediterranean climate, and that on a typical dull and rainy day "Cool alcoves turn into dank rat holes... and the overwhelming sea of grey cement and the ubiquitous drip of water in moist and murky corners crushes the spirit."[2] Hampton Court or Dublin's Trinity College, Watmough asserted, were not ruined by leaden skies. One could build for rain, and Erickson and Massey had not.

The university's chancellor and board of governors had grave misgivings themselves about what they regarded as design deficiencies. When SFU opened, Arthur and Gordon Shrum spoke respectfully of each other, as suited the occasion. Shrum said in a ceremonial speech that "in beauty and concept, I doubt that the university can be matched."[3] But it wasn't long before Arthur and Geoff had to face a different state of things. "I'll never forget," Arthur told Gene Waddell,

> that after the opening... we were called before the Board of Governors, and Geoff and I went in thinking we were going to be congratulated. We went in and they gave us such a dressing down... Here we felt we had really accomplished something, working our guts out to get this thing done, and we were very proud of it. All the things to be corrected—that's all they talked about—not one complimentary statement. So that was the mentality we were working with. We had to fight for absolutely everything. We were always under suspicion.[4]

Arthur dropped his usual Zen-like acceptance and openly complained to Shrum about his "adverse reactions to whatever we do."[5]

A sore point for Shrum was the mall roof. He saw it as purely ornamental, covering a space of no specific value—in his view, a waste of money. Instead, he wanted to build a field-house auditorium west of the gym where ceremonies like convocation could be held. To his surprise and chagrin, Shrum was outvoted by the board, and the roof was authorized early in 1965—as long as it would cost no more than $250,000. The board, however, made it clear that Erickson and Massey's reputation would be on the line. Especially discouraging for Arthur and Geoff was the fact that the university's president, Patrick McTaggart-Cowan—a meteorologist, a weather forecaster, and a former student of Shrum's—was pretty much willing to do the old man's bidding. As for the architecture promoting interdisciplinary education, "[the president] didn't grasp the idea at all."[6]

Shrum and the board began negotiating other campus projects without Erickson and Massey's consultation or approval; these included a winter sports complex west of the gym, a house for the university president (without their knowledge, the project was given to Zoltan Kiss), and a gas station paid for by Shell Oil. Arthur and Geoff's response was a progress report, dated February 15, 1966, that was essentially a request to let them complete the design of the university.[7] It did not mince words: "Unfortunately in the latter stages of Phase I construction, the architect/planners experienced a serious breakdown in communications with the university and have not been able to re-establish rapport or a communication line since." They asked that their shortcomings be measured against what they had achieved: "Excellence cannot be achieved without difficulty, but it has been our experience that the problems accompanying excellence, which at times were large, are soon forgotten, whereas the standards are enduring." The gist of the report was that the university continued to need planners, not just a board that responded to financial and enrolment pressures by bringing in temporary trailers that become permanent. Planners were needed to gather data, create preliminary designs for development, supervise the work, and maintain records of construction. Otherwise, the campus would be developed haphazardly, without reference to the master plan.

For a board meeting on April 19, 1966, Shrum drew up a list of what he titled "Problems with E/M." These included tardy completion of working drawings, numerous design errors, inaccurate cost estimates, and what Shrum saw as the root problem: that Erickson and Massey were "more concerned about aesthetic than functional aspects of design."[8] While the board was indebted to Erickson and Massey for the original concept of the university, Shrum said, there had been much to cause the board annoyance: poor drainage of the mall, delays in finishing the roof, and major leaks in the transportation centre that had not been repaired. Erickson and Massey seemed not to realize they were employees of the board, and a contract allowing them to be "consultants and coordinators to safeguard the integrity of the overall design" was the university's final offer. Determined to be free of Erickson and Massey, the board had offered the next building phase, a classroom complex on the north slope, to Zoltan Kiss: an offer that was withdrawn when they discovered they had already paid for the Erickson design. Further architectural planning, Shrum said, could be done by faculty and staff as the occasion arose.[9] Not even the conferring that year of two awards on Erickson and Massey from organizations as diverse as the Prestressed Concrete Institute (based in Chicago) and the Architectural Institute of British Columbia could change the minds of the board members.

Arthur and Geoff were furious when the board decided at its December 14, 1966, meeting that a competition should be called for a design to landscape the quadrangle garden, because landscaping for the whole campus had been included in their original design. Arthur protested this in a letter dated February 14, 1967, to Arnold Hean, chair of the building committee, in which he identified once again the overall concepts for landscaping the campus and the specifics for the garden. The harmonious siting of the university on the hillside, he argued, was based on three principles. First was terracing, in this case both the buildings and grounds. Second was keeping the trees cut so that, approaching the campus, there was the drama of

Contemplating this tea house at the Saiho-ji temple garden in Kyoto, Arthur came to a new understanding of the relationship between buildings and the natural world. PHOTO: MARY-ANN STOUCK

above After seeing Maekawa Kunio's newly opened concert hall, Bunka Kaikan, in Tokyo in 1961, Arthur was inspired to design long, horizontal structures in concrete. The building's gently curved eaves, suggesting Shinto shrines and Buddhist temples, showed him how modernism could also embody tradition. PHOTO: DAVID STOUCK

facing, top Arthur's Japanese language teacher, Mrs. Griffiths, poses in her former pupil's famous garden. ERICKSON FAMILY COLLECTION

facing, bottom The sculptured rice terraces of Bali. PHOTO: GLYNDWR JONES

above, top The winning design: a single structure in a series of terraces on Burnaby Mountain. SFU ARCHIVES. GORDON SHRUM FONDS, F-32-1-0-0-6

above, bottom Chancellor Gordon Shrum (*right*) with Geoffrey Massey and Arthur Erickson, winners of the Simon Fraser University design competition, July 1963. ERICKSON FAMILY COLLECTION

above Simon Fraser University, 1965: "A delicate crown on Burnaby Mountain," wrote Ron Thom. SFU ARCHIVES

left Simon Fraser University academic quadrangle. SIMON SCOTT PHOTOGRAPHY

right Arthur's long-time partner Francisco Kripacz.

below Arthur and Francisco in Beijing 1973, with Pierre and Margaret Trudeau, Moshe and Nina Safdie, and Paul and Eileen Lin. Paul Lin had arranged the trip.

above Eppich House 1 interior with moon window and canti-levered staircase. SIMON SCOTT PHOTOGRAPHY

left Eppich House 1, West Vancouver: "A waste site reclaimed." PHOTO: GEOFFREY ERICKSON

above, top University of Lethbridge at sunrise from the coulee.
SIMON SCOTT PHOTOGRAPHY

above, bottom University of Lethbridge: "A pierced wall with narrow fenestration, something akin to a fortressed medieval city."
PHOTO: MARY-ANN STOUCK

breaking into an open field "recalling the classical acropoli, which were similarly situated." Third was bringing vegetation as much as possible within the buildings themselves—on the mall in planters and in the courtyards to create a kind of hanging gardens.[10] The only formal landscape design on campus was in the quadrangle, where a long pool symbolized the Fraser River and a heather-covered hill suggested the mountainous country through which the river flowed. (Later, a terraced mound would be added to represent the top of Burnaby Mountain, similar to an earth pyramid at Monte Albán.)

When the board was apprised that the quadrangle landscaping had been included in the original design, they voted to cancel the new competition, and Arthur's design went ahead. But President McTaggart-Cowan insisted: "I am not going to feel happy until the glass is on the roof and until we have the numerous deficiencies and mistakes in the mall... cleared away fast."[11]

Problems surrounding the mall roof had proved intractable. Erickson/Massey had assumed initially that it would be constructed of lightweight aluminum and Plexiglas, but Jeffrey Lindsay, an innovative structural researcher based in Los Angeles and a follower of R. Buckminster Fuller, had designed instead a corrugated glass roof held in place by a steel rod and wooden truss system that impressed Arthur. As work was underway in the autumn of 1965, a steel nut had fallen off one of the rods. That should have been impossible, but some of the nuts reportedly were the wrong size for the rods, with tradesmen forcing them and stripping the threads. The whole roof had to be taken down and rebuilt. It was a manufacturing flaw, but the board viewed Erickson/Massey as responsible for the delay. Geoff's misgivings about glass had grown, and he recommended Plexiglas, but the idea was rejected because it would cost $1,660 more than glass—which, in a budget of $250,000 for the roof, seemed a paltry amount to the architects. With SFU's construction costs turning out to be half as expensive per student compared to other North American universities, this quibbling seemed ludicrous.

The roof was completed in the summer of 1967, and the mall continued to elicit the lion's share of praise in the media. But in the winter of 1969, an unprecedented snowfall caused 1,900 of 4,224 panes to break. The glass had tested at seventy-two pounds per square foot, and the snow load was only thirty-two pounds. What had gone wrong? The exact cause was never determined, though interested parties had their theories: that the contractor had ordered an inferior glass, either through error or because it was cheaper; that the metal bars between the glass had warped; that the panes had been wider than designed, and the bars thus set too far apart. Bruno Freschi held that the wire fusing in the glass itself was faulty. The university was rumoured to have made its own study, but as it did not sue the architects, Arthur and Geoff concluded that the initial failure to use Plexiglas was probably the best assessment of the problem. They could not overlook the irony that maximum snowload predictions for Burnaby had been provided by McTaggart-Cowan, the university's meteorologist president. When the roof was rebuilt yet again, the mullions supporting the glass panes were doubled. That darkened the mall slightly, but it was the only solution.

In the end, Erickson and Massey executed only one more building for Simon Fraser University: the classroom complex on the north slope, which was terraced in half-storey increments, connected with ramps instead of elevators. When the building was completed, the gravelled roofs were flooded—"I was romantically recalling the landscape of Bali and its flooded rice fields," Arthur later wrote[12]—but frozen drains in winter would become such an acute problem that wooden platforms were substituted instead. On January 3, 1968, McTaggart-Cowan wrote to Erickson/Massey to say that the university had "decided to broaden the basis of architectural advice we will receive for the year ahead."[13] Simultaneously, he wrote to the other winners of the architectural competition, asking them to comprise an advisory committee on future planning.[14]

By the late sixties, Simon Fraser University was famous throughout the country for political unrest: for students occupying the administration offices in the library and faculty going on strike in support of teaching assistants and colleagues who were being dismissed. The administration was censored by the Canadian

Association of University Teachers, and SFU was dubbed the Berkeley of the north. The campus seethed with unrest. The question
arose: what role did the architecture play in this upheaval?

In fact, the first protests at SFU were *about* preserving the architecture. All parties agreed that the campus needed a service station for fuel and auto repairs, but the siting of the Shell station in
a way that obscured the most spectacular view of the North Shore
mountains became a controversial issue at once. The fact that the
men's residence was going to be called Shell House raised further
suspicions regarding corporate business practices among the university's Marxist-oriented faculty, of which there were many. Arthur
quickly weighed in: to the board he wrote in September 1965 that
the oil company should not be allowed to choose its location, and
more pointedly he asserted "that Shell's architects, without preliminary direction, are not capable of producing a design that would
comply with the standards that have been set up for the university
so far."[15] He wrote directly to the chairman of the Siting and Building Committee that the proposed location and architecture of the
station would be a "visual outrage"; the design he had seen with its
false fins, for example, would make "a mockery of the design of the
university—an incompetent caricature."[16] Arthur and Geoff wanted
the station situated six feet below the road, with pumps facing north
and out of sight. The board felt such aesthetic concerns were irrelevant, but in the summer and fall of 1966, students, sometimes
joined by faculty, held a protest march and sit-ins at the construction
site, which stopped work temporarily. Eventually compromises were
made—Shell would not exhibit its large yellow trademark sign, there
would be no pennants streaming; the front would be a modest stone
wall in keeping with the colour and design of the university, and
much of the station would be obscured by plantings along the road.

The following years of demonstrations and strikes, during which
both Shrum and McTaggart-Cowan were forced to resign, were
often attributed to the architecture of the university, which provided
a central meeting place—the mall—where rallies were held and no
one could avoid being part of the events, however peripherally. But

Arthur and many others took the opposite view—that the architecture brought the members of the university community together in a shared space to solve their problems, "because there was no escaping them." Arthur liked to point out that, unlike at Berkeley in California or Sir George Williams University in Montreal, no physical damage had been done at SFU, because there were no individual buildings the students could target as the enemy's. (The separate administration building had not yet been built.) And the communal nature of the campus defused violence. The involvement of the total community, Arthur would argue, was the basis of culture. He would also say repeatedly that it was the students, not the administration, who became the conscience of the university.[17]

ALTHOUGH ARTHUR AND Geoff felt harassed by the ongoing issues at SFU, media attention and Arthur's eagerness to talk to the press brought in other commissions for them to focus on. The next major project they undertook was a downtown office building for MacMillan Bloedel, B.C.'s lumber company giant. Arthur had been approached in 1965 by J.V. Clyne, chairman of the board, to look at plans produced by Thompson, Berwick & Pratt for a new company headquarters downtown. "We like the building," Clyne told him, "and we like the price, but we don't like the outside."[18] Arthur asked Clyne to give Erickson and Massey two months to come up with a counter proposal; he was eager, as he had been with the university, to reinterpret one of the world's most important urban spaces—the office. He was remembering, perhaps, that Peter Behrens, a modernist precursor in Germany, had called upon architects to regard the office building as one of the most significant aesthetic challenges in the utilization of public or universal space in the twentieth century.[19] Most office blocks, in Arthur's view, were disasters: staff were tucked behind heavy columns and portable partitions, beneath low-hung acoustic ceilings, surrounded by the clutter of radiator shells, coat cupboards, and filing cabinets, all lit with fluorescent light. Most secretaries worked with little exposure to daylight. To reverse these oppressive conditions, Arthur liked to say that he turned his back on modern technology, specifically the high-rise structural frame clad with a light-weight curtain wall, and returned to the oldest and most traditional of building techniques—the solid, external load-bearing wall with openings cut into it. This way, the interior was free of the structural members that broke up floors and complicated the workplace planning. To further reduce confusion, he created a storage wall, leaving the offices with only desks and chairs—unobstructed areas for communication. Each office had a seven-foot-square window set deeply into the concrete wall and, because the building was narrow, no one was far from natural daylight. "Interior design," he would argue, "is as much an architectural problem as the design of a building shell. Concepts which generate the overall building logically extend to organize and articulate spaces, equipment and furnishings of intimate contact and use."[20]

The MacMillan Bloedel building consists of two concrete towers, slightly offset from each other, attached by a core containing elevators and other mechanical services. To take into account potential earthquake stress, and perhaps Japanese design, the walls are tapered from a ten-foot thickness at the base to one foot at the top and start below sidewalk level, separated from the street by a narrow moat. Reflecting on what Arthur referred to as the chaos and unintelligibility of the modern city, where there is no differentiation of movement or vista from one street to another, architecture critic Nicholas Olsberg would later argue that this building, dropped down a level and set back from the street, widens the vista from traffic and gives different routes to pedestrians moving at different paces.[21] Arthur liked to refer to it as his "Doric building, uncompromising in its simplicity."[22] In a complementary vein, *Architectural Record* described it as having an "elegant leanness."[23]

Work on the MacMillan Bloedel building went relatively smoothly. The most difficult task Arthur faced was convincing the contractors to dispense with construction joints and corner chamfers to give the concrete a smooth, sharp-edged finish. They argued that unbevelled corners would chip away, but he wanted exactly those irregularities in the concrete to contrast with the "sheer liquidity of glass" in the neat rows of windows. Arthur had begun by this time to herald concrete as his "muse," a material he believed to be as noble as limestone. He liked its earthiness and its mass and how, like the brush strokes of modern painting, it left traces of how it was made. In the MacMillan Bloedel building, he was "very conscious of bringing out the beauty of concrete," its rough, expressive strength, and he wanted its irregularities as surface patina.[24] He would frequently say to his critics that he liked a few flaws, that the imperfections of nature never worried him.

There was a grand sense of ceremony at the November 1968 opening for the city's tallest reinforced concrete building. Since then, the building has been both admired and scorned by Vancouver's citizenry. It gives variety and character to a monotonous urban landscape, but on rainy days this concrete monolith with its rows of windows seems to many to draw into itself the greyness of the northwest climate. For some, it remains a remarkable building; to others, it is too stark, a cold piece of brutalist modern architecture. It quickly acquired many nicknames: "Fort MacMillan" was one, or, more affectionately, "the waffle iron." For critics like Nicholas Olsberg, the MacMillan Bloedel building represents a particularly strong example of modernist purity—the repetition of identical units, the coarse, dull surface. Increasingly surrounded by glass towers, it soon became old-fashioned in appearance. But that, observes Olsberg, has enhanced its appeal—it has a serenity within the midst of what look like transitional and temporary buildings.[25]

ALTHOUGH THE CONSTRUCTION of the MacMillan Bloedel building went smoothly, this was not the case with a commission Arthur undertook for David and Jean Catton, with whom he had been close during his days at McGill. Twenty years later, having returned to the West Coast, the Cattons asked Arthur to design a house for them in West Vancouver on a sloping lot looking out to Howe Sound. But after initial enthusiasm for his design—a rhomboid suggested by Swiss farmhouses on mountain slopes—they became alarmed when they saw that the scale of the house was being considerably expanded and no costs on the project had been fixed. In a two-page letter, David states bluntly that he and Jean are "disappointed and frustrated" to see the latest set of drawings for a house that is now "quite beyond our means or our wishes at the present time." The Cattons wanted something that felt spacious, like the Smith house, but not large, and David set "firm limits on size and cost"—1,700 to 1,800 square feet, not exceeding a cost of $40,000. Since the project had been underway for nearly a year with little progress, he set deadlines of June 15, 1968, for finished drawings and a house to move into before the year was over. "Finally, I am disturbed about the fact that we have never received from your company any indication as to how much your fees will be. Much time and effort has been wasted up until now . . . Presumably we must make a fresh start. But, frankly, I would like to have it on a much more business-like basis than it has been up until the present."[26]

There is no record of Arthur's reply, but there is a file of unhappy correspondence between the Cattons and Geoff Massey and Garry Hanson, the project manager. In September 1969, the Cattons were still not in their new home, which was plagued with a variety of problems—a shattered skylight, movement in the building possibly related to a design flaw in the roof beams, bedroom walls needing reinforcement, a cabinetmaker refusing to finish the job, unacceptable painting. Two years later, David wrote to Geoff to explain that he was withholding final payment on his account (just $442), because he was so unhappy with the supervision of the job, rehearsing again his grievances over all the delays and errors.

Arthur was increasingly aloof from the matters of supervision and deadlines. In 1968, he hired Nick Milkovich, one of his former students, to coordinate the activities of the various trades for his clients—but particularly "to serve as 'Arthur's voice' on the job."[27] For this function, Arthur was well served by Nick, a practical and exceptionally diplomatic young man. Nonetheless, Arthur was reluctant to do more private residences; henceforth, he would be interested only in clients of means who could afford additional costs and delays. He told a reporter for *Maclean's* in 1970 that the

Catton house would probably be his last, because private residences involved as much work as a major building but earned the company much less. Houses were time consuming; to know what was needed and get all the details straight, he added, "you practically have to marry the wife of the family you're designing for."[28]

But he still enjoyed the challenge of a difficult site, such as the Craig house fifty feet above Okanagan Lake, or of a commission in a different geographical region. Dick and Laurette Hilborn, living in the Cambridge area of southern Ontario, were excited by the modern architecture they had seen at Expo in Montreal. They met with Arthur in 1969, showed him their lot sloping down to the Grand River, and were eager to proceed, but no plans materialized. In 1970, when they heard he would be passing through Toronto airport, they arranged to meet him there, hoping he would have a design ready for them to discuss. Instead, like Frank Lloyd Wright, Arthur quickly picked up an envelope and began sketching out an idea for the house.[29] He had to let it germinate for an indefinite period before setting it on paper, he explained. That rough sketch, however, would result in one of his finest private homes—a terraced structure in four sections, dropping down a slope between vertical walls of brick that held beams and sod roofs in place; the rest was glass. The owners called it "The Ramparts," and Arthur observed that the Hilborn home played curiously with time. Brick, the traditional building material of Ontario, made the house, even when new, seem long established, perhaps recently excavated but sinking back into the earth. Part of that effect was achieved by the sod roofing, with its thick mats of ornamental grasses and a section discreetly portioned off for growing vegetables. The Hilborns were charmed by Arthur's personal interest in specific details—his concern, for example, that they find in Mexico a large wooden door for the house. He supplied an Italian catalogue from the Museum of Modern Furniture to help them make decisions on furnishings and had Francisco take Laurette shopping in New York for linens and china.

Arthur, in fact, remained always the courteous gentleman in his relations with clients. He listened with sympathy to their cries of distress and conveyed a sense that he was as much a victim of the vagaries of contractors, labourers' wages, and the price of goods as they were. He reassured his clients that what they had paid for was a work of art, pointing out to the Cattons, for example, that their home of exposed surfaces, completely covered in three-inch-wide cedar boards, read like a piece of sculpture carved from a single block of wood. They were eventually convinced, and the friendship survived. But Arthur insisted that a house was the most complicated of buildings to design. As he said many times: "If you can design a house, you can design anything. It's a lesson book."[30]

Arthur was similarly successful in his relations with those who worked for him. John Keith-King, employed by Erickson/Massey in the late 1960s, has described the way Arthur generated excitement at the office by making people feel they were doing something that not only solved a current problem but would change lives and be part of architectural history. Arthur would look over their work and make suggestions; the office culture was based on a shared belief that every design could be improved. As Jim Strasman, another young employee, later observed, the improvements were invariably a matter of simplification. Everyone worked hard to eliminate detail, aware at the same time that such austere designs could scare away clients.[31] Employees would willingly work late into the evening, because much happened then. Famous people Arthur had met might walk into the office—Yousuf Karsh, Harry Belafonte. Arthur's mother might turn up with his laundry.

Another impressionable young employee was Simon Scott, a British-trained architect who immigrated to Canada in 1965 and was hired in 1968 to work on drawings and models. With his masterful photography and slide presentations, he soon became the principal photographer of Arthur's work. Scott observed at close hand the pains Arthur took to present his buildings as works of art. Arthur needed photographs of the Craig house in Kelowna but was disappointed by the owners' furnishings. Lois Milsom, however, had exquisite taste, and so while she and her husband were away, Arthur and Simon rented a U-Haul truck, filled it with the Milsoms' furniture, and drove to Kelowna for the photo shoot. It was 2 AM when they returned to the city. The Milsoms had returned in the meantime and assumed they had been robbed; they were even more alarmed when they heard people entering their house in the middle of the night. But once Lois recognized Arthur's voice, it became another story to tell about their remarkable friendship.

Yet, for all his charm, Arthur kept what Keith-King describes as an "intelligent distance" from his employees. He exhibited "a dominating but quiet personality, an articulate self-consciousness that bore no trace of vanity."[32] He gave great parties for his staff, and Keith-King remembered one at Wreck Beach near UBC where Arthur arrived first and had everything prepared. Their employer was very affable, but once the party got underway he left. Arthur had a sense of theatre about everything he did. His interests were always aesthetic, seldom practical. It was said, for example, that he never knew the current cost of two-by-four lumber but could quote the price per foot of Thai silk.

Yet, for all his vagueness, Arthur was centred; he knew exactly what he wanted and didn't want, knew the kind of people whose friendship he wanted to cultivate. He often had Sunday dinner at the home of John and Nerina Bene, who lived on Vancouver's afflu- ent Southwest Marine Drive. The Benes were Europeans: John, Hungarian-born and the chair of Weldwood Lumber; Nerina, from Florence, a potter, a painter, and a good friend of Arthur's mother. The ambience of the home comprised elegant furnishings—grey Brazilian suede sofas, a collection of Japanese pottery—food pre- pared simply by a Mennonite cook to emphasize the flavour of each item, and walks along the trails in Southlands. But it was also an ambience coloured by ritual. When guests arrived, Nerina would greet them in a mid-calf-length dress of raw silk made for her by a Madame Wiener, and John would pour them a glass of Campari. The air would be scented by Nerina's favourite perfume, Indiscret by Lucien Lelong. Arthur occasionally brought Francisco, who was made welcome. Most of the guests Arthur encountered here were friends from Vancouver's small community of artists: musicians Harry and Frances Adaskin; composer Barbara Pentland and her husband, John Huberman; Gordon and Marion Smith; Abraham Rogatnick and Alvin Balkind. According to Melanie Friesen, then a UBC student who often spent weekends at the Benes, dinners were "quiet, intelligent, and good-humoured—not gossipy." Occasionally the Masseys were invited, because Nerina and Ruth painted together and critiqued each other's work.[33]

THE REPUTATION OF Erickson and Massey had begun to spread. In 1967, they started work on a summer home for W.C. Lam in Cotuit, Massachusetts, and, with Jeffrey Lindsay, designed offices for the Chappellet Winery in Napa Valley, California. At home, they built a Sikh temple for the Khalsa Diwan Society on Ross Street, a project that required Arthur, for the first time, to imagine a building for worshippers from a culture far removed from what was then the Canadian mainstream. His vision for the temple was a white lily rising from a pond, the latter to be suggested by a moat surrounding the building.[34] To meet its traditional requirements, the temple had to be simple, symmetrical, and contained. A high wall covered in marble tiles was a straightforward requisite, but how to create the roof was the challenge. Arthur modified the plan he had used for the Expo 67 pavilion, stacking a series of diminishing rectangular prisms on three levels, each shifting 45 degrees on its axis. He was amazed to discover that this was typical of roof construction in northern India, where available timber was short in length and could only span corners. The temple was crowned with a delicate metal dome and, to enhance its privacy, surrounded by a berm. Avtar Gosal, who negotiated for the Sikhs, felt Arthur loved their community and that mutual respect resulted in one of the smoothest business transactions Arthur was ever engaged in.

But the project that preoccupied Erickson and Massey throughout the late sixties took them to the other side of the world. Before Expo 67 closed, they won the competition to design the Canadian pavilion for Expo 70 in Osaka, Japan. With the Tokyo trade fair of 1965, this made their third exposition. In a talk, Arthur observed that idealists give world fairs noble-sounding themes like "Man and His World" (Montreal) and "Progress and Harmony for Mankind"

(Osaka), but he wondered if extravagance and foolish waste weren't the real point, reminding his listeners that fairs had always been rather crude displays of prowess and excess—the biggest squash, the fattest lady. Festivals from ancient times expressed the bizarre and released the stops of civilization, even if just for a moment, but they also served the deep-seated need for communal celebration and stretched the imagination. "Expositions," he counselled, "are the catharses that let us burst forth in unrestrained folly and learn of the impracticality of our innermost dreams." Expositions, he said, were one of the most complete and engrossing forms of universal communications.[35]

Arthur and Geoff made separate trips to Osaka in August 1967 to meet the fair organizers and tour the suburban site. Back in Vancouver, they were deluged with offers from Japanese firms to work with them as co-architects. They chose Nikken Sekkei for its highly regarded estimating department. Tange Kenzo, now regarded as Japan's foremost architect, was in charge of the Osaka fair, and he invited Arthur to a cocktail party that included Marcel Breuer and the American landscape architect Lawrence Halprin. In a thank you letter, Arthur wrote that he felt humbled to be under the great man's guidance. This major venture in Japan had a promising start.

It also promised major challenges. First, there was the problem of constructing a building in a foreign country. Second, because this was a Canadian commission, one had to work with numerous government functionaries. But the biggest challenge for Arthur was the architectural one: how to build a pavilion that would represent a nation with an identity as ill defined as Canada's. The log cabin at the Tokyo trade fair in 1965 had depicted the country's largeness and rawness. But this time he wanted something more sophisticated. With his team, he struggled to pin down ideas. "We lived, ate and slept Osaka for months," recalled Bruno Freschi. "We were striving for an invisible something that would make people feel they had experienced something of our country. We all worked on it, but it was Arthur finally who settled on the appropriate symbols."[36]

To convey the immensity and emptiness of Canada, he proposed a pavilion sheathed in a mirrored surface, whose pyramidal walls, sloped at 45 degrees, would stand like mountains of glacial ice reflecting the sky. By reflecting its surroundings, the building itself would seem to disappear, conveying Canada's almost invisible presence on the world stage but especially its responsiveness to the world at large. The mirroring would be carefully detailed so that no edge was visible, allowing the building to merge with the white skies of summer in Japan. As Bruno Freschi later put it, the pavilion was an invisible building—"an incredible combination of nothing and something: magic."[37]

The building was distinctively Western with its emphasis on the sky, but its simultaneous reach towards infinity—like a tree's branches and roots—reflected something pervasive in Japanese aesthetics. The constant change in the building's reflected sky also referenced the profound feeling of the Japanese for impermanence, mutability. This theme was to be expanded within the pavilion, where five giant umbrellas, patterned by Gordon Smith and engineered by Jeffrey Lindsay, would perpetually rotate, endlessly rearranging themselves in kaleidoscopic colour.

In late summer 1968, Arthur submitted the design to Patrick Reid, commissioner general of the Canadian Government Pavilion. In October, Reid sent the firm a report from the National Research Council in Ottawa, warning of dire results if the plan for a mirrored surface was pursued. One of the effects, it stated, would be to radiate the surrounding vegetation: "The result of this solar bombardment will be the total destruction of plant life in a very short period." But more disastrous for the fairgoers would be temperatures of 300 degrees Fahrenheit—it would be impossible to enter the pavilion. Passing crowds would experience extreme discomfort and would be forced to look away.[38] Reid had a reputation as an anxious civil servant fretting over details, a man who was difficult to work with: "Everyone will have ulcers with him around, including himself," Arthur's coordinator wrote to Geoff Massey.[39] It was nearly a year before Arthur responded to the NRC report, dismissing out of hand its concerns about heat and blinding reflections: "You must be aware that mirror-coated glass is being used extensively now in North America for the outside sheathing of buildings, and that these present no less a reflection problem in a city than in our pavilion. People are always looking into the reflection of the sun in glass walls, off water surfaces, and simply have to turn away from it." As for people being fried at the entrance, he said, they should not be allowed to line up in that area during hot, sunny periods. It would be a matter of crowd control.[40]

In December 1969, Arthur was insistent that everything was going well: the spinners were on schedule, and the furniture for the pavilion was in the last stages of production. But his coordinator, Vagn Houlbjerg, was less confident about meeting the deadlines for the mid-March opening. In February, Houlbjerg wrote to Arthur that heavy rains had revealed numerous leaks in the exhibit area of the pavilion, possibly caused by an autumn earthquake, and the weeping grasses had not been seeded early enough, the landscapers delayed by the bad weather. Roy Kiyooka, working on site, was having trouble finishing his sculpture. Further, money was running low, and Houlbjerg didn't know how the workers were going to be paid. Arthur's replies made only faint reference to these problems; instead, he described the silver service and all-white chinaware selected for the pavilion's dining facility, and noted his concern to find a blue flower to replace pansies later in the season. Arthur asked Houlbjerg to give attention on his behalf to special guests arriving before the opening—the Duchess Pini di San Miniato and her party and the Canadian ambassador to Pakistan and his wife. The preceding fall, he had asked Houlbjerg to show Blackie Lee's mother around the pavilion ("She is rather ancient, but peppy, an old friend of mine") and to give her a tour of Osaka as well.[41]

The demands on Arthur from all sides often led to confusion and sometimes comic episodes. Racing down to Seattle to catch a plane for Osaka, Arthur was late, as usual, when his badly used car stopped and he could not get it started again. In an adjacent field was a small plane being used by a farmer to dust his crops. Desperate, Arthur asked the farmer to fly him to Seattle airport. The farmer said no at first, since it was illegal to enter airport space unscheduled, but Arthur could charm a bird out of a tree, and the farmer finally conceded. Arthur caught his plane to Japan. A few weeks later, back in Vancouver, he could not figure out what had happened to his car. He searched everywhere—streets near his office, back lanes. Then one of his friends suggested the road to Seattle. Sure enough, there it was, still parked on the edge of the farmer's field.[42]

Arthur made several trips to Osaka, but he and Geoff, with other commissions at home, depended on Houlbjerg and his team to keep the fair project on schedule. Just before the opening, Arthur flew to Japan with Jeffrey Lindsay and Gordon Smith to see that everything was in place. Frank Mayrs, the Canadian government's creative director for international exhibitions and a skilled photographer, was on the trip as well, and Arthur was anxious that a photographic record of this ephemeral project be made. One evening there was an alarming incident. The group went out to the exposition site and climbed up to the emperor's special box to see what the pavilion would look like from that perspective. Relaxing, they passed around a joint of marijuana, but when Arthur inhaled he had an immediate and violent reaction. He could not breathe and quickly passed out. His frightened friends got him down the difficult passageway and took him to a medical centre, where it did not appear he would live. Japanese laws were very strict regarding drugs, and Arthur had to be taken to a hospital at some distance, where he was put on a respirator. While his friends paced the waiting room, he gradually recovered. It was the only time in his life that Arthur used a drug.[43]

He was well again for opening day, and to his great delight the Emperor of Japan visited the Canadian pavilion. Shortly afterwards, his mother and Nerina Bene were in Osaka on a Vancouver Arts Council tour. When Mrs. Bene saw Arthur's pavilion, she clasped her friend and cried, "Oh, Myrtle, he *is* a genius." This was the first world's fair held in Japan, and there was much for Canadian visitors to see—a piece of rock brought from the moon in 1967, the first IMAX film, and a bizarre, gigantic Japanese structure that would eventually be known as the Tower of the Sun.

But in early June, a series of crises arose. On June 9, Patrick Reid telegrammed Erickson/Massey asking for immediate advice on a glare problem off the mirrored face of the pavilion—it was blinding those who passed by and those who worked at the adjacent pavilions.[44] Was there something that could be applied? Arthur's first reply was to recommend that the other pavilions put up shielding screens, because to apply an opaque coating would be "an aesthetic disaster for the Canadian pavilion." In a series of telexes fired back and forth, there was discussion of a transparent purple shadow dye to cover the building, as recommended by Jeffrey Lindsay, but testing suggested the dye might create heat buildup that would cause the mirrors to break. The Japanese co-architects at Nikken were insistent that a semi-opaque vinyl paint be applied. Another suggestion was that coarse-meshed cargo net be hung from the top until late July. On July 5, Erickson/Massey's office was informed that the north flank had been partially painted with off-white enamelled epoxy resin that included a reflection-proof material. The message also reported that some mirrors had been falling off and that reglueing was a nightmare. Soon, Reid reported the threat of lawsuits from neighbouring pavilions, who were suffering sharp loss in profits because of the intense glare.

A heat crisis came next. On July 7, Reid sent this angry telegram:

(1) The problem is immediate. There is boiling sun today and tour just completed at 14.00 by Canadian group around perimeter indicates conditions to be intolerable on two flanks. Have accordingly given instructions for opaque coating to be painted over entire surface of north flank asap. (2) Have mercifully had only one mirror fly off during stormy weather just concluded. (3) Find it indefensible that many visits of principals at E&M were apparently necessary during pre Expo period, but [they] are insensitive to assist on site at time of client's quite desperate need.

Arthur's response appears to have taken more than a week, because he asks on July 15 for details about the coating material so he can test it in Vancouver. Conditions at the neighbouring pavilions—Quebec, China, Sanyo—were growing worse, and heat buildup for the

Philippines, Uganda, and Sierra Leone pavilions was now intolerable. The Canadian pavilion could barely keep cool enough to operate its cafeteria. Before Arthur could run his experiments, Reid reported on July 17 that the whole of the north flank of the pavilion had now been coated with a greyish opaque paint and that the rest of the walls would likely have to be treated in the same way. On July 19, Reid wrote that the weeping love grass used in the landscaping had become infested with rats and would have to be cut. Arthur's only concern in his replies was that the pavilion be photographed extensively, including aerial shots, because he planned to enter it for a Massey Medal.

Eventually, there would be a Massey Medal for the Osaka pavilion, but more important for Arthur was that, from seventy-seven entries, it won the Architectural Institute of Japan Award for the best pavilion at the fair. Arthur and Geoff were apprised of this triumph on August 20, but six days later received notification from Patrick Reid that the award was given for "exhibit integration as well as architecture per se" and that the AIJ had been under the mistaken impression that Erickson and Massey were personally responsible for the total design and integration of the pavilion's exhibits. Accordingly, Reid, the commissioner general, would accept any awards on behalf of the whole nation. When Arthur queried this claim with the AIJ, he received word from Japan that the prize was for the architects, not the administrators. He telegrammed Reid on August 31: "Arrive Osaka Thursday to receive award. Will phone on arrival," and to George Tsujino: "Arriving Wed or Thurs for award. Respectfully request attendance of Nikken representative at Ceremony."[45]

Arthur regarded the Osaka pavilion as one of the most beautiful buildings he had ever created. Its opalescent beauty was all the more precious because it was probably not destined to last. He hoped that the Japanese government would arrange for its preservation, since the grounds were to become the Expo Commemoration Park, with Tange's Festival Hall roof, Okamoto Taro's garish Tower of the Sun, and the National Museum of Art building already identified as permanent structures. But like the other undesignated structures, the Canadian pavilion was demolished after the fair closed in

September. All that remained, as with Mies van der Rohe's elegant German pavilion for the 1929 International Exposition in Barcelona, were photographs and memories.

When designer Frank Mayrs was interviewed by Edith Iglauer, his reflections on Arthur's participation in three exhibitions were both critical and generous, anticipating the responses of many future clients. "You set limits for Erickson," he said,

> and his proposal is always more than you anticipated. You want to do it, and you immediately run into the problem of cost. He treats his buildings like sculpture and tries to preserve the architectural spaces he creates, even to leaving them empty, when our job demands that the space be booked up, in the traditional exhibit manner. Our pavilion at Osaka was fantastic but we worried about what effect the reflection of the sun would have on people's eyes, on adjoining buildings, and on the inside temperature. "You never get direct summer sun in Japan," Arthur said, but by midsummer the sun was coming straight down, and some buildings around us had to reroute their queue lines ... When you deal with Arthur, you have to accept heartaches and worries, but the essential thing that must *never* be lost sight of is that the building works.[46]

14

University
of Lethbridge

THE UNIVERSITY OF LETHBRIDGE first took shape
in the imagination of Dr. Evangelos Christou, whose passionate
feeling for the landscape of southern Alberta inspired Arthur, in
turn, to design one of his most powerful buildings. Van Christou
was born into a small community of Greek immigrants who had fled
the wars and ethnic tensions of the Balkans for the coast of Oregon.
But they found the grey skies and cool temperatures of the Pacific
coast inhospitable, and when a scout described a dry, sunny climate
in the southernmost region of Alberta, several families relocated in
1900 and made Lethbridge their home. As a successful orthodon-
tist and patron of the arts, Van Christou embraced his heritage and
the destiny of the region by taking a leading role in public affairs,
specifically as chair of the education committee of the Lethbridge
Chamber of Commerce.

Until 1957, the only post-secondary institution in the province
was the University of Alberta in Edmonton. That changed when
Lethbridge Community College, Canada's first publicly funded
junior college, was opened to provide advanced technical skills
training and first-year university courses for students in southern
Alberta. From the outset, the problem for the downtown college
was the value of its university credits, because it lacked an adequate
library. Van Christou started a campaign to change this. Soon, Kate

Andrews, chair of the college governing body, persuaded Dr. Christou to join her in meeting with Premier Manning to discuss the idea of a combined college and university. Christou, however, believed that Lethbridge needed a separate university.[1] He was committed to the Greek ideal of a liberal education in the arts and sciences, which he saw as the most important foundation for democracy.

There was strong resistance at first, but Christou commissioned a demographic survey that demonstrated the area's growing need for a university. A group of like-minded citizens met frequently at his home to discuss strategies. By 1966, the University of Calgary had been opened, but the government was convinced by Christou's efforts, and so that same year a third university for Alberta was approved. Christou was appointed to the founding board of governors.

The university's archive reveals that Dr. Christou wasted no time in implementing his vision. Arthur was in Paris in January 1967 when he received a telegram from Garry Hanson advising him to contact Christou immediately. Christou was planning to show a CBC film on Simon Fraser University to his board of governors on January 23, and he hoped Arthur might join them in person to discuss the possibilities of designing a university for Lethbridge.[2] Arthur did stop on his way home for the film presentation, and on January 24 made an "exhilarating morning flight over the city," during which a news reporter asked him where the university should be located. Arthur was said to have nonchalantly offered, "'There,' pointing vaguely downward." The reporter claimed that the famed architect had pointed to the coulee, which ignited a dispute already simmering between merchants who wanted the university downtown and a much smaller group who wanted the campus on a "virgin site" on the coulee, removed from commerce and with unlimited room for expansion. Opponents pointed out the expense that would be involved in building a highway across the coulee to the west side of the river.[3] Arthur wrote to Van Christou apologizing for "making judgments too quickly... particularly with the press." Nonetheless, he felt the cross-coulee site should be explored "as having legitimate potential." Seeing the landscape and listening to Christou and his wife, Helen, tell stories of their parents' lives in this arid, sunny part of the world inspired Arthur to embrace the project wholeheartedly.

The going would not be easy. A letter from Van Christou to Arthur dated February 20 made clear that the opponents of the coulee location were not going to give in without a fight. The board of governors had voted to secure the services of a Toronto group, the UPACE (a consortium of university planners, architects, and consulting engineers), to advise them on their next move. Christou reassured Arthur that this was a necessary move to deal with "certain local political undercurrents," and he hoped the board would have a free hand to select their own architectural firm once the smoke cleared.

In late April, Van Christou, with the acting university president and two board members, attended a conference on university planning and building at the University of Illinois campus in Urbana. Arthur was not present, but Geoff Massey and Ron Bain were there to explain the concept of the integrated campus. This was the opposite of what the UPACE had created at York University, a campus composed of separate, competing colleges spread out on a windy expanse in north Toronto. In the U.S., the Students for a Democratic Society movement was disrupting campus life with protest marches and building occupations, and the Erickson campus design, where all the spaces were for students, was proving capable of meeting that challenge in a positive way. Van Christou and his team came back convinced that Erickson/Massey was the firm they wanted to plan and design their new university.

After the Urbana meeting, Van Christou urged Arthur to revisit Lethbridge to consider the competing locations and put together a report that could be voted on by the board. Arthur made several visits to assess the public mood, the physical attributes of the sites, and the sociological context in which the future institution would function. He took pains to talk with college students, faculty, administrators, and governors, searching for unifying concepts that could be given physical embodiment in the new campus buildings. He continued to believe that a university should provide a place for exchange between the academic community and the public at large, but his meetings with the public did not go smoothly. On one occasion, he was besieged at his hotel by a delegation determined to keep the university downtown. The west coulee location, they claimed, was hazardous because it had been destabilized by mining tunnels and would crumble; to build a highway across the coulee would cost more than the city could afford and would limit what could be spent on the university itself. Arthur listened politely to their views, but the mood was tense. On that same visit, he was walking alone one evening in the coulee when a shot rang out; whether it was an accidental bullet fired by an overprotective farmer or a deliberate scare could not be determined.

In a letter Arthur had written to his family from Spain in August 1951, he had described an ideal sun-drenched landscape in Andalusia where he would like to build a house in which to spend the rest of his life. The house would be on the edge of a cactus-covered cliff from which he could look out over the wheat fields and the threshing of grain—chaff thrown into the air like yellow smoke. In the evening, the setting sun would blacken the faces of the distant hills. This idealized scene came to mind as Arthur explored the coulee terrain of Lethbridge, looking for the perfect site.

Lethbridge also reconnected him to his childhood experience of landscape when travelling in the summers with his family to visit relatives in Winnipeg; he was still in awe of the prairie's vastness and the sensuous spareness of a land where nothing was hidden by foliage. "A single tree becomes a monument in such a landscape; a house, a fortress; fences and roads and the ploughlines form an overlying all-pervasive geometry. Human habitation on a land of such scale and simplicity seems paltry... Only the looming clusters of blind-faced grain elevators somehow possess a nobility to match the landscape." The one built exception to this in Lethbridge was the "light tracery" of a high-level railway bridge spanning the Oldman River for a mile. Overwhelmed by the beauty of the coulee's undulations as they dipped in long ravines down to the river, Arthur concluded that his university would sit just below the tableland in an uncompromising straight line that, like the bridge, would both define the flatness of the land and reveal its rich contours.[4]

Over pleasant dinners with the Christous and their friends, Arthur discussed the site and his ideas for the university. Their enthusiasm was encouraging, but he knew the support of well-placed friends was no guarantee that he would win the contract. His wartime comrade George Swinton had backed Arthur's design for the new Winnipeg Art Gallery, in part meant to house the donation of George's collection of Inuit art, but the commission had gone to another company.

It was nearly eight months before Geoff Massey wrote to the university president, W.A.S. (Sam) Smith, to confirm the company's continued interest in the commission and to report that the west Lethbridge coulee, in Erickson and Massey's opinion, was superior in almost every aspect to the existing college location. Geoff's argument stressed the importance of "seizing upon a site which is a challenge to the imagination of all concerned." As tactfully as possible, he suggested that a spectacular setting like the coulee might help to attract faculty and students to a small city that had no long-standing tradition in higher education. The growth of the university would, in turn, have positive benefits for the whole community.[5] Fortunately, the attitude in Lethbridge to Erickson and Massey had altered visibly after their spectacular success at Expo 67. Many Albertans had attended the fair and become aware of the high profile these architects had achieved nationally. In May 1968, Erickson and Massey received a letter from President Smith commissioning them to develop a master plan for the campus at a fee of $75,000 and urging them to proceed "immediately."[6]

The first stage was to gather data on the physical site—especially important given claims that the coulee was geologically unstable. Soil types and stratifications, ground water and drainage patterns, and flood levels of the Oldman River, old mining faults and potential earthquake zones: these were the initial matters to investigate. But also the climatic factors needed to be assessed: the direction and velocity of the wind, the forms of precipitation, and the amount, duration, and angles of the sun. The contours of the land had to be mapped, and the best vistas and land formations had to be selected. No significant obstacles were identified as disqualifying the west coulee location, and on November 29, 1968, Sam Smith wrote to say that the board of governors had chosen Erickson/Massey as the university's architects and that they should proceed with planning for Phase 1A. Smith reminded them of "the urgency of rapid progress." In an announcement to the public, Smith noted that Erickson and Massey had "demonstrated wide experience with the problems of higher education, and a real sense of unique and beautiful design with an awareness of the limit of dollars."[7] Without realizing it, perhaps, Smith was identifying two issues that would curse the project for nearly three years to follow—timetable and budget.

Like Simon Fraser University, Lethbridge was under the pressure of baby-boom demographics. Another "instant university" was needed, and the president and board were setting their sights on a new campus for September 1970. In 1969, Arthur was occupied with more projects than he had ever handled before, including a major addition to the Bank of Canada in Ottawa, a biological sciences building for the University of Victoria, the Canadian pavilion for Expo 70 in Osaka, and a design for Village Lake Louise, a major development that in the end did not go forward. His first design for Lethbridge bore a strong resemblance to the academic quadrangle at SFU—a long building raised on a series of piers with fins at the windows and rows of steps approaching and receding from the main platform. The office team worked with this design for several months, but Arthur grew unsatisfied; vertically the design was too busy and would distract from, rather than enhance, the setting. On Christmas holidays in Bora Bora with Francisco, he suddenly wired Ron Bain, the project manager, to say columns would not look right in a coulee; it should be "a pierced wall" instead.[8] From that idea, the building took its destined shape, with its great horizontal beam structure and narrow fenestration something akin to a fortressed medieval city.

But much time had been lost. Arthur shifted some blame for delays to the university, where a budget cut necessitated new drawings. The biggest change involved building material. Originally, the university was to have been constructed out of a light, earth-coloured brick from Medicine Hat. In his development plan, Arthur had written: "Buildings must grow out of the ground, clustered with other buildings or trees, but never sit blatantly on top of the ground. Forms must be simple and geometrically concise, as elaborate forms and fussy detail show weakness... Just as the prairie landscape has been reduced to essentials, so must its buildings be elemental, of the earth." It was hard to relinquish brick, but concrete being much cheaper, Arthur now had little choice. The reduced budget also meant sacrificing underground parking for two thousand cars. Especially painful to Arthur, it meant abandoning the construction of a waterfall and a series of reflecting pools in the coulee, with future buildings planned to extend down to the warmer microclimate of the Oldman River.

But in spite of these compromises, time and money, the curse of every architect and client, still worked their poison. Plans for a September 1970 opening had long been abandoned, with Arthur citing revision and the desire for excellence as the cause for delays, but the chair of the board of governors wrote to Arthur on May 14, 1970, to express his alarm that a 1971 opening might also not be possible. In a tone both grievous and angry, he wrote: "It is impossible for me to stress too strongly how important I believe it is to stop engaging in vague promises, and to produce what is expected... we have now reached a point where decisive action must be taken to ensure occupancy, even if compromise in excellence is necessary."[9] In a reply assuring the chair that he understood the seriousness of the situation, Arthur reminded him that the "drastic" budgetary revisions of 1969 had put considerable pressure on his office. At the same time, he asserted firmly that "since the schedule is so tight there seems little chance of advancing it appreciably."[10] And indeed that was the case. Although some classes were held in unpainted rooms that had been roughed in by fall 1971, the university held its official opening in September 1972.

Like Simon Fraser, the University of Lethbridge attracted enormous interest. Seen from a distance, it was the most striking of Arthur's buildings to date and was repeatedly compared to a ship riding the waves. A reporter for *Time* magazine described it as "a tour de force of form, scale, and siting," observing that from across the river it appeared to nestle discreetly below the horizon, but up close it became a massive piece of minimalist sculpture.[11] The entrance suggested to one critic "a gateway like the portal to a medieval city," and the roof of the heating plant, with its starkly sculptural heating stacks and surrounding steps, assumed for another "the profound dignity of an ancient religious enclosure."[12] Built of concrete beams, it also made a contemporary reference to Tange's Kurashiki city hall. The light colour of the local materials used in the concrete mix gave the building a warmer colouration than the grey concrete of Simon Fraser University.

The building's fame over time was greatly enhanced by the photographs of Simon Scott. His images reference the sea: from ground level, one looks up to what appears to be the hull of an ocean liner; from the other side of the coulee, one sees the university breasting the undulating surfaces of the land. But from down in the coulee comes the most powerful image of all—the horizontal span of the building between a sea of grasses in the foreground and a high prairie sky.

Arthur more than once called the University of Lethbridge his supreme achievement. In it he created a single nine-storey building, 912 feet long, in which there was no spatial differentiation between the humanities and the sciences and where faculty offices and student residence rooms were the same size. Except for areas with specific functions, such as laboratories and administration offices, spaces could be assigned across faculties. More so than at Simon Fraser, instruction took place in small seminar rooms, with only major lectures held in the theatres. Because of severe weather conditions on the prairie, the space where the occupants could interact was a concourse running the length of the building—a "main street" with access to library, cafeteria, and student centre furnished with upholstered lounges in tiers. In his description of intent, Arthur had referred again to the universal space of Cairo's Al-Azhar University mosque, "where students, merchants, and beggars sat or lay on the carpeted floors, listening, praying, reading, or just sleeping."[13] In the same way, the main concourse was designed for both teaching—an "educational marketplace"—and relaxation.

With riots at the University of California in Berkeley and Sir George Williams University in Montreal, then killings at Kent State University, student unrest had reached a crisis level in North America. Destruction to university property was a costly part of its manifestation, and Arthur had forestalled this possibility by placing student residences in the same building. This, he believed, would give students a sense of proprietorship: "With learning taking place in their own domestic territory," he wrote, "the university was theirs."[14] The first students in the building seem to have grasped something of this experiment. An early editorial in the student newspaper began by calling the University of Lethbridge "the ultimate in ivory towers, the final white room," but went on to propose that life could be pumped into the building "without dynamite and fire... Probably the outstanding characteristic of Erickson's architecture is its admittance of human potential and possibility, its need for fulfilment. The choice is ours."[15]

While the University of Lethbridge was still under construction, an article about Arthur's work appeared in an Italian journal, *Lotus*.[16] The author was Giuseppe Mazzariol, a Venetian architectural critic and a close friend of Abraham Rogatnick. Mazzariol's overarching idea was that Erickson's work was a dialogue between history and utopia; that with inspiration from the past, his buildings interpreted the present (the reality of rocks, trees, folds in the land, other buildings, the social situation) to give expression to the human imagination—its dreams, conscience, love of beauty. The university as a medieval city-structure offered a glimpse of utopia, making manifest a timeless, ideal human community where all members share equally in remaking the world. For Mazzariol, the distillation of this enterprise in one communal building took the dream of utopia further than did any of Arthur's other creations. It also exemplified Arthur's belief that "nothing has an existence of its own; nothing is seen in isolation but is modified by, and in turn

modifies, its surroundings." The coulee and the building were inseparable. This was knowledge, Arthur observed, that the Greeks had
used eloquently.[17]

But Lethbridge was also Arthur's greatest disappointment. The
master plan was for construction in two initial phases, as dictated
by enrolments and funding. The second phase would be a parallel building offset so that it would largely extend beyond the first
one—the effect likely to suggest a train running through the coulees.
But despite the public praise, official dissatisfaction with Erickson/
Massey had been brewing—as it had at SFU. The delays in completing Phase 1 and the cost overruns made administration and government reluctant to give Arthur a contract for Phase 2. Moreover,
they were already suing the architects for potential damage repair:
because of shifts in the land, some of the pre-cast concrete beams
were close to slipping off supporting ledges. (Erickson/Massey won
this legal battle by citing the engineer's report, the best information
possible at the time.) Complicating matters was a letter from Arthur
to the university president to say that the firm of Erickson/Massey
was dissolving, that Geoff would have a separate business, and that
he, Arthur, would be the one to carry on with the work at the University of Lethbridge.[18] This announcement especially concerned
the university because it was Geoff Massey to whom they had
turned with some confidence for business matters. Phase 2 went on
hold, but when the university expanded, it did so, to Van Christou's
dismay, without Arthur Erickson. The new buildings climbed up to
the top of the coulee, asserting their presence and distracting the
eye from the dramatic shapes of the landscape. Arthur was sickened
by what transpired.

Arthur's experience of universities made him question their
methods of teaching and especially their modes of governance. He
believed that the convergence of intellectuals in a university had
a singular capacity to advance knowledge and prepare students to
be creative citizens, but he recognized, at the same time, that such
an environment sharpened human weaknesses—that creativity in
universities was frequently stifled by ambition, jealousy, and, most

dangerous of all, the lust for power. He believed this lay at the root of his struggle with university bureaucracies.

In public addresses, he began making some radical proposals. Students, he believed, were the university's greatest resource. Professors should abandon their pedantic avocation, he argued, and regard students as a workforce; students shouldn't simply sit and listen but should work on real projects and thereby become responsibly involved in their field of knowledge. Both rank and tenure should be abolished, Arthur asserted, with security established instead through membership in international associations. Also, "faculty should have only a three-year maximum tour of duty in any one place." Administration would be a matter of duty rather than the consolidation of power. And students should be on the move, with some part of their training taking place in another part of the world. All these changes, he argued, would produce a new kind of mind—one more objective, less provincial, less national: "We can no longer... risk the small point of view."[19]

The University of Lethbridge, focussing inwardly, did not escape from the ills Arthur envisioned, and in this light, one architectural critic's description of University Hall eclipsed by unsympathetic expansion seems resonant. Georges Teyssot writes: "Today the massive building sits like a beached vessel run aground... it stands like a megalith commemorating an ideal of sociability that the changing society around it made impossible to realize."[20] Only from a distance, across the coulee, or in early photographs, does the university still speak to that earlier promise.

Part III

Master
Builder

15

Robson
Square

IN *TIME* MAGAZINE, February 1972, Geoffrey
James wrote, "Arthur Erickson has been showered with more acclaim
and awards than any other Canadian architect before him." With
a picture of Arthur on the cover, this brightly illustrated article put
Arthur front and centre in the national public eye.[1] In addition to
numerous professional prizes and an honorary degree, Arthur had
recently won two top awards for public service in Canada—the
$15,000 Molson Prize and the $50,000 Royal Bank Award—heady
sums in 1972, the equivalent of five years' wages for the average
worker.[2] But what James, both author and photographer, found
remarkable was that Arthur was enjoying a high degree of public recognition in a profession that increasingly favoured the anonymity of
group effort. "In an age of team design," he wrote, Arthur Erickson
at age forty-seven "epitomizes the idea of the individual creator, the
architect as superstar"—a phrase that would later be contracted by
the media to "starchitect."

With celebrity his theme, James tried to bring the individual out
from the shadows of myth, while preserving the mystique of uniqueness. Erickson, he wrote, was a handsome man with fine features,
including a regally aquiline nose and attentive blue eyes, and was
on the surface a sunny, gregarious individual, much sought after by
hostesses. Dressed impeccably in suits tailored in Rome, "he rarely

appears to be even faintly ruffled." Alvin Balkind affirmed for James that Arthur "is never abrupt, curt or intemperate, and he resists pressure charmingly." When he was on occasion angered, "it's a gentle rage, as though he were shaking his head with despair that someone could be so stupid." But "there is always the secret Arthur," insisted Abraham Rogatnick. "Something always remains closed... Intimately, he is unreachable and that reserve is reflected in his work."

James's article made fascinating references to Arthur's jet-setting lifestyle (by now, he was rarely in one place more than a week) and to the elaborate parties hosted in his garden. Sometimes as many as two hundred guests were looking for parking in the quiet neighbourhood. One party had a theme of early music and featured outdoor musicians with lutes and harpsichords, with Arthur welcoming such notables as British economist Barbara Ward (a.k.a. Baroness Jackson of Lodsworth), anthropologist Margaret Mead, and novelist James Clavell. But it was a cold spring evening, the partygoers squeezed inside, and eventually Arthur could no longer hear his musicians. Stepping out to see if they wanted a warm drink, he found the players in scarves and mitts. But cold wasn't the only problem, they said. The real problem was frogs: every time they started to play, the frogs' song drowned them out. Arthur supposedly shuffled through some music by Handel and solved the problem, for he found a frog cantata, which the musicians subsequently added to their repertoire.[3] Another soiree featured things Japanese, including two musicians— one playing a Japanese flute, the *shakuhachi*, another playing a *koto*. For this summer entertainment, Francisco had illuminated the garden with paper lanterns, and from the moon-viewing platform, Arthur released a jar of fireflies that had been flown in that day from eastern Canada.

Most notorious was the party Arthur had given in July 1967 for members of London's Royal Ballet performing at the Queen Elizabeth Theatre who, because it was a hot summer's night, doffed their clothing and went skinny-dipping in Arthur's pool. This event acquired mythic status because Margot Fonteyn and Rudolf Nureyev were touring with the company, and it was rumoured throughout the city that the lead dancers had not only been skinny-dipping with the others but the well-endowed Tatar had done a marvellous nude solo—the whole length of the garden.

Certainly, famous guests were frequently in attendance, none more famous perhaps than Pierre Trudeau. Arthur had known Pierre's younger brother, Charles (nicknamed Tip), as a gifted architecture student at McGill in the late 1940s, but Arthur and Pierre did not meet until the latter became prime minister in 1968 and convened a group of the country's leading artists for a dinner in Ottawa—about twenty-four composers, painters, writers, and filmmakers. Trudeau was intent on hearing their views about the country's national identity. Arthur was the sole architect. The gesture of a politician turning to artists for advice seemed extraordinary, and Arthur's meeting with Trudeau was one of instant rapport.

While outwardly they were a study in contrasts, Pierre strong willed and physically aggressive, Arthur gentle by nature and calm, they had much in common as private men—self-discipline, reserve, and enormous ambition grounded in a sense of their superiority. They both loathed regimentation of any kind; they held themselves at an emotional distance from other men, and the education they both valued most had been acquired on their ascetic, backpacking travels when they were young. What they quickly recognized in each other, behind the self-confidence that to many suggested arrogance, was a solitary individual whose intelligence and sensitivities made him feel vulnerable and defensive in relations with the public at large. Each was a leader in his field, and so they met as equals, taking pleasure in the rarified atmosphere that superior leadership created. Further, Arthur was aware of the rumour that Pierre was gay and that this had made the former prime minister, Lester Pearson, uneasy about his successor. Indeed, Trudeau was poised to make his famous statement that the state has no place in the bedrooms of the nation.[4] The close friendship between prime minister and architect fed the public perception that the prime minister needed a wife.[5]

Their friendship soon blossomed into a commission to redecorate the prime minister's offices. It was an assignment chiefly for

Francisco, who still had the apartment in Montreal. Francisco sent Arthur a list of general suggestions about the repositioning of cabinets and doors and making more horizontal work surfaces available for the ready study of files and current documents. His work memo was casual in the extreme: "Room to fool around," it noted, "storage of coats, rubbers, visitors' paraphernalia is desperate—help!" "Tilter chairs marking the walls... a disaster." More specifically he told Arthur: "I think you should give a lot of thought to doing something with the map in Tim Porteous's office. It is the usual display of everywhere in Canada the PM has visited. Very important to the VIP from Woop-Woop Sask." He concluded the memo "Rots of Ruck!!"[6] Arthur and Francisco delighted in ordering fine furnishings for the offices—carpeting from Hong Kong, marble tables from Italy, suede sofas and chairs from New York. Arthur promised Tim Porteous, the prime minister's executive assistant, that all such information would be kept "in house," and when ordering the chairs from New York, he requested that they use padding that would be supplied from Canada—to avoid any "political embarrassment." To that same end, Arthur selected an Inuit print, some Salish weaving, and a painting by Joyce Wieland for the walls, so that the renovations could be said to be Canadian in content. The total cost was more than $121,000.

When work on the prime minister's office was completed in the fall of 1971, Arthur was interviewed by the *Toronto Star*. He downplayed his efforts; the job, he said, consisted largely of stripping dark varnish off panelling and "bringing in a few pieces of furniture." The office had been "unbelievably dark and depressing," he stated. "I doubt if there was another executive in the country working in such poor conditions... Now at least he's got a place to sit down." Interviewed by a reporter for the *Vancouver Sun*, he was equally vague. But rumours were rife, and they ignited the fury of a Mrs. Vivian Say in Vancouver who, when she saw the article, wrote a personal letter to Arthur denouncing the prime minister for the "nonsensical spending and unnecessary waste... of the worst Liberal Government ever known in history." This wealthy prime minister, "a hard-hearted dictator," she asserted, should not be wasting money in a country where inflation was high and senior citizens were starving.[7] Arthur sent Mrs. Say a firm but respectful reply, pointing out that the office did not belong to Pierre Elliott Trudeau but to the prime minister of Canada; redecoration was undertaken so that this individual could function more efficiently as the country's chief executive officer and be better able to consider the economy "and in particular the plight of the senior citizens, about whom we are all concerned." That same day, January 17, 1972, Arthur wrote to Tim Porteous to reassure him: "We naturally treat all information regarding [the commission] in due regard and within house." Porteous replied on February 15 to say that Trudeau was "grateful that you succeeded in convincing *Time* magazine not to mention your work on his office."

An announcement from the prime minister's office on March 4, 1971, had caught everyone by surprise, and a few days later Arthur wrote to Tim Porteous: "We here have all been stunned, immensely pleased, and utterly charmed by the recent events of matrimony!" While Arthur had had no inkling that Pierre would marry, he felt he understood the rationale. As Trudeau grew increasingly unpopular with the public, speculation on his ambiguous sexuality grew louder. Dating a high-profile performer like Barbra Streisand had not been convincing; but his marriage to an attractive woman thirty years his junior was acting out the fantasy of many red-blooded, middle-aged males. In Arthur's view, the marriage, with its possibility of children, represented for his friend the necessary consolidation of political power in a patriarchal society.[8]

Arthur warmed to Margaret Trudeau's vivacious, impulsive nature and recognized in the marriage a similar pairing to his own with Francisco.[9] When the Trudeaus were in Vancouver that summer, at Margaret's request he arranged for the couple to meet Gordon and Marion Smith—to see their by now famous house and Gordon's paintings. Arthur liked to tell the story that he had volunteered his caterer so that Marion would be free of worries about providing lunch, but when the caterer saw Margaret and the prime minister arrive fresh from the Black Tusk meadows, Margaret wearing a crown of alpine flowers, she fainted and, recovering, burst into tears in a nervous fit and left. Marion brought out a backup supply of fresh shrimp and crab, and they had an informal, amusing time instead.[10]

In October 1973, Arthur and Francisco made a month-long trip to China, where they eventually joined the Trudeaus and Moshe and Nina Safdie in Beijing. The trip was facilitated by Dr. Paul Lin, a veteran of the Chinese Revolution, who was the head of Chinese Studies at McGill and later at UBC. Arthur and Francisco began their trip in the Soviet Union, with a memorable first stop in Armenia; Arthur was fascinated by this unique culture trying to survive the historical odds of a landlocked, mountainous landscape and invading, sometimes genocidal, neighbours. He was thrilled by the haunting sound of Armenian music. Russia, he thought, seemed a drab place, with its restrictions on one's movements and its endless lineups for food—chiefly cabbage soup and potatoes. Arriving in China, the contrast was extraordinary—the streets and shops contained every kind of food, and the overladen stalls gave him an immediate sense of physical well-being and contentment.[11]

Arthur's response to communist China was characterized by the kind of epic idealism with which he imagined the Middle Ages. Unlike the oppression and hardship he saw in Russia, he could say that in China "in no way do you feel the weight of government; you feel very much that everyone is enthusiastically participating, that there is no sense of constraint, no lack of freedom." Freedom, he argued, was a culturally specific concept, and was very different in the East. In China, he naively posited, no one was forced to do anything against their will. A student on graduation was told where he would work but did not experience this as a curtailment of his freedom because, as part of a communist society, he was only too glad to accept the job. "Commune-ism," insisted Arthur, had always existed in China. Villages were structured that way, and there had always been a great deal of co-operation. He identified Mao's genius as his ability to adapt Marxism to ancient rural ways.

Everything in China thrilled Arthur. Industrial buildings, he claimed, were situated aesthetically, so that if you were a worker in an oil refinery, for example, you would be looking out at pine-covered hills. The big dams looked especially handsome in their physical settings. China, moreover, had already enacted a green revolution, for everyone was given trees to plant after the liberation, and people were riding bicycles instead of driving cars. Everything, he insisted, was spotlessly clean. And everywhere there was happiness. In a village foundry (one of those myriad places for rendering bits of iron during what is now known as the disastrous Great Leap Forward), Arthur observed that most of the workers were women, "carrying the molten steel and having a marvelous time and wearing only sunglasses." He explained the government restrictions on his own movements as simply the hosts wanting to provide guests with the best hotels and food. The restrictions in China, he added, made him think of Canada during the war, "when everybody was dedicated to a cause . . . There were restraints on what you did, what you could eat, but there was a lot of encouragement, a lot of spirit."

In Beijing, Arthur and Francisco joined the Trudeaus for their famous state dinner with Premier Zhou Enlai, who congratulated Margaret on exhibiting her pregnant condition with pride and contrasted her to Chinese women who still hid their bodies in feudal fashion. Trudeau, who had been to China before, shared Arthur's idealism about the country, and historians generally understood that Trudeau's enthusiastic response encouraged Chinese leaders to invite Richard Nixon and Henry Kissinger to their country, thus establishing a thaw in the relations between the East and West. A more feudal, imperial-style event took place a few days later when Francisco managed to arrange a surprise birthday lunch for Pierre in what had once been the Empress Dowager's personal dining room in the Summer Palace.

IN VANCOUVER, WHEN angry Mrs. Say wrote to Arthur about the wasteful expense involved in renovating the prime minister's office, she concluded her letter with a warning: "Keep your hands off our Christ Church Cathedral, it will not be torn down." Her reference was to a debate raging over Vancouver's then eighty-two-year-old

Anglican structure, situated on highly valuable real estate in the city's downtown core. The congregation was dwindling and could no longer support itself; and since the building was not distinguished architecturally—it was described by George Woodcock as "a little grey Gothic structure that cowers like a sleeping tortoise under lofty office buildings and hotels"[12]—there was enormous pressure to tear it down. With the support of the cathedral's dean, Herbert O'Driscoll, Arthur did drawings for a development that would feature a twenty-two-storey office tower with the unique feature of bevelled corners, making it a seven-sided tower instead of the conventional four-sided glass box. The tower was to be sheathed in mirrored glass and to stand in the centre of a plaza, with the church below grade. The congregation would enter from the lower side of the sloping lot and—like the early Christians, suggested Arthur—would go underground. The walls of the subterranean church would be made from the stones of the old cathedral, and light would be reflected down into the sanctuary from a crystal affixed to three stainless steel pillars, five storeys in height, standing in front of the office tower. "Light is particularly important to religious buildings," Arthur wrote. "It is the essence of life and representative of its mystery." His design showed the crystal refracting light from the sun directly onto the altar in a prism of colours. Above the crystal, a sculptured cross marking the church's underground location would be reflected for the city to see in the mirrored glass of the business tower.

A majority of church members, hard-pressed financially, reluctantly supported the plan. But city heritage groups and antiquarians argued that Vancouver could ill afford to lose a landmark from the nineteenth century. J.V. Clyne, who had hired Arthur to design the MacMillan Bloedel building, opposed the scheme for historical reasons, and the premier, W.A.C. Bennett, was said to have been teary-eyed at the thought of a church of such stature being torn down, its parishioners being banished to a subterranean crypt. Vancouver City Council voted eight to three to defer the redevelopment of the church site, and in 1976, after much lobbying, the cathedral was named a Class A heritage building in both the municipality of Vancouver and the province of British Columbia. Parishioners opposed to the new church said it was "the answer to a thousand prayers." Dean O'Driscoll called it a "failure of imagination."[13] Arthur was deeply disappointed that his ideas for redeveloping Christ Church Cathedral had foundered, and his regrets grew stronger when five years later he saw a plan similar to his implemented in Manhattan. The design for the office building and the crystal of light, however, would be used later in one of his office buildings offshore.

Since the time of his rejected Plan Voisin for Vancouver's West End, Arthur had remained vigorously involved in city planning, and in May 1966, the city's Community Arts Council had commissioned Erickson and Massey to develop suggestions for a new courthouse and government skyscraper on Block 61, immediately south of the existing courthouse on Georgia Street. Envisioning something much larger, Arthur, Geoff, and Bruno Freschi, a lead member of their team, proposed eliminating all vehicle traffic on streets in the heart of the city, for a pedestrian zone that retained shopping at street level with glass-roof protection. Vancouver's mild climate didn't require underground shopping plazas, they said. More radically, they proposed a ring road leading to a new bridge to the North Shore that would be situated between the two existing bridges. The city's proposed twin bridge to the Lions Gate—eventually defeated—would, Arthur argued, ruin Stanley Park, Vancouver's greatest treasure.

In Erickson and Massey's scheme, the provincial government buildings would be four skyscrapers that covered three blocks. In his presentation to the arts council, Arthur urged that "the moment is a critical one in the city's history [with] a rapidly increasing population and great buildings planned . . . suddenly, overnight, we find that we are a city. It is no longer possible to build in the downtown area without taking into account all of its surroundings."[14] But the newspaper headlines next day said it all: "Planner's Viewpoint Beautiful, Unrealistic." Director of city planning William Graham estimated that the Erickson/Massey scheme would cost the city half-a-billion dollars: "It doesn't relate to the dollars and cents available at any level of government to carry it out . . . it's simply not in the ballpark." Some city councillors found it "stunning, breathtaking," but they agreed it was unrealistic. Alderman Bob Williams urged working with the architects to incorporate some of the scheme's best aspects into the city development plan. Park commissioner Andy Livingstone observed, "Something like this will have to come... this business of going through town in second gear burning out clutches has to end sometime."[15]

The following year, 1967, a San Francisco firm was hired by the city to do a feasibility study for a waterfront freeway through Vancouver, including a link through the heart of Chinatown. There was surprise when Erickson and Massey took the job of consultants in collaboration with the American firm, but their purpose was a deliberately subversive one—to study the drawings so they could demonstrate weaknesses. Arthur warned the public that a freeway system would destroy the city's natural beauty. "Most people probably do not realize," he said to a reporter for the *Vancouver Sun*, "that a waterfront freeway would be as high as Hastings Street—not low down on the railway tracks," and that the view to the North Shore would be obstructed by the freeway. Seattle, he argued, has been compromised that way, and "it will take many years for it to be a whole city again."[16] Shirley Chan and others in the Chinese community were stirred to action by the proposal; it went no further than the city's feasibility study. Arthur was viewed by many as a civic hero.

A TALK ARTHUR gave in 1966, "Man Plans His Future: The City," was something of a blueprint for many of his lectures in the years to follow. The question underlying his thinking was how, in the face of an exploding world population, efficient and salutary cities could be created. He began his talk by recounting a lab experiment in which the gradual overcrowding of well-fed rats in an enclosure resulted in stress, disease, cannibalism, and the collapse of the species. From this grim observation, he moved to generalizations about rapid changes in the human condition and about space being telescoped by the modern means of travel and communications, such that the world had become a "global village," as Marshall McLuhan phrased it. This would force changes in forms of government, Arthur argued; perhaps a "universal infragovernment" would be needed to ensure human survival. And with the collapse of nations, a new stratification might emerge, according to generations rather than class—the young, the middle-aged, and the elderly linked for self-defence to parallel generations in other parts of the world.

In the face of these major changes, Arthur said, the North American city of the mid-twentieth century was an absurdity—the downtown was a morass of parking lots and towering buildings; the suburbs consisted of private houses on a grid, with little relation to site or the movement of traffic, each house inside "barren, catalogue-bought, and the same." Living areas remote from the areas of work, shopping, and entertainment required many trips downtown in private or public vehicles, usually in the same peak periods, causing traffic jams, frustration, and nervous tension and leaving downtown streets empty the rest of the time. The alternative—to live downtown in an apartment building with a bleak and narrowly functionalist approach to human habitat—was a form of hell.

In the future, he argued, individualism would no longer be a viable modus vivendi. The medieval period of Western history, with its organic cities expressing a coherent view of life, the individual subsumed as part of the larger whole, would be preferred. In the counterculture of the sixties, Arthur glimpsed a similarly contingent view. "In architecture . . .," he said, "attention is shifting from the inner individual space to the external public space."

As pollution and damage to the ecology increased, Arthur posited, government would have to determine the use of land, especially vital in terms of agriculture: in B.C., for example, "It will be necessary that we build on unarable land such as the mountainsides of the Fraser Valley so that the fertile valley floor is left for food production." He believed (somewhat naively, it must be said) that governments, well informed through computer networks, would be able to set acceptably intelligent policy, and all members of the community could be engaged in working towards a common goal. The role of cities as major centres of culture would increase in importance.

As in the medieval world, he foresaw the city state having as much administrative validity as a large nation linked only by language, commerce, and political interest. And he envisioned the city core becoming denser rather than more dispersed.

His 1966 talk ended with a fantasy of the future, in which people moved about and checked in to hotel rooms that they owned, rather than homes, anywhere in the world. (A form of this did come to pass, of course, with the time-share plans that many have bought in to for vacation purposes.) In a later, shorter version of this talk, titled "The Next Hundred Years: The Architect,"[17] Arthur proposed the end of twentieth-century "vaingloriousness," describing a world in which humankind would be "returned to innocence, having physically created God in his own image to trust in for all the answers." This optimistic and curiously nostalgic conclusion echoed both his early exposure to Christian Science and Rilke's idea of the artist creating God. This version of the future, however, can be seen in a negative light to echo the totalitarian vision of Le Corbusier, or of the fictional Howard Roark, who believed only the architect—the supreme individual—could imagine, control, and bring this new order into being.

But Arthur's radical proposals for redesigning cities, his concern for the environment, and his startling visions of the future revealed him also to be in tune with the new modes of awareness expressed in the peace movement, the celebration of Earth Day, organic foods, recycling, and the sustainable use of natural resources. Throughout the 1970s, he gave lectures—part architectural history, part cultural analysis, and part jeremiad—that seldom failed to rouse his audience's full attention. At a 1971 conference on cities in Indianapolis, he asserted, "Everything we have enjoyed in Western civilization we owe to the city. Our art, our science, our philosophy, have all been born from and nurtured by the city." But he opened his talk by bluntly asserting that the real symbol of America was not the Statue of Liberty but the bulldozer. Sections of cities were increasingly being cleared for urban renewal and freeways, and there was no greater act of aggression against a city or one's fellow man, he insisted, except war itself.[18] The destruction of human environments was bred in North Americans by the early settlers' need to clear the land, but it continued needlessly in both the countryside and cities as an extension of "mechanistic thinking," which led us to believe that we could control all aspects of who we are and where we live. That meant we could not accept much of what a city is actually about—crime, blight, disease, and other things essential to its vitality. In contrast, the Eastern mind, he urged, realized that things of great courage and great beauty and light always stand alongside things of great ugliness in the world. Until we can accept these necessary opposites, we would be unable to think about a real city.[19]

Most damaging of all, Arthur said, mechanistic thinking bestowed a legacy of organization on the city through grid pattern and zoning that is hostile to community. The grid is not a natural form but an abstract pattern of real estate and power—a sewage and transportation network. The street, Arthur insisted, should be the common living room, but instead, it was the place for deliveries and gathering up wastes—and for escape.

Arthur had come to admire Jane Jacobs, the urban activist who left New York for Toronto in the late 1960s. She identified the vitality of the slum as an argument for mixed zoning; she proposed that in dense, mixed neighbourhoods of shopkeepers and houses, the street should serve as the community living room. It was the role of government, she asserted, to make this happen. In the same vein, in one of his lectures, Arthur insisted that a city could never be an act of design—"That is the reason for the failure of capitals such as Brasilia, Chandigarh, Islamabad, Canberra (even Washington and Ottawa to some degree). You can *grow* a city, but you can't create it."[20] Arthur was in accord with popular theorist Robert Venturi that urban modernism was depriving the city of its rich variety and its vital drive for change.[21] There was an urgent need to recover a holistic view of reality. The failure of urban renewal, the flight of the middle class from the inner city, and the heaps of undifferentiated high-rise boxes everywhere were proof to Arthur that the bureaucrat's prospectus and the real estate developer's budget sheet had disastrously replaced the architect's role in planning and designing cities.

Arthur's vision of North American cities and their need to "develop naturally" as a composite of mixed-use neighbourhoods would eventually be implemented in Vancouver by city planners such as Ray Spaxman and Larry Beasley. In his own time, he generated hostility with his aloof stance and his assumption that the architect's role was that of the supreme planner—an attitude all too suggestive of a figure at the controls in a totalitarian state. The contradiction, however, likely never occurred to Arthur; his motives, as he understood them, were not just visionary but selfless.

ARTHUR'S HABIT OVER the years of referring to Vancouver as a "disastrously ugly" city won him few friends in local politics.[22] When the city was trashed during a Grey Cup parade, he suggested, "If you have a shoddy place it is treated shabbily."[23] What civic pride there was, he said in an interview, was artificial—pride in a beautiful setting that was a fact of nature, not a human accomplishment. He intended to remain in Vancouver, he added, because the potential was "fantastic... there are few places left in the world with this emergent aspect."[24] Nonetheless, he told reporter Lorne Parton of the *Province* newspaper, "Every time I come back to Vancouver I get a shock. Migawd it's such a shanty town. No city in North America is as basically shacky as this one... littered streets, sagging fences, houses in need of paint... and I don't see any attempts to improve things."[25] In a program for CBC titled *A Sense of Place*, he said that having no windows in his Vancouver office protected him from the sight of so many ugly buildings.[26]

Arthur's sneering pronouncements would seem to have aligned him with the city's wealthy class, but it was when the NDP government came to power in August 1972 that he finally got a chance to realize his ambitions for Vancouver. In February 1973, the *Province* announced that Erickson had been retained by the provincial Department of Public Works to design a three-block building complex for the centre of the city—government offices, law courts, and other civic uses that would be known collectively as Robson Square. Arthur would "finally have a role in the destiny of [his] hometown."[27]

It was the same site for which, seven years before, Arthur and Geoff had proposed four high-rise towers for government office space and a scheme for closing off traffic. Now, in a temporarily adventurous political climate, and with the specific support of city councillor Bob Williams, Arthur was encouraged to propose a more radical design for the heart of the city. But there were significant obstacles to overcome.

First, there was the three-block space itself: the old courthouse on Georgia Street and two undeveloped blocks to the south of it. For years, there had been talk of creating a green square in the centre of the city, but attempts to secure such a space were invariably trounced by the powerful manoeuvres of land developers. Arthur needed to create office spaces for government and law courts while still finding a way for people to meet and mix in a park-like setting. He could not help but think of the streets and squares in cities like Florence, where "people emerged from the buildings and there was a marvellous mixture of people."[28] Arthur and Geoff's earlier proposal had called for an H-shaped high-rise straddling the middle block, with the block to the south left open, but the idea seemed increasingly out of joint with the public mood. Moreover, the design had come from the office of Erickson/Massey, which no longer existed.

The famous partnership had dissolved in the summer of 1972. On the surface, the split was amicable, the result of an internal study undertaken to see how the firm's workings could be improved. Asked by a curious reporter for a statement, Geoff said simply that their interests over the years had changed, and he and Arthur both thought "it might be more satisfactory to go separate ways."[29] When further pressed, Geoff conceded that he wanted to return to more creative work. In his gossip column for the *Vancouver Sun*, Jack Wasserman speculated that having the professional honours consistently go to Erickson must have been hard for his partner.[30] Possible envy aside, Geoff had other concerns—one of which was financial. Arthur's inability to keep costs down and to meet deadlines was an increasing problem, with Geoff trying to bring order to the books and answer the demands of frustrated clients. He feared bankruptcy if Arthur continued this way. The problem of lavish expenditures was greatly aggravated by Francisco, whom Arthur wanted in the partnership and whom Geoff frankly disliked. Geoff later said he felt he could do more good as a member of city council; he was elected in November 1972. From Arthur's point of view, there was only one reason for the split: Geoff wanted to do more design work, and they had very different approaches.[31]

Arthur had assumed that his employees would continue working with him, but in a July letter to the president of the University of Lethbridge, he explained that Ron Bain, Ken Burroughs, and Garry Hanson had seized the moment to form a separate partnership. Bruno Freschi had already departed to establish his own practice. This left a staff of four architects, including Nick Milkovich, plus a secretary and several specialists. Arthur planned to remain a fairly small design studio, working with other firms to execute larger projects, but when the Robson Square complex became a reality in 1973, he established a full-service office after all.[32] His new staff included Alan Bell, Rainer Fassler, and Bing Thom.

Thom was made project coordinator for the Robson Square complex, and he hired and trained a large company of architects and business staff, most of whom were young and inexperienced. Yet there was no lack of confidence or excitement as this new group took up its various tasks. As one remembered, "There was a thrill to walk into an office that you knew was cutting edge in the field and where your work was always welcome."[33] The team would generate ideas in response to an often vague set of indications from Arthur, invariably resulting in a wide range of possibilities.

Arthur made all the major design decisions, with the office staff and design team then refining each component of the overall scheme and undertaking technical resolution and documentation. The arrangement harked back to the Middle Ages: a studio or atelier where the master presided, apprentices supplied labour, and specialists provided additional technical expertise. It also had elements of Wright's Taliesin fellowship. But it was not without problems; some members of the design team were frustrated by Arthur's inability to articulate precisely his ideas and by his inability to explain why he liked the work of some team members and not others.[34] In an interview, Arthur admitted that his method, crudely put, was "by the seat of the pants," allowing the unconscious to prevail. He realized that was often "confusing and disturbing to those working around me since it meant postponing decisions and pursuing explorations for as long as possible without making any emotional, intellectual, or sensible commitment."[35] Some of those who worked for a time for Arthur felt there was no structure to the office and that they got little credit for the work they did. But Bing Thom said they all knew what they were getting into: "It was Arthur's office and the credit [went] to the name on the door."[36]

For the Robson Square project, Arthur first set a team led by Alan Bell to do an urban design study of the downtown peninsula to better understand its essential structures—particularly its growth patterns and needs.[37] One component of the study was the identification of character areas and corridors; this new form of urban design control was eventually refined and implemented by the city under Ray Spaxman. The study suggested to Arthur how street lighting, curbs, paving, and the planting of trees could define the character of the three-block area he was designing, and that led to the city's first set of character guidelines for the blocks immediately surrounding Robson Square. Underlying the study was Arthur's conviction that in a city there was no such thing as a free-standing structure; buildings could not exist without the specificities of their siting.[38]

But the big question was where to put the park. The old provincial courthouse, which was to be transferred to the city to become the new art gallery, was a heritage building in the neoclassical style, designed by Francis Rattenbury and opened in 1912. Its status was inviolate. The new courthouse would have heavy security requirements. So the park had to fill the block in between, assigned to government offices. How could the two functions be accommodated simultaneously? Rather than a high-rise surrounded by shrubbery and walkways, the decision was made to put the building on its side and create a green space on its roof, in a multi-level configuration consisting of steps and ramps (dubbed "stramps" by the design team), a three-hundred-foot-long pool that would cascade down three levels, and plantings that would cover one-third of the roof—a hanging garden. The stairs would terminate in a sunken plaza containing an ice-skating rink, restaurants, theatres, and other meeting spaces. People could walk the three blocks from the art gallery to the new law courts without encountering traffic. On reflection, this bold concept suggests that the power in Arthur's buildings and designs springs from the tension between their type (people's expectations) and their unique execution—a house cascading down an embankment, a church as an underground crypt, an office tower lying on its side.

But the most innovative aspect of the Robson Square complex was Arthur's plan for the law courts. Before he submitted his design, he had made a business trip to Saudi Arabia, where he learned that punishment was public and severe; as a consequence, presumably, there was little crime. He had accidentally left his own wallet in a public place, and it was still there when he returned the next day. "It seemed," he wrote, "that their justice system, carried out in public squares, encouraged a remarkable honesty." J.V. Clyne, Vancouver's chief justice at the time, made a similar observation, telling Arthur that in his opinion justice had last been carried out effectively in London in the seventeenth century, with public hangings in the streets. From these violent examples, Arthur drew a benign, positive conclusion—that justice had to be seen to be appreciated. Accordingly, his idea for the law courts was to open the justice system as much as possible to the public and make it less an ominous house of retribution and more a civics lesson in community standards.[39] "Why not open up our corridors to the street and then justice will be part of the education of our citizens!"[40] A passerby should be able to see justice at work.

To many, Arthur's approach to justice seemed naïve, just as his views on city planning seemed riddled with contradictions. What was remarkable, however, was his ability to translate ingenuous thinking into innovative design. The law courts building was designed with a great deal of glass, allowing a maximum exposure of light; he wanted the courthouse to be not a depressing place but "a cheerful one, with all sorts of things going on." The main gallery with its glass roof would become one of Vancouver's grand public spaces. Arthur also wanted Vancouver's individual courtrooms to be light and welcoming. People should be able to enter the building, see where the court was, and approach it in pleasant surroundings. "In no way," he insisted, "should one be intimidated by the courts."[41] A courthouse should be as uplifting as a church, university, or museum. Only the courtroom itself should be solemn.[42] Here, however, the architect's vision and the administrator's purposes came into conflict over the matter of security. Arthur wanted glass interior walls, but judges insisted on solid walls on the pedestrian hall side. In the end, only skylights slanting up from the streetside windows would bring daylight into the courtrooms. The wood on the walls and tables was pale American elm, though the carpet was a bright crimson, and the chairs were covered in soft tan leather. Some judges felt the colours were not rich enough, that the effect was too modern, but with J.V. Clyne's support Arthur's choices prevailed.

Arthur's creation of the law courts as a physical monument to the "transparency" of the Canadian legal system was directly connected to Pierre Trudeau's legal reforms. Their friendship always involved a vigorous exchange of ideas. On one occasion, while Lois Milsom was driving them to an event in her Rolls-Royce, Arthur tried to persuade Pierre that Canada should have only five provinces, with the Atlantic and prairie provinces collapsed into one each. Simultaneously, Pierre was telling Arthur that in the new courtrooms there should be no lighting over the judge's podium; everything should be done to make figures of authority seem more human. No doubt such suggestions had significant influence on Arthur's thinking about justice. Trudeau's legal reforms in 1967 had redefined Arthur's relationship with Francisco and Arthur's very status as a citizen.

Another of the pleasures for Arthur on the Robson Square project was to work for the first time with landscape architect Cornelia Oberlander. Bing Thom had hired two landscapers to work on the complex, but it was Cornelia's expertise with plant materials and

her burgeoning interest in roof gardens that drew Arthur's attention. The collaboration that ensued would continue for more than
thirty years.

Cornelia Hahn, a refugee from Nazi Germany, had arrived in
the United States in 1939, where she attended Smith College and
later enrolled in the Harvard Graduate School of Design. There
she studied with Walter Gropius and met her future husband, Peter
Oberlander, who was studying city planning and would become a
leader in that field after they moved to Vancouver in 1953. Arthur
knew of Peter as a McGill graduate who had studied under John
Bland, and he befriended the Oberlanders when they moved to British Columbia. While raising three children, Cornelia established
her own small practice and developed a reputation for the landscaping of social spaces, especially children's play areas. In the 1970s,
she quickly adopted the new thinking about urban green spaces:
how trees and shrubbery improved the air quality and thus the physical health of city workers and residents; how the sounds of water-
falls and wind running through trees reduced noise pollution and
relaxed and replenished those who spent time in parks.

Arthur and Cornelia were in tune in their thinking and in their
seriousness of purpose. Hers was a "minimal palette," as she liked
to phrase it, but one conceived to extend the architect's gesture.[43]
Selecting materials for the terraced roof gardens for Robson Square,
Cornelia, like Arthur, preferred the use of native species—pines,
dogwood, vine maples, laurel, and rhododendrons, with junipers at
the higher levels, and hardy white memorial roses spilling over from
the "flying planters." Their shared ideal of beauty was a white azalea,
not beds planted in gaudy annuals, and water should be a pool or
waterfall, not a fountain, which they regarded as artificial. Similarly
to Arthur, Cornelia liked to think of her work as having historical
reference; a good example was the planting of bonsai plane trees,
grown from seed that was said to be from the tree in Greece under
which Hippocrates took the oath of medicine. The reference also
resonated with Arthur's idea of an urban landscape having healing
powers.

The roof garden's "stramps," a combination of stairs and ramps forming something like a goat path up a hillside, allowed people in wheelchairs or with prams to move from one level to the next.[44] Here, as at SFU, Arthur seemed to be creating a walking course reminiscent of climbing a mountain. And as Cornelia subsequently pointed out, the roof garden is designed so that you find your own path—you can go straight or proceed at a diagonal. This choice negates the imperative of the street grid and invites the pedestrian to find a quiet, contemplative spot in which to relax for a while. The collaboration resulted in North America's largest roof garden, and in 1979 the American Society of Landscape Architects gave the President's Award of Excellence to the provincial courthouse complex for its "extraordinary integration of landscape architecture with architecture—consistent and coherent."[45]

Collaboration on the Robson Square complex extended far beyond Cornelia Oberlander; it was also the modus operandi of the atelier. If Arthur was the producer, to borrow film terminology, Bing Thom was the director, and a list of distinguished credits would include, in employee Eva Matsuzaki's words, "a hundred underlings who keep up the appearance that he [Erickson] does it all."[46] That list would include Jim Cheng who, like Bing Thom, would become one of the city's leading architects. For a magazine article, Cheng described some of the fun at the office in trying to meet Arthur's expectations. First, it was important to "establish the horizontals"— those beams that seem to extend unrealistically past the walls they surmount; then it was "slip and slide" as they struggled to design the "stramps" ("they seem to melt diagonally as you climb over Robson Square"); when all else failed, it was time to "shrub it up": cover it with plants. That final solution to a problem that could not be resolved was a standing joke at the office.[47] The good humour of these employees revealed how loyal they were to Arthur, a role model in his purity and dedication to their profession.

One former employee, Barry Johns, has observed that the Robson Square complex, with its stepped garden terraces, "challenges the early Modernist notion of vast empty plazas and anonymous office spaces."[48] Critic Nicholas Olsberg extended this view in an interpretation that pleased Arthur greatly. Olsberg wrote, quoting Arthur, that beginning with the law courts, the pedestrian moves through the gallery along "a street arcade in which the action of justice [can] be seen." Descending northwards, the walkway moves over "a hardscape of waterfall and pool" under which is the administrative machinery of government. It descends under Robson Street—"the dip making the street the visual focus of the whole scheme"—and then mounts towards the neoclassical building of the art gallery. The symbolism, Olsberg suggested, is elaborate: justice raised on the south end is made visible as the basis of civil society; the functions of government on the everyday street level are discreetly unassertive; the arts, rising on the north end, are dependent on civil order but wholly independent of its mechanism; the street as the moving citizenry is the focus of all three.[49] Arthur was eager to emphasize the significance of the skating rink and art gallery, for his long-held belief was that "a city matures when the citizens flock to the centre— not for work but for pleasure."[50]

The reception of Robson Square over time, however, has been a mixed one. Two aspects of the project have received almost unanimous praise. The gallery off the courtrooms has been referenced as basilica-like and one of the great interior spaces from which one had, at the time of building, a panoramic view of the city. The addition to the art gallery, which included a second-storey indoor and outdoor cafeteria, is viewed as one of the most functional and pleasurable places in the city for a casual meeting. On a flight of outdoor steps, one can sit at different levels to watch the surrounding activities, a feature especially attractive to large crowds during the 2010 Olympics. But the central roof garden, despite its ingenious structure and plantings, has not drawn pedestrians in large numbers, partly because the mix of stairs and diagonal ramps is aggravating, and partly because it climbs to what is largely an exposed terrace. Over the years, however, the heaviest criticism has been directed to the below-street-level skating-rink area. For architectural critic Lisa Rochon, dropping below grade disrupts a natural flow of sidewalk space that evolves from the streets.[51] Perhaps the greater problem is that in a climate starved for light, people are reluctant to go under the street to a place where the ceiling is low and there is little artificial light provided. Restaurants and other businesses did not thrive there, and much of the space was eventually turned into an introverted downtown centre for the University of British Columbia.

The Robson Square complex would turn out to be Arthur's only major public building project in the city's centre. With his team of now nearly eighty employees, he prepared ambitious designs for two more major public building projects during the 1970s, but neither scheme was implemented. One was for a Government of Canada building to be situated on the eastern edge of downtown, near the city's Queen Elizabeth Theatre complex and the Canadian Broadcasting Corporation building. Arthur's design was based on a conceit that was perhaps too playful: because the federal government had no deeply rooted presence in the West and was viewed with some antipathy, his 1978 drawings proposed two six-storey steel-truss pods that would hover "Zeppelin-like"[52] on piers several storeys above the site. Below would be a children's park, a museum, and a library. Then-mayor Art Phillips was reported to be "very excited" by Arthur's proposal, but not all Ottawa politicians wanted to project this image of aloofness.

Arthur was more seriously engaged with a proposal for the redevelopment of the Shaughnessy Hospital site. From childhood teachings in Christian Science, he carried negative associations with medicine: he was "unable to shake the impression that hospitals are places that *cause* sickness."[53] He felt that health was a matter of positive thinking, and the key to that was environment. He had been ill himself a few years before with a severe and demoralizing attack of colitis. He concluded that it had been caused by nervous tension from overwork, that what he needed was to relax in a soothing environment. He remembered that the ancient Greeks believed healing came through a renewed harmony with nature and a faith in one's culture, the best example being at Pergamum where the "hospital" was built in idyllic natural surroundings and included a theatre, bath, gymnasium, and library.[54] With this in mind, he designed a low-rise hospital extension with balconied rooms that looked onto garden terraces. There were plans for patients' families to be housed close by. The technologies of health—laboratories, operating rooms—were to be underground, with the main floor as a "health mall" for education and preventive medicine. Arthur's work on the project was terminated after the change in B.C.'s provincial government in late 1975. When he was chosen in 1984 as part of a consortium to design a hospital in Saskatoon, he incorporated some of these ideas—specifically a park view from the patients' rooms and an atrium that connected the patients' wing to the rest of the hospital, a welcome space in the prairie winter. But he was deeply disappointed not to build in Vancouver and continued to denounce the traditional hospital as "ugly and damaging to the soul, designed like a garage for spare parts."[55]

His disappointments were financial as well, and he concluded, as had Louis Sullivan more than half a century before, that "only through good patrons is good architecture born. Unfortunately, many projects that do not have such strong backing are stillborn."[56] The matter of patrons would remain crucial throughout the rest of Arthur's career: the path to further major achievements and a direct road to his downfall.

16

The Museum of Anthropology, UBC

IN THE MID-1970S, in his early fifties, Arthur was at the peak of his career, running two successful offices and compiling a growing list of prospective clients abroad. He continued to enjoy a public image akin to that of a film celebrity. His name was often in the headlines and even more frequently in the social columns. In an article for the *Montreal Gazette*, Paul Grescoe gave this description of Arthur: "Fifty-two, his lean body [is] still tanned from Christmas yachting in the Caribbean, his high-browed face handsomely sculpted by middle-age lines, hair a pewter grey, eyes a pale but compelling blue—he approximates the Paul Newman vision of the architect as hero—the part the actor played in *The Towering Inferno*."¹ *The Groundstar Conspiracy*, a popular Hollywood science fiction movie released in 1972, was even filmed using Simon Fraser University as the setting. Grescoe makes much of Arthur as a jet-setter. Certainly, the essence of his high-profile life was the steady travelling that had become a necessary part of his work. But for Arthur, travel played an important role in the creative process as well; it was on extended flights that, with his fine-point, black felt-tip pen, on standard sheets of vellum, he made preliminary drawings of his buildings. Above the clouds, undisturbed, his imagination was unfettered. As he put it, "I float in marvellous detachment... and, cut off from all such worldly involvements as the telephone, I return to myself again, and on the one by two foot table in front of me, allow myself to dream. I return to a state of almost original bliss."[2]

Part of the glamour attached to Arthur was his bachelor status—"He lives alone, cooks for himself...," Grescoe wrote, "with a once-a-week maid and a Japanese gardener; he has no permanent romantic attachments. He is too involved in what he is doing." For reporters and the public in general, Francisco was kept offstage, but in fact he frequently travelled with Arthur, and business was invariably combined with pleasure—scuba diving in the Caribbean, shopping in Florence, partying in Rome. Francisco was a thrill-seeker, and Arthur's verbal extravagance came to the fore when he described their experiences for reporters: it was "extraordinary," he said, being dropped by a helicopter on "'a little handkerchief of ice'" in the glaciers of the Swiss Alps, "then skiing five thousand feet to the bottom of a valley and being picked up there by the helicopter and transported to the top of another glacier... 'absolutely incredible.'" They might visit for a day with friends like Pat and William Buckley in Connecticut, or with Blackie and Al Sparzani wherever Al had a posting in Latin America or the Caribbean. "I get restless after ten days, anywhere," Arthur was known to say frequently.[3]

But he seldom stayed away from Vancouver for long stretches, because his physical home had enormous appeal as both a refuge from the pressures of work and a place of relaxation—a "decompression chamber." To visitors surprised that the country's most influential architect lived in such modest circumstances, he would say that architecturally his house was terrible but that, practically speaking, he needed a small place he could close up and leave without worry and that he could withdraw into when he returned to the city. "I need to be able to look inward, to not have my innermost privacy disturbed by intrusion of the world outside, however beautiful, unless I want it to. Then I can go outside and look. Privacy is terribly important."[4] On the gate of the tall cedar fence surrounding his home, he placed a weathered brass door knocker in the figure of a chrysanthemum, the flower sacred to the Japanese as representing serenity. His garden, which he continued to describe as his clearing in the forest, was his sanctuary.

Although his house struck visitors as modest in the extreme, the interior was now decorated in the elegant simplicity that was Francisco's trademark style—the living-room walls upholstered in small beige squares of Italian suede; the floors, fireplace, and tabletops of travertine; and the walls of the study done in yellow Thai silk. In spite of friendships with Gordon Smith and Bert Binning, there were no paintings on the walls—"I found I couldn't put anything on them because they are so rich." Instead, the eye was drawn to the pieces of pottery on Plexiglas shelves to the sides of the fireplace and the eighteenth-century Japanese goddess of mercy on the mantel. Originally Arthur had slept in the living room, on the straw couch made of trolley car seat backs, but after Francisco came to stay frequently, he created a sleeping loft over his study reached by carpeted stairs. He liked to tell people that a Saudi Arabian prince had once visited and laughed uproariously when he saw where the famous architect slept. Later, at a cocktail party, the prince pointed to a canopy over the bar and said to Arthur, "If you get tired you can sleep up there."[5] Sometimes Arthur would say that he still wanted to do a house for himself but never had enough money. Only second-level architects make money, he would add with some asperity, since for them principles never got in the way. Or he would say that he was like the shoemaker whose children go without shoes; he was always too busy designing homes for other people to live in. One of his most pleasurable commissions involved spending a weekend with Pierre and Margaret Trudeau designing a chalet for their private lake in the Laurentians north of Montreal. It was to be burglar proof with no exposed glass or wood, finished in corrugated aluminum, as private as any home could possibly be. After a scheme had been worked out, Arthur and Pierre stripped and went for a swim *au naturel,* and Margaret prepared a picnic that they ate sitting on the rocks by the silent lake.[6]

Arthur liked to tell stories about the domestic dramas involving his garden. Especially troublesome were the raccoons that came in the night to feed on his goldfish and take fruit from his persimmon tree. From the Canadian pavilion at Expo in Montreal he had brought back a golden carp, two feet in length; it was a pale metallic gold and much admired by his friends. But the morning after he placed it in the pool, all that was left were some scales—"'floating like gold coins.'" The raccoons would wake him up in the night, making raids on the local garbage cans and clambering about on his roof to eat the grapes when they were ripe. One night he found himself explaining to a policeman why he was running down the street after a raccoon in his nightshirt. Feeling beleaguered, he phoned Alan Best, head of the Stanley Park Zoo, for advice, wondering if it would be possible to put a crocodile in the pool to get rid of them. Instead, Best sent him a box trap baited with sardines. A couple of days later, his neighbours Abe Rogatnick and Alvin Balkind stopped by for drinks and in conversation mentioned their cat was missing. "'So, a surprised Puss was all that I caught in that trap.'" When Arthur reported his failure, Alan Best came over late at night, climbed a pear tree, and managed to shoot one of the raccoons, but it was barely five minutes before several police cars appeared—the neighbours had reported an armed robbery.

Best made one last try to solve the problem: he sent over two black Australian swans. But that too proved unworkable. The swans required a case of lettuce each day; otherwise, they would eat everything in the garden. They soon became bored on such a small pond and made a mudslide of the berm; the grounds were covered with their droppings. They were, however, much admired by Arthur's party guests. Abe Rogatnick remembered an evening when Arthur had placed performing musicians at the far end of the garden with the swans gliding on the pool in the foreground. Francisco had even tried to fit them with little gold crowns. The effect, said Abe, was "too lovely for words."[7] But eventually, the swans became unmanageable, banging on the glass doors for attention. One day they succeeded in getting into the house, lunging repeatedly at Arthur and leaving digested lettuce everywhere. He resigned himself to raccoons, filling his pond every spring with a hundred little bait-size goldfish.

If Arthur was asked to dinner, he would invariably say yes, but friends knew there was a good chance that he might not appear, that he could be in another country. If he was home, he might forget he had another engagement. At best, he would be late. Some made sure to invite him for an hour or two before the dinner party was scheduled to begin.

His social habits were not unlike his mother's. Myrtle, still a "wonderfully funny woman,"[8] lived close by, and when Arthur returned from a trip, he invariably went to see her first, filling her in on his most recent experiences. She would reciprocate with detailed accounts of her latest adventures, stories that usually ended with her capsized in laughter. It was gratifying to Arthur that she had lived into old age and could enjoy his phenomenal success, much of which he felt he owed to her example. After his father's death, he had found her a coach house apartment at The Crescent, which belonged to his clients, the Keevils. There, with Donald's family also close by, she managed for herself into her eighties. The arts in Vancouver remained the focus of her interest; she was still a volunteer at the Vancouver Art Gallery and active with the Yellow Door painting group she had helped organize. It was said that she started the planting of Japanese cherry trees that now beautify the streets of Vancouver. The story most often told about Myrtle at this time concerned her shoes. She was still painting them to match her outfits, drying them in the oven. For her eightieth birthday, she was invited to a party of family and friends. Next morning there was a vexed-sounding voice on the telephone: "Myrtle, did you paint your shoes yesterday?" The hostess's white carpet was now streaked green. Arthur dropped off his washing at his mother's and she would sometimes bring a lunch to his office, one day bringing her garbage bag by mistake. When Arthur received the Order of Canada award in 1973, she attended the ceremony with him in Ottawa, wearing a silk dress that he had bought for her in Asia.

Other awards, medals, and honours came thick and fast; by the end of the decade, they would number more than thirty. They included an honorary membership in the Architectural Institute of British Columbia (AIBC) in December 1973 and the prestigious Auguste Perret Prize from the International Union of Architects (1974), a prize named for the seminal Parisian architect whose work represents the first effective expression in reinforced concrete.

Arthur received Vancouver's "Man of the Year" citation and three honorary degrees in quick succession—from Simon Fraser University (1973), McGill University (1975), and the University of Manitoba (1978). These were occasions for public lectures in which Arthur addressed those issues that concerned him most.

But one of the most important addresses he gave in the 1970s was to the Institute of Canadian Bankers in October 1972, wherein he attempted to interpret the "Sixties Revolution." "Overpopulation, resource exhaustion, and environmental pollution," he argued, "have brought about a growing and powerful reaction against the historical course of western man... a revolution of a much more profound and fundamental nature than the social and political revolutions of [Russia, Cuba]—a revolution so subtle and yet so encompassing that we will only gradually (and after the event) be aware that everything has changed, completely changed, and that nothing is as it was before." With reference to what he called large alternating historical cycles of action and "meditation," he likened contemporary history to the gradual collapse of the Roman Empire and the Dark Ages, during which the human conquest of the universe subsided, Christian churches replaced the banking halls of Rome, order, justice, material well-being, and the comprehensive planning of great road networks, dams, and reclamation projects were replaced by the fervent beliefs and practices of "a few unarmed dropouts who talked about love, poverty, simplicity, and non-action" and contemplated the imminent end of the world. "Rome was as confident of the immutability of its world and the continual expansion and improvement of the human lot as we are today," he observed. Yet all that slowly disappeared.

What was so different in the mysterious Dark and Middle Ages, he argued (as he had done in earlier talks), was the diminishment of the individual ego. Although it was one of the greatest periods of inspired art and architecture in human history, medieval sculptors and architects never "signed" their work; it was virtually anonymous. This common purpose and form of expression rendered the medieval town a tightly knit, unified structure, "with even the palace and the cathedral part of the same fabric." The cultures of Asia understood this, too. Westerners, he lamented, were "hopelessly and helplessly immersed in ourselves and our effect on things." But the events of the sixties and early seventies gave him hope.

There is a slow but increasing awareness of the interrelatedness of things. We are becoming less prone to accept an immediate solution without questioning its larger implications. And perhaps the greatest single influence on this change of attitude has been the issue of the environment and ecology... which has resulted in an increasing consciousness of the interrelationships of systems. The DDT issue caught us just as we were beginning to poison ourselves as a consequence of poisoning the insects that preyed on our crops; the Aswan dam brought power to Egypt, but affected the very basis of Egypt's existence—changing the fertility of the Nile Valley and eliminating the bountiful fish crop at its mouth. We are learning to be respectful with eco-systems.

He concluded his talk by throwing out a challenge to his audience. Human cultures were now under threat from worldwide tourism. "The tourist," he observed in strong language, "far from being a sensitive explorer, transports his values and demands to his destination and implants them like an infectious disease decimating whatever values existed before." Two cultures especially precious in his view were Bali and Nepal. "Nowhere else in the world do the highly developed musical, dance and art forms still play a vital and central role in community life instead of being relegated to the realm of performance. All other great cultures are in stasis or abandoned." He urged his audience of bankers to be vigilant about the consequences of the projects they financed: what was being done to the natural environment and to human cultures "at some future time may be considered crimes against mankind. As lending institutions, you have enormous power over development in this and other countries, and with that, an enormous responsibility."

In his lectures to the public, Arthur spoke not simply from the discipline of architecture but from the perspective of a cultural historian and an anthropologist. His convocation address at Simon Fraser University opened with a charming discourse on the rituals of spring:

We are here today to witness an ancient ritual, where the young are initiated into the society of elders, having proven their mastery over the mysteries of the tribe. In this ceremony we guilelessly enact rituals older than history—as old as when the human animal first realized the power of his own magic and the urgency of passing it on in sacred riddles, songs, and dances for the survival of his offspring. Not only do we obey such distant impulses of the blood and carry them out with fitting solemnity—but we do it at the height of spring. When else to celebrate achievement, fruitfulness, and going forth, than when, from the remoteness of the human past, it has always been celebrated. Tied to old wheels of ritual we echo down the valleys of time innocently, thinking that this celebration is ours and unique to our ways when, in fact, we only turn an ancient wheel yet another time.

The celebration of spring became a way of talking about the renewal of civilization in different periods of human history—the Golden Age of Pericles, the Medici in Florence, the Sung in China—and a prelude for Arthur's sense of a new era unfolding in the last half of the twentieth century. He called himself "an inveterate optimist" about the steady disintegration and transformation of all that had been familiar. "The American 'Good Life' with its smug pretences is slipping into the past," he argued, "and the materialism that brought it about is being called into question." To master the universe, humans had put their trust in science and technology at the expense of religion and art. Ironically, from a man who spent part of every week on transcontinental flights, he posited that great highways and waterworks, complex cities, rapid transportation and communication, and extraterrestrial flight had prevailed to our detriment. Echoing Rilke, he said we had yet to give voice to the new gods that would emerge triumphant. Mechanistic materialism had created in North America one of the ugliest civilizations in history, proliferating in Holiday Inns and hamburger outlets all around the world. North America's cities were alive with fake building styles, its homes filled with fake antiques; plastic flowers gathered dust in hotel lobbies. Disneyland was rife across the continent. But that was about to change as holistic thinking prevailed again. He offered SFU as an example: "The design of this university for better or worse was an attempt to put the heretofore fragmented university campus back together, in the hope that the gaps between the separate intellectual disciplines themselves might be bridged." He concluded by pointing to the arts: "Of all the panoply of pursuits, of all the roads to reality open to us, the arts stand almost alone as synthesizers of human experience. In our search for wholeness, they are critical. They are the source of meaning, and with meaning, the means of joy in life."

IT WAS DURING this period, while Arthur's creative life was in full flood, that he was approached by a German couple in Vancouver about building them a home. Arthur had forsworn involvement in any more house-building projects: they took too much time and did not earn enough for his practice. Moreover, domestic space no longer interested him; his attention was drawn to public spaces and monumental buildings. But when he met the Eppichs, he recognized that they were unique among those who sought his services. They were not affluent people who wanted a beautiful home to reflect business success and social prominence; rather, they were a modest couple of some means with a strong enthusiasm for the arts. Indeed, they would turn out to be ideal clients.

Helmut and Hildegard Eppich, both born in the ethnic German enclave of Gottschee, in present-day Slovenia, did not meet until they had emigrated to Canada. Helmut arrived in Vancouver in 1953, and with his twin, Hugo, established a small tool and die shop that quickly grew into one of the city's most prominent businesses, becoming with time a multi-faceted group of companies under the name of Ebco Industries Ltd. It was an enterprise with high-profile achievements in numerous fields. Its manufacture of cyclotron components was crucial for the production of radioisotopes essential to medical imaging and nuclear biomedical research. As a heavy equipment manufacturer, Ebco would one day produce the machine used to bore the service line for the underground tunnel between England and France. The Eppich brothers also oversaw the production of sophisticated computer data collection systems. Having come to maturity in three different countries, they knew first-hand the sting of bigotry and were dedicated to its elimination in their workplace. By the 1980s, the company would number more than nine hundred employees from forty ethnic and religious backgrounds and be known for a spirit of tolerance and co-operation.[9]

In early 1972, Arthur was impressed by the integrity and the enlightened aura that surrounded this family. He was equally impressed by Helmut and Hildegard's knowledge of and feeling for the arts. Helmut was excited by modernist architecture, an enthusiasm fostered by an older brother, Egon, who was a painter, sculptor, and art critic in Germany. Austere modernism as practised by Mies van der Rohe, Walter Gropius, and Le Corbusier embodied for Helmut the values of plain living conducted with style, and this is what he saw exemplified in Arthur's buildings.

The Eppichs, enamoured of Vancouver's natural setting, were searching for a wooded property with a stream running through it on which to build. A park-like property in southwest Vancouver, close to the family business, fulfilled their requirements, except for one thing—it was on the Musqueam First Nation's land and came with a ninety-nine-year tenancy, a condition reminiscent of the often troubled landowning systems in Europe. Their search led finally to the city's North Shore and a large, steeply sloped property in West Vancouver. It was situated ideally at the end of a cul-de-sac on Palmerston Avenue, with a creek flowing on the east side, though it had been used by local residents as a dump for landfill and house-hold garbage—tin cans, tiles, broken glass, rusted bedsprings—and was viewed by the municipality as unbuildable. Moreover, there was an easement splitting the property in two lengthwise. But the Eppichs pursued the possibility (the price was only $17,000), and when, with some trepidation, they brought Arthur to view the site, his first response was "very tricky but very interesting."

Two factors came into play in Arthur's decision to design and oversee the building of another home. First, there was the sobering reality that when Arthur and Geoff split up the company in 1972, Arthur was left for a time with little work. Second, and more decisively, the Eppichs explained that they wanted something in masonry rather than wood (to their European perspective, wood was flimsy, subject to fire). It was a chance for Arthur to do something new—a house in glass and concrete.

The first design Arthur produced was for a house built around a courtyard at street level—something like the second Smith house, except in concrete. The courtyard was designed to enclose a clump of lacy hemlocks—the clients' favourite trees—and from street level, the house would enjoy a view of the sea. The Eppichs fell in love with this plan; to them, it embodied the romantic ideal of a forest home. The five-lot property tumbling down the slope, once cleared of refuse, suggested Beethoven's *Pastoral* Symphony in all its possibilities for wilderness landscaping. They felt house and grounds would be the perfect setting for some of Egon's paintings and sculpture.

But after the Eppichs had, in their imaginations, "lived in this house for seven months," Arthur returned with a completely different set of plans. To him the original design had not engaged with the setting—it was just a house sitting on the edge of a ravine. His new idea was to build a house on four descending levels that was set into the landscape in such a way as to shore up and become part of the slope. This was one of the most dramatic opportunities in his career to put into practice Frank Lloyd Wright's radical proposal about the relationship between "architecture and acreage." In *The Living City*, Wright had stated: "Architectural features of any democratic ground plan for human freedom rise naturally by, and from, topography. This means that buildings would all take on, in endless variety, the nature and character of the ground on which they would stand and, thus inspired, become component parts—organic features of that ground."[10] With the Eppich house, not only would the architecture conform to and secure the landscape, it would erase the environmental abuse that occurred when it was used as a dumping ground.

At first, the Eppichs were dismayed. This new design seemed too massive, almost pompous; Helmut knew, moreover, that all the reinforced concrete would be very expensive. But their faith in Arthur's architectural genius was unwavering, and so, in their own words, they let themselves be "re-educated."

Rarely had Arthur found clients so sensitive and pliant. Eager to please them, he created what they came to view as a home in a "classical" style. In terms of function, the Eppich house descended logically down the slope, with garage and storeroom at road level; the entry and the four children's bedrooms at the second level; dining room, kitchen, and living areas on the third; den and master bedroom on the fourth. Part of the stream was diverted to form a small lake at the foot of the house, so that in certain lights the house appeared magically doubled by its reflection. Its lateral reach of flying beams and regularly spaced matching columns created a particularly eloquent example of what Arthur called the rhythmic "cadence of light and line." At each level the house was terraced to catch the daylight, and at the lowest level the lake reflected the northwest sky, bringing light into the depths of a lot shadowed by cedars, hemlocks, and large-leafed maples.

Arthur's second design for the Eppich house reflected his thinking at this time, which was opposed to the Western humanist tradition modelled on God making the world from the void. That concept of creativity, Arthur said in a lecture, "requires a separate and distinct ego over and against an entirely neutral and passive nature." He pointed out that it was not the norm in the rest of the world.[11] Instead, most cultures were established through long processes of selection and adaptation to geography and climate, and the artist in such cultures was the individual who responded with the greatest sensitivity to those conditions. In Zen terms, the artist was like an empty vessel waiting to be "filled." Arthur described this experience of creativity with reference to Jungian psychology:

> In this condition of non-thought the supra-conscious intelligence comes into play, providing a basis of judgment superior to conscious thought. For on this unconscious level we are open, antenna-like to peripheral stimuli, and this much wider range of information is

absorbed without our knowing it to become part of our intuitive perception. It is only then that we are capable of perceiving what is culturally significant, because we are then at the level of the "collective unconscious.[12]

In this view the physical and temporal contexts are the source of ideas for a work, and it can often take a long time for the artist to "intuit" what those needs are.

Many of Arthur's clients were hard-pressed by his application of aesthetic philosophy, but the Eppichs were trusting and patient, even as the estimated costs rose from $75,000 to $360,000 and completion of the project stretched from "a few months" to nearly four years. Arthur's ambitions for the house included a role for Francisco as interior decorator. Again his clients were willing to be "educated." When Francisco telephoned to say he had found ideal carpeting in Hong Kong, Hildegard flinched to learn it was a thick chocolate brown—she envisioned carpeting that would show every footprint and bit of lint. "But you will love it," Francisco swooned over the phone (the carpeting had already been cut) and, after it was installed, they did. He told the Eppichs it had required eighty thousand silk worms to produce the raw silk curtains he had chosen for their living room.

There were three features of the house that drew particular attention: a concrete cantilevered staircase descending from the second to the fourth level in a direct diagonal line, a moon window created in latticework in the dining room, and an outdoor swimming pool off the tiled terrace of the living room. The pool was designed to be an infinity pool that would connect visually with the artificial lake below and, from there, with the ocean in the distance. But the motor that was installed, five horsepower instead of fifteen, was too weak to handle both the overflow and the return. Arthur had proposed and sketched an even more ambitious plan for a grand study cantilevered over the stream. That, and a suggested sauna and pool house, would have raised costs higher, and Helmut was already selling shares in his company to cover the growing expenses. Although the Eppichs said no to the idea, it suggested itself to more than one critic who likened the Eppich house to Frank Lloyd Wright's Fallingwater.[13] On one occasion, photographs of the house were exhibited with the title "Cascade House."[14]

The Eppichs developed a special relationship with Myrtle Erickson while the house was being constructed. She would say, "Don't rush Arthur," knowing that his method was slow and intuitive. At the same time, she did not hesitate to identify problems; she urged the Eppichs in friendly fashion to have a railing built along the cantilevered stair—"or someone will fall."[15] Myrtle would drive herself over to Palmerston Avenue, and one day, sitting by the pool, she confided to these friends her motherly wish that Arthur would marry. But to the Eppichs Arthur was an exemplary instance of the artistic genius for whom celibacy was crucial, and they cited Leonardo da Vinci, Michelangelo, Beethoven, and "poor" Tchaikovsky. Thinking of these musicians and two of their greatest works—Beethoven's Seventh Symphony, completed in 1812, and Tchaikovsky's *1812 Overture*—they persuaded the West Vancouver municipality to let them number their house 1812 instead of 1814.

The Eppichs felt themselves richly rewarded when their house was identified as a masterpiece of modern architecture—Erickson's finest work in the domestic genre. It was photographed for numerous magazines in North America and Europe, including *Architectural Digest* and *Town & Country*,[16] and in years to come would be used frequently as a setting for films and advertisements. The Eppichs, who lived quietly, often found themselves entertaining high-profile visitors: their guest book included signatures from Manfred Wörner, the secretary general of NATO (attended by two Mounties for security); B.C. premier Bill Vander Zalm; Roman Catholic Archbishop Carney; broadcaster and future governor general Adrienne Clarkson; and pop art icon Andy Warhol. One day, Lois Milsom brought Margaret Trudeau who, entering the master bedroom, threw herself down on the bed and said, "I'd do business from here." Simon Scott's wedding was held in the garden as was a launch for Arthur's book about his architecture. With time and the resurgence of vegetation, the house seemed to stretch out into the bushes and the trees as if it had no end. Realizing for Arthur one of his most important goals, it looked as if it had always been there.

EARLY IN 1971 Arthur had received an invitation to spend an evening with his friends Audrey and Harry Hawthorn of UBC's Anthropology Department. They wanted to discuss with him their long-envisioned plan for a museum to house the artifacts that had been accumulating in the basement of the university library for more than forty years. Audrey recalled in a memoir that Arthur came to their house "one beautiful and snowy evening" and her husband built a glowing fire. They talked in front of its warmth about the concept of visible storage; requirements for teaching, research, and display; and the interplay of public and university needs. The three were oblivious to the increasing roar of the fire until Audrey realized that the chimney had caught. But while "spectacular clouds of sparks drifted around outside with the snowflakes," Arthur and Harry talked on, unperturbed, merely raising their voices.[17]

Arthur had already spent many hours with Audrey, looking at items in the vast collection. "Every drawer or cupboard was stuffed with containers, boxes and tins. She would patiently take out one, unwrap the layers of cotton and tissue to reveal a minutely carved spoon from an antler or a sheep's horn, perhaps a headpiece carved in the image of a bear with luminous inset eyes of abalone, or a box of steamed wood bulging from its rectangular prototype on all four carved sides with a tight-fitting lid supporting a deftly carved frog—or a rattle intricately carved with frogs in conjugal union and tongues unified in one slender arc from beast to beast."[18] It was in that library basement that his own vision of a permanent museum first took place.

Knowing of Arthur's friendly relations with the prime minister, the Hawthorns appealed to him to use his connections to see what might be possible. The government department National Museums of Canada was headed by Bernard Ostry. In his many trips to Ottawa, Arthur had met Bernard and his wife, Sylvia, an economist, and felt well-positioned to plead the case. For several months, the Hawthorns heard only rumours. Then, on July 1, they received a call from Ottawa telling them to listen to the radio at 10:30 that morning. It was the day marking the centennial of British Columbia's entry into Confederation, and Prime Minister Trudeau stood on the steps of the Parliament Buildings in Victoria to announce that the government was providing $2.5 million for the building of a museum of anthropology at UBC. To Audrey's great relief, the university's notoriously capricious bureaucracy put up no objection to her declaration that "there is only one architect for this building and that is Arthur Erickson."[19]

Arthur had a profound admiration for the arts of the Northwest Coast First Nations. The works represented for him, in both their practical functions and their ceremonial aspects, fine examples of art arising directly from the conditions of geography and climate. But he understood that the First Nations were struggling to preserve and nourish what remained of their once flourishing culture. One of his first observations was of a general nature: "Our aim will be to try to convey the idea to all of those who visit the Museum, and those who study in it, that at one time, on this coast, there was a noble and great response to this land that has never been equalled since."[20] Arthur's statement, while strongly personal, echoed the claim of the French anthropologist, Claude Lévi-Strauss, cited by Audrey Hawthorn, that "the culture of the Northwest Indians produced an art on a par with that of Greece or Egypt." It was a culture, Lévi-Strauss asserted, that reached back ten thousand years and had the highest standard of living of any people in the world without agriculture as their base.[21]

For the building, the university allocated a priceless stretch of land on the high cliffs of Point Grey that looked out over the straits beyond Vancouver's harbour to the glaciated peaks of the coastal mountains. It was the scene Arthur had often enjoyed as he visited the Swintons, whose home was on that same stretch of land. He tried to approach the site without ideas, but he could see that it replicated in archetypal fashion the situation of an aboriginal coastal village between the sea and the forest.[22] There were, nonetheless, obstacles to work around. The sandstone cliffs were subject to slow but inexorable erosion, and so the museum had to be set back at a reasonable distance from the edge. There were already permanent human marks on the site in the form of three concrete turrets, fifteen feet thick, that had been poured for gun emplacements during the Second World War. These somehow had to be incorporated. And to preserve the scenic view from Marine Drive, the museum had to be a low structure. But working within restraints, for Arthur, was necessary to create "a thing of Beauty."[23]

From the outset, Arthur envisioned glass windows towering forty feet high so that the totem poles standing inside the building would look out to the sea and mountains beyond. There would be a pool in front of the museum to give the illusion that it was actually situated on the shore of an inlet. The museum was to be structured in such a way as to lead the visitor on a path that replicated a walk through the forest towards the ocean. Equally important was the arrangement of artifacts along that path to identify the uniqueness of each nation as determined by geographical location. Arthur's theory was that the fully rounded naturalistic figures of animals and humans released from wood by the Salish carvers should give way to the more symbolic masks of the Kwakwaka'wakw and Nuu-chah-nulth, and then to the unpainted poles of the Haida and Tsimshian, in which the form of the tree still dominates and the shallow carving is abstract, almost mystical. He especially wanted to illustrate in the Great Hall at the front of the museum the powerful contrast between the flamboyant and eclectic character of Kwakwaka'wakw art and the "classic control" of the Haida and Tsimshian, a contrast best visualized in terms of the beak-snapping activity of massive cannibal bird masks compared with the quiet, weather-worn serenity of the Haida pole fragments. He thought of it as the dramatic difference between the art of Italy and that of Scandinavia, or of the Corinthian and the Doric.

As with each of his earlier projects, Arthur set out to rethink the genre of the building he was designing. Just as the function of universities, office buildings, and law courts was radically altering along democratic lines, so too was the museum on an altered course. In a lengthy outline titled "A Functional Program for the Museum of Anthropology," Arthur provides a historical overview of the evolution of museums.[24] Works of art and collections of writing in European and Asian empires were originally owned by rulers and members of the ruling classes, and public access was limited to distant viewing in places like cathedrals. Scholarship was insignificant, but this changed with worldwide exploration and the invention of the printing press, which made possible the distribution of knowledge previously concealed in manuscripts. But it was the Industrial Revolution, bringing large concentrations of people to the cities and fostering social reforms such as universal education, that created the demand for public museums. The British Museum had been founded in 1753 to house a large private bequest consisting of manuscripts, books, drawings, natural specimens, and ethnographic materials, and free admission was granted to all "studious and curious persons." By the late nineteenth century, the museum had become a place where the public could see the growing wealth of materials from colonial collections, hear lectures, and learn freely.

Arthur wanted to take this democratizing of knowledge an important step further—to make all the anthropology museum's holdings available to public access by means of open-drawer storage. He described his thinking this way: "I had always resented the practice that some other person should determine what I was supposed to see. A closed collection is a censored one. Curators, like teachers, may often shield us from the truth. We need our own broad sources for comparison to understand reality or make value judgments."[25] The Hawthorns, having arrived at a similar point in their own thinking, agreed that Arthur should develop the idea to its full potential. This resulted in what is now known as "visible storage," with the entire collection open to the public in glass-fronted cases and in chests of Plexiglas-covered drawers.[26]

Once Arthur had conceived of the building as embodying a walk through the forest to the sea, it was a matter, he would say, of "inevitabilities hardly involving design at all."[27] The structure would be

post and beam, in columns stepping up in seven intervals from sixteen feet at the entrance to forty-five feet in the glass-covered front
hall. Acknowledging the aboriginal use of enormous split cedar logs
and luxurious disregard for structural requirements, Arthur made
both the columns and the channelled roof beams the same width
and thickness, as he had done with the second Smith house, to give
the building a monumental serenity.[28] Such monumentality also
makes reference to the scale of the trees found in the Pacific Northwest.[29] He cast the building in unfinished, light grey concrete since,
as he would write, "the superb, sea-silvered carvings, sometimes still
bearing traces of paint, needed a simple background for contrast."[30]
The exhibits, he believed, should be bathed in the transparent,
watery light of the Northwest Coast; to achieve this, he used bands
of double-glazed, barrel-vaulted skylights between the channelled
beams, which contained unobtrusive artificial lighting.

There were the inevitable delays in construction and a short-
age of funds. Arthur wrote to Trudeau in October 1974, asking for
$300,000 from the federal government's museum board to be sent
early, so that they could complete the MOA on time. "The intention
of the Museum, as you will remember, is to architecturally link up
with the environment in somewhat the same sense as the native cultures linked with and were dependent upon the environment, thus
the landscaping of the roofs ties the building to the ground as the
pond-like setting for the massive carvings reiterates very vividly the
relationship of the original villages to the forest and to the sea. This
vital aspect of the Museum will be lost unless further funding is
available."[31]

The formal opening with Governor General Léger, Premier Bennett, and two thousand guests was held in May 1976. Although that
was a year later than projected, everything had gone smoothly until
a few days before the public was invited in. At that point, Arthur,
returning from one of his many trips, was shocked to find what
the display expert had done with the exhibits. The three entrance
galleries—the walk through the forest—had been hung with so
many masks that it "looked like a bargain basement." Even more

distressing, all the massive carvings in the Great Hall had been made to face inward—towards the visitors. To Arthur, one of the great mysteries of the Acropolis was that the caryatids stare off into the distance to the unknown. In a rare fit of uncontrolled anger, he convinced Harry Hawthorn that something had to be done at once. Cranes were brought in and the poles reset. The great carvings, he insisted, "with their expressionless, primal eyes, their beaks and snouts," should gaze again "at nothing" as they had once gazed out to sea. In making this change, he felt he had transformed the Great Hall into "a sanctuary."[32]

While the museum was being built, Walter Koerner, a major benefactor of the Northwest collection, mentioned to Arthur that he had located a large block of yellow cedar and was saving it for a commissioned work by carver Bill Reid. Arthur began thinking about a special site for the carving. Two of the Second World War gun mounts were being incorporated into the Great Hall—one on the edge of the west wall, the other intruding into the centre of the hall, disguised by displays. Arthur suggested that Bill Reid plan his work to rest on the third gun mount: Arthur would provide a round skylight overhead so that the carving would be naturally illuminated, as if by a shaft of light coming through the forest. Reid accepted the commission and eventually presented Arthur with a tiny intricate carving that interpreted the Haida myth of creation. Reid and his team completed the full-size piece, and Arthur was present in 1980 as it was lowered through the museum roof to rest on its podium. To Arthur, the glowing, golden image in yellow cedar was not only ravishing to behold but radiating with humour and sly wit. There was Raven, the eternal Trickster figure, opening a clamshell to find the first tiny humans, one of whom is unsure about emerging and in breech-birth fashion is turning his backside to the world. More pointedly, by choosing to place on the gun turret a haunting portrayal of creation, Reid, by means of a Haida narrative, was replacing the evils of imperialism with the triumphant birth of a new order.[33]

Bill Reid's masterwork *The Raven and the First Men* became one of the most popular features of the museum. But two other aspects of the overall museum composition would be a source of lasting frustration and some bitterness for Arthur. First, there was the matter of landscaping. Cornelia Oberlander began bringing to the site plants that the aboriginal peoples had used for food, clothing, and medicine, creating an ethnobotanical display in harmony with the setting. But the university's arborists regularly trimmed the sheltering broadleaf maples, and the native ecosystem, thus exposed, gradually died. Even more disturbing to Arthur was a perceived problem with the pool. Although the bottom was sealed with impermeable clay, reports argued that water from the pool could seep into the sandstone and further erode the cliffs on which the museum stood. Consequently, in Arthur's lifetime the pool was filled only on rare occasions, and the public at large was never able to view the museum in what Arthur regarded as its completed form.[34] He decried this as the attitude of Philistines; his critics labelled him unrealistic and seemed almost pleased when leaks appeared in the skylights. As always, Arthur would reply that such imperfections never worried him—they were part of nature.

Although the MOA was fraught with controversy at times, it has probably earned more praise than any of Arthur's other creations. Most critics of architecture regard it as Erickson's masterwork and reference its vitality not just to the aboriginal longhouse but to influences as far distant as the torii of Japanese shrines and the buildings of ancient Egypt, which stare into the wilderness with the totemic power of the Sphinx.[35] Certainly, as Rhodri W. Liscombe has asserted, "The MOA is rich in historical understanding."[36] But the description of his building that outweighed all others, in Arthur's opinion, was published in *artscanada* the year the museum opened.[37] The author, Joan M. Vastokas, arguing that architecture might prove to be the future's most significant art form, touched on what Arthur regarded as the fundamentals in his work: post and beam as the purest, most elemental component of architectural design; tradition as vital in the creation of new forms of art; the crucial relationship of architecture to its setting; and the role of the architect as one who "listens" not only to the client but to what the environment has to say.

What especially thrilled Arthur was Vastokas's attempt to articulate what the visitor experiences when moving through the building. The visitor enters and moves down a relatively narrow passage, "compelled to follow this route by the promise of a brightly lit space at the end... as if moving through a funnel." After the low ceilings of the introductory galleries, he or she experiences a sudden visual release and is "propelled into a vast, open, and light-filled space of psychological repose—a feeling of physical weightlessness and almost beatific well-being." But the visitor, she says, does not experience absolute repose and containment, because his or her vision still moves—"outward, beyond the vast glass walls that open to sea, sky, and mountains, and beyond these, through space to an unknown world beyond. For visually, there is no precise distinction between the interior space of the gallery and the exterior space of beach, sea and sky."[38] What was suggested, she wrote, was an "an almost mystical opening, not only to an exterior landscape environment but to a cosmological beyond, to other worlds and realms where only the imagination can travel."

It is not surprising that Arthur felt that no finer language ever clothed his artistic vision. Vastokas's choice of words is resonant with his admiration for Rilke who wrote that the artist's work was to create God. For Arthur, that meant that every building he designed had something like a religious purpose, that it was his Promethean duty to give his work a mystical dimension, his phrase "the weight of heaven" embodying both the restraint and release of his spiritual tectonics.

17

The Canadian Chancery

FAME ENTAILS CLOSE PUBLIC scrutiny, and Arthur's frequent references to wealthy patrons drew attention to a contradiction—his expressed views were often inconsistent with his style of living. He talked repeatedly about democratizing public buildings, but at the same time he clearly identified with society's wealthy class and those who could serve as his financial supporters. He extolled his connection to students and working people, yet dressed like a film star and ate at the best restaurants. He professed his great love for Vancouver and Canada, but was now spending much of his time out of the country. His seemingly affluent lifestyle was necessary for business, he said in his own defence; he could not realize his ambitions for public architecture without cultivating a certain image in the world of finance. Further, he would remind his critics, he still lived in a garage; although he wished for something better, he could not afford it. But his detractors knew that Arthur's best friends included not only the Trudeaus but William F. Buckley, America's most articulate spokesman for conservative social and political views.

The opportunity to critique both Arthur's buildings and his apparent politics came when he published the first book about his work—*The Architecture of Arthur Erickson*, a fairly lavish volume with a rich selection of photographs chiefly by Simon Scott. The book contained a succinct and eloquent presentation of Arthur's aesthetic principles, under the headings of site, light, cadence, and space, but local reviewers were not generous. In the *Province*, Barrie Cook praised the photography but focussed his review on two issues—the egocentricity of the architect in writing a book about himself, and the stark, angular quality of Erickson's buildings. Arthur was uneasy about the appearance of self-promotion, and he gave several accounts of how the book had come about—among these that he was approached by Tundra Books of Montreal and had only agreed to such a book "as long as I didn't have to get involved."[1] He claimed in a prefatory note that the text originated in taped interviews for Geoffrey James's 1972 *Time* magazine article, and that his brother, Don (at that time teaching English at BCIT), had edited Arthur's "random observations" for the book. He accurately attributed much of the organizational effort to Simon Scott.[2]

Donald Gutstein, reviewer for the *Vancouver Sun*, also questioned the suitability of a self-authored book, calling it a "paean of self-praise," and he examined in a harsher light the architect's person and his politics.[3] What emerged from the book, Gutstein wrote, was no ordinary mortal but "a remote super being," whose view of architecture was elitist and whose attitude towards people was arrogant. This "godlike creator... mystifie[d] architectural design in order to overwhelm the average person." A year earlier, Gutstein had published an article titled "Arthur Erickson: The Corporate Artist-Architect," in which he examined Arthur's relations with land developers and large corporations.[4] Gutstein gave as a striking example the 1971 Village Lake Louise project, a proposal by Imperial Oil Ltd. for a $37-million ski resort in Banff National Park. As a publicly identified environmentalist, Arthur was viewed as the ideal architect; his participation in the scheme would allay local fears of damage being done to the park. But Gutstein was not convinced, and he pointed out that the high-cost development was not intended for local residents but for eastern and international jet-set vacationers.[5] In his review of Arthur's book, he asserted that Erickson's view of the environment was superficially limited to the visual and ignored its social, political, economic, and cultural components. Although Bess Harris had praised Simon Fraser University as "a living work of art . . . one that expresses the inner life of the artist and also the land," Gutstein wrote, Arthur's architecture "illustrates his lack of concern for the needs, interests, and values of the users of the buildings." SFU had enormous problems as a result. It was not possible, Gutstein insisted, to equate architecture with art; architects relied on clients to pay for the execution of their work, and if the client was a corporation, the architect's aesthetics must serve profit-making interests. Although Arthur could dismiss this review as a heavily Marxist reading of his work, he could not ignore the fact that he was being criticized locally in an unfriendly fashion. Moreover, the negative reception of his book came at a time when some of his most ambitious designs—for Christ Church Cathedral, the federal government building in Vancouver, and the Shaughnessy Hospital redevelopment—had failed to be realized.

Arthur would subsequently answer the charge of elitism by pointing to an idea that he and Bing Thom developed for the UN-HABITAT conference, held in Vancouver in June 1976. The principal theme of the conference was housing in the Third World. To get the attention of the community at large, the two architects decided to involve schoolchildren in the construction of two large reception pavilions placed in front of the old courthouse. Except for wooden posts and metal joints, the pavilion roofs would be made of papier mâché finished with a plastic coating. Children brought newspapers from home and were bussed to a factory warehouse; wearing construction helmets, they pasted newspaper to premade moulds. When the paper had dried, they returned to decorate the different sections with motifs from the conference. Arthur felt this activity accomplished three goals. First, it demonstrated that recycling was one of the world's crucial activities. Second, if a child could do this, anyone could build something. Third, making a building could be a community activity, not just the work of an individual architect. He compared the HABITAT project to the work of the early cathedral builders, the effort of many artisans, none of whom knew exactly what the outcome of their individual contributions would be. Unfortunately, heavy rains at the time of the conference made the whole idea seem doubtful at best.

SOME OF THE negative feelings about Arthur were generated by the large amounts of time he spent away from the city. In 1969, he had opened an office in Toronto to give his practice a national profile, something he felt necessary if he was someday going to be an architect of international stature. The Toronto move was occasioned by his being selected to design an addition for the Bank of Canada in Ottawa. At a private dinner party hosted by Pierre Trudeau, Arthur had met Louis Rasminsky, then governor of the bank. Shortly thereafter, Rasminsky phoned Arthur to say that the Bank of Canada and the Department of Public Works, located directly across Sparks Street from the bank, wanted to develop the two blocks they were on together. "The potential was terrific," Arthur told a reporter, "and we proposed a glassed-in mall which would be a kind of winter garden between the two properties," an escape from the cold and greyness of Ottawa winters. "Wouldn't it be marvellous," he suggested, "to have a public area where you could go for a drink and be able to see your Senator at the next table or the Ambassador from Senegal!"[6] But the minister of public works vetoed the proposal.

The Bank of Canada assignment was a prestigious government commission nonetheless, though Arthur's design again met initial opposition, this time from the governing board of the bank. The one thing they did not want was another glass tower; they wanted something in limestone to match the original neoclassical-style building from the 1930s and to blend with the other government buildings on Wellington Street. Arthur patiently explained that one would not take a piece of Baroque gold and place it in a setting of new gold; rather, one would find a contrasting material. And so, his extension (undertaken with the firm of Marani, Rounthwaite & Dick) enclosed the original limestone building on three sides with a glass atrium flanked by two glass towers. The atrium between the towers contained a tropical garden bordering a pool and became a welcome public space, popular for weddings, though in Arthur's view it was just a vestige of his larger vision encompassing Sparks Street, "hardly worth mentioning."[7] The atrium also served as a forecourt for the bank's numismatics museum on the ground floor. But what distinguished the building most was its combination of the contemporary and the traditional. The copper columns, spandrels, and mullions of the new building were treated with acid to give them a green colouration that tied in with the roofs of surrounding buildings on Wellington. The choice of copper also reflected this metal's historic role as a fundamental of monetary currency. The walls were made of mirrored glass, so that the older Gothic surroundings were reflected in, and thus part of, the new building. As with the Osaka pavilion, this made the new building fit its setting by disappearing into reflections—by becoming, as Arthur sometimes phrased it, a "non-building." As time passed, the bank addition would also reflect the evolution away from the heavy buildings required for the symbolic protection of cash to the virtual world of electronic monetary transactions. Arthur's fondest memory of the project was watching a team of Japanese specialists treating the copper with acid to achieve the desired verdigris patina.

Keith Loffler, an energetic and affable young architect, quickly became an important employee in Arthur's Toronto office. Upon his arrival in Canada from Australia in 1969, Loffler was awestruck by Simon Fraser University, then much discussed in architectural schools. After completing a graduate degree in the University of Toronto's architecture program, Loffler saw a notice that Erickson was hiring for his Toronto office, applied, and was taken into the practice. A new concert hall for Toronto was the focus of the advertisement, but the work at hand was the Ottawa bank.

Loffler's initiation came when he was assigned to design a new landscape plan for the atrium. Arthur's plan and that of Marani, Rounthwaite & Dick were at odds, so Keith came up with a possible resolution. But when they flew to Ottawa to meet with the other architects, Arthur instructed Keith not to present his compromise. Instead, Arthur recalled at the joint meeting with some asperity how short-sighted the Sparks Street Mall Authority had been in vetoing his original design for the bank's atrium. Now, he said, they were all meeting to make the best of a bad situation. He called for some tracing paper, which he placed on the table over the other architects' plan, and proceeded to sketch out his own new proposal, different again from Keith's. The others objected that this was different from the design the Bank of Canada had tentatively approved, but Arthur replied that what they had seen was out of date. When called on, Keith said the new plans, which Arthur had just sketched, were on his office desk awaiting final approval. With that, Arthur characteristically looked at his watch and said he had a plane to catch.

On the return flight, Keith expressed his fear that there would be trouble getting approval for the changes; he felt he had no real leverage for keeping the Ottawa architects on track. But Arthur advised Keith to remind the others that Arthur would "take matters to the highest authorities" if there were any objections. Keith issued such threats as diplomatically as possible—and with success. On that trip, he recalled, he also became aware, going to and from Toronto airport, of how fast Arthur drove: "He would have made a champion racing-car driver."[8]

ARTHUR'S FIRST MAJOR commission in Toronto itself came in 1973, from the city's transit authority, which hired him to design the Yorkdale Subway Station. In the end, the building took the streamlined shape of a subway train, including its rounded skylight roof and windowed steel sides. As Arthur suggested, the building was best appreciated from the outside, from a moving automobile. But within, Rhodri W. Liscombe would observe, "The excitement of travel, even commuting, and the sensation of movement are articulated by the overall shape."[9]

Whenever Arthur was asked how he liked Toronto, he made the kind of disparaging observations that typified his assessments of Vancouver. Especially as compared to Montreal, he would say, in Toronto there was a great lack of style. "I guess it's the English and Scottish background. You dress down and live in a very low-keyed way and tend to be very insensitive to your surroundings."[10] When he and Francisco looked for a place to live in the city, they were also struck by a lack of privacy: "All the homes looked into one another's windows," and the apartment buildings were equally "appalling" in that respect. Eventually, they rented a coach house at 7 Highland Avenue in Toronto's exclusive Rosedale district, an area with more gardeners per capita than probably anywhere else in the country. The coach house belonged to Larry Heisey, the publisher of Harlequin romances, who lived in "a majestic house directly across the street." Arthur and Francisco took shameless advantage of their landlord's friendliness, going as far as to knock out a wall to accommodate a lengthy mural by American pop artist Roy Lichtenstein. A magazine article would later attribute the interior decor to Arthur's modernist aesthetics,[11] but it was more likely Francisco's decorating scheme that determined the white walls and the monochromatic furnishings: chrome-and-black-leather Mies van der Rohe dining chairs, grey suede Le Corbusier armchairs, grey broadloom. Only freshly cut flowers and a few carefully selected art objects lightened the austere mood. These included two Claude Tousignant oils facing each other across the living room, a small sculpture of coloured acrylic panels by Venezuelan sculptor Jesús Rafael Soto, and a bronze bust of a Sung Dynasty princess. The only touch of vibrant colour was found in the bathroom, the walls of which were covered with Thai silk "the colour of a blood orange." The coach house included a tiny walled garden with a fern-edged goldfish pond. Arthur told the magazine writer that "somewhere in my nature there's still a longing for a monastic existence, a retreat."[12]

Toronto was a key location in the Montreal–Toronto–New York triangle. In a very real sense, Arthur was living in all three cities simultaneously. Francisco still had his furniture business on Sherbrooke Street in Montreal and kept an apartment there. In New York, with the assistance of Lois and Geoffrey Milsom, they located an apartment in the Olympic Towers on Fifth Avenue, which they purchased and remodelled at great cost. Guests remember a handsome steel dining table custom made by the Eppich brothers, a showing of Ellsworth Kelly paintings on the walls, and a glass floor that Francisco was always anxious that guests might scratch or chip. In

Manhattan, he and Arthur had a dazzling list of friends and acquaintances, including one of the country's wealthiest and most generous patrons of the arts, David Rockefeller; the leading New York interior designer Joe D'urso, architect Philip Johnson; dramatist Edward Albee; and painters Roy Lichtenstein, Mark Rothko, Ellsworth Kelly, and Frank Stella. They also knew Andy Warhol, who for a time was talking to Arthur about designing him a home. The pair mixed easily with this company and with various habitués of Studio 54.

To give their social life in New York a creative focus, Arthur built in the mid-1970s a house on Fire Island, a narrow spit of land off Long Island famous for its nude beaches and gay enclaves. The two-storey house was a composition of simple cubic frames expressed in cedar and glass, its transparency clearly a reference to Philip Johnson's Glass House. The white walls, white glazed tile floor, and white furnishings set against the blue of the ocean registered every subtle shift in atmosphere and light. Two extravagant mechanical devices emphasized that it was a beach house—though an unusually elegant one. One of these was hinged fences: when they were upright for complete privacy, they were like the sides of a ship, and the house seemed ready to set out on open water; when the beach was empty and the fences lowered, there was a full view of the breakers. The other was a retractable roof over the living room that opened with the press of a button and on a summer evening let the occupants sit around the fireplace under the stars.

The Fire Island house was the scene of many parties. One of these, for jazz and soul singer Roberta Flack, was given a touch of glamour by the presence of Pat Buckley and Philip Johnson. In the summer of 1979, for one of the most memorable events, Francisco filled the living room with gold and silver balloons. When midnight came, the roof was opened and the balloons ascended into the sky. Simultaneously, amidst clouds of dry-ice fog, singer France Joli appeared upstairs to belt out her disco hit "Come to Me" for the guests boogying below. Later, this party would be described in several memoirs as a "last waltz" before AIDS began to cast its long shadow over Fire Island and the gay world.[13]

LATE IN THE summer of 1979, Myrtle Erickson died at the age of eighty-four. Diagnosed with cancer earlier in the year, and living for a time with old friends Kay and Dewar Cooke until she went into hospital, Myrtle had requested no funeral but a party instead.

Arthur was bereft, for his mother was the link to his most intimate sense of self and purpose. Along with an all-encompassing love, she had given him self confidence, which allowed him to live the life of an artist with assurance and exuberance. In the list of precious individuals who had awakened Arthur to his calling—Jessie Faunt, Lawren Harris, and Gordon Webber—the originary, determined presence of his mother stood first.

A measure of Myrtle's impact on others was reflected in the expressions of sympathy Arthur received. Jeffrey Lindsay, from whom Arthur had been estranged for several years, remembered Myrtle in a letter with a special kind of love. His McGill classmate and European travel companion, Ken Carruthers, who with his wife, Kaye, now lived in Ohio, wrote that they had found his mother delightful when they came to know her for a time in Vancouver: "She was an unusual and wonderful woman. I remember you talking about her in England in 1951 and before, while we were at McGill, and she certainly lived up to your accolades." Carruthers reminisced about the trip he and Arthur had made to Spain, his departure from Granada for Greece, and his first meeting with Kaye, but the "lasting impression" Myrtle made was his reason to write.[14]

When Pierre Trudeau's mother died in 1973, Arthur had written to his friend: "She must have been an exceptional woman for what she bestowed on you and Tip. And she must have felt a great sense of fulfillment for what you stood for and what you have done for this country. You must at least feel content to have given her that and to have brought to her life a special richness in return. It is a matter for wonder to witness a life lived and finished so fully."[15] These were some of the consoling thoughts he was now having about his relationship with his own mother.

Although Arthur was sometimes in Vancouver only two days in a three-week period, he was still designing some of his best work for clients on the West Coast. In 1978, John Laxton, for whom he had built a cliffside home in West Vancouver, approached Arthur about a ten-storey office building in the Coal Harbour area of Vancouver's downtown. The space was constricted, but it offered a spectacular view of the yacht basin in Burrard Inlet and the mountains beyond. Thinking especially about the approach from the water, Arthur designed a building of stepped terraces and hanging gardens, with every office having access to an outdoor patio space. It was soon known as the Evergreen Building and became a symbol for buildings in the city core being made hospitable to a natural environment. A similar project was King's Landing, a luxurious condominium complex of 320 units located on the Toronto waterfront. Again, the site was restricted—wedged between a freeway and Lake Ontario—but by stepping back each level of the building and opening each apartment to the lake and the light by means of a glassed-in conservatory, Arthur created an external effect that has been likened to a waterfall, an effect best appreciated from a ferry to or from Hanlan's Point on Toronto Island. Of both buildings, Arthur said the concrete street side made them fall into the category of "Queen Anne front and Mary Jane behind."[16]

Arthur would sometimes refer to the houses he had built for the Grahams and the Eppichs in West Vancouver as villas, by which he seemed to mean luxurious residences in a natural setting, although the Roman term *villa* more precisely referred to an agricultural estate where the wealthy city dweller went to check on the management of property and to relax in natural surroundings. In the twentieth century, the luxury residence in the country, sans agriculture, continued to represent removal from the city. Leading architects such as Wright (Fallingwater), Le Corbusier (Villa Savoye), and Mies van der Rohe (Farnsworth House) created for these dwellings some of their most innovative forms. The fine houses Arthur built for the Grahams and the Eppichs were not country retreats but their owners' principal residences, well within the orbit of the city, from which they went to work each day. The ideal of a country retreat for most North Americans, including the Eppichs, was a modest weekend cottage. Arthur only once designed a building in this genre—a 1,400-square-foot summer house for Norman Keevil on the waterfront of Savary Island. Although it referenced in both form and function the pioneer cabin and fisherman's shack, its elegant post-and-beam structure, glass walls, and flat roof identified its modernist origins. It also evoked the aboriginal buildings of the Northwest Coast, facing the water on the margin between forest and sea. Since it was built, the exposed cedar wall boards have weathered to a silvery grey; the flat roof is now covered in moss. The uniquely Erickson touch is the slight terracing of the house's three square grids and an outdoor deck floating above the sandy beach that is surrounded by shoreline grasses and salal.

Two properties that Arthur designed in Washington State in the early 1980s came closer to being villas in the historical sense. One of these, known as Puget Sound house, had grazing fields for Arabian horses, fruit orchards, and berry fields, as well as a conifer forest. Because the property had such a rich variety of distinct views— Puget Sound, the Cascade Mountains, meadows, and forest—and was also a family vacation ranch, Arthur produced a design for four separate pitched-roofed pavilions angled away from each other. He had seen such family compounds in Bali, but he had also for a long time been mulling over the mystery of the Athenian Acropolis and the geometry of its loose arrangement of buildings.

The other house he designed in Washington was for Bagley and Virginia Wright. In a second book about his architecture, Arthur referred to the Wrights, without naming them, as "very special clients"—partly because he had known Virginia, daughter of Prentice Bloedel, from an early age, but also because Bagley Wright, a prominent real estate developer, was an active patron of the arts. A theatre in Seattle was named for his substantial support, and the Wrights were collectors of contemporary painting and sculpture. What they envisioned was a nine-thousand-square-foot country home.[17]

The property was nine acres of thick forest in the Highlands gated community north of Seattle. Arthur's first session with his clients in 1978 included a visit to the Bloedel family estate on nearby

Bainbridge Island, where he saw "a remarkable string of gardens wrested from the glens, meadows and swamps of a similar forest property."[18] In the Pacific Northwest, a forest setting has inevitably a melancholy aspect, and so Arthur's decision, an uncharacteristic one, was to clear-cut a swath east to west through the forest that could accommodate the house at the centre. The clearing he had made flowed through the principal interior spaces—reception area, art gallery, and living room. Above this rectangular space, a glass-block roof allowed a source of ever-changing patterns of light to enter. On either end was water, bringing reflected light from the sky: to the east, a swimming pool; to the west, a shallow sculpture pond, which connected visually to the distant waters of Puget Sound. The classical severity of the concrete house and its setting was emphasized by the removal of the lower branches of the firs and cedars to about fifty feet, so that the 150-foot trees suggested an *allée* of stark architectonic forms. This was further interpreted by the architecture, which included a series of H-shaped concrete portals combining the strong horizontals of the house with the almost overwhelming verticals of the forest. The effect was softened by Cornelia Oberlander's creation of wildflower meadows from the cleared land.

The chief purpose of the house was not domestic (the Wrights' four children were grown); rather, it was to display the owners' remarkable art collection. Accordingly, its architectural logic and detailing were calibrated to the exhibition of specific works of art. Several of the paintings would each fill one-quarter of a wall— pieces by Mark Rothko, Andy Warhol, Jeff Koons. A lead painting by Jannis Kounellis would dominate the front hall; Helen Frankenthaler's *Picture with Frame* would rest over the fireplace. A sculpture by Anthony Caro titled *Riviera* required a terrace of its own by the pool. The house, too, was a sculpted work of art. Kasota limestone was used for flooring indoors and out with stunning effect, but especially successful, in Arthur's opinion, was his experiment in dyeing concrete. The result was what he described as a "tawny parchment hue," a warm yet neutral tone that changed with the moving light of day and was the perfect complement to the art on the walls. At night, the house glowed in the midst of the black forest, and the forest was itself illuminated by strategically placed floodlighting.

But, as so often, the execution of the project did not go smoothly. From Arthur's point of view, it was necessary to go slowly with such a fine building to get it right. "Arthur, I know the pyramids took longer," Bagley chivvied, "but . . ." The Wrights saw a first set of designs in 1979, but it was another two years before concrete was poured. The cost had been estimated at $1 million, but when it was finished in 1982, nearly $4 million had been spent. And almost from the beginning, problems were evident: the glass-block roof leaked, the outdoor limestone terraces stained. It was the presence of Nick Milkovich, Arthur's tactful associate, that encouraged the Wrights to believe their expectations for the home would eventually be realized.

The presence of Francisco as interior decorator was a persistent vexation, especially for Virginia. In the early planning stages, he had visited the Wrights' existing home and, looking about dubiously, asked which items of furniture they planned to take with them to the Highlands. He made them feel that most of their possessions were rubbish; when Virginia said she would be keeping the family dining table and the swan chairs, she caught Francisco rolling his eyes. Virginia had to remind herself that she was the one who had started the family's art collection with her purchase of a Mark Rothko in 1951. Francisco indicated that the idea of a home serving as an art gallery would be a difficult balance. Despite Virginia's objections, he chose black and steel for everything in the kitchen— counters, flooring, utilities—and arranged for the bed in the master room to be placed on a raised platform, as if the Wrights would be holding levees there. But Virginia was determined that her home be livable as well as beautiful, and when the construction and decorating were finished, she soon changed these things.

Arthur remained above the fray in his calm, detached way. He took special pride in his house for the Wrights, because it was a showplace for contemporary art and for fashionable gatherings. Shortly after they moved in, they hosted benefits for the Seattle Ballet Company and the Seattle Opera. Some of the largest gatherings, attended by upwards of two hundred guests, were held to mark the opening of shows at the Seattle Art Museum. But most memorable was an evening entertainment in 1982 that Arthur and Lois Milsom viewed as an "opening" for the house. The composer Philip Glass was there, playing a new composition the Wrights had commissioned. The Wrights felt bombarded by "noise" and noted that some of their guests were fanning themselves nervously,[19] but to Arthur, the pulsing minimalist rhythms resounding from the glass roof were an exact parallel to the cadences of his architecture.

AN OPPORTUNITY TO leave a significant architectural imprint on the city of Toronto had come in 1976, when Arthur was chosen to design a major new concert venue. It was known during planning and construction (stretching into the early 1980s) as the New Massey Hall but would eventually be renamed in memory of financier Roy Thomson. The hall was to be part of an $80-million development, including a park with a cascading waterfall. This was a chance for Arthur to "rethink" another archetypal building, the concert hall, which he believed in the twentieth century was conceived of on such a grand and impersonal scale as to insult the sensitivities of both artists and music lovers. The earliest concert halls, by contrast, with tiers of boxes and small orchestra platforms, had made the musical experience immediate and intimate. In the nineteenth century, painted ceilings and brilliant chandeliers had added a visual delight to the experience.[20] The idea of the intimate spectacle in a park-like setting was at the heart of what he wanted to recover in his interpretation, but as so often with public buildings, it became the source of much controversy and frustration.

The first disappointment for Arthur was the cancellation of the three-acre music park setting, so that the concert hall would have to stand on its own in a congested area of downtown Toronto. The board of governors wanted a jewel-like design for the new hall that would help them launch an effective fundraising campaign. His second disappointment, trying to meet that expectation, was his inability to find glass workers in the Toronto area who could craft a slanted oval roof and canopy without mullions that would give the roof the appearance of a glacier. Arthur was trying to give building materials more plastic forms, as Frank Gehry would do to great acclaim a few years later, but budgetary restraints and a lack of available technical expertise made that impossible. After seemingly endless trials with the design team, Arthur presented a curving steel mesh that swept down from the edge of the circular roofline over the low canopy above the entrance level—a honeycombed glass net that would be reflective by day and make the crowds visible at night.

The board was enthusiastic, but the problem for Arthur was how to achieve intimacy in a building of this size. After "some thirty-two exercises," his answer was an oval structure of concrete piers, from which were hung individual balconies that could be entered separately, dividing some of the audience into small groups. No balcony seat was more than 107 feet from the stage. The concrete slabs of the ceiling, supported by the piers, formed a steel structure shaped like a bicycle wheel. It suggested a chandelier and had two functions— a lighting system for the hall maintained from a ring of catwalks on the "wheel" and an acoustical system of banners. For the latter, an accomplished fibre artist, Mariette Rousseau-Vermette, created three rings of tapestries, consisting of two thousand tubes of wool. The two outer rings were retractable for reverberation control—to ensure clarity for early and contemporary music and a fuller sound for romantic music. Portions of the tapestry moved out of sight or descended, signalling dramatically a change to the next number. Interspersed among sparkling lights, the tubes ranging in colour from ivory through grey to scarlet, purple, and burgundy created a subdued sunburst effect—in Arthur's words, it was "a consummate work of art."

The hall was completed in 1982, and there was a black-tie gala opening concert on September 13. A special fanfare was commissioned for the event, followed by sharply contrasting musical selections designed to show off the hall's versatility. These included an organ concerto by Francis Poulenc, a song by Canadian composer Ernest MacMillan, a choral work by Murray Schafer, and Ravel's

Daphnis et Chloé, performed by the Toronto Symphony and Men-delssohn Choir conducted by Elmer Eisler. Afterwards, Arthur and Francisco hosted a "celebration" at their Rosedale coach house. Police organized the parking, and caterers came and went through-out the evening. On the list of roughly two hundred guests were fam-ily names well known across the country—Bronfman, Eaton, Keevil, Thomson—and individuals accomplished in a variety of fields—pho-tographer Roloff Beny, opera singer Maureen Forrester, ballet dancer Karen Kain, furniture designer Klaus Nienkämper, politician Mitch-ell Sharp. It was a triumphant, glittering occasion.

The design of Roy Thomson Hall was unanimously praised as the work of a master builder; further, it was an outstanding work of modern architecture in Canada's largest city. But the reputation of the building was tainted in various ways. One controversy arose at the time of the opening, when the name of the late Roy Thomson was placed on the hall because the financier's multi-billionaire son, Ken Thomson, had only donated $5.4 million of the total $39-mil-lion cost. It was the first time a major building in Toronto was named for a benefactor who paid for less than half. "My God! You've got to be kidding," exclaimed Pierre Berton, pointing out that more than $6 million had come directly out of the pockets of Toronto tax-payers through property taxes, whereas Thomson's donation would be spread in equal amounts over five years and was tax deductible. Further, Roy Thomson had not been a sophisticated patron of the arts but preferred lowbrow culture—vaudeville, fast-action thrillers, the films of Doris Day. He was reported to have said, "The sweetest music to me is a radio spot commercial at $10 a crack."[21]

But the controversy that would surround Roy Thomson Hall for years concerned the building's acoustics. Because the hall was fan shaped, sound did not carry evenly to all areas. A series of acrylic discs over the concert platform, serving as baffles, did not help to distribute the sound. But the real acoustical problems were said to derive from the wool tubes that formed the sunburst design in the ceiling. In January 1983, eight hundred of the tubes were removed—"the desecration of a work of art," cried Arthur to a reporter for the *Globe and Mail*. He was deeply disappointed that the famous acoustician from Boston, Theodore Schultz, with whom he had worked closely, had so completely misjudged the degrees of sound absorption and reflection. The ceiling had been carefully designed as the focal point of the auditorium, and its redesign, Arthur warned, would be costly. "It is the site of complex features, including lighting, air-handling, banners, and catwalks. With Madame Rousseau-Vermette, we tried to make something that didn't look like a Meccano set."[22] The public was quick to respond with its own similes, comparing the hall to a turbine engine, the baffles to flying saucers, and the wool tubes to cigarettes dangling in the air.

In the *Globe and Mail* interview, Arthur was also asked to comment on the maintenance costs for the building—the permanent crew required to clean the glass exterior, the chrome and glass interiors, and the carpet. Francisco, in charge of the interior, had chosen cream leather seating, silver chrome, and soft pearl-grey carpeting to complement both the bare concrete walls and the Toronto businessmen "in their good grey suits." The Rousseau-Vermette design in the ceiling and women in glamorous evening gowns would provide the animation of colour in the hall. To the reporter, Arthur said the carpet was extremely durable and could withstand as much cleaning as was necessary. "The only way to hide stains is to have a strong pattern. To do that, you have to have something really ugly." Arthur's recourse to aesthetic standards over practical ones was held up to the public for ridicule when he was quoted as saying that "people also hear with their eyes." The negative view of the hall grew. In 1990, architectural critic Lisa Rochon described it as moving far away from the earthy, humanitarian roots of [Erickson's] best architecture and called it "a cold-hearted flirtation with geometry that ultimately stands isolated from the city."[23]

THE NEGATIVE FEELING that accumulated around Roy Thomson Hall was no doubt generated in part by the scandal that broke around Arthur in 1982. In February, the federal government announced that he had been chosen as architect for the Canadian chancery in Washington. (The term chancery was used instead of embassy because an ambassador would not reside there.) For several months, a panel of civil servants and architects had met to examine some three hundred applications for the commission and had narrowed the candidates down to a list of eleven, which included Arthur, and then to a choice of four, among which he no longer figured. Although the committee's final selection was the firm of Zeidler & Roberts of Toronto, Prime Minister Trudeau directed his minister of public works to award the commission to Arthur. The Opposition Tories screamed patronage: Trudeau was denounced as Canada's Sun King and Erickson characterized as the arrogant *architecte du Roi*. Even worse, in the press, Arthur was likened to Albert Speer, Hitler's official architect. When that comparison was taken up in question period, Trudeau crooked his forefinger at MP John Fraser, indicating that the two should step out into the hall, schoolboy-style, to fight.

Trudeau soon issued a statement to the press implying that Arthur had been unanimously regarded by the panel as the best architect in Canada, all agreeing that "Arthur Erickson stands out most clearly on the international scene as expressing Canadian architectural concepts." He stated further that, in his opinion, it was right for the government, rather than an external committee, to decide on the architect for the chancery. The reaction from the Conservatives was swift. MP John Crosbie asked the Commons: "Why did he [Trudeau] attempt to deceive the Canadian people with this shabby and mendacious release which twisted the truth out of all shape entirely?"[24] The Conservatives demanded the prime minister's resignation.

There was, of course, a backstory. Recognizing in each other uniquely kindred spirits, Arthur and Pierre had continued to spend time together whenever possible, most famously when Pierre, now separated from Margaret, was briefly out of office in the fall of 1979 and they travelled to Tibet. It was a difficult journey, complicated by political restrictions imposed by the ruling Chinese government, but this trip to the top of the world, "with its salubrious plateau air," further bonded the two men in a friendship that would last the rest of their lives.[25]

And so it was not surprising that Arthur had written a confidential letter to Trudeau on December 14, 1981, when he learned from his old McGill classmate, Guy Desbarats, now part of the government, that he had not made the final short list for the chancery commission. Arthur appears to have typed the letter himself in secrecy, casting himself in the rare attitude of a supplicant. The Washington chancery, he wrote, "is for me that rarest of opportunities—to design a building of distinction, a place of renown on a site of high visibility and significance for this country of ours. Nothing in my career as an architect would be as worthwhile as the chance to make a Canadian statement in the American capitol." He pointed out that he had turned down the opportunity of designing the embassies in China and Saudi Arabia in order not to prejudice his chances for Washington. Accordingly, "it was pretty devastating" that he should have been "blackballed through personal envy" and by rumours that he frightened clients because the quality of his work meant higher costs. Plaintively, he stated: "I wouldn't care as much if I had been rather facile in my approach to architecture, but my reputation has been won through continuous hardship and disappointment that has never weakened my dedication."

He made his case forcefully on the basis of his achievements and reputation:

> What is particularly galling to me is that I have done more to put our Canadian architecture into the world picture than any other architect in the country. In fact, Vancouver has become a place of architectural pilgrimage from all over the world and, particularly now, the United States... For what the Canadian Pavilion of Osaka accomplished for the image of Canada abroad—for that alone I would expect to be given a commission such as this. I would think that External Affairs would recognize my international stature (I am the only Canadian architect to have been made an Honorary Fellow of the American Institute of Architects for outstanding design) in such an important diplomatic post as Washington.

He concluded by speculating how Trudeau might act in his favour: "It seems to me there are many possibilities: to ask for another selection board and repeat the process; to revert to a competition among the eleven finalists; to ask for my name to be included by Ritchie amongst the top five, simply because of my stature in the international architectural community (and not because I am a friend of yours); or, perhaps politically the most difficult, to have me named directly."[26] Trudeau chose the latter.

Architectural circles were in an uproar over the decision, especially as no design or model had been required for the competition. There had been significant costs in putting together a bid, which included a Washington site analysis and an account of how one would proceed to do business in that city, and some of those on the short lists, including Zeidler & Roberts, Moshe Safdie, Raymond Moriyama, and Thompson, Berwick & Pratt, spoke of seeking compensation. The Architectural Institute of British Columbia (AIBC) and the Royal Architectural Institute of Canada (RAIC) stood firmly with those protesting both the government's handling of selection procedures and the final choice. The AIBC considered lodging a formal complaint with the federal cabinet, because it had rejected the work of an independent selection committee. The feeling of outrage was compounded by the rumour that Arthur had been assured two years in advance by Guy Desbarats that the commission would be his.

Journalist Peter Newman, with a quick eye for scandal, published an unfriendly editorial on Arthur in *Maclean's* on May 31, 1982, titled "Arthur Erickson's Lollipop." Arthur's lawyer, Bryan Shapiro at Bull, Housser & Tupper, demanded an editorial retraction on behalf of his client regarding certain inaccuracies: specifically, Arthur had not known two years in advance from Desbarats that the commission would be his; the committee had been established as an advisory, as opposed to selection, committee; the story was full of negative insinuations regarding Arthur's international jet travel—that his buildings were dreamed up on the back of envelopes on aircraft. Especially offensive in this context were Newman's references to Erickson and Trudeau travelling together to China, Tibet, and Saudi Arabia. The article implied that Erickson was best at auditoriums and world's fair pavilions, not more functional buildings. Arthur's lawyer also sent warnings to the AIBC, the RAIC, and the *Vancouver Sun*, the latter for a May 17, 1982, editorial titled "Lingering Doubts," said to be full of inaccuracies and innuendos.

As the controversy ensued, noted architectural critic Adele Freedman was describing Arthur in her columns as a witty, semi-mystical, but not at all humble man. This view was reinforced when Arthur wrote to Douglas Miller, then president of the RAIC, on July 29, 1982. Selection panels, Arthur asserted, of the kind favoured by the RAIC and set up for the chancery commission, were very suspect, especially because they involved interviews, which "too often depend upon personal chemistry, appearance, manner of speech, colour of tie, sense of humour, gossip, innuendo, etc. It is virtually impossible to make an objective assessment of any kind in an interview. One has to judge on the basis of feelings and these can be way off base." Only a competitor's accomplishments should count, he argued. Without something objective to judge, the process was wholly "shadowed by the clouds of envy, vindictiveness and political vendetta." Arthur's usual calm had given way to anxiety. He feared that, in future, potential clients might now avoid him.

Arthur was relieved to find a strong supporter in Washington in the person of Allan Gotlieb, Canada's ambassador to the U.S. When they met in March, Gotlieb assured Arthur he could count on him to fight the bureaucracy, if necessary. In a diary entry, Gotlieb wrote: "I was told by an embassy officer that the property officials down from Ottawa are furious with me for showing 'favouritism' to Arthur. I could have vomited on them."[27]

The public was treated briefly in May to a series of cartoons by Andy Donato on the subject. The *Calgary Sun* ran one of Trudeau as a scantily dressed prostitute leaning against the Canadian embassy in Washington twirling her change purse, saying, "The *difference* between what I give the *general public*, and what I give my *friends*, is the difference between *business* and *pleasure*." In another for the *Toronto Sun* on May 13, 1982, Arthur is shown reclining like an unclothed woman, Trudeau pouring money over him from a bucket marked "embassy." The much larger bucket over which Erickson reclines is marked "Pork Barrel," and Trudeau says: "If a man can't help his friends, Arthur, who can he help?"

Not so humorous was the editorial that accompanied the *Toronto Sun* cartoon, which summed up the general view of events. "What is so infuriating," it said, "maybe even criminal—is that the selection process was an empty ritual that didn't influence Trudeau in the slightest. His mind was made up. His chum Arthur was going to get the contract and to hell with propriety, decency, maybe even legality. It is grossly unfair to those architects who invested thousands in time and money to make a presentation—all for naught." Fraud charges should be laid, the editorial said, but it was not likely to happen, since Canadians were "ruled by a demagogue who abuses his trust as no prime minister in our history has done... The Erickson case, regardless of whether or not his appointment as architect was known two years ago as is claimed, is another example of morally corrupt leadership and ethically bankrupt policies. Canada will remain thus until we rid ourselves of Trudeau."[28]

Arthur wrote to his friend on July 30 in an apologetic vein: "I want to tell you how deeply grieved I am for how you had to suffer on the floor of the House—and for how much precious time was squandered on that matter. How you are able to keep your integrity and not abandon yourself to the utter cynicism of politics only proves how strongly principled you are." Arthur told Trudeau about all the spitefulness he himself had endured, the infantile letters received, but said, though it had all been "very uncomfortable, it gives me some furtive pride to have been included in the same copy as yourself!" He enclosed with his letter an article by Stanley Meisler that appeared in the *Los Angeles Times* on July 11, 1982, titled "Canada's Trudeau: Sexy, Brilliant, Arrogant and an Enduring Enigma." Meisler observed that many Canadians could not understand Trudeau, "simply because he is so different from them and because the novelty of this difference has worn off... He is a man of style and flair in a country that often prides itself in its grayness and its deference to authority... He is a leader unwilling to court the common man. 'A society which eulogizes the average citizen,' Trudeau once said, 'is one which breeds mediocrity.'"

Arthur infuriated the public when he was interviewed by Benjamin Forgey of the *Washington Post* and asked to describe the new chancery building. He demurred, replying obliquely, in the manner of Frank Lloyd Wright, "It's very hard to speculate. I think the most dangerous thing is to have ideas before it is time to have them." The reporter, in parody, likened Arthur's answer to Le Corbusier's oracular pronouncement when given an assignment: "I have the habit of committing it to memory by not allowing myself to make any sketches for several months... Then, one day, the idea, or child, emerges."[29] Otherwise, Forgey's piece was fairly positive. He described Arthur as "a flexible modernist whose work is hard to classify, perhaps a bit like that of Alvar Aalto, the great Finnish architect. His penchant for wholeness, spatial drama and strong sculptural form was boldly announced in his design for SFU."

When the design and model for the chancery were finally unveiled two years later, Adele Freedman in the *Globe and Mail*, on May 9, 1984, said she was surprised by how much fussy detail there was—the building looked "overworked," though Arthur had said in the past that he "want[ed] to build with all details suppressed."[30] To Freedman, the penthouse, for example, with its jumble of window types, was "composite and confusing." Forgey's response in the *Washington Post* was similar: "Things don't quite come together with the authority or naturalness one expects of Erickson." To Forgey, the design combined late modernism with the work of the postmodern generation. There was complexity and contradiction, not classical unity. There was an unwanted fussiness.[31]

Arthur's design reflected the complicated requirements of the assignment. It had to conform to Washington's strict building guidelines for Pennsylvania Avenue, which mandated a vocabulary of neoclassical architecture from base to attic. The building's height was set by these guidelines, and its other measurements were determined by the requirement that it fill out the whole lot. At first the neoclassicism of Washington, D.C., seemed pretentious to Arthur, as if by imposing Greco-Roman formalities on the capital city, a great republic could be proclaimed. But he soon found that, as with difficult ravine or cliff sites, the restrictions on Pennsylvania Avenue were a source of inspiration. A rotunda with twelve pillars on the surface seemed to pay homage to the classical porch of the nearby

Federal Trade Commission building, but it was designed specifically to symbolize the (then) twelve regions of Canada—its ten provinces and two territories. A row of six stately columns on a totally different scale, which would normally support the heavy architrave, were made of aluminum and set back so they supported nothing but a skylight. Arthur was meeting the guidelines but, at the same time, mocking them.

In his original design submission, Arthur had quoted an unnamed former ambassador to the U.S. as saying that the chancery should reflect both the similarities and the dissimilarities of Canadians and Americans.[32] Erickson later put it this way: "I wanted the chancery to express an image of Canadian reserve and good manners, coupled with a characteristic gesture of openness and invitation, to affirm our similar heritages and, at the same time, to project an element of freshness and forgivable naïveté."[33] The usual symbols of Canada's physical identity were represented in the building's structure and decor: the long horizontals reflecting the country's breadth, an ample courtyard its light and spaciousness, a pool in the courtyard its water resources. Eventually, a waterfall around the rotunda would represent Niagara Falls, the famous site on the Canada–U.S. border, and white azaleas and white roses hanging from planters would suggest Canada's falling snow.

The word "naïveté" in Arthur's statement carried a sly connotation, given his intent to subvert the historicist scheme of the Washington setting. Canada's "difference," then, could be read as a matter of irony—or even satire. This seemed overt in his choice of a sculpture for the courtyard's reflecting pool. Rather than an abstract representing the Great Lakes by Greg Snider—as in his first proposal—he decided that a humanistic sculpture would be more suitable, and so he asked Bill Reid to carve an aboriginal welcome pole.

To Arthur's delight, Reid took the idea in a different direction, creating an eighteen-foot bronze canoe for the reflecting pool instead. Reid said he first got the idea from observing a fractious family on a canoe outing on Stanley Park's Lost Lagoon, and his initial title for the sculpture was "Sunday Afternoon on Lost Lagoon."[34]

But he began thinking about all the embassies in Washington and about the world's nations quarrelling, and so he filled the canoe with figures from Haida mythology at odds with each other. Extrapolating to the international level there was the humour of, among others, the French frog, the Russian bear, and the American eagle, all in the same boat together. This was in keeping with a building where the main columns held up only a glass roof, not doing much work, and those in the rotunda were not symmetrical. These are jokes, too—architectural ones.

The Spirit of Haida Gwaii, as the sculpture came to be known, has been likened to Emanuel Leutze's memorable painting of the American Revolution, *Washington Crossing the Delaware*.[35] Reid's work was also suggestive of revolution, for he was indicating in his sculpture the idea of a distinct nation within Canada with its own mythology and proposing that "Haida Gwaii" should replace the colonial "Queen Charlotte Islands" as the name for the Haida homeland. His work on the sculpture had become entangled in Haida land claims and a protest to stop logging on Lyell Island. When talks with the federal government broke down, Reid stopped working on the large plaster model that he and his assistants were constructing in preparation for the bronze casting. He would not sell symbols of the Haida people, he said, to a government that refused to settle these matters. When negotiations moved forward, he resumed his work.

DESPITE THE CONTROVERSY surrounding the Canadian chancery, Arthur was enjoying a period of unprecedented fame and adulation in the early 1980s. He was made a Companion of the Order of Canada and received three more honorary doctorates. A series of articles about his life and work written by Edith Iglauer for *The New Yorker* in 1979 was published in 1981 as *Seven Stones: A Portrait of Arthur Erickson, Architect*. But Arthur took the greatest pride in the awards and honours that came directly from the architectural community. The first of these was the gold medal from the Royal Architecture Institute of Canada in 1984, followed that same year by the first Chicago Architecture Award, which Arthur shared with Philip Johnson.

Johnson, then in his seventies and regarded as the dean of American architects, had given Arthur's career a huge boost when Edith Iglauer in *The New Yorker* reported him as saying: "Arthur Erickson is by far the greatest architect in Canada, and may be the greatest on this continent."[36] An award of even greater prestige also came in 1984, when the French Academy of Architecture gave Arthur its gold medal. In his acceptance speech on June 26, 1984, he said:

> Vancouver is a beautiful setting without a city. Much of my work has been to rectify that situation. And of course, Paris has always been a model—of the courage, vision and refinement that can shape a city—of the passion of its citizens that nourishes it. Working in the far northwest where everything is yet to be created—it is a lonely challenge, just as it must be very humbling to you, my colleagues, to create anew amongst the magnificent witnesses of your past. Paris is your masterwork, members of the Academie—was, is, and will be—a masterwork for all mankind.[37]

June 14, 1984, his sixtieth birthday, was declared Arthur Erickson Day in Vancouver. In 1985, a major exhibition of his work, *Arthur Erickson: Selected Projects 1971–1985*, was mounted in New York at the Center for Inter-American Relations. It was curated by Barbara E. Shapiro, a PhD candidate in architectural history at Harvard.

But the highest honour came in 1986, when the officials of the American Institute of Architects awarded Arthur their gold medal in recognition of a lifetime achievement in design. In his view, this was the equivalent of a Nobel Prize for architecture. Lois Milsom flew to San Antonio for the ceremony, as did Francisco. In addition, there was Francisco's family—his flamboyant mother, Sara; his brother, José; and José's excitable wife—all generating confusion.

The elegantly worded citation was a fine summation of Arthur's strengths and his approach to architecture:

> The American Institute of Architects is honored to confer the 1986 Gold Medal, the Highest Honor it can bestow, on Arthur Erickson,

FAIA, global architect, passionate advocate of cultural awareness, and fervent explorer of human and natural environments, whose buildings, though remarkably diverse, share deep respect for context, incomparable freshness and grace, and the dramatic use of space and light. He has journeyed to the far corners of the earth, looking deeply into the heart of human cultures and, in so doing, has brought to his work an understanding of the community of man that, when filtered through his insightful mind and fertile imagination, gives birth to a singular architecture that is in dialogue with the world.

In receiving the AIA's gold medal, Arthur joined the ranks of the world's most famous modern designers, including Frank Lloyd Wright, Mies van der Rohe, and Le Corbusier. He was the first Canadian. He addressed the audience in his customarily urbane, witty, and self-deprecatory fashion, saying, "I've always counselled others that to choose architecture you have to be a fool. I'm happy to see that the American Institute of Architects suffers fools gladly... I think all of us, as practitioners, know the difficulties, the hardships, the terrible risks of the profession. And somehow or other we accept every humiliation, every difficulty as if somehow we deserved it."[38]

This award marked the pinnacle of Arthur's career. But as his speech portends, it was also prelude to an extended period of almost insurmountable difficulties. The same month that he received the gold medal, a travel agency in Toronto was preparing for a legal action to recover $50,000 in unpaid airplane fares.[39] According to Keith Loffler, the chancery cost $50 million to construct and Arthur received a fee of approximately $6 million, more than half of which was paid out in costs to engineers and subconsultants. But at the project's conclusion he would owe the Canadian government $4.6 million in disputed cost overruns.

Stories in Canada about Arthur's extravagance and unrealistic estimates were impairing his ability to get more work. The most obvious reflection of this was the fact that Canada's most famous architect was not awarded a single commission for Vancouver's Expo 86. The design for one building that he submitted—an amphitheatre with a retractable roof on False Creek—had been welcomed at first, but in 1984, it was rejected as not meeting the requirements of the site. Earlier, he had lost the bid for Canada Place, the federally funded convention centre on Vancouver's waterfront. In response, Arthur had written to Trudeau in August 1982, asking him to intervene. Trudeau, who likely replied with a phone call, noted at the top of the letter from Arthur that he had investigated and discovered that British Columbia wouldn't do it any other way. The prime minister was not going to interfere this time.[40] Arthur was also turned down for the new CBC centre in Toronto; the Toronto opera ballet theatre; and the National Gallery, which he had coveted for years. Friends and associates were beginning to feel that Arthur had made something like a Faustian bargain, selling himself to get the chancery, with everything afterwards turning to ashes.

A DEDICATION CEREMONY for the Canadian chancery took place on April 28, 1988, and reviews of the new building appeared shortly thereafter. They were mixed. Benjamin Forgey, in the *Washington Post*, had a fairly positive response—"a powerful building in a place that calls for one"—but expressed some reservations: the chancery was "a mighty battleship of a building," "an edgy flawed masterpiece." Paul Goldberger, the chief architecture critic for the *New York Times*, steered a middle course, describing the chancery as an odd mixing of contrary elements—the grandiose and the graceful, the pompous and the inviting—but concluded it was "one of Mr. Erickson's less-successful works." Adele Freedman, for the *Globe and Mail*, did not like the building and did not spare the architect her sarcastic assessments. And although there were accolades on the street—George Wright, the cautious chief architect for the Capitol region, said to a reporter: "It's a lasting design, which is also human-scaled and accessible"[41]—hostile views were the most articulate. Michael Stanton, the architecture critic for *Washington City Paper*, the local entertainment weekly, denounced the building as "an unresolved hodgepodge," embodying "the worst aspects of late modernism and postmodern architecture: the former's senseless sculptural acrobatics, and the latter's cavalier disregard for the historic details and compositions that it distorts." Like everything associated with this building, Stanton's views were steeped in politics. He questioned whether Canada's embassy should be so close to the U.S. Capitol and at such a distance from all other embassies: "Perhaps Canada is pressing to become the 51st state." This was a continuation of some of the debates that had preceded the construction of the chancery: should a foreign power be permitted to own property on America's main street? Why should the previous tenants of two decrepit buildings that occupied the site be made homeless?

Arthur did not feel it necessary to comment on these issues. He remained concerned, however, about the interior decorating of the building. Francisco was designing all the public areas, using a cream and grey palette with the startling contrast of vermilion furnishings. The theatre, for example, was given grey walls and a metal curtain but red seating. Arthur's attempt to persuade Trudeau to intervene so that Francisco could design the private spaces as well had been unsuccessful, chiefly because Trudeau left office in 1984. More than four years later, not all the decorating issues had been resolved. Allan Gotlieb wrote in his diary entry for August 5, 1988:

> Amidst all the grand battles going on regarding the future of Canada, I am dealing again with a small poisonous one. Arthur Erickson called me three times to tell me that the External Affairs decorators have insisted on substituting a different shade of red from the one he chose for all the upholstery in the executive offices. The External decorator czars said the upholstery had to be the same colour as the flag. Arthur said it conflicts with the limestone wall and floors that dominate the building. Arthur lost. He had every reason to be upset. I called the associate undersecretary in Ottawa and told him that to substitute the taste of the departmental decorators for that of the architect was an affront to the architect. The guerrilla warfare goes on and on. The anti-Erickson feeling in the department still runs high.[42]

Gotlieb would learn a few months later that external affairs decorators were still trying to prevent Francisco from doing the chancery's executive furnishings. "Will the assault on Arthur ever end?" he wondered.[43]

The critical puzzle the chancery posed would not be solved by the passing of a few years. In 1992, Witold Rybczynski would describe it as "a very beautiful building" with great attention to detail, and he praised its overall sculptural impact. But he found the postmodern symbolism puzzling: "It sends ambiguous messages."[44] Twenty years later, Nicholas Olsberg would find the building awkward in its merger of two antithetical styles and, particularly, in its lack of the repetitive framework that was Arthur Erickson's signature strength. Its long horizontal beams on three sides established its kinship with some of Arthur's best and most characteristic work—Simon Fraser University, the University of Lethbridge—but its multi-level roofing with complicated fenestration, and especially its aluminum columns and rotunda of twelve pillars, were in the postmodern style Arthur professed to despise. It was a heavily decorated building, a postmodern collage, and Arthur's best work was always minimalist.

Olsberg believed that Arthur was being satirical, making fun of the restrictions placed on him by the Washington building code. But Arthur was never a successful satirist, which was reflected when one untutored observer was reported to have said, in response to the rotunda and columns, that no building so clearly before "showed me how imperial Washington is." Arthur would eventually argue that with this building he was making fun not of Washington's building codes but of postmodernism itself. One questions how strictly the neoclassical style was actually imposed on the chancery, because its neighbour, I.M. Pei's extension to the National Gallery of Art, completed in 1978, is invariably described as "rigorously modernist." Had the regulations changed in six years? And did Arthur really set out with such a negative goal in mind? It was not like him. The puzzles that surrounded this building from commission to completion will likely remain part of its reception far into the future. The chancery continues to have many admirers, but it also appeared on *Forbes*'s list for 2002 as one of the ten ugliest buildings in the world—described as "simply bizarre by any aesthetic standard."[45]

A formal ceremony was held on May 3, 1989, to open the chancery. It was a day when glory and disaster nearly collided for Arthur.[46]

In Washington, Prime Minister Brian Mulroney and U.S. Secretary of State James Baker cut the ribbon, and opera singer Louis Quilico sang the Canadian and American anthems. Arthur was in the audience of VIPs. On that same day in Toronto, there appeared a notice in the *Globe and Mail* cancelling a May 4 auction of the contents of Erickson's Toronto office. Krugarand Corporation, the landlord of 80 Bloor Street West, had run out of patience and was suing Arthur for more than $75,000 in outstanding rent payments. An auctioneer had been hired to sell everything in the office that had been seized by a bailiff: not only equipment but all the architectural drawings on the premises. But the day before flying to Washington, Arthur had called a meeting with Krugarand and offered part of the money owing. Not wanting to be demonized for bullying a national hero, the company cancelled the auction, and the lawsuit was dropped. Returning to Toronto, Arthur moved his office to an unfurnished space on Queen Street. Only four employees made the move with him; a dozen others started looking for work elsewhere. By September, Arthur Erickson Architects had been replaced on the two or three remaining projects in Ontario and the United Arab Emirates, and the Toronto office ceased to exist. What, the public wanted to know, had brought near ruin to the country's foremost architect, its master builder?

Part IV

Celebrity

18

The Middle East

ONE REASON FREQUENTLY GIVEN for Arthur Erickson's plummeting fortunes in the late 1980s was his firm's involvement in the Middle East. In 1988, twenty years after his initial engagement there, he had to admit that "for all the creative energy invested, only a temporary structure and a single tall building have seen the bright light of the desert day." It was hubris, he acknowledged, to challenge the world in all its diversity of climates and cultures, and yet such projects, even when unrealized, were nonetheless "important acts of learning... and the honest assertion of ideas that are part of me."[1]

Arthur's lengthy foray into the Middle East brought into focus the global aspirations he had for his architectural practice. But while bringing something of world architecture to Canada proved successful for him, he found it difficult to establish himself as a celebrated player on the world stage. Until 1980, all that he had designed and built in the U.S. was a summer house and a winery office. Larger schemes, such as his designs for the West Seattle Freeway, the Portland Municipal Services Building, and a condominium complex in Reno, Nevada, were unsuccessful. His entry in the Centre du Plateau Beaubourg competition in Paris (the Centre Georges Pompidou) did not place, nor did a submission for urban renewal in Venezuela's capital, Caracas. His one triumph abroad was a laboratory complex for the Napp pharmaceutical company in Cambridge, England.

Arthur had first experienced the Middle East in 1950, when he set out with his McGill scholarship to see the world. Travelling through the treeless desert of Syria by train, he was spellbound by the geometry of the mud villages and the stark, dry terrain. Fourteen years later, he was further awakened to the visual impact of the desert and the human culture it produced, especially the importance to architecture of strong light. "In the desert," he told an interviewer in 1964, "you begin to see forms clearly... the sunlight plays on shapes and you become more conscious of form. There is a more heightened sense of life."[2] Later he would tell an audience that the desert of the Middle East was a landscape of purity of form; it had given rise to mathematics and geometry. The pyramids of Egypt, the domes of Iran—they were a response to hard, brilliant light; any subtle, alleviating details (a finial or bas-relief) would be trivial.[3] He now viewed the Alhambra in Spain, with its exposed arches, screens, and fountains, as luxurious and decadent, because it did not highlight from the outside essential forms like the square, octagon, and circle. In the desert, complicated, layered forms of architecture using arches and screens were lost in strong shadows; they were for internal use in the harems.

Although the desert terrain was a landscape of essentials, it produced, in Arthur's view, some of the world's most sensuous cultures. The artists of the deserts imprinted written script and patterns from nature on the flattened surfaces of their buildings—the precise but shallow incisions of hieroglyphics turned surfaces into "a shower of sparks in the light."[4] The interiors of buildings were decorated in layered patterns that did not relate to each other: gracefully patterned tiles on the lower walls, carved plaster above that, carpets with rich colours and designs, and patterned ceilings. Arthur attributed this to the hostility of the climate; desert dwellers stayed inside most of the time and thus craved this richness—an illusion of diversity.[5] Arab traditions in the arts were both graceful and very tactile—not an architecture of bones (like the Gothic) but one of volumes and surfaces. What also fascinated Arthur was the people: the striking appearance of men in formal dress wearing banded headcloths, white tunics, robes, and rustling silk skirts—the women hidden behind curtains of black cloth. He found Arabs welcoming and hospitable, and he met many individuals of great personal charm. They were people, moreover, with a passionate love of poetry.

In February 1967, he travelled to the Middle East to share the experience with Francisco, and shortly afterwards he sent for a list of government projects he might compete for. Before the year was out, he had submitted a proposal for the university city of Riyadh in Saudi Arabia.[6] This was followed in March 1968 by a series of letters that went through the Canadian embassy in Beirut, Lebanon, exploring the possibility of a contract to build Kuwait University.[7] The striking success of Simon Fraser University, Arthur argued, originated in the Middle East, for it was modelled on one of the world's oldest institutions of higher learning—the Islamic Al-Azhar University in Cairo— which merged secular and theological studies. The tenth-century format of Al-Azhar, with its non-compartmentalized form of learning, had been the model for his university architecture, and so he was proposing what was, in fact, an indigenous form of architecture for his potential Middle Eastern clients. He was also proposing pure geometric forms as the essence of Islamic architecture.

Kuwait University had a number of bright young faculty members who were being advised by an Irish architect in the Ministry of Education. The latter had seen magazine articles on Simon Fraser University that impressed him greatly.[8] As a result, Arthur received a direct invitation to be the architect for the new university campus, based on the outline he submitted. But when Canada sided with Israel at the time of the Arab-Israeli War of October 1973, Arthur's proposal was rejected, and the commission went to a Spanish firm. His interest in the region, if anything, grew keener. In 1974, he secured a commission to design a condominium complex for a ski resort in the mountains north of Tehran. But it was the Arabs, rather than the Persians, who attracted him. From the outset, he found the Arabs had a way of showing politeness and hospitality that was unparalleled—"a courtesy in their way of dealing with people that you don't find elsewhere."[9] So when an invitation came from the board of the National Housing Authority of Kuwait (the board included some of the young professors he had met at Kuwait University), he and his team submitted an elaborate design—the result of nearly a full year of work.

The Sawaber Project in Kuwait City was a government plan for a luxurious, multi-storey housing complex on a sixty-acre site in the centre of the city. In the drive to Westernize, many newly oil-rich families were moving to the suburbs where they were building, in Arthur's words, pseudo-palaces. Attracting them back to the city was central to the political and design strategy behind the Sawaber project. Arthur had a dedicated team led by Kiyoshi Matsuzaki, with Alan Bell as project planner and designers Wilbert Breugger and Larry McFarland. Designing a residential project, however, was a challenge in a culture where "infidels" were unwelcome in private homes. How to envision interiors without seeing the way people actually lived? This was an intensely private culture. One thing the team knew for sure was that these desert people were reluctant to sacrifice their newfound privacy and the pleasures of the family courtyard, so each unit would have to include an extended balcony that was wholly screened off. To achieve this, Arthur and his team designed a series of residential blocks, each consisting of two "stacks of villas" in stepped-back formation from grade to apex, where each balcony had exposure to light and air from above but was visually hidden from any neighbour. This open A-frame formation of the buildings created a shaded and naturally ventilated inner street below, where children could play and men could sit and talk. A heavy sandstorm that occurred while they were starting the planning process guided their decision to align the buildings for wind exposure as well as sun. At the centre of the whole development was a park mounded over a disused cemetery and spaces for community facilities—schools, mosques, local shops.

Arthur wrote to Pierre Trudeau on November 11, 1977, urging the government to view Kuwait favourably. After a prolonged visit to the Middle East—through Iran, some of the Emirates, Kuwait, and Saudi Arabia—Arthur was convinced that Kuwait was the most promising place for Canadian enterprises.

We, as you perhaps know, have a major housing project of around
$300 million there which we expect to proceed into its working
drawings phase by the end of this year... Our reception by various
government agencies has been very good indeed and I think our
contribution to all accounts has enhanced the Canadian reputation
in that area. However, we are only too aware of the enormous asset
the Canadian Trade Mission in Kuwait would be to our efforts and
I do hope that the opening of the Mission there, which the Kuwait
Government is expecting, will proceed as soon as possible. Our
links with that part of the world can be tremendously profitable to
Canadians... There is no doubt in my mind that Kuwait has the
pivotal role and that we need representation there.[10]

But although the Sawaber urban study and plan became well
known and was highly praised, when the project was put out to bid,
the government "lost sight of its original objective," as Arthur phrased
it, and the southern half of Sawaber was built by a Singaporean-
Korean contractor. "Only the unique outline was vaguely ours,"
wrote Arthur, "and no Kuwaiti of means would live there."[11] Alan
Bell put it more bluntly: "The basic idea was ours, but the Kuwaitis
chose to build a cheap bastardized version that omitted most of
the key features intended to attract Kuwaitis. It negatively affected
Arthur's reputation in Kuwait."[12]

The Sawaber plan did lead to Arthur being awarded the contract
for another major project in Kuwait. By this time he had opened an
office in Jeddah, Saudi Arabia, and potential clients in the Middle
East knew he was serious about doing business there. His second
assignment was to design a new town centre at Fintas, on the coast
south of Kuwait City, to serve a population of 250,000. The challenge, he understood, was to create a design that would provide
for modern needs—an air-conditioned shopping mall with parking, office space, cinemas, and various government services—but
would, at the same time, serve the Bedouins recently arrived in the
city with a bus station, fresh food market, and extensive, naturally
ventilated souks. Shopping was the main recreation of the wealthy
and, except for a garden area, the mall's focus was entirely on shops,

which would include, Arthur assumed, the main couturiers—Pierre Cardin, Yves Saint Laurent, and so forth.

As Arthur saw it, except for the mosque, the peoples of the Arabian Peninsula had no architectural traditions that marked their structures externally. The appearance of a building from the outside was of no importance; only inside did one see the arches and courtyards. Arthur saw this external plainness as connected to the Islamic democratic view of everyone being equal before God. He liked to point out that when King Faisal died, he was buried out in the desert, becoming part of the earth, with nothing marking his grave. And so, in cities no one building was more important than another. Some might be exceptionally rich inside, like an individual might contain great resources of intellect, learning, and sensitivity, but from the street, all buildings appeared much the same.[13] The explorer and travel writer Wilfred Thesiger saw indigenous Arabic architecture as beautiful in this external plainness, but he had written in 1959 that this architecture was doomed, "for the Arabs taste is easily corrupted. New and hideous buildings . . . are already rising in their ancient cities."[14] With the development of the oil industry, the traditional societies of the desert peoples were indeed disintegrating, and the fragile settlements of the peninsula were being transformed along Western lines into modern metropolises—most of which were, in Arthur's view, "terrible abominations."

Convinced that great architecture was grounded in the simple vernacular of the past, Arthur came to see the wall, the ancient defence against the desert, as the essential structure of the Middle East. This was not the wall of modernist architecture—the largely transparent skin of glass—but a solid form, like the walls of Lethbridge University, into which windows were "pierced." Accordingly, his design for Fintas was to wrap the western half of the shopping complex in a wall of parking garages that would simulate the traditional walled city. The circular ramps leading to the parking garages at the four cardinal compass points would suggest the turreted corners of a walled Arab town. Adjacent, to the east, there would be a two-level structure: a bus station and external pedestrian bridge across the main road, separating the eastern and western halves of the town centre; below, one would descend by means of stepped gardens and water basins in the Mughal style to an open plaza with the Friday mosque and a food market. Further east again was to be a covered version of the traditional souk, except here there would be no air conditioning. But again, Arthur was disappointed by his clients; they could not agree on how to actually realize the town centre, and the project fizzled out.

Why did Arthur continue to pursue work in the Middle East when major projects like Sawaber and Fintas came to nothing? Certainly there was the lure of a major commission in public housing or a commercial development that would bring his company huge, solidifying profits. Large-scale projects like Simon Fraser University or the Robson Square complex, which involved rethinking traditional building types and urban forms, were becoming scarce in Canada. At this time, every major international firm was pursuing work in the Middle East. But financial gain was never Arthur's first motivation. Nor was he principally motivated to further his status as an architect with a global reach. Rather, it was the romance of a landscape and a people that held him there. As a child, he had heard the tales from *One Thousand and One Nights*, but a fuller experience came when, during the war, he read T.E. Lawrence's *Seven Pillars of Wisdom* and thrilled at Lawrence's descriptions of the austerely beautiful desert landscape and weather. Lawrence made him see in colour when he wrote, for example: "[We] watched a sunset, which grew from grey to pink, and to red; and then to a crimson so intolerably deep that we held our breath in trepidation for some stroke of flame or thunder to break its dizzy stillness."[15] This hallucinatory style of expression seems to have imprinted itself on Arthur's own poetic descriptions of landscape in his early travel letters and diaries. Lawrence also let him experience the violence of the desert: "The wind, which had been scorching our faces with its hot breathlessness, changed suddenly; and, after waiting a moment, blew bitter cold upon our backs. It also increased greatly in violence, and at the same time the sun disappeared, blotted out by thick rags of yellow air over our heads. We stood in a horrible light, ochreous and fitful. The brown wall of cloud... was now upon us with a loud grinding sound... wrapping about us a blanket of dust and stinging sand, twisting and turning in violent eddies."[16]

Lawrence, who had studied architecture at Oxford, also had a way of seeing landscape architecturally. His description of the Wadi Rum (Valley of the Moon) was powerful reading for Arthur. Moving through the precipitous walls of the valley in sunset, Lawrence wrote that the perspectives "grew greater and more magnificent in ordered design, till a gap in the cliff-face opened on our right to a new wonder... an amphitheatre oval in shape, shallow in front, and long-lobed right and left. The walls were precipices, like all the walls of Rum, but appeared greater, for the pit lay in the very heart of a ruling hill, and its smallness made the besetting heights seem overpowering." Then, the dying glare of the sun "flooded with startling red the wings each side of the entry, and the fiery bulk of the further wall across the great valley... About the feet of all the cliffs lay boulders greater than houses, sometimes, indeed, like fortresses which had crashed down from the heights above."[17] Lawrence's writing contained exquisite mirage-like images, such as "camels swaying curiously, like butterflies, under the winged and fringed howdahs of the women."[18]

But for Arthur, reading Lawrence was also, in his words, "like meeting oneself."[19] And here one might speculate. Arthur, who sometimes bewailed his own essential shyness, was described by friends as modest, even self-deprecating. What might he have thought when Lawrence, a small man, tells his reader that he was always provoked when described as shy and modest? To Lawrence, shyness was a matter of conduct, but modesty was very different. "It irritated me, this silly confusion... For I was not modest, but rather I was ashamed of my awkwardness, of my physical envelope, and of my solitary uniqueness which made me no companion, but an acquaintance, complete, angular, uncomfortable as a crystal."[20] Arthur possibly thought of Lawrence when his architectural competence was challenged. At times he referred to himself as an amateur, because he lacked the technical expertise of so many professionals. Lawrence had similarly described himself. His war, he wrote, was overthought because he was not a soldier, his activity overwrought because he was not a man of action. Perhaps it was also the sexual ambiguity of the speaker in Lawrence's text that Arthur found compelling; here was the voice of an unmarried ascetic who, nonetheless, described the pleasure that young Arab men took in each others' bodies.

Pierre Trudeau also had a strong affinity for Lawrence, the scholar and warrior, and in the fall of 1980, on a trip arranged by the Saudi Arabian oil minister, he and Arthur explored together for a few days the northern Hejaz region. Arthur later remembered how they went "tramping through the Nabataean Tombs in northern Saudi Arabia, near Lawrence's bombed out Turkish railway depots unaltered by time."[21]

ARTHUR WROTE THAT while he had tried to do business in Kuwait, "Saudi Arabia was the prized client."[22] When he lost the detailed development of the Sawaber project to another firm, he simplified and refined the design for an imam who wanted to build a hotel and residential complex in Medina, the city of the prophet's birth.[23] But the proposal with drawings went no further, and this would be the pattern with a series of projects in Saudi Arabia for the next several years. These included designs for two different universities, the Saudi Air Force Academy, the national science centre, a private boys' school, and the Saudi air defence headquarters. The coveted prize of these was King Abdulaziz University at Jeddah—a $2-billion mini-metropolis for twenty thousand students. The only design of Arthur's that went forward was for a temporary government building in Jeddah, quickly erected to house the Ministry of Foreign Affairs until a permanent one could be constructed in Riyadh, the capital. Still standing, it is a simple cubical structure, with teak screens hung before a glass curtain wall for protection against the sun.

Looking through the illustrations for the chapter titled "Counterpoint: Other Ways of Seeing," in *The Architecture of Arthur Erickson,* one is struck by both the originality of the designs and the ingenuity of local references that were worked out for more than twenty building projects in the Middle East. The proposals for the Saudi Air Force Academy (or Technical University) to be situated in the centre of Saudi Arabia are notable for the way they respond to the severe climate of the region. The site offered Arthur little direction other than the need for walls to defy the wind and driving sand, and for buildings that would shade each other and the pedestrian. His design philosophy remained rooted in the traditional Islamic *madrasa*, where communities of students lived and studied with their teachers. Three storeys were identified to fulfill these needs: an uppermost plaza with communal facilities such as the library, dining hall, and mosque; below that an academic street of classrooms and offices; and below that another street for dormitories. The whole was to be contained inside a building hunkered down to withstand the onslaughts of the climate, but it was a building to be finished in sand-coloured concrete that would have looked "like an enormous stepped pyramid, deceptively simple yet extremely complex."[24] The academy was to be connected to the nearby town by means of a shared sports complex and a Friday mosque for both students and townspeople, inspired by the great ninth-century mosque with multi-columned arched walls that Arthur had seen in Kairouan, Tunisia.

At home, Arthur's publicity office was working overtime to celebrate the company's increasing international business. The *Vancouver Sun* announced in January 1980 that Arthur had secured a contract to design and build the men's campus of King Abdulaziz University of Jeddah: "The biggest design contract any Canadian firm or consortium has ever had." The men's campus would be one of three parts of the future university and would occupy five million square feet and include medical facilities. The university was being designed to accommodate twenty thousand students eventually. It was Erickson's fifth major project in the Middle East, the newspaper reported.[25]

At the same time, an invitation came from Iraq to participate in an urban renewal plan for the city of Baghdad, specifically the Abu Nuwas, a two-mile district of the city lying directly across the

Tigris River from Saddam Hussein's presidential palace, now known as the Green Zone. Certainly, this was a dream project, immensely attractive to Arthur for its rich associations with history and poetry. Saddam wished to identify his military regime with the years of Baghdad's greatest glory, the period of the Abbasid Dynasty in the eighth and ninth centuries. At war in 1981 with Iran, a Muslim but non-Arab state, Saddam wanted to boost nationalist pride by reminding his citizens of their country's golden age, when the power and prestige of the Abbasids in the areas of industry, commerce, science, and arts made Baghdad the capital of the Muslim world. The American advisor to Baghdad's chief architect, Rifat Chadirji, had selected the Erickson team over several other international consultants to undertake this prestigious project because he saw Arthur's office as having both a visionary leader and a strong urban design and planning team.

Abu Nuwas was named, as Arthur ingenuously phrased it, for "a celebrated poet of pleasure" who lived from 756 to 814 during the period of the Abbasid caliphate. Chief among the pleasures the poet celebrated was his love of beautiful boys. Born in what is now Iran of a Persian mother and Arab father, Abu Nuwas (nicknamed "Father of Curls" for his long hair) eventually came to live in Baghdad, where he satirized the worn but revered poetic tradition of nostalgia for the Bedouin way of life and celebrated the contemporary life of the city—especially the joys of the tavern and pederasty. His panegyrics earned him favour with the ruling caliphs, but writing freely about sexual subjects was forbidden by Islamic law, and many times Abu Nuwas was put in prison for drunkenness and lewd behaviour. His sense of humour and irony became legendary, and he appears in *One Thousand and One Nights* as a ribald folklore character. The section of Baghdad that bore his name was, fittingly, a popular recreation area, famous for its cafés and fish restaurants, but by the late twentieth century it had become rundown, and Arthur's commission was to present a design that would revive its waterfront.

Research for the project began in the hot summer months of 1981. Ted Scott went to Geneva and Copenhagen to document their waterfronts and urban recreational activity areas; Alan Bell and Sonya Lukaitis visited conservation projects and historic architectural sites in other Islamic countries. Jonathan Barrett, David Siverson, and others were engaged in a broad urban planning study and a detailed inventory of the site, plus an investigation into the city's heritage materials. With these findings at hand, and in response to his client's intention to hold an international conference and exhibition on the planning and design of Baghdad, focussed on the Abu Nuwas area, Arthur did felt-pen sketches of two possibilities. These were developed by the team in the form of diagrams and plans, large-scale models, and fine pastel-coloured drawings by Michael McCann that evoked for Arthur the magical "storybook" feel to this project. The first scheme proposed a bridge across the river from the Abu Nuwas district to the presidential palace, in the middle of which would be an island with a science museum, aquarium, and astronomical garden. A second scheme was to return the river, by means of a canal, to its original banks on Abu Nuwas Street, with the land between the canal and river transformed into walled gardens of various types in the traditional Arab/Islamic foursquare format.

In designing a scheme for the Tigris riverfront, Arthur was aware that during the period of the Iraqi monarchy, several prominent twentieth-century architects had been engaged by the city's planners and had left their imprint—Walter Gropius most substantially, as architect for the University of Baghdad, and Le Corbusier in designing a sports hall as part of Baghdad's failed bid for the 1960 Olympics. (It was eventually built in the late 1970s and named the Saddam Hussein Gymnasium.) Alvar Aalto had designed an art museum and a post office, neither of which were built. But most interesting to Arthur was the Iraqi invitation to Frank Lloyd Wright to design an opera house. Wright arrived in Baghdad in May 1957, just one month short of his ninetieth birthday, and after an audience with King Faisal II, he left with permission to incorporate the proposed opera house into the development of a site in the middle of the Tigris River, an uninhabited stretch of land known then as Pig Island. Wright had fastened on the idea that this was the original site of the Garden of Eden, and he renamed it Isle of Edena. Back in the

United States, he referred to Baghdad as "the once beautiful circular city built by Harun al-Rashid." Baghdad's circular design was, in fact, the work of the city's original caliph and planner, al-Mansur, but Wright perhaps deliberately attributed it to the later al-Rashid, whose court is associated with the magical world of the Arabian Nights tales. Wright's design for the opera house itself was to include a large proscenium arch like a crescent rainbow that would contain mosaics and roundels depicting scenes from *One Thousand and One Nights*. The building would be topped with a statue of Aladdin holding his lamp and a spire to represent the sword of Mohammed. Wright made the cultural complex "worthy of a king," but his grand scheme came to an end, as did the king, when in 1958 a military coup terminated the Hashemite monarchy.[26]

For Arthur's team in Baghdad in the summer of 1981, the atmosphere was far from magical. The heat and humidity that year were exceptional: whether in their local office or on site, for long stretches they experienced temperatures reaching more than 122 degrees Fahrenheit. Frequent power outages in the city, because the Iranians had disabled several power plants, meant both electricity and air-conditioning were intermittent. Some members of the team got sick. Hanging over the project was the knowledge that the proposal would have to please a brutal dictator. In fact, Rifat Chadirji, the Iraqi chief architect with whom they were consulting, had been serving a jail sentence for currency violations before he was plucked out for a two-year stint as counsellor to the lord mayor of Baghdad. But Arthur appeared to his staff to be little concerned with these issues when he made his "visits."

In November 1981, Arthur joined Baghdad's deputy lord mayor and a panel in the central chamber of the National Assembly hall to discuss the proposals for redesigning the Abu Nuwas area. The team had prepared two models, each twelve feet in length, which were placed for study in the lobby of the chamber. Arthur was in the pit of the assembly hall lecture theatre, explaining the different features of the two schemes, when the doors were flung open at the back and soldiers entered, followed by the president. Saddam initially wanted only to listen, and Arthur continued to describe the water gardens, pleasure gardens, and scented gardens of the second scheme (roses, oranges, jasmine, and lilies), while about the room, spaced out at strategic intervals, stood soldiers with machine guns. The president then made it known he did not want a bridge leading directly into the government zone, and at the conclusion his one instruction to Arthur was to develop Abu Nuwas Street as an Abbasid street. It was clear from further discussion with city planners that Abu Nuwas should be redesigned to suggest once again al-Mansur's round city. Contrary to populist preference, Saddam wanted new cultural buildings that would be monumental in scale.

Billboards everywhere proclaimed "Iraq Fights On/Iraq Builds On," and Arthur was told that in the national treasury there was an account for war and a separate account for culture. But the country soon ran out of money. Arthur and his team continued with the project, crafting a final model that retained some elements of both initial schemes, but a sizable part of their fee was never paid, and plans to revitalize the Abu Nuwas district were shelved. It was one of the sharpest disappointments in Arthur's career. When the U.S. bombed Baghdad in 2003, he consoled himself that he did not have to watch his work being destroyed. But as a journalist observed close to the time, from the outset he should have mistrusted a scene that found him discoursing with President Hussein on paradisiacal gardens while vast ranks of soldiers were engaged in war.[27]

There were still other projects in the Middle East. In 1984, Arthur and his team (including several Montreal firms) won a competition to build a government complex in the Hamma district of Algiers, directly below the hilltop Martyrs Monument. The design was a merging of French and Arabic elements: a wide formal avenue leading from a monumental gateway in the manner of Baron Haussmann's Paris, with all porticoes, pavilions, and roof forms in a simplified Arabic style. The gateway was designed as an Islamic triumphal arch, accommodating a deputies' residence and spanning between two major new buildings, the Assemblée Nationale and the Palais des Congrès. But after photos were taken of the Algerian president with the model and congratulations extended all around, there was silence. Eventually, rumours surfaced that Algerian architects were introducing major changes to the plan, that Bulgarian architects were being engaged inexpensively to execute working designs, and that Chinese workers would construct the complex. Arthur heard nothing further.

Ironically, the two projects that went into construction in 1986 had in their design almost no references to the Middle East. The first was a competition-winning design for a headquarters tower in Abu Dhabi for Etisalat, the Emirates Telecommunications Corporation (the word *etisalat* means communications in Arabic). A twenty-four-storey tower was alien to the region's architecture but, as Arthur had observed, extravagance was not; and so one side of the tower was a curtain wall clad in green-tinted mirror glass. On top was a Teflon-coated sphere, housing communications dishes and antennas, that served as an illuminated landmark. The success of this concept resulted in a similar commission for Etisalat that was eventually built in Dubai.

But the lack of government funding, the failure to establish appropriate implementation mechanisms, the intervention of rivals, and the volatile political climate all contributed to the abortive conclusions to most of Arthur's projects in the Middle East. But human relations also presented stumbling blocks. Arthur found his discussions with clients in the Middle East bogged down at times in complications that echoed the region's ancient tribal feuds. At one point, dealing with two rival Saudi princes, he unwittingly spoke to the wrong one about matters that should have remained confidential; for some months, the atmosphere was tense, though one prince eventually took out shares in Arthur's company. Something else unfamiliar to Arthur was that socializing in the Middle East was always with men. He missed female company in these situations, the relaxed pleasure of women's conversation, the occasional confidence. In this world of ritualized manners and friendships, there was a constant concern among men for loss of face.

He was always aware, too, that many men in the Middle East would not want to do business with a gay man. Only Arthur's friendship with King Hussein of Jordan seemed exempt from these tensions. He considered a lack of human resources another major problem. It proved extremely difficult to find individuals with the education and determination to guide large, prestigious projects through the complexities of government approvals, financing, and construction. On several occasions, just when it seemed someone suitable might be engaged to advance one of Arthur's projects, that person was promoted to a post elsewhere.

Some of those who worked with Arthur, however, saw things differently. In their view, he did not cultivate or pursue clients in a way that would keep a project going forward. Arthur might meet with a prince or sheik or cultivate a national figure in the arts, like Chadirji in Iraq, but he did not connect with the local urban planners and engineers who made things happen. He was too often absent from important meetings, and if he did attend, he would usually arrive late, appear distracted, and leave before the meeting turned, in the natural course of such events, into a social occasion. Arthur was always telling clients he had a plane to catch. And when clients in the Middle East caught wind that Arthur's firm was having financial problems, further projects dried up. The last of his new project offices in Abu Dhabi was closed.

In this period, only three of the twenty-two projects designed in the Middle East were built, and none of them had Arthur's involvement through all stages and aspects of design. While he was sometimes paid handsomely for the designs his office produced, he lost the more lucrative profits of overseeing the construction phase. When a project stalled or grew difficult, he disappeared and seemed to leave it to "fate." When asked how he felt when he saw his designs altered and built by rival companies, he would say, "I can't afford to waste my time and energy by being angry."[28] What remained of his twenty-year venture in the Middle East were some splendid designs, but they were mostly paper architecture or, as Arthur said of the Abu Nuwas scheme, "a magic carpet stored for better times."[29]

The Museum of Anthropology at the University of British Columbia.

above Pierre Trudeau and Arthur at the Museum of Anthropology, UBC, C. 1976. ERICKSON FAMILY COLLECTION

above, top In Los Angeles, *left to right*: Jasmine Lindsay, Arthur, Lois Milsom, Donald Sutherland, Liona Boyd. PHOTO COURTESY LOIS MILSOM

above, bottom Arthur with Veronica Milner, Prince Charles and Princess Diana, and Hilary and Galen Weston at Qualicum, B.C., May 1986. ERICKSON FAMILY COLLECTION

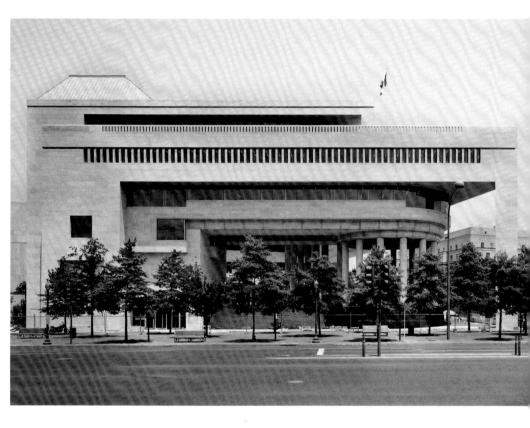

facing, top Bagley Wright House, Seattle Highlands:
"An art gallery in a forest clearing." PHOTO: MARY-ANN STOUCK

facing, bottom Roy Thomson Hall, Toronto. PHOTO: GEOFFREY ERICKSON

above The Canadian chancery, Washington, D.C. PHOTO: TIMOTHY
HURSLEY

facing, top Arthur and Lois Milsom at the Vancouver Symphony Lover's Ball, 1990s. PHOTO COURTESY LOIS MILSOM

facing, bottom Arthur and Hugo Eppich, c. 2005. ERICKSON FAMILY COLLECTION

above Eppich House 2, British Properties, West Vancouver. SIMON SCOTT PHOTOGRAPHY

Museum of Glass, Tacoma, Washington. SIMON SCOTT PHOTOGRAPHY

19

Bankrupt

ALTHOUGH ARTHUR'S DREAM of being a global architect was not realized in the Middle East, his long engagement there was not the cause of his financial ruin; as several of his employees observed, the firm was often well-paid by Arab clients for the designs produced.[1] Instead, the source of his precipitous decline lay in the United States. While he was busy designing and overseeing the construction of the Canadian chancery in Washington, D.C., he was simultaneously pursuing his quest for international fame in California. That opportunity came in 1980 when, with Toronto developer Jack Daniels of Cadillac Fairview, he won to everyone's surprise a billion-dollar contract for the design and construction of a five-block site in the heart of Los Angeles. It was one of the largest architectural projects in North America, and among his competitors was a consortium of luminaries in the profession, locally dubbed the "L.A. superstars," including Frank Gehry, Charles Moore, Cesar Pelli, and Lawrence Halprin. California Plaza, as the project would come to be known, was regarded as the crowning jewel in a major effort to rejuvenate the centre of the city, specifically the elevated area known as Bunker Hill. It was to consist of three office towers on Grand Avenue, one of which would be 52 storeys high; a 750-unit residential section; a 450-room luxury hotel; an acre-and-a-half of public space; and a museum for contemporary art that would open onto a plaza connected to shops and restaurants at various levels.

Although Arthur's attachment to a developer with a strong financial proposal was crucial, he believed their first-place win was for his design of the spaces in between major buildings—the idea of an extensive and lavish park with dense plantings of feather palms, jacarandas, bougainvillea, and roses unifying the eleven-acre site. He viewed Los Angeles as similar to London—a loose collection of boroughs with no real centre. In London, a series of parks, originally royal hunting grounds, allowed one to walk from Kensington to Picadilly Circus. Los Angeles was connected instead by a framework of freeways. Arthur viewed his design for California Plaza, which drew together in a park-like setting the disparate strands of government, business, popular markets, food, and entertainment, as a model for the integration of the city as a whole.

He was excited to be working in Los Angeles. "We will celebrate the central role that Los Angeles plays in the film world with a 12-theatre cinema complex," Arthur said to an interviewer. His initial project director, Bing Thom, told a *Vancouver Sun* reporter, "Downtown Los Angeles tends to be quite dead at night, with not many eating facilities, so we have decided to give a lot of emphasis to food facilities with restaurants based on movie themes—like recreating Rick's Cafe from *Casablanca*."[2] There was something, however, almost fatal in these references to Hollywood and its dream-like excesses—as if, from the outset, the life that Arthur would lead in California would be given to fantasy and would exceed the restraint that had always been the source of his creativity and success.

The scale of the California project necessitated the opening of an office in Los Angeles. To the surprise of many, Arthur put Francisco in charge of the new office, perhaps because he had a U.S. green card to work there. Arthur's employees were alarmed by this choice, because Francisco was notorious for his extravagance and lack of business sense, but those who knew this mercurial man were aware of his ambition and of his chafing under what he viewed as the "limitations" of Canada. Francisco harboured contempt for Canada, especially Vancouver where he was viewed skeptically by many of Arthur's close friends, and he wanted to establish himself as a designer of interiors on the larger stages of Europe and the U.S. In southern California, he would enjoy not only the sybaritic pleasures of its physical climate but the Hollywood-style fame that accrued around successful architects and interior designers.[3]

Arthur was easily seduced into this good life as Francisco arranged it, and in the 1980s, they lived in extravagant luxury. Their first move was to buy a house on the upper reaches of Schuyler Road, one of the palm-lined avenues in exclusive Bel Air. The purchase was made in Francisco's name because, as Arthur explained to his friends, Francisco's insecure childhood as a postwar refugee meant that he needed, above all, the security of a home of his own. The situation of the house was ideal: from its location in the hills there were shimmering perspectives all over greater Los Angeles; there was a garden with an infinity pool; and Rock Hudson lived on the next street. But the house itself was decorated in French provincial style, compelling Francisco to set about on major renovations. Lois and Geoffrey Milsom were making changes to a house they had purchased in Newport Beach, and Francisco arranged for Lois's contractor to work on the Bel Air residence. The interiors were gutted and the house soon became uninhabitable, forcing Arthur and Francisco to rent a house on Sunset Plaza Drive in Beverly Hills. The rented house had only two bedrooms, but there was a cottage across the street where guests and servants could stay and where they stored their excess belongings, including, at one point, four cars. All of this was costly. Arthur was paying $20,000 a month in interest on the bank loan for the Bel Air property and a stiff $15,000 a month rent for the house on Sunset Plaza Drive. It was not long before they had hired a full-time cook and a butler-valet and had regular gardening and housekeeping services.

Rock Hudson provided an introduction to the Los Angeles gay community, and through him, they also came to know a number of Hollywood's eminent personalities, including Hudson's close friend, actress Elizabeth Taylor; producer Ned Tanen at Universal Pictures; Tanen's wife, Kitty Hawks, a noted interior designer and daughter of legendary director Howard Hawks; and David Geffen, the record company executive and co-founder of DreamWorks. It was Francisco's delight to entertain in the garden all year round, to give themed dinner parties, and to fill the house with lavish sprays of flowers. Guests almost always carried away a dinner menu in calligraphy. One of those parties was an eighteen-course Japanese dinner with a *koto* player on a bridge in the garden. Another was reported this way in a Los Angeles paper: "Dashing Francisco Kripacz gave a little dinner party at his hilltop home Wednesday night for that grand gentleman of fashion, Hubert de Givenchy. The setting for dinner was dramatic—black china on black cloths with vases filled with white narcissi and other pale flowers for contrast."[4] Francisco enjoyed equally the weeks of preparation and the gossipy aftermath, in which guests were praised, caricatured, and sometimes excluded from further invitations. He was himself sometimes caricatured as the architect's hysterical wife, but for many, his still youthful exuberance and charm were the perfect balance to Arthur's sedate, reflective presence.

In contrast to Francisco's Hollywood coterie, Arthur was drawn to a different crowd. On a flight from New York to Los Angeles, Arthur, in first class, entered into a conversation about spirituality with a woman in the next seat who turned out to be actress Shirley MacLaine. They were well into the subject before they became aware of each other's respective accomplishments. It was a conversation that would continue for several years. Through MacLaine's Russian émigré lover, the film director Andrei Konchalovsky (best known in America for *Runaway Train*), Arthur came to know Mel Ferrer and his wife, Elizabeth, a granddaughter of Leo Tolstoy. With their roots in European culture, Ferrer and his wife appeared to Arthur more sophisticated and informed than many who attended the parties he and Francisco hosted. His pleasure was in smaller gatherings, which might include the Ferrers and Shirley MacLaine, Canadian actor Donald Sutherland, and a troubled young Richard Gere, whom Arthur found very attractive. At these parties, nobody gossiped about facelifts and where to eat; instead, they were likely to spend the evening listening quietly to Arthur or Shirley talking about Buddhism and other spiritual disciplines. Richard Gere was especially fascinated with Arthur's stories of Japan and his views on the Dalai Lama, and eventually, with Arthur in mind, Gere would portray an architect in the film *Intersection* shot in Vancouver. When Katharine Hepburn, occasionally present at those small gatherings, was in Vancouver in the fall of 1985 to make a film, she phoned Arthur, and he invited her for an informal dinner that he prepared himself.[5] She wanted to see the Museum of Anthropology, so Lois Milsom made special arrangements to take her there when it was closed to the public. Hepburn was struck not only by the museum and its historical collection but by Bill Reid's *Raven and the First Men*, and Lois subsequently arranged for the two shaky veterans to meet.

Throughout much of the early 1980s, while his reputation remained at its peak, Arthur spent much of his time socializing with the rich and the famous; later, when called to accounts, he explained it was a necessary part of his profession. For a time, he and Francisco also kept their Fifth Avenue residence in Manhattan, where they gave especially elegant parties. For one of Pierre Trudeau's visits to New York in 1981, they invited, among others, Arthur's old friend and conservative socialite Patricia Buckley, fashion guru Diana Vreeland, political analyst and author Theodore White, *New York Review of Books* editor Robert Silvers, entertainers Diana Ross and Shirley MacLaine, and two Canadians: television producer Stephanie McLuhan, daughter of Marshall McLuhan, and financier Paul Desmarais.[6] Arthur and Francisco, in turn, were frequently guests in the Hamptons and at wealthy retreats on the Mediterranean. Liona Boyd, the celebrated guitarist, who knew Arthur through her close friendship with Trudeau, described in memoirs how "on impulse" she, Arthur, Francisco, and Lois Milsom flew for a couple of weeks to Italy, where Arthur was very much part of the aristocratic society of Rome and where multilingual Francisco, as another friend observed, "would swan into the Hotel Hassler in Rome, as if he had been doing so since puberty."[7] They dined for several evenings "in the glamorous company of Italian countesses,

barons, tycoons, fashion designers, and film directors," because
Arthur and Francisco cultivated the international set "like Mikimoto
pearls."[8] It was, Boyd wrote, "*La Dolce Vita* come to life." The group
subsequently headed for Capri, where again, "dinner parties with
jewelled countesses and playboy industrialists kept us entertained."
One afternoon, Boyd introduced Arthur and his friends to Adnan
Khashoggi, the infamous Arab arms dealer, and they spent several
hours on his enormous yacht (with its own helicopter pad and a
crew of fifty). Stretched out on the deck of this floating palace, with
Mozart playing from hidden speakers, Boyd noted, one never had to
contemplate "the real world."[9]

In another "enchanted" social space, Arthur came to know
Prince Charles and Princess Diana. Arthur had met Charles
through a mutual Italian friend, Vittorio Annabaldi, and in 1975,
Arthur and Francisco joined Charles and Vittorio midway on an
excursion in Canada's Far North, taking some choice cuts of steak
and fresh asparagus with them to vary the fish-and-seal diet. They
met again in April 1980, when Charles unveiled the Bill Reid sculpture at the Museum of Anthropology. But it was when Arthur was
engaged in the design and construction of the Napp pharmaceutical laboratories near Cambridge that he and Charles saw each other
more frequently. Working with the Sackler brothers, Raymond and
Mortimer, the owners of Napp Technologies, was another enchanting experience for Arthur. The Sacklers, then in their sixties, were
surrounded, Medici-like, by advisors and experts of all sorts, and
their "court" moved from place to place, from one Sackler house
to another: New York, London, Gstaad, Antibes.[10] Francisco had a
lively involvement as confidant of Mortimer's second wife, Gheri,
who was thirty-four years younger than her husband. The brothers
had a keen interest in modernism and wanted a design that would
challenge the boundaries of architecture, as they were doing with
medical technology. Although they vetoed his first design, using
glass blocks, in favour of double-glazed mirrored glass walls, Arthur
found them excellent clients to work for, and he was gratified that
Charles, with his strong but conservative tastes in architecture,

approved of the buildings. Apparently, Charles liked the minimalist rhythm of the design, "its massive ribcage of columns and mirrored glass over a flat roof," and would take visitors there to show them how progressive British industry could be.[11]

Arthur probably met Diana through her cousin Desmond FitzGerald, whom he had known when he was teaching at UBC. At his father's death, FitzGerald had become the twenty-ninth Knight of Glin, and Arthur and Francisco visited him in Ireland in September 1981. Arthur later wrote: "We enjoyed our brief but enchanting visit with you and your family. I shall not lose the vision of Glin Castle that early Sunday morning with dew on its vast lawns, its charming 'folly' appearing over the brow of fields sloping down to the Shannon, its great trees hugging the embattlement wings, our morning walk and most precious of all, the children in their outsize but very au-courant and chic dress-up, even to a matching purse but containing a doll set of china!"[12]

When Charles and Diana came to Vancouver for the opening of Expo 86, Arthur spent an extended period of time with them. He took them to see the Museum of Anthropology and, joined by Galen and Hilary Weston, travelled with them in a private yacht to Qualicum Beach, where they visited Desmond's mother, Veronica Milner, a Spencer cousin to Diana. During the course of the visit, Arthur became something of a confidant to the troubled princess, who subsequently stayed in touch, phoning him on Christmas Day 1992 after she had separated from Charles and, the year before she died, sending thanks to Arthur for arranging a possible holiday visit to B.C.'s Gang Ranch, where he had assured her privacy for herself and her sons.[13] Earlier that same year, she had been with Arthur and Francisco at the K-Club on Barbuda; there she and Francisco had talked at length about health food and exercise. (There were often surprising connections within the world of the rich and famous, Arthur discovered, when a few years later he learned that Diana's lover, Dodi Al-Fayed, was the nephew of the arms dealer Adnan Khashoggi.)

Arthur's enlarged sympathy for Diana was rooted in his own experience. By 1982, Francisco had been his partner for twenty years.

They had worked together on many design projects, had holidayed in luxurious resorts, and had travelled to parts of the world with legendary names—Machu Picchu, Kathmandu, the Hindu Kush—but their relationship was changing. For many years, Arthur had had a recurring dream in which he and Francisco became separated. They had arranged to meet for a holiday in the Caribbean, but Francisco did not show up at the appointed destination. In the dream, Arthur flew from one small island airport to the next, but there was no trace of Francisco. He would wake up shaken. The separation, however, did not happen quite like that. Rather, one day when Arthur arrived at their rented home on Sunset Plaza Drive, Francisco introduced him to a new friend, a handsome student named Jan, still in his teens, who was going to be staying at the house. Arthur knew at once that something irreversible had happened. While their relationship had always been an open one, they had never brought casual acquaintances home to stay. This change made Arthur painfully conscious of being fifty-eight years old.

Their working relationship had also changed. Being put in charge of the Los Angeles office had empowered Francisco and made him overweeningly self-confident. Where previously he had deferred to Arthur, he was now making many of the office decisions on his own. To the staff, his exuberant playfulness had become tinged with a sinister arrogance. The opportunity to work on the California Plaza project had attracted a number of bright young architects in the United States, but they found an office being run inefficiently by a parvenu with no architectural background. Arthur Erickson, around whose name they had gathered, often seemed a shadowy figure in the background, busy elsewhere. More disturbing, he seemed to be taking directions from his very lightweight office manager.

None of this played well in the business world. California Plaza was a giant redevelopment project with one hard-nosed goal—to increase, with the participation of several real estate developers, the residential and commercial activity at the financial heart of the city. For Arthur, there were parallels in this megaconstruction to the building of Simon Fraser University: while he had charge of the overall plaza project, he was involved at the same time in coordinating the activities of developers, contractors, and other architects and engineers. "The project is prodigious," he told Edith Iglauer, "with six groups brought together under one management."[14] For SFU, most of the coordination had been done by Geoffrey Massey, who negotiated firmly with businesses and governments alike and kept the building on track. But Francisco was no Geoff Massey, and in his published account of California Plaza, Arthur tellingly refers to "shifts and changes... fits and starts" and to "the forces of economics prevailing."[15]

The original master plan linked the five-block, eleven-acre site by means of a chain of pedestrian parks, so that one could walk from the Colburn music centre on the northern periphery to Pershing Square, the city's symbolic heart, on the south. Arthur's design placed the office towers at the south end, adjacent to other city towers, with the hotel and the 750-unit residential complex to the north. But what especially interested him were design opportunities related to the arts: a dance gallery, a museum for contemporary art, and a performance plaza with a covered outdoor stage to attract both tourists and far-flung city dwellers. In his book, he explained that the best presentation of contemporary Los Angeles art he had seen was in a series of converted stables on the outskirts of Milan, Italy, where each artist was given an individual "stall" entered from the loggia. In his determination to rethink the genre of every building in light of its contemporary use, he designed the Museum of Contemporary Art to replicate a series of shops and placed them along the base of the condominiums. But this movement away from the art-museum-as-temple was rejected by the museum board and, to Arthur's dismay, another architect was hired to provide a more traditional design.

His plan for an outdoor performance plaza with a covered stage for television specials became even more fraught. With public input, the idea for this space was to create something like a modern version of Shakespeare's Globe theatre below street level, with seats in circular tiers above an orchestra level, onto which restaurants opened. The theatre area could function as a cabaret at night and a marketplace during the day. But this plan was rejected by a new developer who favoured an informal space where unplanned, spontaneous events could be staged. Still, the Community Redevelopment Agency wanted California Plaza to be an appealing hub for the downtown area. To this end, Arthur played with turning the plaza into a garden, like Copenhagen's Tivoli Gardens, featuring a small lake as a setting for restaurants, cafes, and performance spaces.

Central to this scheme was the involvement of the English artist David Hockney, famous for his paintings of Los Angeles swimming pools, who Arthur believed could give the water garden a fantastic dimension. Hockney's designs could also be carried into the construction and decorating of shops, restaurants, service costumes, even tableware, so that everything in the plaza would be part of a huge stage. But Arthur frequently failed to appear at meetings to promote his vision with city planners and developers, and in Francisco, businessmen and politicians saw no assurance that such fantastic schemes could be successfully realized. The water garden project was put on hold and eventually dropped. The dance gallery met a similar fate. As in the rejected design for Christ Church Cathedral in Vancouver, the gallery was to have been situated below the plaza, with a skylight on the plaza level and, to mark its presence, a spiral of glass gesturing skyward, suggesting the arrested grace of a dancer's movement. But it, too, was shelved.

Phase 1 of California Plaza, including the first office tower, the hotel, and the Museum of Contemporary Art, was given the go-ahead in 1983 and was completed in 1985. Everything was held to a strict budget, and Marcelo Igonda, one of the project architects, spent what seemed like unreasonable amounts of time searching out inexpensive materials as they proceeded.[16] On opening, although a great deal of critical praise was given to the contemporary art museum designed by Japanese architect Isozaki Arata, the project as a whole was met with indifference. Rem Koolhaas had seemed to anticipate this when he wrote in 1981 that building on this neutral site would be like "designing for a void."[17] About the tower, the reviewer for the *Los Angeles Herald* wrote that "a first-rate designer gives his second best for Cal Plaza"; the plaza was disappointing—a series of bland, glass-wrapped semicylinders jutting from a vast deck—altogether a watered-down invention.[18] Photographers agreed in subsequent years that the tower was best viewed from the fountain plaza looking south, with Isozaki's red sandstone museum on the right; but the vitreous high-rise of reflective glass, while giving the city centre a focal point, remains anonymous and sleekly generic in the California sun.

Arthur had lost the design of not only the art museum at California Plaza but the hotel as well, and this would become a pattern. In the early 1980s, he won a competition for the Orange County Performing Arts Center at Newport Beach, California. He would be working with a budget of $20 million. But when his future employers asked if what was said in Edith Iglauer's book was true—that he was never in one place more than three days—Arthur answered cheekily that in fact he was never in one place more than two days. When asked, "Who makes decisions from day to day?" he replied that contractors usually went ahead; if anything was wrong, he would have them start over again. The hiring team came to Vancouver to check this out; hearing the same account of Arthur's arrogance, they cancelled the contract. Arthur said in response: "You can't own me, only my designs."

Arthur's unco-operative aloofness and his extravagance were viewed by many as the result of Francisco's influence. Lifestyle, it seemed, had now become more important to Arthur than architecture. What his friends and employees did not fully realize was how fragile that lifestyle was. When Arthur was in L.A., he usually had to stay in a hotel, because Francisco had filled their rented house with his own friends. Arthur found himself a new partner in 1982, a married man from Seattle with a daughter, but someone who was again twenty years younger. His name was Allen Steele, and they met when Allen was bartending for Bagley and Virginia Wright the evening of the Philip Glass concert. Blond, square-jawed, Allen was a handsome but shy man whom Arthur's friends in Vancouver welcomed. But Arthur was less successful at integrating Allen into

the company of Francisco's California friends. They tried vaca-
tioning together—Arthur and Allen, Francisco and Jan—but it was
not entirely comfortable, perhaps because the age differences now
spanned three generations.

Not all the projects originating in the Los Angeles office were
disappointing. The concrete-and-glass San Diego Convention Center, designed in 1981, is regarded as one of Arthur's most successful
later buildings, certainly his major accomplishment in the U.S. The
challenge with this commission was how to give a gigantic building
a friendly, human face. Arthur had a particular dislike for convention centres; to him, they were barn-like structures centred around
an exhibition hall and, like their cousin the covered sports stadium,
were often situated in prime locations but were "not very friendly
to surrounding urban life."[19] His competition-winning strategy in
San Diego (with Muramatsu Yasuo's significant input) was to tie
the building to its harbour setting and to "submerge" the exhibition and meeting spaces as much as possible, behind and beneath
bright public spaces and landscaped terraces, so that a convention
would have the aspect of a pleasurable, holiday-style occasion. This
was achieved to a great extent by the glass vaulting over the lobbies,
which gave the interiors transparency and lightness, but also by the
roof terraces, where concrete gantry-like structures supporting the
glass vaults suggested the boiler plate and riveted steel construction
of ships and dockyards. Sail-like roof membranes gave the terrace
a festive, nautical air. The San Diego Convention Center opened
in 1989 to positive reviews, and Arthur was asked to develop a second phase of expansion. But none of his other California buildings—
chiefly university laboratories and private homes—were regarded by
the public or critics as especially distinguished, and his failure to
generate much new work was becoming a concern.[20]

ANXIETY ABOUT THE lack of new work had already formed a dark
cloud over the Toronto office. In 1986, Keith Loffler and five other
senior employees prepared a seven-page memorandum addressed to
Arthur in which they outlined the strengths and the weaknesses of

the business and demanded immediate action on his part to address their concerns.[21] Investment opportunity in Toronto, in their opinion, could not be stronger, but the severe lack of cash flow made it almost impossible to run the office. Long-standing unpaid accounts in Toronto (at least $650,000) meant that everything had to be paid for in cash, and numerous suppliers (travel agencies, taxi companies, couriers, fax machine repairmen) would no longer render their services. Office staff were demoralized because their salaries had been frozen for a long period. Worse, the company was in danger of not being able to meet its contractual commitments with clients and thereby risked legal trouble. These problems were becoming well-known in the community and were scaring away potential clients.

Above all, the memorandum to Arthur stressed that "things are ready to fall apart in the office." The pressure created by lack of funds was destroying the group's motivation and ability to perform with a sense of pride, "particularly frustrating after the intense personal investment each one of us has in the office." Knowing that money was always available for the Los Angeles office, those signing the memo gave Arthur an ultimatum: that in thirty days there be funding for at least 50 percent of the current accounts payable; that the balance of accounts payable be structured and agreed on with the firm's creditors; that a system of incentive payments be introduced for senior staff; and that the firm "invest in itself" (staff development, product/material resources, labour-saving technologies) "to compete in the 1980s and restore the pride and image it once had." There is no reply from Arthur in the office's archives beyond a secretarial note, "Seen by A.E.," penned on the cover of the memorandum.

Arthur was in deep financial trouble. In a lengthy article for *Report on Business* magazine in April 1990, Canadian architecture critic Lisa Rochon gave the public a detailed account of Erickson's dire situation, presenting under the title "Blueprint for Chaos" the history of his practice for the preceding five years.[22] If Rochon had not been so respectful of Arthur's architectural genius, this article could have been described as an exposé. Nonetheless, it was fairly sensational. To structure her overall narrative, she seized on the story of young Adam Koffler and his wife, who in the mid-1980s had taken steps to realize their dream of creating a health resort north of Toronto. They had first thought to engage Jack Diamond as architect, but when Erickson's Toronto office expressed an interest in discussing the project, they were thrilled to think they might be able to work with Canada's leading architect. At their first meeting, Arthur arrived without the square footage detail that others had offered but proceeded to enrapture them with an account of the Aesclepeion at Pergamum, where in ancient times patients were treated in a facility of surpassing architectural beauty known also for the greatness of its library, where, indeed, parchment had been invented as a recording medium. The young couple was sold. They told Rochon: "He'll say one sentence. It doesn't sound like much. But the full meaning of the sentence, when you finally see the direction that it's taking you, has tremendous impact... the first few months we didn't really know what we were going to get." An April 18, 1986, outline of the proposed King Ranch Health Spa and Fitness Resort suggested Arthur's influence. It listed concepts to strive for at the ranch, including well-being, regeneration, sharing, nurturing, and healing; a list of feelings for clients to experience included calm, balance, openness, soaring, intimacy, dynamism, repose. Overall, it proposed the pursuit of equilibrium in body, mind, and spirit.[23]

In 1986, the Kofflers received conceptual drawings rooted in what Rochon called "Erickson's spiritual, low-lying work," and Arthur was hired, his fee set at the standard 5.5 percent of the $22.5-million construction cost. They were eager to proceed, but by 1988, when building was finally underway, they had become aware of major problems. Construction documents from the Toronto office, with its heavy employee turnover, were not coherent: the plans did not make clear how parts of the building with its different wings were going to fit together, or even how hot tubs, for example, would be installed. Further, the consulting engineer reported that the fees Koffler had paid (in one case $5 million) had not been distributed to the construction companies but remained with Arthur.

One group threatened to stop work when eight months had passed without payment. Anxious but still inspired by Arthur's visions, the Kofflers advanced more funds until they learned in May 1989 that a Toronto bailiff "pursuant to a landlord's distress warrant" had been instructed to seize and sell by auction the contents of Arthur's office, which would include the drawings for the King Ranch Health Spa and Fitness Resort. They felt they had no option but to drop Arthur as their architect, though they had to hire one of Arthur's former employees to help his successor wade through the sketchy documents that were on file.[24]

The Kofflers were not alone, Rochon reported. An addition to the Robert McLaughlin Gallery in Oshawa and the competition-winning Markham Civic Centre were major projects underway in Arthur's Toronto office in the late 1980s. Arthur had won these commissions over solid Canadian competitors like Raymond Moriyama and Barton Myers Associates, but when payment to engineers and construction companies was delayed and then ceased altogether, his office was removed from these high-profile jobs. Arthur had led clients like the Kofflers to believe that his financial problems were with his Middle East accounts, but Keith Loffler, who had left the Toronto office in 1988, explained it differently to Rochon. It was clear, Loffler said, from having worked with Arthur for fifteen years, that there were two fatal problems. First was the vexing matter of an absentee boss who refused to share administrative control or profits with anyone else in the firm. Arthur was the first to admit he had no business skills; nonetheless, he had the final say on all aspects of the business, though he was seldom there to attend to them. He badly needed equals on the job, but senior architects would eventually leave the firm, concerned about its ability to survive and giving up on the prospect of becoming partners someday. Second was the Los Angeles office, where out-of-control spending had reached crisis proportions. In Loffler's view, the Los Angeles office could only be described as "a black hole." When clients like the Kofflers advanced large sums to complete the next phase of their project, Arthur would transfer them to Los Angeles.

When Arthur and Francisco established the firm at 125 North Robertson Boulevard in L.A., they spent nearly a million dollars renovating an office for which they initially had only a three-year lease. In addition to the house on Sunset Plaza Drive, they also rented, during the long summer months, a three-bedroom cottage on Malibu Beach from film director Robert Altman. Most burdensome remained interest on the bank loan for the Schuyler Road home. The renovations there had stalled for lack of ready cash to go forward. When Gordon and Marion Smith visited, they found Arthur driving a Maserati, Francisco a Lamborghini. They could see their ascetic Vancouver friend led quite a different life in Los Angeles.

When the L.A. press caught wind of his money problems, Arthur lamented to a reporter that it was "terribly frustrating" doing business in Canada: "Canadian banks wouldn't give adequate credit on overseas receivables, and we were left hanging. We then exhausted American and Far Eastern banking systems in an attempt to give the firm a better base... So many of the projects we were hoping to be involved with have been abandoned, or have fallen through for us." He added what had become a familiar refrain: "Business is not my strength. I wish I knew more about it, but I am interested in design, and that's where I still want to concentrate my energies."[25]

In an extraordinary gesture of philanthropy, a group drawn from Canada's financial elites came to Arthur's rescue in January 1988. Identified as friends, ex-clients, and admirers, the group included Conrad Black, then chairman of Hollinger Inc.; Peter Bentley, chairman of Canfor Corp.; Larry Heisey of Harlequin Enterprises Ltd.; art patron Isabel McLaughlin; clients Helmut and Hugo Eppich of Ebco Industries Ltd.; Peter Munk, chairman of American Barrick Resources Corp. (now Barrick Gold); Galen Weston, president of George Weston Ltd.; Dr. Norman Keevil Sr. of Teck Cominco; and financier Samuel Belzberg.[26] Chiefly, these were self-made millionaires for whom the work ethic was primary, but they knew that their support of the arts gave them a special status; they could make good use of the tax credits if the investment went sour. Under the direction of Richard Gordon, Arthur's financial management consultant

in Los Angeles, the Arthur Erickson Capital Group Ltd. was formed
to create a minimum of $3 million in capital so that Arthur's Cana-
dian offices could remain in business. Potential investors were provided with a history of Arthur's company, which identified naïve tax
practices, delays in collection procedures in the Middle East, and
inflationary economics as the principal sources of his financial crisis. It was proposed that each participant would be offered a "Limited Partnership" share worth $250,000, on the understanding that
every effort would be made to make the partnership a commercial
success.[27]

The investors, though alert to the substantial risks involved for
their money, were not quite prepared for what transpired. Once the
money was in place, providing services similar to that of a commercial bank, Arthur again directed large sums to be sent to the Los
Angeles office. The members of the syndicate began to lose faith
when they learned that Arthur's creditors were still banging down
the doors to the Toronto office and especially when they learned
about Arthur's expensive properties in Bel Air, Malibu, and Fire
Island and his Maserati. In her article, Rochon described a telecon-
ference meeting with the investors in which Arthur's detachment
from the "real" world became clear to them. "Arthur, you are our
friend," they are reported to have said. "We love you. You're Canada's national treasure as a designer. But you can't go on like this.
You're making fools of us all." His answer was, "You obviously don't
understand what architecture is all about." Maybe so, they replied,
but they did know what business was all about—they knew the difference between "money" and "no money." Confronted this way by
his backers, Arthur felt like his fictional heroes Jean-Christophe and
Stephen Dedalus and the poet Rilke—the artist misunderstood by
Philistines for whom great art is just another commodity. His backers, however, saw themselves as sympathetic individuals providing
"Red Cross Money" to bail out their friend.

Arthur showed no signs of implementing an austerity plan: even
after the stiff warning from his investors, he left with Allen for a
holiday in Fiji, and Francisco went skiing in Colorado. When a few

months later Arthur turned to the Capital Group for more money, he was refused. Heward Stikeman, who had served as legal director of the Canadian backers, was quoted by Rochon as saying, "There was always a gap between what was needed [from Erickson] and what was put in. The picture kept changing for the worse." Stikeman Elliott, Arthur's solicitors, dropped their client because he had not paid them for years. In 1989, Arthur directed Richard Gordon to establish a new group of financial backers, giving him names like Jack Daniels, the former chairman of Cadillac Fairview with whom Arthur had won the California competition, and Toronto lawyer Hal Jackman, board chairman of several investment and insurance companies and a strong supporter of the arts. But word was out, and this time no one was willing to step forward. The Toronto office continued its downward spiral. In September 1989, the four remaining employees left, and the office was quietly vacated.

The staff in the California office could see they were on a similar course. Arthur did not make himself a public presence in Los Angeles. Because he was so frequently somewhere else, he was perceived as just a "Canadian architect." And when he was in the city, he was with his private circle of friends. Accordingly, he got almost no press in the United States, and his buildings received no awards. To those in the field, his prestigious gold medal from the AIA in 1986 seemed a complete mystery. The work at the office turned more and more to variations on familiar genres—university laboratories and private residences.

Francisco was increasingly in charge in the L.A. office—not just delegating work to the employees but taking control of the company's assets. Staff were alarmed to see him ordering Arthur about, insisting on changes not only to his designs—a round window here instead of square—but to his personal grooming: "You *must* get your nails done, Arthur, *today*." In spite of his giddy sociability, Francisco had a deep lack of interest in other people, focussing everyone's attention on himself and his perceived needs. These were numerous and invariably excessive: diving holidays with Jan in Phuket, an apartment in Trump Tower in New York, a Porsche to replace his

Lamborghini. His "lesser" needs included a daily luncheon delivery of salade niçoise from high-end restaurateur Michel Richard and a vast collection of costly, often fragile sweaters, maintained by a Japanese weaver who did repairs. All of this was charged to the company with the same claim that Arthur made—these were lifestyle choices important to making business contacts.

Those most often impressed with Arthur and Francisco were artists, actors, and fashion designers. Melanie Friesen, whom Arthur knew from his friendship with the Benes, was now vice-president of Martin Scorsese's production company, making frequent trips from New York to Los Angeles, and she was often invited to their parties. One of the most memorable was a "black and white" party Francisco arranged under a white tent on the beach at Malibu, where guests dressed thematically and were served such delicacies as black Russian caviar and white peaches in champagne. Office staff members were often sent on complicated errands in connection with these parties, and for this one, Ann Videriksen, Arthur's executive assistant, had spent a day searching the city for a set of black teaspoons.[28] The most exquisite touch remembered that evening was a little bowl at each place setting in which swam a black goldfish with a long, flowing fantail.

Melanie, who occasionally stayed the night, saw that Arthur's bedroom was spare, a painting by Ruth Massey the only decoration on the walls. Francisco's bedroom, however, was like "something from Versailles." At breakfast, the cook would offer a selection from thirty-seven jars of jams, marmalades, and honey. "You never know what someone might want," quipped Francisco.[29] For a weekend with Jan in Arizona, Francisco had their bicycles shipped ahead. Almost every trip involved the purchase of new equipment: diving gear for the South Seas, the latest camera lenses, new skis for the Alps.

The mood of the remaining L.A. employees turned from amazement to outrage as they saw their working lives reduced to hardscrabble conditions. When Susan Oakley, one of Arthur's stalwart architects, one day asked Arthur for $14 to buy tracing paper (for toilet paper the women at the office were using coffee filters), he said he couldn't help her, he was in a hurry, at which point a chauffeured limousine pulled up to take him to the airport. Arthur was only a great architect, Oakley asserted, "when he paid attention," and that was no longer the case.[30]

Arthur's failure to take the helm was perhaps best explained by his personal life. In the late 1980s, Francisco's partner, Jan, still in his twenties, had become ill. He was the first of their close friends to show evidence of the newly identified human immunodeficiency virus, the pandemic scourge known as AIDS. Rock Hudson had died in 1985, and his doctor, Michael Gottlieb, one of the early AIDS researchers, attended Jan as well. The day Jan died, Arthur was on his way to China. When he heard the news, he turned around in the Tokyo airport and flew back to be with Francisco. Several friends rallied around, including Elizabeth Taylor, who had become passionately active on behalf of HIV/AIDS research. William Wilkinson, the popular California hotelier and chef who had planned several social events for Arthur and Francisco, managed the rituals surrounding Jan's passing. At a small gathering in Malibu, Shirley MacLaine scattered Jan's ashes. Francisco, realizing he was possibly infected, reacted with more determination than ever to live life to the fullest.

Arthur's companion, Allen Steele, was also ill. In character, Allen was the opposite of Francisco—an undemonstrative man whose physical attractiveness and serving nature suggested to some a male odalisque. Allen had been given the heavy task of putting together a text for the second edition of *The Architecture of Arthur Erickson*, published by Douglas & McIntyre in 1988. Some of the materials were drawn directly from the 1975 Tundra volume, but much of the sequel was compiled by Allen from what Arthur referred to as his "scribbled fragments."[31] During this time, Allen was identified as HIV-positive. Quiet, introverted, and never wholly at ease with his gay identity, he now saw himself as a guilty man being punished for the abandonment of his wife and daughter. In the summer of 1990, a friend of Arthur's, Hugh Brewster, observed that Steele had become deeply angry over his failing health and the firm's collapsing fortunes and would vent his rage on Arthur. But in this difficult time, Brewster noted, Arthur's Buddhist sensibility was such that he continued to express great love and compassion for his suffering friend, his calm and equanimity remarkable.[32] Shortly after a visit from his daughter, Allen died in Vancouver at St. Paul's Hospital on October 20, 1990.

By 1991, the Los Angeles office had met the same fate as Toronto's: there was no money to pay the employees, and creditors had ceased providing goods and services. Arthur's design was used for the second tower in the California Plaza development, but the third tower, part of the original design, was never built. The only viable projects still in the works—an addition to a mall in Blaine, Washington, and a house in Colorado for Shirley MacLaine—were being designed in the Vancouver office. The landlord at Robertson Boulevard served notice; in June, Arthur closed the office down, amidst bitter allegations from employees that he had siphoned off massive amounts of cash from the business for personal use. Arthur countered that he had hired Richard Gordon, a Los Angeles attorney and financial advisor, as far back as 1985 to put the firm on sound financial footing, and that had not happened. By 1990, Gordon had decided to sue Arthur himself for unpaid consulting fees, describing himself as Arthur's "largest single creditor." He told Lisa Rochon that he had "spent a year and a half cleaning up a decade of destruction and decadence. He's a very self-destructive man... it's a black eye [for] Canada."[33] Arthur's Canadian financiers, though, were made to understand that Gordon had confiscated much of their invested money on the grounds that it was owing to him for services rendered.[34]

When Arthur was advised to declare bankruptcy in the U.S., Shirley MacLaine, with whom he had taken refuge, suggested he disclose everything to the press. But when he told a reporter that he hadn't trusted his accountant, someone within the office mistakenly felt she was being accused instead of Gordon; in fact, Arthur had hired a series of accountants in California, giving none of them a clear outline of how the business was being run. The American press played with the story for several days, describing the nearly

$10 million owing. A reporter from the *Los Angeles Business Journal*, sent to investigate the rumour that Erickson had closed his office without warning, found a dumpster in an alley behind the building "stuffed with blueprints, renderings, sketches, and various architectural documents." These included the plans for California Plaza.[35]

The Canadian press was equally curious about Arthur's situation, and in a period of economic recession, evinced little sympathy for the architect notorious for his free-spending lifestyle. An article in the *Globe and Mail* drew attention instead to the plight of unpaid subconsultants left behind in the wake of Arthur's business failures. Erickson, the writer said, was so arrogant that "he will only be photographed for an article if it includes one of his works as well."[36] A piece in *Maclean's* reported that Arthur had simply walked away from the L.A. office, leaving the door unlocked, drawings and blueprints scattered everywhere.[37] Arthur continued to insist in interviews that what was perceived as lavish living was appropriate to his times; he was spending to attract more business. He had not spent the money on himself, he said, but on company investments and promotions. Between 1988 and 1990, he said, his office had entered several high-powered competitions that failed to produce results, including two university projects, the Chicago Public Library, and the World Bank headquarters in Washington. "We lost a lot of money putting together the submissions," he claimed, pointing out that each presentation cost approximately $150,000.[38] But his retreat position was that of the great artist scorned in his time. He liked to quote Emerson, so admired by Lawren Harris: "To be great is to be misunderstood. For non-conformity, the world whips you with its displeasure."[39]

ON FEBRUARY 28, 1992, Arthur entered the Vancouver courthouse he had designed and filed for personal bankruptcy. His creditors in Canada and the U.S. were legion; some 270 statements of claim were filed in Vancouver alone. He was reported to owe in excess of $10.5 million. One of the largest debts, $4 million, was to the federal Department of Public Works that, from the Trudeau era, had

provided security for Arthur's firm. The external affairs department
was also owed more than a quarter million in connection with the
design and construction of the chancery in Washington. Many
claims had not yet been made, including one from the Arthur Erickson Capital Group, who, as the *Globe and Mail* phrased it, "were on
the hook for almost $3 million." The same article claimed that the
bulk of the creditors were still in the U.S.[40] Because British Columbia bankruptcy law allowed an individual to keep only $2,000 in
tangible personal property, Arthur lost most of his art collection—
the Ellsworth Kellys, the Lichtensteins, his mother's gravy-stained
Emily Carr. That evening, he went to Lois Milsom's for dinner. In
her words, they had a relaxed, lovely evening together, and it was a
shock for her to read about his bankruptcy in the paper the next day.

Arthur's only other asset was the small cottage and garden in
Vancouver's Point Grey neighbourhood, which was listed with
three mortgages against it totalling $3.5 million. One of the holders,
Power Corporation of Canada (the others were National Trust and
the Arthur Erickson Capital Group), ordered the property to be sold.
From a realtor's point of view, the house was negligible, but it was
situated on a double lot that could accommodate two new houses,
so it was put on the market with an asking price of $650,000. In
the meantime, landscape architect Elizabeth Watts had organized
a group of heritage-minded Vancouver residents who were looking for ways to persuade the city to step in and preserve the house
and garden, which they regarded as a national treasure. "It was
a source of inspiration and reflection for Canada's most notable
architect," they argued, "who otherwise lived most of his life out of
a flight bag." They insisted their cause was not charitable: "We're
not saying 'Poor Arthur. Don't take his home away.' We're saying
this is a heritage resource and is of value to all Canadians."[41] Phyllis
Lambert, the architect-activist who founded Héritage Montréal in
1975 and was instrumental in saving large parts of Montreal from
the wrecker's ball, joined the campaign to save the property. From
her office as director of the Canadian Centre for Architecture, she
wrote to Mayor Gordon Campbell: "As the locus of work, thought,

and experimentation of an outstanding Canadian, and the country's most renowned architect, the house and garden deserve the highest respect and must be preserved as a historical and architectural monument."[42] The realtor received as many as a dozen offers but was held back while city council pursued a heritage designation for the property.

In January 1997, after five years of petitions and fundraising, the group known as the Arthur Erickson House and Garden Foundation achieved its goal of getting the property listed on Vancouver's "A" inventory of post-1940s heritage buildings. This was accomplished when both the Capital Group and the Power Corp. agreed to forgive what was owed in the mortgages they held and when Peter Wall and Phyllis Lambert provided $350,000 and $150,000 respectively to refinance the mortgage held by National Trust. A number of others, including Bill Reid, Jean Southam, Hugo Eppich, and the Bronfman family, made important contributions towards saving the house and garden. The arrangement was that Arthur would have occupancy for life and that the public would have access in guided tours of the garden arranged by appointment. A long-term goal was to make the property a national heritage site and an education centre.

Not everyone in Vancouver loved Arthur Erickson. A large number of architects could not forget the way he had been awarded the prize commission in Washington. Office workers were aggrieved that they should be suffering the discomfort of cold windows and leaking roofs in Erickson-designed buildings. Still others were outraged by Erickson's continued King-Arthur-and-his-court public image. Writing in the *Vancouver Sun*, Jamie Lamb described seeing Arthur at a public reception, saying it was "like attending a papal reception: you half expected anybody approaching him to genuflect, kneel, and kiss the papal ring." Lamb concluded his article with sarcastic praise for a man who had mortgaged a $450,000 property for more than $3 million.[43]

Celebrity had become notoriety, but Arthur was largely unfazed by public criticism. He knew that many of his employees were angry and hurt by the collapse of his business and that his friends sometimes felt ashamed on his behalf. Nonetheless, if he enjoyed someone's company, he would still phone and ask them out to lunch as if nothing had happened, his dignity intact.[44] When reporters pinned him to the wall for a statement about his financial disasters, he would fall back on Eastern philosophy and say that a crisis is always an opportunity for growth: "Nothing should be treated as negative." "My brother, no denying, has had a lot of problems lately," wrote Donald Erickson to Arthur's old girlfriend, Diana (Chesterton) Whittall, "but he is a remarkably focussed human being. He floats above it all."[45]

20

Local
Celebrity

A FEW MONTHS AFTER declaring bankruptcy in 1992, no longer eligible for insurance, Arthur Erickson, at sixty-seven, quietly merged his Vancouver office with Aitken Wreglesworth Associates (who themselves later merged with another firm and renamed themselves Architectura). David Aitken had worked briefly for Arthur in 1972, and it seemed to some a cruel reversal of fortunes that Arthur should be working for a former employee. But once he had adjusted to his diminished status (in his own words, "a difficult time"), he was comfortable enough working as a design consultant and not being harried by the "treacheries" of business. Arthur was employed on a project-to-project basis, and it worked very well, he told friends. At AWA, there were local projects that he took up with enthusiasm, especially the expansions to Simon Fraser University (the student services building and west mall expansion) and the Koerner Library at UBC. But he had no control over the final implementation of his designs. As he would say of the squat, disruptive appearance of the SFU student services building, with its tinted glass fins and eyebrows, "They were sometimes manifestly clumsy in their misunderstandings."

Over a slightly earlier project, Arthur had retained a master builder's control. The second Eppich house had been designed and built while Arthur was still in business on his own, and he continued to take charge in matters of fine tuning. Impressed by the house

Arthur had built for Helmut and Hildegard, Hugo Eppich was eager to follow in his twin brother's footsteps. After Hugo purchased a 1.3-acre sloping lot in the British Properties in West Vancouver, Arthur arranged for a meeting with the whole family to get everyone's ideas about what the new house should be like. Hugo's wife, Brigitte, did not like concrete, and so the house was not going to resemble the one built for Helmut and Hildegard. And the three teenaged children wanted their rooms not on the highest but on the lowest level of the house—for greater privacy. Hugo himself was open to whatever Arthur suggested.[1]

That first meeting had been in 1977. The following year, Arthur had offered his clients plans for a house of steel and glass, the metal parts of which could be milled at the Ebco plant in Richmond. But a lengthy delay followed, caused by the financial setback Ebco experienced in the recession of the early 1980s, and construction of the house had not begun until August 1985. Arthur's special interest had been to create shapes that would reveal the malleable nature of metal and, at the same time, meet the challenge of a rugged, irregularly shaped site. The steel-and-glass house stepped down the hillside in three large arcs, with the curvilinear steel beams giving a cascading effect. This sensuous quality was reinforced inside by the contrast of high-tech stainless steel columns with rough-sawn hemlock board ceilings and warm, tactile sandstone floors.

The exterior was also a drama of contrasts. The house was reached from the street by a path that meandered through a remnant of forest underplanted with indigenous rhododendrons, salal, and sword ferns and brought the visitor to an entrance framed by stainless steel panels treated with dichromatic acid, producing a rainbow of coppery hues. Some of the contrasts suggested the originary influence of Frank Lloyd Wright. The house was set on concrete terraces defined by fieldstones recovered from the site, which were set into the outer surface of the forms before the concrete was poured. The resulting wall recalled the walls at Wright's Taliesin West, where irregular stone, like indigenous plant species, was part of a work of high artifice. A natural creek ran through the lot and widened into a water garden that captured an inverted, mirror-clear reflection of the house. The children's lower-level sleeping quarters were cantilevered over the stream in Wrightian fashion. The interior brought the natural and artificial worlds together: each level ended in a half-vault of curving glass blocks, creating a greenhouse or conservatory-like space which on the middle, living-room level was occupied by two podocarpus trees, Arthur's favourite form of vegetation. Hemlocks nestled up to the northeast window of the living room, and the southwest window opened to Vancouver's fabled views of city and ocean.

The family had taken up residence in December 1987. But the house was far from finished, since Arthur had persuaded his clients that its furnishings and accessories should also be one of a kind. Francisco, who from the outset had taken charge of the interior design, had followed Arthur back to Vancouver, and now he continued meticulously with his work at the Eppich residence. The result was a *Gesamtkunstwerk*—a house that was a complete work of art in every aspect. All the furnishings had been designed for the house—as were such smaller items as candlestick holders and metal placemats—and they referenced each other in a dialogue of curving forms and straight lines. The house became a gallery for the sculpture and paintings of Hugo's brother Egon, who had died in a car accident in the early 1980s. The Hugo Eppich house was featured in the twentieth-anniversary issue of *Western Living* and in the expensively produced Japanese publication *Global Architecture*, with photographs Arthur thought especially fine.[2] An *Architectural Digest* crew spent five days photographing the house and furnishings, but Arthur's American reputation having collapsed, they eventually abandoned the idea of a magazine feature.

WHEN ARTHUR CLOSED his Vancouver office, his long-time employee Nick Milkovich decided to set up a business on his own rather than join Aitken Wreglesworth, an organization already numbering more than one hundred employees. Subsequently, Nick created a congenial place for Arthur in a new practice called Nick Milkovich Architects, which provided Arthur with fairly steady work for the rest of his life. The work promoted Arthur's name, but Nick's office took full business and ultimate professional responsibility. The first of the projects from Milkovich's office to catch the public eye was the Portland Hotel, a housing facility for hard-to-house residents of Vancouver's drug-ridden Downtown Eastside. Some saw the Portland Hotel as a metaphor for Arthur's own career; like the Portland residents, he had been publicly humiliated and was virtually homeless. It seemed amazing, as one journalist put it, "that the man who befriended Pierre Trudeau and Shirley MacLaine, who dined with royalty and designed some of the most celebrated buildings in North America . . . would be crafting a home for paupers with mental illness and diseases such as tuberculosis, AIDS, and hepatitis," designing what another reporter called "an elegant flophouse."[3] But Arthur did not see this as strange: "I'm always curious about how other people lead their lives," he told a journalist from *Maclean's* when the building eventually opened in 2000. Arthur had been given the history of each prospective resident, and he observed with keen interest that "some of them came from quite wealthy families." But he did not feel personally threatened by their adverse fortunes. Securely grounded in Christian Science and a Buddhist sensibility, he would say to reporters: "I've always been lucky. I'm never concerned about personal tragedy because something positive always seems to happen."[4]

What interested Arthur in the Portland Hotel was the challenge of designing individual and communal spaces for a group of people regarded as socially dysfunctional. There were three main challenges that he and Nick Milkovich worked out together. A tight budget meant paring each room down to what was absolutely essential, such as one sink per unit (that being in its kitchen instead of the bathroom) and devising a furniture module that combined a rollaway Murphy bed (also serving as sofa) with a wall unit. There was the challenge of making everything as resistant to abuse as possible—the toilet cisterns were built into the wall, for example, so as not to be damaged. But most important in Arthur's view—extending his concept of the people-friendly courthouse—was to make the residence an open and cheerful place that would encourage communal activities. "For all [the residents'] problems and eccentricities," Arthur noted, "they are a community and you want them to interact as much as possible. This is not a jail." To that end, each unit was designed with a Dutch door, allowing tenants to keep the top half open to see who was in the hall. Corridors were made wider than normal, because that is where people liked to stop and visit. Communal laundry and kitchen facilities were clustered together on each floor as social spaces, and there was a projects room and a roof garden, designed by Cornelia Oberlander, with blueberry bushes and dwarf apple trees, to encourage people with poor social skills to talk to each other.

When the building was finished, Arthur said—perhaps only half joking, given his affinity for small, spare personal spaces—"I wouldn't mind living here if I could get all my books in . . . I'm really fascinated to know whether it works—if the things we did in design improve their life."[5] With reference to the hotel's clean modernity, he pointed out, "These are people used to dark corners to hide in and I am putting them in a highly illuminated place."[6] Journalist Alexandra Gill described a return visit Arthur made a year later when the residence was fully functioning. Of Arthur, she wrote: "There is absolutely no trace of the imperious arrogance often attributed to this graceful, silver-haired man in the neat navy suit as he tours the concrete courtyard and the sunny yellow 'ballroom' smelling of stale pizza and apple juice left over from today's TB-testing clinic." Arthur floated serenely above the messy scene around him, she said—the "revolting mash of milk-bloated corn flakes splattered over the walls and floor . . . the sight of a vacant-eyed man with a chartreuse crust rotting in his beard, who staggers by and bangs face-first into a shatterproof glass door." Standing with a group of residents around the waterfall in the front lobby, Arthur said in all sincerity, "You should really get some English ivy in here."[7]

For clients at quite a different place on the social ladder, Arthur designed the Waterfall Building in 1996, a mixed commercial and residential complex of five concrete-and-glass buildings encircling a central public courtyard. He seemed here to have been under the spell of Le Corbusier's play between coarse and refined, the dull and the shining, manifest in the Waterfall Building's contrast between concrete and glass walls, the brittle sheen of external metal staircases, and the soft texture of roof gardens. The staircases evoked a raw, industrial aesthetic that referenced the history of the area on reclaimed industrial land. The central public space in the courtyard was organized around a pyramid-shaped glass gallery that has since been used for exhibitions and social occasions both public and private. The "waterfall," a thin curtain of water that plunged down by the entrance, creating something like a portcullis, helped to muffle the sounds from the street, distancing the city. When the building was finished in 2001, it was praised as an independent urban village with a unique blend of stores, art gallery, work spaces, and living spaces. The rhythmic minimalist blend of steel, glass, and concrete was said to create "urban poetry."

But if one building were to be chosen as being the most important from Arthur's later years, it would surely be the Museum of Glass in Tacoma, Washington. Located in a part of the city that had become a crime-ridden industrial wasteland, the project was conceived, in part, to speak to the renovation and sustainable development possible for the city's waterfront district. Working in collaboration with Nick Milkovich, and with Wyn Bielaska as project architect, Arthur designed a museum of workshops, studios, and galleries situated beneath an expansive rooftop plaza that orchestrated the harbour, freeway, and warehouses into a coherent concrete landscape.[8] With wide staircases evoking again an ancient acropolis and terraces of intersecting planes reminiscent of Robson Square, the visitor approached the entrance to the museum on something like the mountainside path that Arthur conceived of for Simon Fraser University.[9] The focal point of the plaza was a monumental ninety-foot leaning cone covered in diamond-shaped stainless steel plates, which housed a "hot shop" amphitheatre where visitors could watch glass-making in progress. The shape of the cone made historical reference to the sawmill wood burners of the sawmills that once dotted the Pacific Northwest;[10] at the same time, it suggested the volcanic shape of Mount Rainier clearly visible in the distance. Three rimless reflecting pools on different levels created the illusion of water disappearing over the edge into the water of the harbour beyond.

While critical write-ups about the new museum when it opened in 2002 found the Grand Hall typical of the cold, impersonal space "where museums hold events to thank sponsors and donors," they were enthusiastic about the cone's steel framework interior: "There is an elegance and rhythm to the structural steel as it moves up the cone's interior to an apex of perforated metal" that represented the perfect melding of form and function.[11] The design was also praised for its role in the revitalizing of Tacoma—"as a true urban fragment rather than a simple architectural object."[12] In the cone, there was an interesting architectural echo of Maekawa's Automobile pavilion for the 1970 Osaka Exposition, where the pavilion's exhibition halls were made of steel cables and rings, and the whole pavilion, clad in silver-painted canvas, took the form of two truncated cones.[13] But if this was a borrowing, it did not detract from what Arthur always did best, which was to merge his building with its setting in such a way that the viewer sees that setting with new eyes.

BY THE TIME the Museum of Glass opened to the public in 2002, Arthur's life had again drastically altered. Francisco had followed him to Vancouver in the fall of 1991 and found a house to rent nearby—"the perfect set-up," Arthur noted.[14] Although his circumstances were much reduced, Francisco managed to find occasional interior decorating jobs in Vancouver, and he and Arthur would travel together when Arthur's budget allowed. But on a skiing trip to Whistler in late fall of 1996, Francisco came down with "chills" and a heavy cold that quickly turned into pneumonia. Back in the city, he was hospitalized, and after a series of blood tests he was informed that he had AIDS. Despondent for some time and convinced that local doctors knew little about the disease, he turned to international experts for advice and therapies. Many of the leading experimental drugs were then still unavailable in Canada, and in his notes for an autobiography Arthur wrote, "With my income so reduced, we have a difficult time." For food and rent, Francisco was supporting himself on disability insurance; Arthur was paying for most of the costly medications. For nearly two years, Francisco seemed to be slowly regaining his health, the chief marker of the disease being an asthma-like breathing condition that he managed with a portable inhalator. But in September 1999, his breathing grew more laboured and, as Arthur saw it, "local MDs were helpless." They flew to Los Angeles to see Dr. Michael Gottlieb, who had attended Jan and who seemed now to make Francisco feel better with his sympathetic attention. This apparent physical reversal and Francisco's renewed optimism made Arthur think about his earlier theory that his companion might be bipolar, for Francisco had always been given to radical mood swings. Arthur had once made an appointment for him to discuss his periods of depression with a psychiatrist, but Francisco had been consistently buoyant and articulate, and after a couple of sessions, the consultant saw no reason to see him again.

With improved health, Francisco flew to Miami for a month in the sun, and on returning to Vancouver, he made elaborate plans for further travels. But every time his departure day arrived he was unable to get on the plane. As the winter of 1999–2000 progressed, his condition worsened. Arthur told the rest of the story in autobiographical notes:

> April 3, 2000: Five days before [Francisco's] 59th birthday, I return from judging competitions in Washington, D.C., and bring him mail from my office—alarming notices and threats from the insurance company and bank overdraws. He leaves my dinner table in rage and deep depression. I don't realize the depths of his frustration and despair. He rushes out. I follow an hour and a half later, worried, and take $800.00 in U.S. traveller's cheques to offset his draft. When I go in, he is upstairs at his computer typing away—but won't talk. I assume he is resolving the insurance issue—I forget to give him the cheques. I leave assuring him that everything will be alright, as always. I phone the next morning—no answer—assume he has gone for checkups—enter the house to find him hanging from a beam in his bedroom. I am utterly horrified and helpless.

Arthur concluded the sequence of notes about Francisco's death by saying that the events of that evening had preyed on his conscience ever since, and that he had not realized how much he depended on Francisco as a companion, a design critic, and an "organizer of all the loose ends of my life and travels—all the things I prefer to overlook. For me, his death [is] a great, great loss."

GRIEF ASSUMES MANY forms. Self-reproach is one, and Arthur would rehearse in his mind—and in conversation with his closest friends—the events of that fatal evening again and again, lamenting his insensitivity to Francisco's despair, his failure to leave him the traveller's cheques. He sought consolation (his word was "recuperation") in his work, saying nothing to colleagues about his personal tragedy. But the chief expression of his grief, one very uncharacteristic of him, was the anger he directed towards the public when he saw any of his works threatened or his ideas challenged.

"Arthur's War," an article by Frances Bula in the *Vancouver Sun* later that year, gave an account of Arthur's denunciation of the urban expansion taking place on Burnaby Mountain. It threatened, in his view, to destroy the integrity of everything he had achieved with Simon Fraser University.[15] From the university's inception, he himself had envisioned a village developing around it to offset its extreme isolation and make it "more balanced as a community." In the early 1980s, he had tried to press forward with a plan that would put his firm in charge of creating approximately five thousand units built over time by developers on a leasehold or share basis with the university. The plan was to provide not only student housing but residences for the public at large, with retail, recreation, and cultural facilities. An inclined rail system up the side of the mountain would tie in with the city's existing bus service. The university had met with Roméo LeBlanc, the federal minister of housing, who reportedly liked the concept but felt there were too many demands in the rest of the country to give SFU priority. In 1983, Arthur wrote directly to the prime minister to see if he could not "cut through the red tape."[16] Trudeau replied that he saw the proposal as "typically innovative" and that he would pursue the matter with LeBlanc, but to Arthur's disappointment, it went no further.[17]

By 2000, SFU, reportedly for endowment purposes, had embarked once again on "an ambitious project to graft a complete mountain village on to the campus." Arthur had been hired as an advisor, but he was eliminated as the architect in charge of the village's design guidelines. Crushed and humiliated, he lashed out. In letters to Michael Geller, CEO of the Burnaby Mountain Community Corporation, and in statements to the press, he denounced the burial of SFU's visionary principles under a "developer's mercantile blanket." The new design, with a strip mall of shops and restaurants leading to a series of high-rise towers and suburban streets to the east, would leave the university's mall no longer central to the campus. Arthur envisioned growth in terms of low-rise terraced buildings hugging the mountain slopes, instead of "lonely, awkward high-rises," but Geller argued that modern-looking, flat-roof buildings were not what people wanted—"it's just not the most marketable stuff around." In angry notes he made for a discussion with SFU president Jack Blaney, Arthur argued that an architecturally enlightened campus would be turned into "a banal, featureless, middle-class neighbourhood ... the unique smothered in the commonplace."[18] SFU should resist the client only interested in a commanding view. Publicly, Arthur denounced Geller as a "blowhard," adding that Geller had been hired by another "blowhard," Jack Blaney.

Arthur had sought and lost commissions many times before, but being turned down for the expansion of SFU into the twenty-first century was a truly painful blow. For a time, people found him very difficult to deal with. When the board of the Vancouver Art Gallery approached him about opening up the front entrance to the gallery, which would have redirected people away from Robson Square, Arthur brusquely told them to find another architect. He walked away from a residential project at the Bayshore, where Geller was also in charge, because he could not tolerate, he said, "interference with his work." He felt besieged on every front. Initially, he supported the idea of UBC having a presence at Robson Square, but when it transpired that one of the public theatres for cultural events would be converted to classrooms for business courses, he was outraged. He wrote to UBC president Martha Piper on August 8, 2001, that "in its brutal conversion of Robson Square," UBC was undermining the square as an effective forum for civic dialogue. In a biting summary, he stated: "It exhibits the callow indifference to the environment that seems typical of many of UBC's initiatives."[19] Expansions to the University of Lethbridge drew similar ire. The campus was being cluttered with buildings that bore no relation to his master plan, and only from a distance—low in the coulee—was the original idea for the university still visible. He vowed he would never visit Lethbridge again. In a more detached mood, he would note how strange it was that there were so many enmities at universities. Professors and administrators vied for power, but set beside the governance of nations, it was of so little importance.

Also painful were renovations to Roy Thomson Hall, which destroyed what Arthur considered Francisco's best work. In a letter to Ken Thomson on November 20, 2001, he wrote that "the changes brashly destroy the aesthetic quality of the interiors altogether" and said how appalled he was "that the visual trash ... of our cities has so desensitized the public's aesthetic responses that there is little outside objection to the trashing of Roy Thomson Hall."[20] Major acoustical adjustments were being made to the concert hall but what especially upset Arthur was the proposal to change the interior from concrete to wood. He published a letter in the *Globe and Mail* that spoke to both aspects of the proposed renovations. "Originally," he wrote, "the primary goal was to avoid the kitsch of decorative plasterwork often used to provide sound reflection, and instead achieve this through the structure itself. Above all the hall was to be distinguished by its restraint, quiet harmony, and the honesty of its structure and acoustic devices." This serene interior, he continued, was "achieved by designer Francisco Kripacz, who harmonized the concrete in a sophisticated grey and silver [fabric] palette." He reminded readers that the beauty of Roy Thomson Hall had been praised by celebrated musicians like Leonard Bernstein and Cecilia Bartoli, but now he feared it would look like a Chinese restaurant.[21]

IT WOULD BE misleading to suggest that Arthur became com-
bative for the first time in his life in his late seventies. In fact, he
had been embattled in a no less determined way for years over the
issue of postmodern fashions in architecture. In 1980, his design
for the Portland Municipal Services Building was turned down in
favour of a building with wildly varied façades and decorative flour-
ishes. Princeton professor Michael Graves's winning submission—a
chunky fifteen-storey building painted in strong colours, with tiny
windows and a garland of blue concrete ribbons—could not have
stood in greater contrast to the large buildings of glass and steel
filling the downtown streets of North America's major cities. The
selection committee found the design by Graves innovative and
exciting. Arthur described himself as shocked that this "expensive
prank" could be taken seriously.[22] But Philip Johnson was one of the
Portland committee members impressed by Graves's invention, and
within a couple of years, Johnson's like-spirited design for the AT&T
Building in New York was drawing even greater attention and praise.
When the building was completed in 1984, instead of observing the
abstract lineaments of the International Style he had once champi-
oned, Johnson crowned it with a play on a Georgian broken pedi-
ment, so that it looked like a piece of furniture—a grandfather clock
or a colonial bonnet-top highboy. Everyone was now talking about
postmodernism.

As early as 1966, critic Robert Venturi had been arguing that
modernist architects had not sufficiently recognized complexity: "In
their attempt to break with tradition and start all over again, they
idealized the primitive and elementary at the expense of the diverse
and sophisticated."[23] To Arthur, this celebration of diversity was just
historical eclecticism and tedious surface decoration—innovation
for innovation's sake, without meaning. In a letter to Ada Louise
Huxtable, the New York doyenne of architectural critics, he conceded that postmodernism had perhaps one salutary function—its
eclecticism revealed a cultural insecurity and the need to reconsider
the two opposing streams in North American design. The best of
those went back to the root American tradition of utilitarian crafts,
the workman's respect for his materials, and the beauty that came

from how simply, gracefully, even ingeniously an object showed its use.[24] He liked to give as an example the down-to-earth solutions found by the Shakers in their rendering of furniture and houses. The opposing stream turned away from native ingenuity in favour of what he termed nostalgic eclecticism—houses as French châteaux, skyscrapers as Gothic cathedrals.[25] This, he argued, was the effect of Walt Disney, "the great Satan of our period," who had turned everything into entertainment. This had changed the purpose of design; new forms were simply façades—"a costume ball of affectations."[26]

Arthur was characterized publicly as an architect out of touch with new ways of thinking. In a 1994 book about Vancouver as a postmodern city, Paul Delany described the west mall extension to SFU as "defiantly anachronistic, a piece of sixties brutalism replicated in defiance of the contemporary spirit."[27] Arthur saw this new spirit as dominated by academic debate, wherein critics, writing in journals such as Peter Eisenman's *Oppositions*, strove to outdo one another in the abstruseness of their prose and where intellectual contention was replacing design as the currency of the profession. Arthur argued that institutional aesthetics (theories and works of art produced by universities and art institutes) stood in contrast to great canonical works like the Athenian Acropolis, Dante's *Divine Comedy*, or Beethoven's Ninth Symphony, which gained their long-standing worldwide fame from audiences who knew little or nothing of historical and academic analysis. He denounced postmodernism as "a nostalgic preoccupation with maquillage." In a lecture he gave at Robson Square, he asserted that with postmodernism, "out went functionalism and amenity... in came symbol and style." It reminded him of Samuel Johnson's observation about Blenheim Palace: "'Tis all very fine, but where do you sleep and where do you dine?"[28] Arthur may have been temporarily seduced to accommodate the new fashion when he designed the Canadian chancery in Washington, with its fake pillars and busy roof structure, or in a design for the Crowne Plaza building in Los Angeles, with its stepped balconies on the top four storeys, the uppermost capped by a pitch-roofed skylight. Otherwise, he remained firm in denouncing

what he termed "the terrible lapse of architecture into postmodernism."[29] He remained firm, too, in his fight to save his buildings as he
had designed them.

The final volley fired in "Arthur's war" came in the spring of
2003 when he was interviewed at McGill University. Asked what
advice he would give budding architects, he said: "Go into another
profession. Architecture is full of heartbreak. Buildings don't usually
last all that long. Most of them come down. Houses are sold and
changed by their new owners. When you really put your heart into
something, it can be devastating when it all comes apart."[30]

Arthur's consolation was what he called "great art." Friends
invariably found him at home with music playing in the background,
and when he was asked to select music and provide commentary for
a CBC program titled *Music in My Life*, he sent the producer a list
of nineteen pieces that were a history of his emotional and imaginative life.[31] A morning raga marked his wartime experience in India;
a *saeta* with the call of the muezzin evoked memories of Spain in
1951, a Legong the enchantment of Bali in 1961. An Armenian song
recalled his transit through the Soviet Union to China in 1973; a
sirtaki dance composition by Mikis Theodorakis roused his love
for Greece. Some pieces were a record of his public experience of
music: Mozart at a private concert with Leonard Bernstein at the
Buckerfields in 1941, Bach's *Goldberg Variations* played by Rosalyn
Tureck at the Buckleys', Philip Glass performing at Virginia and
Bagley Wright's home. *Der Rosenkavalier* connected to his friendship with George Swinton. A Scarlatti sonata he remembered in
connection with Gordon Webber; Boccherini's *Fandango Quintet*
with "Happy," his paramour in Spain. Koto music recalled sharing a
ryokan with Pierre Trudeau in Kyoto in 1976. For the meaning and
associations of his final selection, Mahler's *Songs of a Wayfarer*, he
simply noted "1946 to the present."

Painting was also a great bulwark in his declining years. The
other source of consolation, experienced on a daily basis, was the
ever-changing, ever-fascinating life of his garden. Art and nature
were one and the same, he held. Gazing at his garden, he said to

Edith Iglauer: "I love that river grass out there. Look at the beautiful pattern. And within the pattern are all the variations of Beethoven compressed into a single image."[32]

WHILE ARTHUR'S FAME had been eclipsed in North America, he continued to pursue work abroad, especially in the Far East. As far back as the late 1970s, he and Bing Thom had toured China with government officials to survey sites where a chain of small inns might be built. Each would preserve something of the local architectural vernacular—the cave dwellings of the north, the pit houses of the central plains, the black-tiled farmhouse roofs of Suzhou. In 1988, while still running his own business, he had won a competition to design a multi-purpose art centre for Shanghai that was to include an opera house, symphony hall, playhouse, exhibition centre, performers' lodgings, and 750-room hotel—all surrounded by a landscaped park. But the upheavals at both Tiananmen Square and his Los Angeles office aborted these undertakings, and the Oriental Art Center in Shanghai was later designed by, and opened to much praise for, French architect Paul Andreu. It was built in the form of a butterfly orchid.

By 2000, Arthur was receiving invitations through a Chinese developer, Jiang Qi, a young architect he had met at Aitken Wreglesworth Associates, to contribute to the great burgeoning of China's metropolises—Beijing, Nanjing, Shanghai—and to participate as a consultant in the planning of a series of new towns. Japan was rivalled now in Arthur's affections by China, with its rich and, in Arthur's view, relatively unspoiled heritage. It was still his mission, he felt, "to help find ways to extend its great architectural traditions into the new era, rather than see them replaced by concrete boxes or some imported language."[33] He was also seduced by the fawning admiration of Chinese contacts, who wrote to him: "My master—it is a real honour."[34] Arthur's designs were incorporated into at least four buildings—a twin tower residential project in Beijing, a yacht club in Kunshan, the Dalian Cultural Centre, and a government building in Weihai—but Nick Milkovich, jointly involved in these projects, viewed the results as disappointing. There had been almost no coordination with the builders, and Arthur and his associates accordingly had little control over the execution of their designs.[35]

More gratifying was the completion of another project of substance in the Middle East. In 1989, Arthur, in joint venture with a Kuwaiti firm of architects, had been selected to design a major office complex, but the work was halted by the Persian Gulf War in 1990. The project was being revived in late 1991. Aitken Wreglesworth did not want to risk doing business in the Middle East, so Alan Bell, Wilbert Bruegger, and Nick Milkovich created a low-overhead virtual firm, Atelier, to take the Kuwait Oil Sector Complex forward. Located on reclaimed industrial waterfront land just outside the city centre, the complex consisted of two towers—one twenty-two storeys, the other eighteen—each with a lens-shaped building in front and a triangular one at back, with a single shared service core. It is one of Arthur's more imposing designs, because of its dramatic siting, interesting geometry, and spectacular atrium at ground level—a main entrance lobby enclosed by frameless glass walls and a free-spanning/truss skylight. The main entrance looks out to an infinity pool that, in turn, overlooks Kuwait Bay. Externally, the sculptural composition features a multi-storey car park covered by tensile fabric sails, ground-level parking, and extensive landscaping with water features, plus a shorefront promenade with two jetties. The complex as finally completed in 2005 respected most of Arthur's original intentions. But especially important was to have a building of substance realized in the Middle East.[36] Atelier (in partnership with Aitken Wreglesworth) had also designed an entrance to Malaysia via Singapore, a waterfront development—like Abu Nuwas in Baghdad—with specifically tropical architecture for ventilation. But as so often with overseas clients, the developer got his zoning permit on the basis of sophisticated plans and then dropped the architects.

ARTHUR STILL LOVED to entertain and travel. In notes left in his office, there was an elaborate set of plans for a small garden dinner party he held in Phyllis Lambert's honour in the summer of

2003. Guests included the Oberlanders and Vancouver architect Richard Henriquez and his wife, Carol, plus six others to make a table of eleven. Lois Milsom was asked to bring chairs, and Arthur's office secretary, Merle Ginsburg, to locate hurricane lamps. Lois and Merle were to be guests at the table, but all week there was a schedule of duties to keep them busy, overseeing the cleaning, weeding, and cooking. Francisco's influence was present everywhere: in the setting of the table with white dishes on a black cloth, a centrepiece of white lilies, place cards, and candles; in the "pink and white" menu of clear rose petal soup, salmon with cucumber and dill sauce, risotto (using beet juice), watercress salad, and raspberry summer pudding. The visual effects were exquisite, and afterwards one of the guests wrote: "The garden was beautiful, and the transition from dusk to dark accompanied by the shakuhachi, the introduction of candles on the pond, and the lights in the foliage was all wonderfully ethereal."

In the fall of that year, Arthur was part of Governor General Adrienne Clarkson's much critiqued company of fifty distinguished Canadians making a circumpolar tour. He had accepted the invitation because he had never seen St. Petersburg, or Finland or Iceland, and he was in a nostalgic, searching mood over the recent death of George Swinton, who had so vigorously embraced northern cultures. But Arthur found himself overwhelmed trying to meet the demands of the trip schedule on his own. In Reykjavik, he did not turn up on time for the island tour because he was ironing his shirt before setting out for the day.

Francisco's death had left Arthur vulnerable on all fronts. But early in the first decade of the new century, someone entered his life who would become his new organizer of loose ends and also a champion and defender of his works. Cheryl Cooper, divorced from a professor of English at UBC, first worked as a director of the Arthur Erickson Home and Garden Foundation. "Seated at his feet," she listened with riveted attention to Arthur describing his theories and practice of architecture.[37] Soon, she was accompanying him to events in the city, dining with him at restaurants, and organizing his timetable for the week. After a disagreement with other members of the foundation, she made the bold move of establishing the Arthur Erickson Conservancy, a separate body, eventually persuading foundation members such as Hugo Eppich, James Cheng, and Nick Milkovich to join her. Arthur began referring all requests outside the office to her attention, and for a time, Cheryl Cooper's attentions provided Arthur with the kind of biased support he seemed to need to function successfully. She recognized Arthur's craving to be a celebrity again, and she spared no effort to make that happen, setting up interviews with journalists and organizing public events to celebrate Arthur and his work. He emerged from these promotions as a wise, elder statesman, still dapper and sophisticated but easily approachable.

With Cheryl's encouragement, Arthur agreed to appear in Toronto on a panel with Moshe Safdie and Frank Gehry in the lecture series at the Design Exchange. The three architects, linked by Canadian residency in their youth, were asked to converse casually on the subject of contemporary architecture. Their exchanges were cordial and informative, but it was what Arthur didn't say that evening that remains most interesting. He had admired Safdie's Habitat building at Expo 67, and he liked Gehry for his low-key manner, but he felt strongly that both architects had taken the wrong path in their work. Probably thinking about Gehry's Guggenheim Museum at Bilbao, hailed as the most exciting building of the era, he told an interviewer at McGill, "Architecture is too often viewed as packaging. Most of our cultural buildings today are built to be little more than wrapping paper. It's a crass way to sell a product."[38] In another interview, he said that architecture's current darling might have been a decent sculptor but asks of his building at Bilbao: "What is he making? There are two structures, one internal and one external, and they don't talk to each other."[39] Arthur regarded Safdie's National Gallery in the same light. He liked the proportions of the individual galleries and the design of the courtyards but thought the larger structure too massive—it was like entering a Gothic cathedral.[40] By this time, he was painfully aware that his own work had been eclipsed in the public eye, not only by these former Canadian residents but by architects like Norman Foster and I.M. Pei, with whom he had enjoyed friendly relations for several years. He especially envied Pei's opportunity to design the Museum of Islamic Art for Doha, the capital of Qatar.

Arthur's friends and family became fully aware of Cheryl Cooper's operative presence in his life at the time of his eightieth birthday celebrations, held at the Museum of Anthropology in June 2004. Many people took part in making this event happen, but it was Cheryl who persuaded the real estate company Concord Pacific to sponsor the evening, thereby convincing UBC to allow the pond in front of the museum to be filled temporarily. The street banners with Simon Scott's images of Arthur's Vancouver buildings, the decorating of the museum and grounds with candles, the presence of people from all walks of life, and the many fine speeches of praise were all heartwarming to Arthur, but nothing thrilled him more than to see water in front of the museum.

The permanent filling of the pond was a project that Cheryl would pursue on Arthur's behalf—in this case with the matching determination and enthusiastic assistance of Cornelia Oberlander. More urgent in 2005 was the future of the Evergreen Building downtown, which the owner, John Laxton, had said he would demolish because the city had refused him permission to add four storeys. The building sat on expensive land, and the Evergreen was not built to the maximum size allowable on the site; moreover, it was said to leak and did not meet earthquake code. A new full-size building would significantly enhance the value of the property. With connections to members of the Vancouver Heritage Commission, Cheryl set out to save the building, a crusade closely documented in the press. Laxton tried to dissuade her, calling it "a futile gesture," and was quoted on April 1, 2005, in the *Province* as claiming already to have put his heart and his wallet into saving the building, which was not economically feasible or technically possible. Arthur said in response that it was "greed, purely and simply."[41] Laxton wrote to Arthur that same day, reminding him that they had long been friends, that he had commissioned Arthur to build him a home before he had become famous, had recommended him to other clients, and was instrumental in getting him the courthouse commission. He asked for a retraction and an apology, which Arthur apparently provided, since their correspondence concludes with plans for a lunch with champagne. During the next several months, Cheryl mustered significant support, and at a public hearing, she convinced city council to approve a heritage revitalization agreement for the Evergreen Building and to add it to the Vancouver Heritage Register.[42] It was an impressive victory.

In 2005, Cheryl was occupied with two other projects. She was preparing a document she titled the "Erickson Garden Conservation Plan," which provided a detailed, professional description of Arthur's garden in all its aspects—history, design, and plant materials—and indicated how it could be maintained in optimum condition in the years to come. Visitors were being given guided tours by now, and the garden was featured in a richly illustrated book about artists' gardens in the Pacific Northwest.[43] Cheryl was also assisting Arthur to select materials for a 2006 retrospective of his work at the Vancouver Art Gallery—an activity from which Arthur's family and friends felt excluded.

For Christmas holidays that year, Arthur went to Cyprus with Greek friends, where it happened that former Liberal prime minister Jean Chrétien and his wife, Aline, were staying at the same hotel. It gave Arthur the unexpected pleasure of talking about art with two serious collectors and of reminiscing about their mutual friend, Pierre Trudeau, who had died the same year as Francisco. But when he returned, he seemed exhausted by the experience of travelling such a distance. Arthur's memory had never been very precise, but he now frequently seemed unable to remember fundamental things. Cheryl arranged for a personal trainer to give him exercise, and she helped him keep track of his commitments, but his friends and colleagues noticed the change with some alarm. At a meeting to discuss proposed changes to Robson Square, Cornelia Oberlander was dismayed to see Arthur had brought the wrong file and didn't

seem to be following the discussion. That year, he had two accidents on the road and was forced to surrender his driver's licence. He
arranged for Seung Ho Hong, a North Korean immigrant known as
Ray, to drive him to the office every day, a task that was soon supplemented with heavy housekeeping and gardening chores. By the end
of the year, Ray was living at Arthur's house, taking charge of meals
and reorganizing furniture; the arrangement suited both Cheryl and
Arthur's family.

DESPITE THE CHANGES that curtailed Arthur's freedom, 2006
brought a number of rewards. Chief among these was the career
retrospective *Arthur Erickson: Critical Works*, which opened at the
Vancouver Art Gallery in May, accompanied by a coffee-table book
of the same name. It occasioned a flurry of public events and interviews. Arthur appeared at the opening in a public conversation with
curator Nicholas Olsberg, and, as always, he was impeccably dressed,
this time in a tailored suit from Leone. The focus of the show was
on concrete as Arthur's muse—its permanence, its strength, and its
response to light—but another theme kept emerging in interviews:
the neglect of the prophet architect in his place and time. Olsberg
said to a reporter for the *Vancouver Sun* that the city had not lived
up to what Erickson expected when he created his buildings. SFU
was designed with an idealistic vision of intimacy between faculty
and students and a utopian absence of hierarchies, but the university,
with three campuses, had ended up being expansionist and impe-
rialist. Similarly, Erickson had hoped Robson Square would be an
oasis in the middle of a bustling city, but the area underneath where
artists and poets should have gathered, creating an intellectual centre, had become instead an empty space.[44] To this same reporter,
Arthur said Vancouver had not yet reached the density to become
a "world class city," and in a CBC radio interview a few weeks later
he lamented that Vancouver had had no buildings to influence him
when he was young. His own work had drawn from the larger world
in the mould and class of Frank Lloyd Wright and Le Corbusier, but
it had had no influence on Vancouver whatsoever. He saw nothing
but frivolity in the buildings that had gone up; local people thought

"small town," he said. Not until the city reached the size he envisioned would his influence be felt.[45] Typically, the interview blended Arthur's gracious speaking manner with a self-confidence often viewed as arrogance.

In the most interesting review of the retrospective, Clint Burnham for the *Vancouver Sun* saw the controversy around Erickson as stemming from Arthur's imperious manner in combination with his democratic ideals. Burnham saw such contradiction in the buildings themselves: "They are both open and closed, heavy and light, totalitarian and democratic, abandoned and finished, regional and global, specific and universal." Burnham gave the Museum of Anthropology as an example: it houses First Nations artifacts and opens up to the landscape and Georgia Strait, which predates European colonization, but does this with Greek (Acropolis), Japanese (the torii of Shinto shrines), and Haida architectural elements. Robson Square is less successful, in his opinion. "Its transparency regarding justice, for instance, now seems voyeuristic in the age of *Court TV*... The area beneath Robson Street is desolate, in pointed contrast to the crowds of bike couriers, tourists, drug dealers, skateboarders and protesters who throng on the north and south sides of the art gallery itself." Concrete, Burnham wrote, is "ugly, utilitarian, everyday. It is everything but beautiful or elegant or graceful." Yet, in places, he conceded, Arthur Erickson had made concrete transcend its humble origins and purposes. "And this finally seems to be the proper way in which to view or inhabit or use Erickson's architecture, as structures that straddle the ugly and the sublime, the ponderous and the ethereal, the transitory and the monumental."[46]

An article that summer by Rhodri W. Liscombe in *Canadian Architect* examined the way Arthur's name was being exploited as both an aesthetic and an investment commodity.[47] From the late 1990s forward, most of Arthur's work had been for a high-end market—a luxurious home for a Vancouver client on the waterfront in Maui, a series of condominiums in the Choklit Park neighbourhood of Vancouver's Fairview Slopes, a high-rise condominium on False Creek that would be known as "The Erickson." Liscombe knew that much of the work was being done by Nick Milkovich and his staff; Arthur's reputation was now more important than his design contribution. But Arthur's name had become an emblem of quality, and this seductive form of marketing was typical of celebrity culture. A low-rise development on Evelyn Drive in West Vancouver, for example, in which Arthur played a minimal role in the actual design process, was advertised on its hoardings as "an architectural statement by Arthur Erickson." Houses that Arthur was not likely to have designed, or even approved, but that had originated with his office, appreciated in value.

In September 2006, Cheryl Cooper organized a major event for Arthur that was purely honorific—a gala dinner in the Great Hall of the law courts building, hosted by the United Nations Association in Canada and the Arthur Erickson Conservancy. It was lavishly sponsored by a range of businesses and public bodies, including Concord Pacific, Phyllis Lambert's Canadian Centre for Architecture, the schools of architecture at McGill and UBC, Bentall Capital, and the Canadian Mortgage and Housing Corporation, all of whose members were represented by dinner speakers introduced by popular radio and television personality Vicki Gabereau. Guests paid $250 a plate and were urged to wear medals and pins indicating their accomplishments; a *komuso* figure played a *shakuhachi* flute. Arthur was scheduled as the final speaker, and although he had been his dapper, relaxed self over dinner, on stage he could not put together a coherent run of words. The audience sat in uncomfortable silence, occasionally throwing him a line or a missing word. The rumour that Arthur was beginning to suffer from Alzheimer's disease now seemed confirmed.

In 2007, Cheryl accompanied Arthur on all his travels: to Ottawa for a commemorative plaque ceremony at the Bank of Canada, to Montreal to celebrate Phyllis Lambert's eightieth birthday. For a conference at Carleton University's School of Architecture, she arranged in advance that he would participate only in a one-on-one conversation with the evening's host, with images of his work running on a screen in the background. This format seemed to work best, because he had very little to say.

That spring, Canada Post featured Arthur and three other Canadian architects (Safdie, Moriyama, and Douglas Cardinal) in an issue of stamps marking the one-hundredth anniversary of the Royal Architectural Institute of Canada. Simon Scott's photo of the University of Lethbridge stretching in a straight line across the undulating coulee was the ideal representation of Arthur's work; it dramatized eloquently how building and site depend on each other for their perceived structure and meaning. Arthur refused to attend the unveiling of the stamp at Lethbridge, because the ambitious, petty administrators had failed to complete his vision.

But events in Arthur's life at this point were not all commemorative. On May 23, 2007, there was a ribbon cutting to celebrate the opening of a new building in Regina—the RCMP Heritage Centre, which had been conceived and designed at the beginning of the decade to tell the story not only of Canada's famous police force but also of First Nations, Saskatchewan, and other aspects of northwestern Canada. The building drew positive notices. D. Grant Black in the *Toronto Star* pointed out it was shaped like a prairie snowdrift, but the roof line was also reminiscent of the tents used by the Mounties. It represented "safe enclosure and inclusion—also the sacred space of the training centre." The result, in Black's view, was "stunning."[48]

In the fall of 2007, ground was broken on Georgia Street for the Ritz-Carlton Tower (also referred to as the Palm Court), a building of sixty storeys, combining hotel rooms and private residences, the latter fetching up to $13 million each. It was to be the second-highest building in Vancouver. Its unique design feature was its spiralling shape; the twist would make it dynamic in what was otherwise a forest of static high-rises. For residents, the rotation would guarantee that each unit had a slightly different view of the ocean and mountains. The twisting, Arthur acknowledged, was not unique (he was likely thinking of Santiago Calatrava's Turning Torso in Malmö, Sweden, named after the architect's sculpture representing a twisting human spine); what was unique was its setting in Vancouver.[49] Malcolm Parry in the *Vancouver Sun* reported that "condo sales mogul Bob Rennie, who 'brokered' the Erickson deal, joked that the latter 'earned every dollar of his outrageous fee.'"[50] Arthur was buoyed once again by the attention paid to his work. "Will this be your last project?" a reporter asked. "It will be my highest project. But not my last," he replied.[51] When asked about retirement, he invariably answered that an artist never retires.

That fall, Cheryl Cooper mounted two more receptions to celebrate Arthur and his work. One acknowledged RAIC centennial awards to Erickson and Massey (Arthur's former employee Kiyoshi Matsuzaki represented the RAIC at the event held at the Waterfall Building); the other featured a screening of Michèle Smolkin's 2003 French-language documentary, *Arthur Erickson: Concrete Poetry*. (Arthur had also been celebrated in CBC's *Life and Times* TV series in 2004.) Both events attracted capacity audiences with entrance fees of $75 per person, proceeds going to the Arthur Erickson Conservancy.

But the year ended bleakly with the demolition of the Graham house near Horseshoe Bay. It had been purchased by an offshore client in 1988 and had fallen into disrepair. The spectacular waterfront lot was now worth more than $3 million, and although the house was on the inventory of heritage homes in the area, it was not protected. Arthur expressed his disappointment in private: "You can't hang on to your work, though it is impossible to walk away from it entirely. What happened to the Graham house is a significant loss, but what has been done to the universities I designed is more upsetting to me—the integrity of the overall designs being compromised. It is like mud being thrown in your face and all you can do is walk away."[52]

By 2008, Arthur's house and garden were under siege while a two-storey house overlooking his property was being built next door. The east side, which straddled the property line, was stripped of most of its vegetation, and the south end was opened, exposing Arthur's garden to intruders—passersby taking a shortcut and finding themselves trapped—and the curious—admirers who had always wanted to see inside this famous but secret garden. The noise of demolition and so much open sky to the east disoriented Arthur. He had grown more fragile in every way, seldom going into the office.

By fall of 2008, there was no doubt that Arthur was in the advanced stages of Alzheimer's and had symptoms of Parkinson's disease as well. Although he retained his gracious manner in public, he could no longer engage in a conversation. When asked questions about his career, "it was as though he knew where he intended to go in answering them, but lost his way en route."[53] Cheryl Cooper took him to sit on the jury for the *Western Living* design awards and to ceremonies at the Ritz-Carlton presentation house, but Arthur could not speak at either event; he was confused and anxious to get back home.

In January 2009, Arthur went over one final precipice. It began with a prostate crisis: unable to urinate, he was rushed to St. Paul's Hospital, where various tests were done. But at the hospital he fell, twisted his back, and then was no longer able to use his legs. A suitable place was found for him at the Finnish Home in Vancouver, where a steady flow of family, friends, and admirers came to visit.

On May 20, 2009, after refusing food for several days, Arthur died in the afternoon, with Lois Milsom; his niece, Emily; and Emily's husband, David, at his side. He was eighty-four.

After Words

A CELEBRATION OF ARTHUR ERICKSON'S life and work took place at Simon Fraser University's Convocation Mall on the clear Sunday afternoon of June 14, 2009, which would have been his eighty-fifth birthday. Close to a thousand people attended the service in the setting of one of Erickson's greatest creations.

The Borealis String Quartet played Arvo Pärt's *Fratres* while Erickson's ashes were carried in and placed on the speakers' platform. Various participants addressed the gathering: Nancy Southam read "The Swan," Rilke's poem about dying; Arthur's niece, Emily Erickson McCullum, read from the *Bhagavad Gita*; his brother, Don, presented selections from Arthur's writings; others spoke of the architect as mentor and friend. Threaded throughout were the haunting solos of a Japanese flautist.

In a memorable eulogy, Abraham Rogatnick spoke of the pathways that shaped Arthur's great works of architecture. His estimate of his friend seemed exactly right:

> [Arthur] was the first person to greet me upon my arrival in Vancouver 54 years ago... Immediately I knew I was in the presence of someone rare, and over the years I marveled at the absence of self-importance he demonstrated, even as his creative vision brought triumph after triumph. To him it was the poetry, not the poet that

mattered. I also came to recognize the nobility, courage, and sto-icism with which he faced the trials, sorrows, and ironies of his pub-lic and private life.[1]

OTHER REMEMBRANCES OF Arthur would bear witness to the con-tradictions in his life. In describing his impact locally, Mary Roaf of the Vancouver Arts Council said, "One feels in Vancouver that we have always known Arthur Erickson. A unique and humble man, coming and going like a character in a fable, he has influenced our thinking and shaped our lives."[2] In a different spirit, novelist and visual artist Douglas Coupland, whom Arthur had befriended, wrote: "Arthur was always in the news... baking on a beach some-where, fleeing nightclubs, or maybe in San Francisco eating a for-eign cuisine... Arthur seemed to live on a heady salad of money, beauty, fame."[3] At a museum showing of his photographs of Arthur's buildings, Simon Scott spliced together the disparate threads in a tribute to his friend: "Arthur was a quiet, kind, simple-living man. He lived a Zen, almost monastic life. But on the other hand he was a superstar, a jetsetter, an international citizen and also a very power-ful man in his own way. He lived his public life among, and catering to, the Pharaohs of our present culture."[4]

Arthur left behind unresolved matters. One concerned his estate and his relationship with Cheryl Cooper. In 2006, persuaded by Cooper to sever involvement with the Arthur Erickson House and Garden Foundation, he had signed a consent form naming her Arthur Erickson Conservancy "the sole artist-authorized agency for the work of Arthur Erickson, in perpetuity." By January 2010, Cooper was being sued by Arthur's brother, executor of his will, for "allegedly exploiting her relationship with the architect for per-sonal gain at a time when his mental abilities had deteriorated."[5] The dominant purpose of Cooper's relationship with Arthur, read the lawsuit, "was to use his name, reputation, and body of work for her own gain." Cooper did not file a statement of defence. Her sup-porters felt the claim was a misinterpretation of her motives, that although Cooper enjoyed being in Arthur's reflected limelight, her conservation activities were to be lauded. But everyone recognized the uncontestable authority of Arthur's will, which left all decisions to his family.

Arthur's house and garden became another matter for speculation. Cooper had envisioned it as a museum that would house his furnishings and function as an archive for his personal papers. But except for the contents, it belonged to the foundation. Meanwhile, Arthur's nephew Geoffrey, with his young daughter, took up residence in the house. Pending a decision on the future of the property, Geoffrey spent a year organizing the significant contents of the house, but whether these items would stay on the property or be redistributed to public archives remained to be seen. The garden was unfortunately altered by a natural dieback of bamboo.

Everywhere, the temporal nature of architecture as an art form was keenly felt by Arthur's admirers. SFU's expansion eastward and the removal of benches and planters from the mall further abandoned the architects' vision for the campus; the Vancouver Art Gallery was anxious to vacate the Robson Square complex; owners of private residences, with the best of intentions, inevitably made renovations—a room divided, a window changed—causing Simon Scott to respond: "Would you move an eye to another part of the canvas in Picasso's *Demoiselles d'Avignon?*"

Arising from the need for shelter, architecture exists to enable other things to happen. When there is a perfect mastery of form and space, as at the Museum of Anthropology, it can transcend the functional and become art. But in that gap between function and pure form resides another dimension—what some critics have described as the ethical function of architecture.[6] Arthur believed that a great building is art and, like Beethoven's *Choral* Symphony or Picasso's *Guernica*, can awaken longings for a better world. His purpose in rethinking building genres was consistently informed by his youthful, utopian ideals—a law court to make justice more transparent, an office building to make working conditions more humane, universities to eliminate hierarchies in the quest for knowledge. These democratic goals, as he stated them, offer a measure by which to evaluate his achievements. What characterizes his best work is not the thrusting spires and skyscrapers or the convoluted "fireworks" of the world's most ambitious architects but the low, horizontal buildings in perfect harmony with their settings that, like the Japanese temple, "accept with graceful resignation the weight of heaven."

Notes

PROLOGUE | AMIENS, 1918

1 An excellent account of the Battle of Amiens from a Canadian perspective can be found in James McWilliams and R. James Steel's *Amiens: Dawn of Victory* (Toronto: Dundurn Press, 2001). They include several references to the 78th Battalion, Winnipeg Grenadiers. See page 183 for specific mention of evening activities for August 8.

2 War diary, 78th Battalion, accessed online November 2007 at Library and Archives Canada.

PART I A Portrait of the Architect as a Young Man

CH 1 | CHILD

1 Information in this paragraph comes largely from a telephone conversation, June 2, 2007, with Henry Erickson's daughter, Muriel Morgan, Toronto, ON.

2 Most of the information in this paragraph was provided in conversation with and in emails from Blackie Lee Sparzani in 2007 and from a conversation with Anna Auer's daughter-in-law, Evelyn Rogers Auer, July 7, 2007.

3 Information about Charlie Chatterson comes chiefly from Donald Erickson in interviews, January 4, 2006, and August 8, 2007.

4 Email from Blackie Lee Sparzani, 2007.

5 Ibid.

6 From a conversation with Lois Milsom, April 20, 2007.

7 Michael Harris, "King Arthur," *Vancouver* (September 2006): 54.

8 The Women's Auxiliary became a formal body in 1943; it was renamed the Volunteer Committee to the Vancouver Art Gallery in 1980.

9 Erickson interviewed by Mr. [sic] Takahashi in "Speeches by Arthur Erickson." This statement from the architect may be viewed as an example of "enacted biography," wherein an artist (or his or her family and friends) recounts details of actual life experiences to give a rational explanation for the puzzle of an artist's creative activity. See Ernst Kris and Otto Kurz, *Legend, Myth, and Magic in the Image of the Artist* (New Haven: Yale University Press, 1979), 131–32. Similarly, Frank Lloyd Wright told about his mother shaping his future as an architect when she gave him Froebel blocks to play with as a child. See Wright's *An Autobiography* (New York: Horizon, 1977), 34.

10 Edith Iglauer, *Seven Stones: A Portrait of Arthur Erickson, Architect* (Madeira Park, BC: Harbour Publishing, 1981), 39.

11 Arthur Erickson interviewed by Ruth Sandwell in July 2001, SFUA, F-223-1-7-1-15.

12 Mary Baker G. Eddy, *Science and Health with Key to the Scriptures* (Christian Science Publishing Society, 1906), 418.

13 Erickson quoted in Iglauer, *Seven Stones*, 39.

14 John Vanderpant, Vancouver's principal photographer, and his Victoria counterpart, Harry Upperton Knight, were ardent Christian Scientists, as were Eric Brown, first director of the National Gallery in Ottawa, and Bess Harris, the painter and wife of Lawren Harris. See Sheryl Salloum, *Underlying Vibrations: The Photography and Life of John Vanderpant* (Victoria: Horsdal & Schubart, 1995).

15 Erickson quoted in Iglauer, *Seven Stones*, 38.

16 Erickson interviewed by Sandwell, SFUA.

CH 2 | PRODIGY

1 Ethel Wilson, "Seen through Waves," Ethel Wilson Papers, UBC Library, Rare Books and Special Collections, Box 7, Folders 24–5.

2 Bert Binning interviewed in a 1974 video by Dorothy Metcalfe, Vancouver Art Gallery Collection.

3 Quoted by Sheryl Salloum in *Underlying Vibrations*, 27. This book contains a comprehensive account of the fragile beginning of the arts in Vancouver in the 1920s and '30s. Salloum quotes a lecture given by Vanderpant in 1928 in which he says that "the voice of art in the west, is the voice of one crying in the wilderness," 60–61.

4 Doreen Walker, *Dear Nan: Letters of Emily Carr, Nan Cheney, and Humphrey Toms* (Vancouver: University of British Columbia Press, 1990), 225–26.

5 Arthur Erickson, *The Architecture of Arthur Erickson* (Montreal: Tundra Books, 1975), 11.

6 Walker, *Dear Nan*, 154.

7 Faunt's work as a painter never achieved significant standing in the art world; although in 1942, Lawren Harris selected one of her abstracts for a local exhibition that went on to Toronto in 1942, and certainly her friends were pleased to have her work on their living-room walls. In 1945, she retired from school teaching and gradually stopped painting, turning her energies to the local art scene in West Vancouver. In 1947, she was instrumental in forming the West Vancouver Sketch Club (now known as the North Shore Artists' Guild) and establishing an annual lecture series featuring speakers such as B.C. Binning, Mildred Valley Thornton, and Gordon Smith. Jessie Faunt is memorialized by the guild with an annual award in her name for outstanding service. See Frieda Ashworth's brief "History of the West Vancouver Sketch Club" (2007), a copy of which has been filed with the West Vancouver Archives.

8 Erickson, *The Architecture of Arthur Erickson* (Tundra), 11.

9 Ibid.

10 Ibid.

11 Information about the Desbrisay family was supplied by Monte Marler in an interview, May 19, 2009.

12 Quoted in Iglauer, *Seven Stones*, 42.

13 Bill Baldwin turned his journal notes into a thirty-one-page essay titled "Island Highway," which was discovered among his papers by his son, John Baldwin. Words and phrases in quotations are taken from that diary essay.

14 The botanical name of this microscopic flora is *Chlamydomonas nivalis*. This snow, which is sometimes compared to watermelon pulp, was one of the strongest memories both Erickson and John Dayton retained from the hike to Forbidden Plateau. John Dayton interviewed on May 17, 2009.

15 Alan Edmonds, ed., "The Architect Who Thinks People Matter More than Buildings," *Maclean's* 83 (June 1970): 45.

16 Arthur Erickson, foreword to Peter Larisey, *Light for a Cold Land: Lawren Harris's Work and Life—An Interpretation* (Toronto: Dundurn Press, 1993), vii.

17 Erickson interviewed by Sandwell, SFUA.

18 Walker, *Dear Nan*, 140.

19 Arthur Erickson, introduction to *B.C. Binning*, Abraham J. Rogatnick, Ian M. Thom, Adele Weder, eds. (Vancouver: Douglas & McIntyre, 2006), x.

20 Ibid.

21 Quoted in Iglauer, *Seven Stones*, 42. Gordon Smith, however, years later, would see Arthur's paintings as full of promise and especially interesting in the way they embodied the influence of abstract impressionists in Canada, like Emily Carr, Lawren Harris, and Bertram Brooker. Smith

interviewed on April 8, 2009. One of Arthur's paintings—an abstract impression of a Mexican bullfight—became part of Simon Fraser University's art collection. Arthur said he painted it for UBC anthropologist Wilson Duff.

22 Sydney Smith, "The Recent Abstract Work of Lawren Harris," *Maritime Art* 2 (Feb–Mar 1942): 79–80.

23 Quoted in Iglauer, *Seven Stones*, 42. In a later account, he told Sean Rossiter: "Anybody could come as long as they arrived before 8 o'clock. Sharp at 8 they turned out the lights so there was no conversation. Then came a half hour of music. Then a 10-minute break. Then more music, and coffee. They would have a night of Delius. Dilworth would read Whitman's 'out of the cradle endlessly rocking...'" "Cleared for Departure," *Vancouver* (August 1984): 35.

24 Walker, *Dear Nan*, 287.

25 Ibid, 301.

26 Erickson, *The Architecture of Arthur Erickson* (Tundra), 12.

27 Bess Harris and R.P.G. Colgrove, eds., *Lawren Harris*, with an introduction by Northrop Frye (Toronto: Macmillan, 1969), 10.

28 Joan Murray and Robert Fulford, eds., *The Beginning of Vision: The Drawings of Lawren Harris* (Vancouver: Douglas & McIntyre, 1982), 35.

29 Dick Wright interviewed on November 19, 2008.

30 Ibid.

31 Donald Erickson quoted in Iglauer, *Seven Stones*, 40.

32 This and the following Prince of Wales quotes are from *Three Feathers Year Book*. Volumes 1940–41 and 1941–42 were loaned to the author by Ruth Killam Massey.

33 Donald Erickson interviewed on August 8, 2007.

34 From a conversation with Blackie Lee Sparzani, August 2007.

35 James Joyce, *A Portrait of the Artist as a Young Man* (New York: Viking Press, 1965), 64–65.

36 An interview with Jessie Binning, January 29, 2006.

CH 3 | SOLDIER

1 *Vancouver: A Portrait with Arthur Erickson*, Marlin Motion Pictures, UBC, 1983.

2 Erickson interviewed by Ruth Sandwell, SFUA.

3 See Larisey, *Light for a Cold Land*, 100. During this experience, Harris was in the company of B.C. Binning.

4 Arthur Erickson, foreword to Larisey, *Light for a Cold Land*, viii.

5 Ibid., vii.

6 Lawren Harris, "Science and the Soul," *The Canadian Theosophist* 12 (December 15, 1931): 298–300.

7 Arthur Erickson quoted from a CBC television interview, 1982. See also Larisey, *Light for a Cold Land*, 151.

8 Rainer Maria Rilke, *The Book of Hours*, trans. Susan Ranson, ed. Ben Hutchinson (Rochester, NY: Camden House, 2008), 19.

9 Rainer Maria Rilke, *The Notebooks of Malte Laurids Brigge*, trans. John Linton (London: Hogarth Press, 1930).

10 Rainer Maria Rilke, *Letters to a Young Poet*, trans. M.D. Herter (New York: W.W. Norton, 1934), 30.

11 For an account of the Japanese language school, I am especially indebted to Saul Cherniak, Winnipeg, interviewed by telephone on February 23, 2008.

12 These headlines appeared in *The Ubyssey*, March 27 and 13, 1942, respectively. Ubyssey.ca/archive.

13 Ibid., November 21, 1944.

14 Mary McAlpine, "Erickson: Architect on the Move," *Vancouver Sun*, June 14, 1975.

15 George Swinton quoted in Geoffrey James, "Erickson: The Architect as Superstar," *Time* Canada (February 14, 1972): 19.

16 Romain Rolland, *Jean-Christophe* (New York: Henry Holt and Company, 1914), 186–87.

17 Diana Chesterton Whittall interviewed on April 30 and October 9, 2008.

18 Mary Buckerfield White, *Buckerfield: The Story of a Vancouver Family* (Vancouver: privately printed, 2011), 125–26.

19 Quoted in James, "Erickson: The Architect as Superstar," 19.

20 George Swinton to Saul Cherniak, December 30, 1945.

21 Quoted in James, "Erickson: The Architect as Superstar," 19–20.

22 James, "Erickson: The Architect as Superstar," 21.

23 Ibid., 20.

24 Some of this information is taken from a letter Erickson wrote on May 22, 2003 (office files), to Richard Bower in London, who was writing a history of British judo. Bower had previously written about five thousand words on Leggett for Britain's *New Dictionary of National Biography*.

25 Quoted in Iglauer, *Seven Stones*, 46.

26 George Swinton to Saul Cherniak, December 30, 1945.

27 Erickson interviewed by Ruth Sandwell, SFUA.

28 Erickson to Richard Bower. See note 24.

CH 4 | STUDENT

1 See Iglauer, *Seven Stones*, 46.

2 Erickson quoted indirectly in George Woodcock, "Future Present," *Weekend Magazine* 3 (January 1976): 9.

3 Abraham Rogatnick, "A Passion for the Contemporary," *B.C. Binning*, 12.

4 Ned Pratt, a registered architect and friend, handled the drafting and signed the blueprints, but the design was almost exclusively Binning's. See Adele Weder, "The House" in Abraham J. Rogatnick, Ian M. Thom, and Adele Weder, *B.C. Binning*, 59.

5 Arthur Erickson, introduction to Rogatnick et al., *B.C. Binning*, xi.

6 Arthur Erickson, foreword to Larisey, *Light for a Cold Land*, viii. Harris's advice was the same given by Rainer Maria Rilke to a young writer: "You ask whether your verses are good... You compare them with other poems... You are looking outward, and that above all you should not do now. Nobody can counsel and help you, nobody. There is only one single way. Go into yourself." Rilke, *Letters to a Young Poet*, 18.

7 Erickson, *The Architecture of Arthur Erickson* (Tundra), 12.

8 See John Bland's essay, "Arthur Erickson and McGill" in Daniella Rohan and Irena Zantovska Murray's *Arthur Erickson: The Middle East Projects* (Montreal: McGill University Libraries, 1999), 15.

9 Erickson interviewed on February 17, 1998, by Jim Donaldson, www.mcgill.ca/architecture/aluminterviews/erickson.

10 "Tribute to Doug Shadbolt," talk given at Carleton University, December 1973, "Speeches by Arthur Erickson."

11 Donaldson, www.mcgill.ca/architecture/aluminterviews/erickson.

12 Quoted in Iglauer, *Seven Stones*, 47.

13 Norbert Schoenauer, "McGill's School of Architecture: A Retrospection" in *Prospectus: Schools of Architecture and Urban Planning* (Montreal: McGill University, 1987).

14 See Bruce Anderson, *Gordon McKinley Webber: Memories of an Artist, Designer, and Teacher* (Montreal: McGill School of Architecture, 1996).

15 Ibid., 7–8.

16 Interview with Blackie Lee Sparzani, July 26, 2007.

17 Arthur Erickson, *The Architecture of Arthur Erickson* (Vancouver: Douglas & McIntyre, 1988), 18.

18 Anderson, *Gordon McKinley Webber*, 32.

19 Gilles Gagnon interviewed on November 13, 1998, by Jim Donaldson, www.mcgill.ca/architecture/aluminterviews/gagnon.

20 Quoted in Iglauer, *Seven Stones*, 48.

21 Douglas Shadbolt interviewed on April 16, 1996, by Jim Donaldson, www.mcgill.ca/architecture/aluminterviews/shadbolt.

22 Harold Spence-Sales interviewed on April 17, 1996, by Jim Donaldson, www.mcgill.ca/architecture/aluminterviews/spence-sales.

23 Erickson, *The Architecture of Arthur Erickson* (Douglas & McIntyre), 18.

24 Donaldson, www.mcgill.ca/architecture/aluminterviews/erickson.

25 "Seeing is Believing," 1967, "Speeches by Arthur Erickson."

26 Erickson, *The Architecture of Arthur Erickson* (Douglas & McIntyre), 18.

27 Foreword by Alfred Barr to the catalogue for Henry-Russell Hitchcock Jr., Philip Johnson, and Lewis Mumford, *Modern Architecture: International Exhibition* (New York: The Museum of Modern Art, 1932).

28 Donaldson, www.mcgill.ca/architecture/aluminterviews/gagnon.

29 Donaldson, www.mcgill.ca/architecture/aluminterviews/erickson.

30 Donaldson, www.mcgill.ca/architecture/aluminterviews/erickson.

31 See William Weintraub, *City Unique: Montreal Days and Nights in the 1940s and '50s* (Toronto: McClelland & Stewart, 1996).

32 Jean Catton interviewed on November 16, 2005.

33 Guy Desbarats interviewed on November 11, 1998, by Jim Donaldson, www.mcgill.ca/architecture/aluminterviews/desbarats.

34 Shadbolt quoted by James in "Erickson: The Architect as Superstar," 20.

35 Frederick (Tex) Dawson interviewed in July 1999 by Jim Donaldson, www.mcgill.ca/architecture/aluminterview/dawson.

36 Ibid.

37 Erickson, *The Architecture of Arthur Erickson* (Douglas & McIntyre), 18.

38 Quoted in Iglauer, *Seven Stones*, 50.

39 Ibid.

40 Donaldson, www.mcgill.ca/architecture/aluminterview/erickson.

41 Erickson interviewed in *McGill News* (Summer 2003).

42 Author interview, October 8, 2005.

43 Quoted in Iglauer, *Seven Stones*, 50–51. In James's *Time* article he said, "I think that anyone who participated in that particular life [at Taliesin] really took a long, long time to recover from it, because it was unreal. It was beautiful, too beautiful." And with a more sinister emphasis, he told a reporter in 2006: "It didn't feel healthy to me. It felt ghostly . . . producing only paper architects, overawed students who never produced anything real." And he mentions the "creepy influence" of Olgivanna Wright with her Gurdjieff mantras. (See Lloyd Dykk, *Vancouver Sun*, June 16, 2006).

CH 5 | TRAVELLER

1 Donaldson, www.mcgill.ca/architecture/aluminterviews/erickson.

2 Ibid.

3 Erickson, *The Architecture of Arthur Erickson* (Tundra), 12.

4 Quoted in Iglauer, *Seven Stones*, 51.

5 Erickson, *The Architecture of Arthur Erickson* (Douglas & McIntyre), 18.

6 Many of these letters made their way to an uncatalogued repository at the University of Manitoba. They may have been sent to the university by Myrtle Erickson, who kept up friendships in Winnipeg, or they may have been left there by an architecture student who was working on an Erickson

project in the 1970s. They were first recorded in a published bibliography on the literature of Arthur Erickson prepared by Jill Wade in 1973. In 2007, at my urging, they were archived as part of the University of Manitoba Archives and Special Collections.

7 Arthur Erickson to John Bland, December 1950. Letter located at the Blackader-Lauterman Library of Architecture and Art, McGill University.

CH 6 I EUROPE

1 The fullest account of Carl Massa's views of Michelangelo appears in Iglauer, *Seven Stones*, 52, which I have summarized and quoted here.

2 Letter quoted by John Bland in his introduction to *Arthur Erickson: The Middle East Projects*, 16.

3 This letter to his family in Vancouver is simply identified as "Florence, December 1950."

4 Letter dated January 7, 1951.

5 See Iglauer, *Seven Stones*, 52.

6 "Christmas in Rome" is the manuscript of an undated talk, probably given in the late 1950s or early 1960s. A copy of this manuscript is part of the Erickson collection at the University of Manitoba Archives.

7 Elizabeth Hardwick, *A View of My Own* (New York: Farrar, Straus & Cudahy, 1962), 77.

8 In his late writings, Berenson railed against academic critics and historians who "rise with leaden wings... to bring down theories, pseudo-histories, misinterpretations, romances, occult theologies" with which to evaluate the work of great artists. Berenson writing in *Caravaggio, His Incongruity and His Fame*, 1953, quoted by Ernest Samuels, *Bernard Berenson: The Making of a Legend* (Cambridge, MA: Harvard University Press, 1987), 538.

9 Larisey, *Light for a Cold Land*, 56.

10 In an undated talk titled "Marzo e Pazzo—March is Mad," some of the details of the Aeolian adventure differ from those in his letter to his parents. The version prepared as a public talk is more dramatically constructed, and places and times are rearranged accordingly. A copy of the talk is in the Arthur Erickson Archive at the University of Manitoba Archives and Special Collections.

11 Donaldson, http://www.mcgill.ca/architecture/alumninterviews/desbarats.

12 Donaldson, http://www.mcgill.ca/architecture/alumninterviews/erickson.

13 From a letter fragment written in the fall of 1951 but mistakenly attached to a letter addressed "Dear Family" and dated January 7, 1951.

14 From Erickson interview by Sandwell, SFUA, expanded by an author interview.

15 Letter to Donald Erickson, October 1951. Quoted by Rhodri W. Liscombe in his introduction to the catalogue for the 1985 Erickson exhibition, *Arthur Erickson: Selected Projects 1971–85.*

16 John Ruskin, *The Stones of Venice* (New York: Da Capo, 1960), 167.

17 Mies van der Rohe quoted by Franz Schulze, *Mies van der Rohe: A Critical Biography* (Chicago: University of Chicago Press, 1985), 290.

18 The Valencia quotations are from an undated letter titled "Spain."

19 This undated letter is identified as "Cordova."

20 These quotations are from a letter to "Dear Family" titled "Spain" and dated August 1951.

21 Ibid.

22 This passage is adapted from the Sandwell interview, SFUA.

23 This account of the Altamira cave paintings is from a letter to "Dear Family" that has no place, title, or date.

24 Arthur's relationship to "Happy" is sketched in his notes for an autobiography labelled in his office papers as "Arthur Erickson Profile."

25 Mary McCarthy, *The Stones of Florence* (New York: Harcourt, 1963), 71–72.

26 There is confusion about Erickson's return date because he liked to say he spent three years travelling Europe on a scholarship. But according to Joanne Sheppard Weghsteen, who travelled back to Montreal on the same ship, they returned in September 1952.

CH 7 | APPRENTICE

1 James, "Erickson: The Architect as Superstar," 16–21.

2 Letter from Toledo, Spain, dated June 1951.

3 Quoted in Iglauer, *Seven Stones,* 54.

4 Arthur Erickson, foreword to Janet Bingham, *Samuel Maclure* (Ganges, BC: Horsdal & Schubart, 1985), n.p.

5 For a brief online survey of architectural firms in B.C. in the first half of the twentieth century, see Sean Rossiter's "Architects and Architecture of Greater Vancouver," www.discovervancouver.com/GVB/vancouver-architecture.asp.

6 Quoted in Douglas Shadbolt, *Ron Thom: The Shaping of an Architect* (Vancouver: Douglas & McIntyre, 1995), 10.

7 Quoted in Iglauer, *Seven Stones,* 55.

8 Zoltan S. Kiss, *Without a Blueprint: Surviving in a Changing World* (West Vancouver: Sandor Press, 2005), 145.

9 Erickson quoted in the Sandwell interview, SFUA, and in *Vancouver: A Portrait with Arthur Erickson,* Marlin Motion Pictures, UBC, 1983.

10 Some of the details about this building were first collected by Danielle Egan for an article titled "Arthur Unknown," published in *Vancouver*, June 2002.

11 Abraham Rogatnick interviewed on December 6, 2005.

12 Brian Hemingway was the architect who in 2001 turned the Stegeman studio into a multi-million-dollar home, and it is an exaggeration to call it an Arthur Erickson–designed residence.

13 Erickson, *The Architecture of Arthur Erickson* (Tundra), 14.

14 The Takahashi interview, "Speeches by Arthur Erickson," 10.

15 Erickson, *The Architecture of Arthur Erickson* (Douglas & McIntyre), 21.

16 George Woodcock, "Future Present," *Weekend Magazine* (January 3, 1976): 8–11.

17 Ibid., 21.

18 Donaldson, www.mcgill.ca/architecture/aluminterviews/erickson.

19 Ibid.

20 Ibid.

21 Brahm Wiesman interviewed on April 17, 1996, by Jim Donaldson, www.mcgill.ca/architecture/aluminterviews/wiesman.

22 Quoted in Iglauer, *Seven Stones*, 42.

23 Donaldson, www.mcgill.ca/architecture/aluminterviews/shadbolt.

24 Donaldson, www.mcgill.ca/architecture/aluminterviews/erickson.

25 From an interview with Douglas Shadbolt's wife, Sidney Shadbolt, March 7, 2008.

26 Brownell Frazier of Oregon's School of Architecture would tell one of her students who was moving to Vancouver that Arthur Erickson was "the one" in that city—"a very dynamic young man." Wayne Elwood to author, January 17, 2010.

27 The letter to Alan Jarvis, dated December 1958, is located in CAA: ERI 4A/76.13, Box 12.

28 Max Wyman, "To Understand the City We Make," *Vancouver Forum* 1 (1992): 146–58.

29 Quoted in Iglauer, *Seven Stones*, 59.

30 Abraham Rogatnick, "A Poem on Arthur's Life," *Canadian Architecture* (October 2009): 22.

31 John Roaf interviewed by telephone on November 17, 2008.

32 "The Seven Crutches of Modern Architecture," an unpublished talk at Harvard University, delivered December 1954. Quoted in Franz Schulze, *Philip Johnson: Life and Work* (New York: Alfred A. Knopf, 1994), 233.

33 Geoffrey Scott, *The Architecture of Humanism: A Study in the History of Taste* (New York: Charles Scribner's Sons, 1924).

34 This statement occurs in a letter Arthur wrote supporting the nomination of Antoine Predock for the Art Institute of America's gold medal,
   October 12, 2001. Erickson office papers.

35 Jim Strasman interviewed by telephone on September 29, 2010.

36 Information about the Buckerfield commission, including a letter from
   Ernest Buckerfield to Arthur dated July 28, 1957, can be found in CAA,
   ERI 4A/76.13, Box 12.

37 Quoting Zipporah Woodward's granddaughter, Sherry Grauer, who was
   interviewed on May 28, 2009.

38 This phrase and the two following are from a short illustrated article by
   Arthur Erickson titled "Cabana in Vancouver," published in *The Canadian Architect* (July 1959): 45–48.

39 References to these submissions can be found in correspondence in CAA,
   ERI 4A/76.13, Box 12.

40 Cecilia Smith, "Rebellion in Home Designs," *Vancouver Sun*, February 20,
   1959, 8.

41 Erickson quoted in Rossiter, "Cleared for Departure," 38.

42 Arthur gave various accounts of how he purchased and developed his property. The best of these is an unpublished essay titled simply "The House
   at 4195 West 14th Avenue, Vancouver, B.C." included with "Speeches by
   Arthur Erickson" at UBC Library. I also found valuable information about
   the house and garden compiled by Cheryl Cooper in an unpublished
   document loaned to me by Hugo Eppich titled "Erickson Garden Conservation Plan."

43 Erickson quoted in Iglauer, *Seven Stones*, 33.

44 See David Laskin, "Design and Neglect: The Garden of Arthur Erickson"
   in Valerie Easton, David Laskin, and Allan Mandell, *Artists in their Gardens* (Seattle: Sasquatch Books, 2001), 98–111.

45 Iglauer, *Seven Stones*, 29.

46 Giuseppe Mazzariol quoted in James, "Erickson: The Architect as Superstar," 16–21.

47 Anecdote from Iglauer, *Seven Stones*, 34.

CH 8 | THE FILBERG HOUSE

1 To date, the best source of information about the Filberg family is in
  Richard Somerset Mackie's *Island Timber* (Victoria: Sono Nis Press, 2000).

2 *The Ubyssey*, January 11, 1945, 3.

3 Erickson, *The Architecture of Arthur Erickson* (Douglas & McIntyre), 31.

4 Arthur Erickson, "The Filberg House at Comox on Vancouver Island,"
  Canadian Architect v (December 1960): 47.

5 Ibid., 48.

6 Trevor Boddy, *Globe and Mail*, June 1, 2007.

7 Arthur Erickson, "The Design of a House," *Canadian Art* XVII (November 1960): 342.

8 Lawren Harris, *Contrasts: A Book of Verse* (Toronto: McClelland & Stewart, 1922), 90–91.

9 Arthur Erickson, "The Filberg House at Comox," 47–56.

10 Quoted in Iglauer, *Seven Stones*, 55, 57.

11 Letter to Alan Jarvis, dated May 20, 1960, is located in CAA, ERI 4A/76.13, Box 12.

12 Arthur Erickson, "The Design of a House," 342.

13 Arthur Erickson's correspondence with Rita Reif and her article are located in CAA, ERI 4A/76.13, Box 12, as are the refusals from *Architectural Forum* and the *Architectural Review*.

14 Abraham Rogatnick, "Criticism," *Canadian Architect* V (December 1960), 57–58.

15 Rhodri W. Liscombe, *Arthur Erickson: Selected Projects 1971–85* (New York: Center for Inter-American Relations, 1985), 8.

16 Christopher Hall, "Canada's Most Fabulous House Makes a Comeback," *New York Times*, March 23, 2003, 34.

17 Erickson, the *Architecture of Arthur Erickson* (Douglas & McIntyre), 31.

PART II The Weight of Heaven

CH 9 | JAPAN

1 Binning interview with Kay Alsop, "The Artistic Credo of B.C. Binning," *UBC Alumni Chronicle* (Summer 1973).

2 The application to the Canada Council is located in CAA, ERI 4A/76 Box 13.

3 Note filed with Canada Council application.

4 Copies of the letters to Gordon Webber form part of the Arthur Erickson Collection at the University of Manitoba Archives.

5 See the interview with Mr. Takahashi, "Speeches by Arthur Erickson."

6 For a fuller discussion of this building, see Jonathan M. Reynolds, *Maekawa Kunio and the Emergence of Japanese Modernist Architecture* (Berkeley: University of California Press, 2001), 187–94.

7 Erickson, *The Architecture of Arthur Erickson* (Douglas & McIntyre), 41.

8 These details about his physical discomfort in Nara are from a short letter to Gordon Webber dated May 17, 1961.

9 The visit to Bishop Sakamoto is described in Erickson's fourth letter to Gordon Webber, marked "Kyoto" and dated June 11, 1961.

10 Information from a telephone interview with Jane Clegg, April 12, 2010.

11 Myrtle Erickson to Arthur Erickson, June 1, 1961. CAA, ERI 4A/76.13, Box 13. Other letters he received while on this trip are in the same box.

12 Interview with Mr. Takahashi, "Speeches by Arthur Erickson."

13 Ibid.

14 Erickson, *The Architecture of Arthur Erickson* (Douglas & McIntyre), 42.

15 Interview with Mr. Takahashi, "Speeches by Arthur Erickson."

16 "UIA, S. Giorgio, Conference on Cities," 1971, "Speeches by Arthur Erickson."

17 Quoted in Iglauer, *Seven Stones*, 57.

18 "Speech to the National Gallery Association, 1972," "Speeches by Arthur Erickson."

19 "UIA, S. Giorgio, Conference on Cities," 1971, "Speeches by Arthur Erickson."

20 Kakuzo Okakura, *The Book of Tea*, 1906 (New York: Dover, 1964), 30.

21 Arthur Erickson, "The Architecture of Japan: A Tendency Towards Formalism—I: The Roots," *Canadian Architect* XI, no. 12 (December 1966): 32.

22 Erickson, *The Architecture of Arthur Erickson* (Douglas & McIntyre), 43.

23 Arthur Erickson, "The Architecture of Japan," 36.

24 Information and speculations about John Howard's life are from an author interview in November 2006.

25 "Expo '70: The Asian Fair," "Speeches by Arthur Erickson."

26 In his letter to Webber, he refers to four days spent in Bali, whereas in CAA, ERI 4A/76, Box 12, there is a travel agency timetable for an eight-day trip, which begins with his flight to Jakarta on July 17 and to Denpasar on July 18, with departure on July 26. "Four odd days in Bali" probably refers to the experiences covered thus far in his journal letter, which is dated July 23.

27 Edith Iglauer, *Seven Stones*, ends her book with this statement from Arthur, 118.

28 "An Address to the Institute of Canadian Bankers," October 16, 1972. In this talk he goes on to say "the World Bank is supporting a 3,000-room hotel development whose impact on that island will be terminal. Bali should be under UNESCO as a world museum, or a world park, like our national parks, for conservation—with visitors restricted to those with genuine interest in that culture." This address is collected in "Speeches by Arthur Erickson."

29 Arthur Erickson, "The Weight of Heaven," *The Canadian Architect* IX (March 1964): 50.

30 This practice is cited in a talk Erickson gave to the National Gallery Association, May 9, 1972. Collected in "Speeches by Arthur Erickson."

CH 10 I PUBLIC LECTURER

1 The Grauer cabana was photographed to advantage by Selwyn Pullan and was featured in *The Canadian Architect* 4, no. 7 (July 1959): 45–48, and in *Weekend Magazine* 9 (November 14, 1959).

2 See "Notes from an Interview with Arthur Erickson, 1964" and "Climate as the Conditioner," 1976 in "Speeches by Arthur Erickson."

3 Erickson, *The Architecture of Arthur Erickson* (Douglas & McIntyre), 44.

4 Arthur discusses this in retrospect with Lance Berelowitz in an interview titled "Erickson: A Turning Point," 18.

5 Even earlier, Arthur had persuaded Lucille and Charles Flavelle to construct a sod roof on their summer house on Hornby Island.

6 In the film *Vancouver: A Portrait with Arthur Erickson*, he praises the work of stonemason "Jimmy" Cunningham, who for thirty-two years oversaw the construction of much of the seawall.

7 John Baldwin interviewed on April 23, 2009.

8 Erickson, *The Architecture of Arthur Erickson* (Douglas & McIntyre), 26–27.

9 Ibid., 43.

10 Quoted in Iglauer, *Seven Stones*, 28.

11 Erickson, *The Architecture of Arthur Erickson* (Tundra), 81.

12 Ibid.

13 Rita Reif, "A House with Motion Built In," *New York Times*, September 19, 1967.

14 Erickson, *The Architecture of Arthur Erickson* (Douglas & McIntyre), 49.

15 Most of this story is pieced together from the Graham file in CAA, ERI 4A/76.13, Box 9.

16 Lois Spence (later Milsom) quoted by Sally Fotheringham in an article on the Point Grey Road townhouses, *Vancouver Life* (November 1966). This article is one of the best sources of information on the subject. It has been supplemented here by an interview with Lois Milsom, May 19, 2009.

17 "Habitation: Space, Dilemma, and Design" was published in 1966.

18 This talk, collected in "Speeches by Arthur Erickson," has no title.

19 Barry Downs interviewed on August 9, 2011.

CH 11 I SIMON FRASER UNIVERSITY

1 From taped interviews with Peter Stursberg quoted by Hugh Johnston in *Radical Campus: Making Simon Fraser University* (Vancouver: Douglas & McIntyre, 2005), 8.

2 The closest parallel to Simon Fraser University was York University, which provided a second university for Toronto, but its creation was not a one-man show and it did not have buildings up and running on a permanent site until the sixth year of its operations. In fact, it remained an affiliate of the University of Toronto for its first four years.

3 There is a vivid portrait of Gordon Shrum in action threaded through the pages of Johnston's *Radical Campus*. Shrum's own version of his busy life, compiled from interview tapes by Peter Stursberg, can be found in *Gordon Shrum: An Autobiography*, edited by Clive Cocking (Vancouver: UBC Press, 1986).

4 Erickson interviewed by Sandwell.

5 This motive is the subject of Allan Fotheringham's article, "How an Old Boy Got Back at UBC," *Maclean's* 78 (October 16, 1965): 67–8.

6 Board minutes, October 10, 1963, 7, SFUA, F 3/1/0/0/1.

7 In his autobiography, Shrum said, "Above all, I wanted an experimental university where no hard and fast rules inhibited faculty from modifying courses, pursuing interdisciplinary studies, or developing creative programs. I wanted Simon Fraser University to be a place where new ideas would flourish and creative people would flock in." Cocking, 110.

8 Gene Waddell, "Design for Simon Fraser University and the Problems Accompanying Excellence," the draft of an unpublished book-length typescript, 1999, 39, SFUA.

9 Johnston, *Radical Campus*, 43.

10 Ibid.

11 Arthur Erickson, "Designing Simon Fraser University," SFUA, F 70/2/0/3.

12 Erickson interviewed by Sandwell.

13 Rossiter, "Cleared for Departure," 38.

14 These points are drawn loosely from Arthur Erickson, "The Architectural Concept of Simon Fraser University," dated September 2, 1965, SFUA, F 11/1/4/1.

15 Waddell, "Design for Simon Fraser University," 64.

16 Erickson interviewed by Sandwell.

17 Erickson, "Designing Simon Fraser University."

18 Arthur may also have been aware of Frank Lloyd Wright's assertion that a building should not be *on* a hill, but *of* it. Frank Lloyd Wright, *An Autobiography* (New York: Horizon Press, 1932), 191–200.

19 Waddell, "Design for Simon Fraser University," 86.

20 Ibid., 85.

21 Shrum is quoted by Randle Iredale and Duncan McNab in Waddell, "Design for Simon Fraser University," 100. Shrum was no doubt thinking here of Thompson, Berwick & Pratt, regarded as the city's leading

architectural firm at that time, and of Fred Hollingsworth and Barry Downs. They were all three cited as honourable mentions in the competition results.

22 Clive Cocking, ed., *Gordon Shrum: An Autobiography*, 104. Shrum added: "I was a committee of one at that stage, and it is a wonderful feeling being a committee of one."

23 Erickson's recollections are from "Designing Simon Fraser University" and the Sandwell interview.

24 Erickson interviewed by Peter Stursberg for the Clive Cocking book on Shrum, SFUA, F 31/2/1/18.

25 Stewart Williams to Warnett Kennedy, August 1963, SFUA, F 32/1/0/6.

26 The quotations in this paragraph are from the Sandwell interview, from Erickson, "Designing Simon Fraser University," and from the Stursberg interview, SFUA, F 31/2/1/18.

27 Erickson, "Designing Simon Fraser University."

28 Ibid.

29 James, *Time*, 21.

30 Information taken largely from Gene Waddell's interviews with Ron Bain and Arthur Erickson for "Design for Simon Fraser University," 79–80.

31 Quoted in Waddell, "Design for Simon Fraser University," 82.

32 Arthur Erickson, "Designing Simon Fraser University."

33 These setbacks are described in Waddell, "Design for Simon Fraser University," 238. The account is drawn chiefly from an interview with Ron Bain.

34 George Bull, *Michelangelo: A Biography* (London: Penguin, 1996), 68.

35 "Notes from an Interview with Arthur Erickson, Architect, January 16, 1964," from "Speeches by Arthur Erickson." This interview has been published in David Stouck and Myler Wilkinson, eds., *Genius of Place: Writing in British Columbia* (Vancouver: Polestar, 2000), 229–38.

36 John Roaf in a telephone interview, November 17, 2008.

37 Erickson interviewed by Sandwell.

38 Some details here were supplied by former SFU instructor Wayne Elwood, August 5, 2011.

39 Erickson, "Designing Simon Fraser University."

40 Ibid.

41 Donaldson, www.mcgill.ca/architecture/aluminterviews/erickson.

42 This tag was first used by Donald Stainsby in an article titled "Instant University" in *Saturday Night* 79 (March 1964): 16–18.

43 This statement was affixed to a display of materials about SFU and the University of Lethbridge for the Arthur Erickson show at the Vancouver Art Gallery in 2006.

44 Waddell, "Design for Simon Fraser University," 74, quoting A.L. Maier, "University," *Burnaby Courier*, September 2, 1965, 2.

45 Nick Milkovich in conversation with the author, January 13, 2011.

46 Waddell, "Design for Simon Fraser University," 74.

47 Edmonds, ed., "The Architect Who Thinks People Matter More than Buildings," 45.

48 Ray Affleck's letter appears in *Canadian Architect* (March 1966): 14, 16.

49 "Canada: Sermon on a Mount," *Interbuild* (February 1966): 12–17; *Architectural Review* published its positive notice in the April 1966 issue.

50 Arthur Erickson, introduction to Carol Moore Ede, *Canadian Architecture 1960–70* (Toronto: Burns, MacEachern Ltd., 1971), 7.

51 R.J. Thom, "Academe on a Mountain Top," *Canadian Forum* (January 1966): 225.

52 Abraham Rogatnick, "Simon Fraser University, British Columbia," *Architectural Review*, Westminster, 854, 968: 262–75. Rogatnick compares SFU to several other "radiant examples of world architecture," including Lhasa, Monte Albán, and Pergamum, to evoke both the poetic and sacred aspect of a hilltop structure in mysterious proximity to the sky.

53 There had also been discussion of a flock of sheep to graze the meadows to prevent alders and eventually forest growing back. The brother of the president, Ian McTaggart-Cowan, a zoologist at UBC and an early, prominent environmentalist, encouraged the idea and even recommended the type of sheep and how to look after them. Geoffrey Massey interviewed on December 19, 2005.

54 Erickson, "Designing Simon Fraser University."

CH 12 | FRANCISCO KRIPACZ

1 Maeve Slavin, "Designer of the Year," *Interiors* (January 1985): 127–36.

2 See Archives d'Etat de Genève: Personnes enregistrées à la frontière genevoise durant la Deuxième Guerre mondiale. 30/07/2009.

3 Melanie Friesen interviewed on March 12, 2011.

4 This vignette is from Bruno Freschi, interviewed on August 20, 2009.

5 Geoffrey Erickson interviewed on May 26, 2007.

6 Arthur Erickson writing in support of Moshe Safdie's nomination for the American Institute of Architects gold medal, November 13, 2002 (Erickson office papers).

7 Arthur Erickson, "Speech to the National Gallery Association," 1972, "Speeches by Arthur Erickson."

8 Maeve Slavin, "Designer of the Year," 132.

9 Erickson, *The Architecture of Arthur Erickson* (Douglas & McIntyre), 128, 130.

10 The 1964 Jamaican invoice is located in CAA, ERI 4A/76.13, Box 89, and the 1971 business note in Box 53. His name and signature do appear on informal memos and postcards.

11 Wayne Elwood interviewed in March 2010.

CH 13 | HUCKSTER

1 Johnston, *Radical Campus*, 54–55.

2 David Watmough, "About Art," *Vancouver Sun*, December 10, 1965.

3 Shrum's words reported in the *Vancouver Sun*, September 8, 1965.

4 Erickson quoted in Waddell in "Design for a University," 276.

5 Erickson to Gordon Shrum, September 29, 1965, Shrum fonds SFUA, F-32/1.

6 Donaldson, www.mcgill.ca/architecture/aluminterviews/erickson.

7 See the Erickson/Massey Progress Report for SFU, dated February 15, 1966, located at CCA in Box 22-01/ARCON 1996.0039:001.

8 Located in the Erickson and Massey file at SFUA, F 11/1/4/1.

9 See Waddell, "Design for a University," 290.

10 Ibid., 315.

11 P.D. McTaggart-Cowan to Geoffrey Massey, January 4, 1967. CAA, ERI 4A/76.13, Box 47.

12 Quoted in Iglauer, *Seven Stones*, 67.

13 P.D. McTaggart-Cowan to Messrs. Erickson & Massey, January 3, 1968, CAA, ERI 4A/76.13, Box 47.

14 P.D. McTaggart-Cowan, January 3, 1968. CAA, ERI 4A/76.13, Box 47.

15 Erickson to the board of governors, September 13, 1965. SFUA, F-32/1.

16 Erickson to Arnold Hean, February 7, 1966. CAA, ERI 4A/76.13, Box 47.

17 Erickson, *The Architecture of Arthur Erickson* (Tundra), 151.

18 Edmonds, ed., "The Architect Who Thinks People Matter More than Buildings," 46.

19 Peter Behrens statements on the office building were first published in the *Berliner Morgenpost*, November 27, 1912. They are quoted (in translation) by Franz Schulze in *Mies van der Rohe: A Critical Biography*, 109.

20 "A Proposal for the Interior Design of the Bank of Canada," September 1972, CCA, 22-TOR-705.

21 Nicholas Olsberg, *Arthur Erickson: Critical Works* (Vancouver: Douglas & McIntyre, 2006), 133.

22 Erickson, *The Architecture of Arthur Erickson* (Douglas & McIntyre), 61.

23 "A Building in the Doric Tradition," *Architectural Record*, 1969.

24 These statements about concrete and about the MacMillan Bloedel building can be found in *The Architecture of Arthur Erickson* (Douglas & McIntyre), 59–61. They echo Mies van der Rohe's earlier frequent claim

that the built forms of the twentieth century would evolve from concrete, steel, and glass.

25 These observations were made by Olsberg in 2006 interviews attending the publication of *Arthur Erickson: Critical Works.*

26 This letter and Catton's subsequent correspondence with Erickson/Massey are located in CAA, ERI 4A/76.13, Box 87.

27 Nick Milkovich interviewed on January 19, 2010.

28 Edmonds, ed., "The Architect Who Thinks People Matter More than Buildings," 44–49.

29 Information from a telephone interview with Laurette Hilborn, July 20, 2010.

30 This Erickson quote is taken from a television interview with Adrienne Clarkson, 1995.

31 Jim Strasman interviewed by telephone on September 29, 2010.

32 John Keith-King and Sherry Grauer interviewed on May 28, 2009.

33 This account of evenings at the Benes' was provided by Melanie Friesen in an interview, March 12, 2011.

34 Jeff Hodson, "Temple Honours Erickson, *MetroNewsVancouver.ca,* June 1, 2009. The moat part of the original design was never completed.

35 Arthur Erickson, "Expo '70: The Asian Fair," a talk given January 31, 1971, to the Society of Architectural Historians in Chicago, collected in "Speeches by Arthur Erickson."

36 Bruno Freschi interviewed on August 20, 2009.

37 Bruno Freschi quoted in Iglauer, *Seven Stones,* 48.

38 The NRC report dated October 24, 1968, is located in CAA, ERI 4A/76.13, Box 6.

39 For example, see the letter from Vagn Houlbjerg to Geoffrey Massey, October 11, 1969. CAA, ARI 4A/76.13, Box 63.

40 Arthur Erickson to Patrick Reid, September 11, 1969. CAA, ERI 4A/76.13, Box 6.

41 The correspondence referred to and quoted in this paragraph is located in CAA, ERI 4A/76.13, Box 63.

42 This anecdote was related to the author by Lois Milsom, October 13, 2009.

43 The story of Arthur's hospitalization for smoking marijuana was told by Geoffrey Erickson interviewed on May 26, 2007, and by Gordon Smith interviewed on April 8, 2009.

44 The correspondence referred to in this and the following paragraph is located in CAA, ERI 4A/76.13, Box 6.

45 The correspondence about the AIJ award is located in CAA, ERI 4A/76.13, Box 6.

46 Mayrs quoted in Iglauer, *Seven Stones,* 72.

CH 14 | UNIVERSITY OF LETHBRIDGE

1 Van Christou interviewed on December 9, 2006.

2 The telegram from Garry Hanson is in Special Collections, University of Lethbridge Library.

3 Owen G. Holmes, *Come Hell or High Water* (Lethbridge, AB: Lethbridge Herald Publications, 1972), 89.

4 This account of Arthur Erickson's initial experience of the prairie landscape and his conception of the university is based on his brief poetic accounts in both the Tundra and Douglas & McIntyre versions of *The Architecture of Arthur Erickson*.

5 Geoffrey Massey to W.A.S. Smith, April 2, 1968, Special Collections, University of Lethbridge Library.

6 W.A.S. Smith to Arthur Erickson, May 22, 1968, Special Collections, University of Lethbridge Library.

7 W.A.S. Smith, "To Whom It May Concern," January 28, 1969, Special Collections, University of Lethbridge Library.

8 Telegram from Arthur Erickson to Ron Bain, no date, CAA, ERI 4A/76.13, Box 6.

9 N.D. Holmes to Arthur Erickson, May 14, 1970, Special Collections, University of Lethbridge Library.

10 Arthur Erickson to N.D. Holmes, May 27, 1979, Special Collections, University of Lethbridge Library.

11 James, "Erickson: The Architect as Superstar," 16–21.

12 "A gateway like the portal of a medieval city" is from Nicholas Olsberg, *Arthur Erickson: Critical Works*, 75; "an ancient religious enclosure" is quoted from Rhodri W. Liscombe's catalogue for *Arthur Erickson: Selected Projects, 1971–1985*, 11.

13 Erickson, *The Architecture of Arthur Erickson* (Douglas & McIntyre), 67.

14 Ibid.

15 Quoted in James, "Erickson: The Architect as Superstar," 18.

16 Giuseppe Mazzariol, "Il linguaggio di Erickson," (tr. "The Language of Erickson") 161–87.

17 From an unidentified lecture to a congress in London, England, May 3, 1978, Erickson's office files.

18 Arthur Erickson to W.E. Beckel, July 21, 1972, Special Collections, University of Lethbridge Library.

19 The quotations here are drawn from a presentation Arthur Erickson made at a conference on cities in Indianapolis, May 1971. The paper was prepared for Panel B1 and can be found with "Speeches by Arthur Erickson."

20 Georges Teyssot, "Western Monoliths: Arthur Erickson's Design for Two Universities," in Nicholas Olsberg, *Arthur Erickson: Critical Works*, 121–22.

PART III Master Builder

CH 15 | ROBSON SQUARE

1 This article, written by photographer Geoffrey James, appeared in the Canadian edition of *Time*, February 14, 1972, 16–21. I have taken the liberty for greater clarity of reorganizing the word order in the statement quoted.

2 In comparison, Erickson reported an income of $9,000 for 1962.

3 *Seattle Times*, October 25, 1981.

4 Actually, it was *Globe and Mail* editor Martin O'Malley's phrase, appearing in the December 12, 1968, issue of the paper, but Trudeau repeated it a few days later and the media subsequently attributed it to the prime minister. See Richard Gwyn, *The Northern Magus: Pierre Trudeau and Canadians* (Toronto: McClelland & Stewart, 1980), 64.

5 In April 1970, the FLQ Manifesto, read on Radio-Canada, said that Quebec would listen no more "to the lies of the 'fairy' Trudeau." Quoted in John English, *Just Watch Me: The Life of Pierre Elliott Trudeau 1968–2000* (Toronto: Alfred A. Knopf, Canada, 2009), 80.

6 This and other correspondence concerning the prime minister's office renovation is located in CAA, ERI 4A/76.13, Box 53.

7 This letter by Mrs. Say written December 9, 1971, and the newspaper articles dated November 18, 1971, and December 8, 1971, are located in CAA, ERI 4A/76.13, Box 53.

8 Erickson in conversation with the author, June 12, 2005.

9 Ibid.

10 Nancy Southam, ed., *Pierre: Colleagues and Friends Talk about the Trudeau They Knew* (Toronto: McClelland & Stewart, 2005), 129.

11 From a taped Vancouver Institute lecture by Arthur Erickson titled "A Personal View of China," delivered December 7, 1974. This lecture is located in Rare Books and Special Collections, UBC Library. I have worked with a transcription made by Michelangelo Sabatino and Adele Weder.

12 Woodcock, "Future Present," 8.

13 See *Living Stones: A Centennial History of Christ Church Cathedral*, Chapter 6, www3.telus.net/kellet-adams/CCCHistory/ accessed June 25, 2010.

14 The account of the presentation is by Dave Ablett, *Vancouver Sun*, May 19, 1966, 18.

15 Keith Bradbury, "Planner's Viewpoint: Beautiful, Unrealistic," *Vancouver Sun*, May 19, 1966, 20.

16 Moira Farrow, "Architect Warns on City Freeway," *Vancouver Sun*, December 11, 1967, 8.

17 "Man Plans His Future: The City," 1966, "Speeches by Arthur Erickson."

18 "Resources for Effective Innovation": Conference on Cities, Indianapolis, May 25, 1971, "Speeches by Arthur Erickson."

19 The ideas in this paragraph are summarized from "Speech to the National Gallery Association," May 9, 1972, "Speeches by Arthur Erickson."

20 "Royal Bank Address," June 9, 1971, "Speeches by Arthur Erickson."

21 Robert Venturi, *Complexity and Contradiction in Architecture* (New York: Museum of Modern Art Press, 1966).

22 The phrase "disastrously ugly" is highlighted at the outset in Edmonds, "The Architect Who Thinks People Matter More than Buildings," 44.

23 "Notes from an Interview with Arthur Erickson," *Genius of Place*, 234.

24 Ibid., 237.

25 Lorne Parton's column in the *Province*, February 27, 1969, 29.

26 The segment of CBC's *A Sense of Place* featuring Arthur Erickson was aired October 11, 1966.

27 Erickson, *The Architecture of Arthur Erickson* (Douglas & McIntyre), 93–94.

28 "Speech to the National Gallery Association," May 9, 1972, "Speeches by Arthur Erickson."

29 "Architects Split," *Province*, July 27, 1972.

30 Jack Wasserman column, *Vancouver Sun*, June 10, 1972.

31 Arthur Erickson to Rhodri W. Liscombe, January 5, 1978, reported in Waddell, "Design for a University," 155.

32 Alan Bell provided the author with a detailed explanation of this transitional period in notes submitted for this biography, August 2011.

33 From interviews with Tony Griffin, November 4, 2009, and Rainer Fassler, January 11, 2011.

34 These observations were made by Noel Best in an interview, January 11, 2011.

35 Quoted by Rhodri W. Liscombe, *Arthur Erickson: Selected Projects*, 11.

36 Quoted in Sean Rossiter, "Cleared for Departure," 40.

37 The complete issue of *Capilano Review* 40 (1986) is an account by Ann Rosenberg of the design and planning process of Robson Square.

38 See Olsberg, *Arthur Erickson: Critical Works*, 144.

39 The ideas and references in this paragraph are taken chiefly from *The Architecture of Arthur Erickson* (Douglas & McIntyre), 118.

40 Quoted in Iglauer, *Seven Stones*, 106.

41 The ideas here were voiced by Erickson in an interview for the *Vancouver Sun*, December 5, 1975.

42 Arthur interviewed for "Around Swedish America," Nordicway.com accessed June 2, 2011.

43 Cornelia Oberlander interviewed by Mechtild Manus in "Walking with Oberlander," in *Picturing Landscape Architecture: Projects of Cornelia*

Hahn Oberlander as seen by Etta Gerdes, Mechtild Manus and Lisa Rochon, eds. (Munich: Callway Verlag, 2006), 52.

44 Ibid., 53.

45 Reported by Lisa Rochon in "Where Architecture Meets the Trees: The Landscape Architecture of Cornelia Hahn Oberlander," in Gerdes, ed., *Picturing Landscape Architecture*, 24.

46 See Sean Rossiter, "Cleared for Departure," 72.

47 The view from the office is given in Sean Rossiter's article, "Cleared for Departure," 40, 73.

48 Barry Johns quoted by Essy Baniassad in an introductory note to *Barry Johns Architects: Selected Projects 1984–1998* (Halifax, NS: TUNS Press, 2000), 12.

49 Nicholas Olsberg, "The Common Ground," in *Arthur Erickson: Critical Works*, 134–5.

50 Iglauer, *Seven Stones*, 105. To date, this vision for Robson Square has been most fully realized during the 2010 Winter Olympics, when thousands gathered at the square to socialize and watch telecasts of the games. The square was also the media communications headquarters.

51 Lisa Rochon, "Where Architecture Meets the Trees: The Landscape Architecture of Cornelia Hahn Oberlander," in *Picturing Landscape Architecture*, 26.

52 Rhodri W. Liscombe, *Arthur Erickson: Selected Projects*, 11.

53 "Royal Bank Address," June 9, 1971, "Speeches by Arthur Erickson."

54 Erickson, *The Architecture of Arthur Erickson* (Douglas & McIntyre), 94–96.

55 Daniel McCabe, "A Fine Balance: The Art and Sciece of Architecture," *McGill News* (Summer 2003).

56 Ibid., 95.

CH 16 | THE MUSEUM OF ANTHROPOLOGY, UBC

1 Paul Grescoe, "Edifice Rex: The Brilliance—and Limitations—of Arthur Erickson," *Montreal Gazette*, Canadian Supplement, February 19, 1977, 4–7.

2 From an address given on the occasion of an honorary degree from the University of Lethbridge, 1981, Special Collections, University of Lethbridge Library.

3 Mary McAlpine, "Erickson: Architect on the Move," *Vancouver Sun*, June 14, 1975.

4 Erickson quoted in Edmonds, ed., "The Architect Who Thinks People Matter More than Buildings," 49.

5 Grescoe, "Edifice Rex," 5.

6 See Southam, *Pierre*, 130. The chalet was not completed until 1984, the Trudeaus having separated and divorced in the meantime.

7 Abraham Rogatnick interviewed on December 6, 2005.

8 This phrase is from a telephone conversation with Joanne Sheppard Weghsteen, March 9, 2007.

9 Information in this and the following paragraphs is from interviews with Helmut and Hildegard Eppich, June 2002, and March 10, 2010, and from www.manufacturing-today.com/content/view/393 accessed March 12, 2010. This website provides a comprehensive overview of Ebco.

10 Frank Lloyd Wright, *The Living City* (New York: New American Library, 1970), 143.

11 "Ideation as a Source of Creativity" is regarded as one of Arthur's most important essays. Basically, it argues that context—geography, climate, history, culture—is the most important source of ideas for creativity. It was presented at a conference on May 6, 1975, in Madrid and is one of the few talks he gave to be published. See W.H. New, ed., *A Political Art: Essays and Images in Honour of George Woodcock* (Vancouver: UBC Press, 1979), 26–33.

12 Ibid.

13 Olsberg, *Arthur Erickson: Critical Works*, 20.

14 The catalogue for this show is titled *The Poetics of West Coast Modernism in West Vancouver* and was published by West Vancouver Cultural Services in 2005.

15 Arthur was always hostile to the presence of railings or banisters and for nearly forty years owners and guests were unassisted in their climb or descent.

16 "Architecture: Arthur Erickson," [anonymous] *Architectural Digest* (March 1978): 98–105.

17 Audrey Hawthorn, *A Labour of Love: The Making of the Museum of Anthropology, UBC, The First Three Decades 1947–1976* (Vancouver: UBC Museum of Anthropology Publications, 1993), 78.

18 This account taken from notes left with Erickson's office files.

19 Hawthorn, *A Labour of Love*, 80. Arthur's company officially received the commission on December 7, 1972, based on the drawings submitted. The cost was not to exceed $4,065,149.

20 *UBC Reports*, January 18, 1973, 2.

21 Claude Lévi-Strauss is quoted by Audrey Hawthorn in an interview with the *Vancouver Sun*, July 21, 1971, 41.

22 In conversation with Joan M. Vastokas, Arthur explained that he was inspired specifically by an old photograph of a Haida village on Anthony Island, at the southern tip of Haida Gwaii (formerly designated the Queen Charlotte Islands). See note 37.

23 Speech to the McGill University School of Architecture, October 21, 2000.

24 This outline, submitted by the Erickson and Massey office and dated May 15, 1972, was written to encompass the facilities required to provide for the activities of a teaching and public museum. It can be found in the MOA Archives, Michael Ames Fonds, Box 1, 1-A-3. The outline of museum history provided here is a summary of Arthur's ideas contained in that document.

25 Erickson, *The Architecture of Arthur Erickson* (Douglas & McIntyre), 88.

26 In an interview on January 6, 2011, Henry Hawthorn said that his parents always laid claim to the "visible storage" idea but that he saw it arising jointly from their concern for function and Arthur's skill in design.

27 Erickson, *The Architecture of Arthur Erickson* (Douglas & McIntyre), 87.

28 In 1979, Erickson would give the same serene, monumental aspect to the twenty individual townhouses at Monteverdi Estates in West Vancouver by using horizontal beams that far exceeded their functional requirements. (The structural work of the roof beams at the MOA is misleading because the roof-supporting function is performed chiefly by smaller crossbeams.)

29 See Michelangelo Sabatino, "Arthur Erickson and Essential Tectonics," *Journal of Architecture* 13, vol. 4 (2008): 493–514.

30 Erickson, *The Architecture of Arthur Erickson* (Douglas & McIntyre), 87.

31 Erickson to Pierre Trudeau, October 25, 1974, LAC Trudeau Papers, LAC, MG 26-020, vol. 4, file 2.

32 Erickson, *The Architecture of Arthur Erickson* (Douglas & McIntyre), 88.

33 Summarized here is a one-page account of "Raven and the First Men" that was located with Erickson's office papers.

34 The pool was filled for the APEC conference in 1997 and for Arthur's eightieth birthday in 2004. In September 2010, the pool was filled, with the understanding that it would remain so permanently.

35 In Olsberg, ed., *Arthur Erickson: Critical Works*, Laurent Stalder refers to the torii in his essay "Europe-America-Japan: In Search of a New Architectural Language," translated by Steven Watt, 61. The reference to Egyptian buildings is quoted by Olsberg in his introduction, 7.

36 Rhodri W. Liscombe in conversation, January 12, 2011.

37 See Joan M. Vastokas, "Architecture as Cultural Expression: Arthur Erickson and the New Museum of Anthropology, University of British Columbia" *artscanada* 208/209 (October/November 1976): 1–14.

38 Sabatino reinforces this sense of the ethereal when he observes that the roof beams of the museum, like those in torii gates, Shinto shrines, and Native longhouses, project well beyond the requirements of the post and seemingly float in the air. "Arthur Erickson and Essential Tectonics," 493–514.

CH 17 | THE CANADIAN CHANCERY

1 Quoted in Barrie Cook's "Architecture Showpiece Stunning," *Province*, November 23, 1975.

2 When the project seemed to lag in 1973, Simon Scott persisted in pushing it forward. Fittingly, he was presented with an award from the American Institute of Graphics for his photography in *The Architecture of Arthur Erickson*.

3 Donald Gutstein, "Buildings, Yes—People, No," *Vancouver Sun*, December 5, 1975, 32A.

4 Donald Gutstein, "Arthur Erickson: The Corporate Artist-Architect," *City Magazine* 1, no. 1 (October 1974): 5–15.

5 Starting in 1969, Erickson/Massey executed elaborate plans for this large vacation complex in the park, but eventually politicians bowed to the pressure of negative public opinion and the project was cancelled in 1972.

6 Erickson quoted in Edith Iglauer, "The 'Never-Builts' of Arthur Erickson," *Interface* (September 1981): 29.

7 Ibid.

8 www.arthurerickson.com/inmemory2.html accessed May 25, 2010.

9 Rhodri W. Liscombe, *Arthur Erickson: Selected Projects, 1971–85*, 11.

10 Grescoe, "Edifice Rex," 6.

11 John Lownsbrough, "Arthur Erickson," *Western Living* (June 1988): 52a-h.

12 Ibid., 52f. See also Judy Ross, "Open Season," *Ontario Living* 4, no. 3 (April 1988): 39.

13 An account of this party appears in Hugh Brewster's "Remembering Arthur Erickson," *Xtra!*, June 4, 2009, www.xtra.ca/public/vancouver /remembering_arthur_erickson-6881.aspx accessed August 20, 2009.

14 Expressions of sympathy from Lindsay (undated) and Carruthers, September 25, 1979, are located in CCA, 22-TOR-722.

15 Erickson to Pierre Trudeau, LAC, Trudeau Papers, MG 26 020, vol. 4, file 2.

16 Erickson, *The Architecture of Arthur Erickson* (Douglas & McIntyre), 125.

17 This account of Virginia and Bagley Wright's home (referred to in print as the Pacific Northwest House) is based on *The Architecture of Arthur Erickson* (Douglas & McIntyre), 106–11; on an author interview with the Wrights, August 6, 2008; and on the Wrights' book titled *Virginia and Bagley Wright at the Highlands* (Seattle: privately printed, May 2007).

18 Erickson, *The Architecture of Arthur Erickson* (Douglas & McIntyre), 106.

19 "Preface," *Virginia and Bagley Wright at the Highlands*, n.p.

20 See *The Architecture of Arthur Erickson* (Douglas & McIntyre), 135.

21 Vic Parsons, *Ken Thomson: Canada's Enigmatic Billionaire* (Toronto: Burgher Books, 1996), 106. See also "The Thomsons: A $23.8 Billion Mess," *Maclean's* (May 9, 2006).

22 Stephen Godfrey, "Erickson Upset at 'Desecration of Art,'" *Globe and Mail,* January 13, 1983, 12.

23 Lisa Rochon, "Blueprint for Chaos," *Report on Business* (April 1990): 62.

24 Reported in the *Province,* May 7, 1982.

25 Arthur drew attention to this journey in a speech he gave honouring Trudeau at a gathering of friends organized by Pat Buckley. A copy of the speech can be found at CCA, Box 22-TOR-708. Details of the trip can be found in LAC, Trudeau Papers, MG 26 020, vol. 4, file 2.

26 Erickson to Pierre Trudeau, December 14, 1981, LAC, Trudeau Papers, MG 26-020, vol. 4, file 2.

27 Allan Gotlieb, *The Washington Diaries 1981–1989* (Toronto: McClelland & Stewart, 2006), 140.

28 Copies of the cartoons are located in CCA, 22 TOR, 725, file 1.9.2a.

29 Benjamin Forgey, *Washington Post,* April 3, 1982, C1, 5.

30 Adele Freedman made similar observations in a brief article for *Progressive Architecture* 65 (October 1984): 24–25, which she pointedly titled "Erickson's Embassy: Post-Modern Pastiche." This would be followed on the opening of the chancery with a critical review in the *Globe and Mail,* November 4, 1989, C6, titled "Where's the Erickson We Thought We Knew?"

31 Benjamin Forgey, *Washington Post,* May 12, 1984.

32 CCA, Box 22-TOR-701.

33 Erickson, *The Architecture of Arthur Erickson* (Douglas & McIntyre), 214–15.

34 Nicholas Jennings, "Haidas on the Seine," *Maclean's* (October 16, 1989): 67–8.

35 Olsberg, *Arthur Erickson: Critical Works,* 140.

36 Iglauer, *Seven Stones,* 11–12. But Johnson was very responsive to the winds of change and, just a few years later, in 1985, Allan Gotlieb would observe at an embassy dinner party given for Johnson that he appeared patronizing towards Arthur and seemed to see Arthur "stuck in modernism." *The Washington Diaries,* 321.

37 A copy of the speech can be found at CCA, 22-TOR-723.

38 Ibid.

39 Rochon, "Blueprint for Chaos," 59.

40 Erickson to Pierre Trudeau, August 12, 1982, LAC, Trudeau Papers, MG 26-020, vol. 4, file 2.

41 Some of these quotes can be found in Colin Mackenzie, "Canada's New Embassy Turns Heads in Washington," *Globe and Mail,* June 29, 1988, A12.

42 Gotlieb, *The Washington Diaries,* 587–88.

43 Ibid., 600.

44 Witold Rybczynski, *Looking Around: A Journey through Architecture* (New York: Viking, 1992), 168–69.

45 Reported in the *Ottawa Citizen*, July 21, 2002.

46 This owes much to Lisa Rochon's excellent overview in "Blueprint for Chaos," 59–69.

PART IV Celebrity

CH 18 | THE MIDDLE EAST

1 Erickson, The Architecture of Arthur Erickson (Douglas & McIntyre), 143.

2 Arthur Erickson, "Notes from an Interview," *Genius of Place*, 237.

3 "Climate as the Conditioner," "Speeches by Arthur Erickson."

4 Ibid.

5 Lance Berelowitz, "Erickson: A Turning Point," 18–19.

6 See CAA, ERI 4A/76.13, Box 53. There appears to be no reply to this proposal in the Calgary archive.

7 See CAA, ERI 4A/76.13, Box 87.

8 Much information in this chapter was provided by Alan Bell in interviews on August 28, 2009, and October 9, 2010.

9 Lloyd Dykk, *Vancouver Sun*, June 16, 2006.

10 Erickson to Pierre Trudeau, CCA, Box 22-TOR-708.

11 Erickson, *The Architecture of Arthur Erickson* (Douglas & McIntyre), 153.

12 Alan Bell interviewed on October 9, 2010.

13 Erickson's views of Arabic architecture described in this paragraph are mostly to be found in an interview with Pierluigi Bonvicini given in Los Angeles, November 11, 1983. A copy of this interview is located in CCA, Box 22-TOR-723.

14 Wilfred Thesiger, *Arabian Sands* (New York: E.P. Dutton, 1959), 72–73.

15 References here are to the first edition of T.E. Lawrence's *Seven Pillars of Wisdom* published for general circulation in 1935, reprinted in 2008 by Vintage, New York.

16 Ibid., 212.

17 Ibid., 360.

18 Ibid., 276.

19 Arthur Erickson in conversation with the author, July 17, 2005.

20 Lawrence, *Seven Pillars of Wisdom*, 579.

21 "A Toast to Pierre Trudeau," April 9, 1981, CCA, Box 22-TOR-708.

22 Erickson, *The Architecture of Arthur Erickson* (Douglas & McIntyre), 153.

23 Ibid.

24 Ibid., 159.

25 *Vancouver Sun*, January 14, 1980, A1. It should be noted that while Arthur was the lead designer, his was only one of several Canadian firms comprising the Campus-Consortium Consultants joint venture team for the project.

26 See John Allison, "Arabian Opera Nights," *Opera* (January 2008).

27 Rochon, "Blueprint for Chaos," 63.

28 Donald Erickson interviewed on August 8, 2007.

29 Erickson, *The Architecture of Arthur Erickson* (Douglas & McIntyre), 162.

CH 19 | BANKRUPT

1 Alan Bell, October 9, 2010; Keith Loffler, June 17, 2010; Randolph Jefferson quoted in Rochon, "Blueprint for Chaos," 63.

2 "How Erickson Won Over the Biggest in U.S.," *Vancouver Sun*, July 18, 1980.

3 Francisco used the term "designer," though he did not have the education that the term implies. Strictly speaking, he was an interior decorator.

4 Jody Jacobs column, *Los Angeles Times*, November 8, 1985.

5 A copy of Erickson's note to Hepburn was left with his office files. She was filming *Mrs. Delafield Wants to Marry*.

6 This list appears in John English, *Just Watch Me*, 396–97.

7 From an interview with Melanie Friesen, March 12, 2011. Friesen was working in London as a literary agent in the early 1980s and would see Arthur and Francisco when they were in Europe.

8 Liona Boyd, *In My Own Key: My Life in Love and Music* (Toronto: Stoddart Publishing, 1998), 214–15.

9 Ibid., 215–17.

10 Email from Peter Gould to Michelangelo Sabatino, May 14, 2011.

11 Information about working for the Sacklers is from emails sent by Peter Gould to Michelangelo Sabatino, May 14, 2011. The Napp laboratory complex in Cambridge's Science Park won the Concrete Society's award for 1984 and has been a favourite backdrop for television commercials and movies in the U.K. But it was not without controversy in the early years. The angle of the glass and concrete walls, meant to evoke the shape of an East Anglian dyke, created a blinding reflection. One woman in a newspaper article said it was worse than looking directly into the sun itself. There was fear of accidents on the highway but a "skin" was put on the glass and bushes and trees planted that broke the glare and prevented the client's potential wrath. Nicholas Olsberg composed the description of the laboratory presented here and reported that Prince Charles liked to show the Napp laboratories to visitors in the U.K.

12 CCA, Box 22-TOR-762.

13 The letter about the Gang Ranch was written March 4, 1996, and copied to the author by Geoffrey Erickson.

14 Quoted in Iglauer, *Seven Stones*, 96.

15 See *The Architecture of Arthur Erickson* (Douglas & McIntyre), 207, 211.

16 Marcelo Igonda interviewed by telephone on March 29, 2011.

17 Rem Koolhaas, "Two Competition Projects for Bunker Hill in Downtown Los Angeles," *Trace* 1, no. 3 (July–September 1981): 10.

18 Leon Whiteson, *Los Angeles Herald*, January 5, 1986.

19 Erickson, *The Architecture of Arthur Erickson* (Douglas & McIntyre), 205.

20 Two exceptions might be Portola Valley's lavish, almost Mughal style, Khosla house, designed for a Silicon Valley executive from India, and the glass house at Newport Beach built for clients who had visited the Maison de Verre in Paris. Marcelo Igonda saw this as an exceptional house because it was built of glass on a beach but achieved complete privacy.

21 The memorandum dated April 18, 1986, was sent by Keith Loffler and five other senior architects with the Toronto office of Arthur Erickson Associates. A copy is located in CCA, Box 22-TOR-718.

22 Rochon, "Blueprint for Chaos," 59–69.

23 CCA, Box 22-TOR-757.

24 The King Ranch Health Spa and Fitness Resort did open in late 1989 but failed to achieve its goals and closed in 1992. It subsequently became a leadership centre for the Canadian Imperial Bank of Commerce.

25 Stephen Godfrey, "Syndicate Puts Erickson on Firmer Ground," *Globe and Mail*, March 17, 1988, A13.

26 This list of "investors," also including Ira Young and Irell & Manella, is contained in a letter dated February 4, 1988, from Richard Gordon to Yves Pratt, Montreal, inviting Paul Desmarais to be an additional member of the Capital Group (also called the Arthur Erickson Syndicate). See CCA, Box 22-TOR-718.

27 Management of the Arthur Erickson Capital Group Ltd. also included two Canadian lawyers: Heward Stikeman of Montreal and Howard Litowitz of Toronto. The amounts invested varied from individual to individual.

28 Ann Videriksen, interviewed in Los Angeles on December 7, 2010, provided several anecdotes about the Los Angeles office.

29 Melanie Friesen interviewed on March 12, 2011.

30 Susan Oakley interviewed in Los Angeles on December 6, 2010.

31 Erickson, *The Architecture of Arthur Erickson* (Douglas & McIntyre), 13.

32 Brewster, "Remembering Arthur Erickson."

33 Quoted in Rochon, "Blueprint for Chaos," 68.

34 From a conversation with Hugo Eppich, March 5, 2011.

35 Brewster, "Remembering Arthur Erickson."

36 David Olive, "Arthur Erickson," *Globe and Mail*, August 10, 1991.

37 Anne Gregor, "Plans Gone Awry," *Maclean's* (July 22, 1991): 34.

38 Annabelle King in the *Montreal Gazette*, April 27, 1993.

39 Ralph Waldo Emerson, *Essays: First and Second Series Complete in One Volume* (New York: Thomas Y. Crowell, 1926), 40–41.

40 Patricia Lush, "Architect's Finances in Ruins," *Globe and Mail*, February 21, 1992, B2.

41 Chris Dafoe, "Group Hopes to Save Erickson's Property," *Globe and Mail*, March 4, 1992, A10.

42 Michael Scott, "Erickson House on Shaky Ground," *Vancouver Sun*, March 1, 1992, B8.

43 Jamie Lamb, "Erickson Home a Monument to Ingenuity in Creative Financing," *Vancouver Sun*, June 25, 1992, B1.

44 In interviews, Susan Oakley, Marcelo Igonda, and Ann Videriksen explained how their friendships with Arthur were sustained beyond the office.

45 This letter remains in the possession of the recipient, Diana Whittall.

CH 20 | LOCAL CELEBRITY

1 Hugo Eppich interviewed on January 2 and March 5, 2011. See also a column by Steve Whysall, *Vancouver Sun*, May 16, 1992, C1–2.

2 See *Western Living* (December 1989): 112–19, and *Global Architecture* 33, 94–105.

3 See Jennifer Hunter, "Back on the Job," *Maclean's* (July 31, 2000): 31–32; Ian Mulgrew, *Vancouver Sun*, May 6, 2000, A20.

4 Jennifer Hunter, "Back on the Job," 31.

5 Ian Mulgrew, A20.

6 Jennifer Hunter, *"Back on the Job,"* 31.

7 Alexandra Gill, "I've Been Very Misunderstood," *Globe and Mail*, February 15, 2001, R1.

8 Olsberg reports this as the architect's stated intention in "The Common Ground," *Arthur Erickson: Critical Works*, 144–45.

9 Trevor Boddy sees this as a typically Canadian commitment to safe and generous public spaces. See his article "Landscape," *Canadian Architect* 47, no. 11 (November 2002): 30–36.

10 There was a personal connection as well. Travelling to Seattle with his parents as a boy, he was fascinated by the shape of the sawdust burners whenever they passed a mill. Burning sawdust was an inexpensive way to

heat private homes and he remembered that as a boy it was his duty to keep the burner filled. From an interview conducted by Kathryn Gretsinger for CBC AM's "The Current," June 6, 2006.

11 Anna C. Noll, "Museum of Glass by Arthur Erickson," *Architecture Week* (October 9, 2002): D1. See also a mention and photo of the Museum of Glass in *Condé Nast Traveler*, April 2003, 98–99, which reports that Tacoma finally has a calling card of its own.

12 Ricardo L. Castro and David Theodore, "The Museum of Glass, Tacoma" in Olsberg, *Arthur Erickson: Critical Works*, 165.

13 See Reynolds, *Maekawa Kunio*, Plate 5, and pages 230–31.

14 "Arthur Erickson Profile" (notes for an autobiography).

15 Unless otherwise indicated, quoted matter in this paragraph is taken from "Arthur's War," *Vancouver Sun*, November 4, 2000, H1, 2.

16 Erickson to Pierre Trudeau, February 21, 1983, LAC, MG 26-019, vol. 52.

17 Trudeau to Erickson, LAC, MG 26-019, vol. 52.

18 Erickson office files.

19 A copy of this letter was found with Erickson's office files.

20 Ibid.

21 This letter appeared in the *Globe and Mail* on November 19, 2001, in response to an article from November 17, 2001, which was titled "Wood to Warm Up Roy Thomson Hall."

22 Erickson, *The Architecture of Arthur Erickson* (Douglas & McIntyre), 178–79.

23 Venturi, *Contradiction and Complexity in Architecture*, 23.

24 Erickson to Ada Louise Huxtable, October 19, 1981, CCA, Box 22-TOR-761.

25 Erickson, *The Architecture of Arthur Erickson* (Douglas & McIntyre), 179.

26 Office notes.

27 Paul Delany, ed., *Vancouver: Representing the Postmodern City* (Vancouver: Arsenal Pulp Press, 1994), 17.

28 The Alcan lectures on architecture, January 1986.

29 Arthur used these words in a letter on October 12, 2001, recommending Antoine Predock for the AIA's gold medal. He believed Predock was outstanding for his sympathetic responses to both natural and cultural contexts and that he had eschewed all the contemporary fashions in favour of pursuing his own architectural vision. Office papers.

30 Quoted in McCabe, "A Fine Balance," 2.

31 Memos to Neil Crory, producer of *Music in My Life*, couriered December 2, 1985, copies in CCA Box 22-TOR-723.

32 Quoted in Iglauer, *Seven Stones*, 48.

33 Erickson, *The Architecture of Arthur Erickson* (Douglas & McIntyre), 151.

34 From a letter dated December 3, 2003, and signed "Fenfang." Others were signed Jian Qi. (Erickson office files.)

35 Nick Milkovich interviewed on January 13, 2011.

36 Some of Erickson's design work for King Abdulaziz University is being executed as well.

37 Her words to a public audience at the law courts, September 10, 2006.

38 Quoted in McCabe, "A Fine Balance," 2.

39 Erickson interviewed in *Saturday Night* (May 2005).

40 He viewed Douglas Cardinal's Museum of Civilization similarly: the vastness of the main hall gallery, for example, diminished the totem poles. He preferred Cardinal's 1969 St. Mary's Church in Red Deer. In conversation with the author, May 28, 2005.

41 *Province*, April 1, 2005.

42 The proposals were passed April 16, 2006.

43 See Easton, et al., *Artists in Their Gardens*, 98–109.

44 Amy O'Brian's telephone interviews with Erickson and Olsberg formed the basis of her article on the gallery show in the *Vancouver Sun*, May 20, 2006.

45 Erickson interviewed by Kathryn Gretsinger on *The Current*, CBC AM, June 6, 2006.

46 Clint Burnham, "Reaching for the Sublime: The Ineffable Vision of Arthur Erickson," *Vancouver Sun*, May 27, 2006, F3.

47 Rhodri W. Liscombe, "Architizing," *Canadian Architect* 51 (August 2006): 26–28.

48 D. Grant Black, *Toronto Star*, May 19, 2007.

49 Cori Howard, *Globe and Mail*, November 24, 2007.

50 Malcolm Parry, *Vancouver Sun*, November 15, 2007, C4.

51 Howard, *Globe and Mail*, November 24, 2007.

52 Erickson to the author, December 2007. He made similar statements to Sandra Martin. See "I Remember," *Globe and Mail*, May 23, 2009.

53 Ibid.

AFTER WORDS

1 See Rogatnick, "A Poem on Arthur's Life," *Canadian Architect* 54 (October 2009): 22–24.

2 Mary Roaf interviewed on October 1, 2008.

3 Coupland quoted in Michael Harris, "King Arthur," *Vancouver* (September 2006): 56.

4 Address titled "The Architecture of Photography," delivered at the West Vancouver Museum, June 23, 2009.

5 Gerry Bellett, "Arthur Erickson at Centre of Lawsuit," *Vancouver Sun*, January 30, 2010; Keith Fraser, "Un-Arthurized," *Province*, January 29, 2010, A1, 12. The fullest account of the lawsuit appears in Frances Bula's "Battle Royal," *Vancouver* (May 2010): 43–47. The family's allegations were further confirmed in a file made available to me by the architect's niece, Emily McCallum. According to the latter, by the time her uncle signed the document designating the AEC as the agency for his work, he had been diagnosed medically as no longer capable of making such decisions.

6 See Karsten Harries, *The Ethical Function of Architecture* (Cambridge, MA: MIT Press, 1998). Paul Goldberger summarizes some of Harries's ideas in *Why Architecture Matters* (New Haven: Yale University Press, 2009).

Sources

ARCHIVES

John Bland Architecture Collection, McGill University
Canadian Architectural Archives, University of Calgary (CAA)
Canadian Centre for Architecture, Montreal (CCA)
Simon Fraser University Archive (SFUA)
University of Lethbridge Library, Special Collections
University of Manitoba Archives and Special Collections
Vancouver Public Library (newspaper clipping collection)

(Note: References to Erickson's "office files" indicate materials located
in his office at the time of his death that were designated for the CAA but had
not yet been transferred there when this biography was written.)

Selected
Bibliography

Anderson, Bruce. *Gordon McKinley Webber: Memories of an Artist,*
  Designer, and Teacher. Montreal: McGill School of Architecture, 1996.
Berelowitz, Lance. "Erickson: A Turning Point." *Canadian Architect*
  (April 1992): 17–24.
Bingham, Janet. *Samuel Maclure Architect.* With a foreword by Arthur
  Erickson. Ganges, Horsdal & Schubart, 1985.
Brewster, Hugh. "Remembering Arthur Erickson." *Xtra!,* June 4, 2009.
  www.xtra.ca/public/vancouver/remembering_arthur_erickson-6881.aspx.
Bull, George. *Michelangelo: A Biography.* London: Penguin, 1996.
Cocking, Clive, ed. and Peter Stursberg. *Gordon Shrum: An Autobiography.*
  Vancouver: UBC Press, 1986.
Donaldson, Jim. McGill Alumni Interviews. www.mcgill.ca/architecture
  /alumninterviews.
Easton, Valerie, David Laskin, and Allan Mandell. *Artists in Their Gardens.*
  Seattle: Sasquatch Books, 2001.
Edmonds, Alan. ed. "The Architect Who Thinks People Matter More than
  Buildings." *Maclean's* 83 (June 1970): 44–49.
English, John. *Just Watch Me: The Life of Pierre Elliott Trudeau, 1968–2000.*
  Toronto: Alfred A. Knopf Canada, 2009.
Erickson, Arthur. *The Architecture of Arthur Erickson.* Montreal: Tundra
  Books, 1975.
——. *The Architecture of Arthur Erickson.* Vancouver: Douglas & McIntyre,
  1988.
——. "The Architecture of Japan: A Tendency towards Formalism—I: The
  Roots." *Canadian Architect* XI (December 1966): 28–36.

——. "The Design of a House." *Canadian Art* xvıı (November 1960): 338–42.

——. "Designing Simon Fraser University." sfu Archives, f 70/2/0/3.

——. "The Filberg House at Comox on Vancouver Island." *Canadian Architect* v (December 1960): 47–56.

——. *Habitation: Space, Dilemma and Design* (Ottawa: Canada Housing Design Council, 1966).

——. "Notes from an Interview, January 1964." David Stouck and Myler Wilkinson. *Genius of Place: Writing in British Columbia.* Vancouver: Raincoast Books, 2000, 229–38.

——. "Speeches by Arthur Erickson." University of British Columbia Library.

——. "The Weight of Heaven." *Canadian Architect* ıx (March 1964): 48–53.

Goldberger, Paul. *Why Architecture Matters.* New Haven: Yale University Press, 2009.

Gotlieb, Allan. *The Washington Diaries 1981–1989.* Toronto: McClelland & Stewart, 2006.

Grescoe, Paul. "Edifice Rex: The Brilliance—and Limitations—of Arthur Erickson." *Montreal Gazette*, Canadian Supplement, February 19, 1977, 4–7.

Harries, Karsten. *The Ethical Function of Architecture.* Cambridge, ma: mıt Press, 1998.

Harris, Bess, and R.C.P. Colgrove. *Lawren Harris.* With an introduction by Northrop Frye. Toronto: Macmillan, 1969.

Harris, Michael. "King Arthur." *Vancouver* (September 2006): 50–57.

Hawthorn, Audrey. *A Labour of Love: The Making of the Museum of Anthropology, ubc, The First Three Decades 1947–1976.* Vancouver: ubc Museum of Anthropology Publications, 1993.

Iglauer, Edith. *Seven Stones: A Portrait of Arthur Erickson, Architect.* Madeira Park, bc: Harbour Publishing, 1981.

James, Geoffrey. "Erickson: The Architect as Superstar." *Time* Canada (February 14, 1972): 16–21.

Johnston, Hugh. *Radical Campus: The Making of Simon Fraser University.* Vancouver: Douglas & McIntyre, 2005.

Kiss, Zoltan S. *Without a Blueprint: Surviving in a Changing World.* West Vancouver: Sandor Press, 2005.

Larisey, Peter. *Light for a Cold Land: Lawren Harris's Work and Life—An Interpretation*, with a foreword by Arthur Erickson. Toronto: Dundurn Press, 1993.

Liscombe, Rhodri W. *Arthur Erickson: Selected Projects 1971–85.* With an introduction by Barbara E. Shapiro. Catalogue published by the Center for Inter-American Relations, New York 1985.

Mackie, Richard Somerset. *Island Timber.* Victoria: Sono Nis Press, 2000.

Mazzariol, Giuseppe. "Il linguaggio di Erickson" (tr. "The Language of Erickson"). *Lotus* 5 (1970): 161–87.

McAlpine, Mary. "Erickson: Architect on the Move." *Vancouver Sun,* June 14, 1975.

McCabe, Daniel. "A Fine Balance: The Art and Science of Architecture." *McGill News* (Summer 2003): 2.

McWilliams, James, and R. James Steel. *Amiens: Dawn of Victory.* Toronto: Dundurn Press, 2001.

Murray, Joan, and Robert Fulford. *The Beginning of Vision: The Drawings of Lawren Harris.* Vancouver: Douglas & McIntyre, 1982.

Olsberg, Nicholas, and Ricardo L. Castro, eds. *Arthur Erickson: Critical Works.* Vancouver: Douglas & McIntyre, 2006.

Reynolds, Jonathan M. *Maekawa Kunio and the Emergence of Japanese Modernist Architecture.* Berkeley: University of California Press, 2001.

Rilke, Rainer Maria. *Letters to a Young Poet.* trans. M.D. Herter. New York: W.W. Norton and Company, 1934.

Rochon, Lisa. "Blueprint for Chaos." *Report on Business* (April 1990): 59–69.

Rogatnick, Abraham. "Criticism: The Filberg House." *Canadian Architecture* v (December 1960): 57–58.

Rogatnick, Abraham J., Ian M. Thom, and Adele Weder. *B.C. Binning.* Vancouver: Douglas & McIntyre, 2006.

Rohan, Daniella, comp., Irena Zantovska Murray, ed. *Arthur Erickson: The Middle East Projects.* Montreal: McGill University Libraries, 1999.

Rossiter, Sean. "Cleared for Departure." *Vancouver* (August 1984): 32–40, 73.

Rybczynski, Witold. *Looking Around: A Journey through Architecture.* New York: Viking, 1992

Sabatino, Michelangelo. "Arthur Erickson and Essential Tectonics." *Journal of Architecture* 13:4 (2008): 493–514.

Salloum, Sheryl. *Underlying Vibrations: The Photography and Life of John Vanderpant.* Victoria, BC: Horsdal & Schubart, 1995.

Sandwell, Ruth. "Arthur Erickson Interviewed in July 2001." Simon Fraser University Archives: F-223-1-7-1-15.

Schulze, Franz. *Mies van der Rohe: A Critical Biography.* Chicago: University of Chicago Press, 1985.

———. *Philip Johnson: Life and Work.* New York: Alfred A. Knopf, 1994.

Slavin, Maeve. "Designer of the Year." *Interiors* (January 1985): 127–36.

Southam, Nancy, ed. *Pierre: Colleagues and Friends Talk about the Trudeau They Knew.* Toronto: McClelland & Stewart, 2005.

Tippett, Maria. *Bill Reid: The Making of an Indian.* Toronto: Random House Canada, 2003.

Vastokas, Joan M. "Architecture as Cultural Expression: Arthur Erickson
  and the New Museum of Anthropology, University of British Columbia."
  artscanada (October/November 1976): 1–14.

Venturi, Robert. *Complexity and Contradiction in Architecture.* New York:
  Museum of Modern Art Press, 1966.

Waddell, Gene. "Design for Simon Fraser University and the Problems
  Accompanying Excellence." The draft of an unpublished book-length
  typescript. c. 1999. Simon Fraser University Archives.

Walker, Doreen. *Dear Nan: Letters of Emily Carr, Nan Cheney, and
  Humphrey Toms.* Vancouver: University of British Columbia Press, 1990.

Woodcock, George. "Future Present," *Weekend Magazine* (January 3,
  1976): 8–11.

Wright, Frank Lloyd. *An Autobiography.* New York: Horizon Press, 1932.

Acknowledgements

MY FIRST DEBT OF GRATITUDE is to Mary Bucker-
field White, who suggested this biography and provided initial assistance to make it possible. Having known Arthur Erickson in his
youth, Mary compiled a list of his Vancouver friends and the families who could help me tell his story, and during the writing of this
book, she pursued on my behalf many of the details that provided
a groundwork for the opening chapters. Mary is the *sine qua non*
behind this book, and to her I extend my warmest thanks.

I am equally indebted to Wayne Elwood, who was the book's first
audience, reading the chapters as they were written and sharing his
knowledge of architecture and his insight into artists' lives as the
story unfolded. I am especially grateful to Wayne for the painstaking
care he gave to editing the manuscript so that it would attract a publisher and for his reassurance that I was on the right track.

Similarly, I owe much to one of Arthur Erickson's close associates
over the years. Alan Bell read the first version of the manuscript, cor-
recting factual errors, but more importantly supplying information
about the work at Erickson's offices and the buildings that emerged
from those design boards. He has made an invaluable contribution
to this project.

At the top of Mary White's list was Blackie Lee Sparzani who,
in person and in a series of emails, provided me with a wealth of

information about Arthur Erickson and his family. Also on that list was the late Kay Holland Cooke, who grew up next door to the Ericksons. Her children, Stephen Cooke and Trish Hurl, provided valuable anecdotes and photographs documenting the architect's early life.

Members of the Erickson family have been generous with their time and their recollections. I thank Arthur Erickson's two cousins: Muriel Morgan, for information about the Ericksons in Toronto, and Evelyn Auer, for stories about her Auer and Erickson in-laws in Vancouver. I am indebted to Arthur's brother, Donald, for his description of the family when Arthur was young, and to Emily McCullum, Arthur's niece, for her memories and impressions of her uncle and her grandparents. I am especially in debt to Arthur's nephew, Geoffrey, the family historian, author, and curator of the arthurerickson.com website, who provided not only vivid and entertaining glimpses of his uncle's life but also many of the illustrations for this book.

For further stories and documents about Arthur Erickson's childhood and early youth, I am grateful to Ruth Killam Massey, Richard Wright, John Baldwin, and John Dayton. For helping me to learn more about his art teacher, Jessie Faunt, I thank Doreen Walker and two members of the North Shore Artists' Guild, Norman Vipond and Larry Achtemichuk.

Diana Chesterton Whittall has been a good friend of this book, cheerfully welcoming its author to her home and providing stories and photographs of Arthur Erickson as a young man. I am deeply grateful for her generosity. For stories and documents related to Arthur's experience as a soldier, I am indebted to the relatives and friends of his wartime companion George Swinton. They include his daughter, Moira Swinton; his sister-in-law, Eileen Swinton; and their friend Saul Cherniak.

At McGill, Arthur Erickson fell under the spell of Gordon Webber. For sending me his excellent monograph on this eccentric instructor, I thank Montreal architect Bruce Anderson. For information about Douglas Shadbolt, Arthur's classmate and friend, I am indebted to the generous memories of his widow, Sidney Shadbolt. Sherry Grauer gave me an account of her family's relations with Arthur in the 1950s, and Jane Clegg told me about her friendship with Arthur in the 1960s. To them, I extend my thanks.

Many of Arthur's close friends were willing to share memories that spanned several decades. I am grateful that Abraham Rogat-nick shrewdly and wittily answered my questions and encouraged me to go forward with this project. Similarly, I am grateful to Gor-don Smith for taking time on at least two occasions to show me the house Arthur designed for him and his wife, Marion, and for sharing anecdotes, professional and personal, about their long friendship.

I feel especially indebted to Geoffrey Massey, who has answered frankly and with a concern for accuracy all my questions about his friendship and business partnership with Arthur Erickson. I thank him specifically for taking me to visit Jessie Binning, a centenarian whose memories of Arthur and his family were still crystal clear, dis-cerning, and entertaining.

My gratitude to Lois Milsom is immense. Like Geoffrey Massey, she was always willing to share her store of memories about her spe-cial relationship with Arthur, who had first been her teacher, then a close friend. Her insights into Arthur's creativity and her knowl-edge of his social life have been significant resources for this book. I thank her specifically for photographs and other documents she shared and for the continuous, friendly support she has given this project.

For their memories of Arthur Erickson as a teacher at UBC and subsequently as an employer, I thank John Roaf, Bruno Freschi, Alan Bell, and Nick Milkovich. I am particularly grateful to Nick Milkovich, Arthur's long-time professional associate, for giving me access to the contents of Arthur's office after his death.

Other architects who worked for Arthur Erickson and shared valuable recollections include John Keith-King, Tony Griffin, Henry Hawthorn, Ted Scott, Jim Strasman, Rainer Fassler, and Noel Best. I extend a special thank you to Simon Scott, who became Arthur's principal photographer; to Cornelia Oberlander, his landscape architect; and to Keith Loffler, who for several years managed the Toronto office. Similarly, I am grateful for interviews with Susan Oakley, Ann Videriksen, and Marcelo Igonda, who worked in the Los Angeles office. They played vital roles in Arthur Erickson's career and their stories have been invaluable.

I have been privileged to meet and know some of Arthur Erickson's clients. Helmut and Hildegard Eppich come first to mind, because they were for a time my neighbours in West Vancouver and, before this project was conceived, they welcomed my wife and me to their home on Palmerston Avenue. I thank them for their hospitality and for telling me the story of their relations with Arthur, professional and personal, as he designed and built his first concrete house. The design and construction of the Filberg house was an equally important chapter in this history, and I thank Robert Anderson and Richard Mackie for providing background information on the Filbergs. I am especially grateful to Doug Field for giving me a tour of his impeccable restoration of the house and for subsequently answering my many questions.

I thank Jean Catton and Virginia and Bagley Wright for telling me about their friendships with Arthur and the designing of their homes. Similarly I thank Laurette Hilborn for answering my questions about "The Ramparts," as her home in Cambridge, Ontario, was once known. I thank Ann Dohanik, Sue Tietz, and John Hueton for helping me to locate the Hilborn house and make contact with its original owner.

Dr. Van Christou has played an important role in this biography as the man who befriended Arthur Erickson and made the dream of a university in Lethbridge, Alberta, a reality. I thank him for all the information he provided and his friendly support for this project. For showing me their spectacular home and sharing their stories, I thank Hugo and Brigitte Eppich. I believe that in his late years Arthur had no kinder friend than Hugo Eppich, and I am pleased to be able to acknowledge that special architect-client relationship.

Many people have provided information, ideas, and impressions that have been woven into the fabric of this narrative. I thank, in alphabetical order: Mark Angus, Adrian Archambault, Tamsin Baker, George Baldwin, Janet Bingham, Cheryl Cooper, Paul Delany, Merle Ginsburg, Glyndwr Jones, Zoltan Kiss, David Laskin, Andrea Lebowitz, Rhodri W. Liscombe, James McWilliams, Joan Mann, Monte Marler, Mary Roaf, Michelangelo Sabatino, Don Vaughan, Gary Watson, and Joanne Weghsteen.

One of the joys of researching a book of this kind is in the unexpected. My debt to Melanie Friesen is of this kind. Without my bidding, she made contact and provided me with stories of Arthur's personal life, both glamorous and humble. In my opinion, they are some of the most charming and telling moments in this narrative.

This biography would not have been possible without professional and institutional assistance. Jill Wade's 1973 bibliography of Arthur Erickson was second only to Mary White's initial idea in making this book possible. Listed in that bibliography was a collection of Erickson letters dating from 1950 to 1961, written during the crucial years of his travels to Europe and Japan. They had not been catalogued, but staff at the Department of Architecture and the library at the University of Manitoba located them for me and they form the heart of this book. I thank Shelley Sweeney and Vladimira Zvonik for their assistance but especially Jill Wade for her early work in preparing the bibliography.

I am grateful to the staff of schools, libraries, and archives across the country for providing materials and information when requested. I thank Richard Dancy, Simon Fraser University Archives; Suzanne Ell and Bonnie Woelk, University of Calgary Archives; Brad Lloyd, Point Grey Elementary, Vancouver; Virginia Lam, Prince of Wales Secondary, Vancouver; Krisztina Laszlo, Museum of Anthropology, UBC; Ann Marie Holland, McGill University Library; and Bronwen Masemann, Genevieve Couture, and George de Zwann at Library and Archives Canada. My working hours at the Canadian Centre for Architecture in Montreal were made pleasant and profitable with the assistance of Renata Guttman and Colin McWhirter. There, I also had the opportunity to meet Phyllis Lambert, the centre's founder, who shared her vivid memories and ideas about her friend

Arthur Erickson. I am deeply indebted to Gene Waddell, College of Charleston, South Carolina, for permission to quote from his invaluable account of the design and construction of Simon Fraser University.

As I moved forward with this project, I had the personal encouragement of two individuals who worked to give this project an attractive public face. Beverly Neufeld, grants facilitator at SFU, led me through the process of securing travel funds from the SSHRC. My neighbour and fellow author, Alex Rose, asked many questions about this project, helping me to see the big picture, thereby making this story more legible and compelling. I thank Professor David Covo, McGill University, for his reading of the manuscript and his suggested rewordings that more smoothly engage the idioms of architecture.

I am grateful to two friends for their interest in and contributions to this project: Paul Comeau, who discussed with me what worked for him as an early student on the SFU campus, and Myer Wilkinson, who accompanied me on a first interview with Arthur Erickson in 1999.

I thank publisher Scott McIntyre for embracing this project with enthusiasm and to those working at Douglas & McIntyre who played a part in creating this book. I am fortunate to be in a position to thank Barbara Pulling, one of Canada's most distinguished editors, for her remarkable skill in reducing the length of this story, sentence by sentence, without eliminating an idea or phrase that was essential. I thank Caroline Skelton, assistant editor, for her cheerful attention to many matters, and Shirarose Wilensky, copy editor, and Peter Cocking and Jessica Sullivan, designers, for their creative labours and patience.

WRITING THIS BOOK has been a family enterprise. Happily, my wife, Mary-Ann, has travelled with me to locations identifying different phases of Arthur's career and has taken photographs crucial to formulating and illustrating this story. My daughter, Jordan, worked for seven years at the University of Lethbridge, which allowed me an insider's knowledge of how the original building works and how its vision was compromised. My son, John, with an interest in Eastern philosophies, provided me with valuable books on Japanese architecture. Several interested cousins, near and far, have provided a clipping service on Arthur Erickson and items about architecture in the news. I thank Frances Cleveland, West Vancouver; Betty Lou Docherty, Edmonton; Estella Howey, London, Ontario; Anne Kear, Toronto; and James Vosburgh, Mission, B.C. Finally, I want to thank my friends Ken Dawe and Eva Kato of Toronto for their hospitality and their abiding interest in my projects over the years.

Index